DEADLY AUSTRALIAN
Women

DEADLY AUSTRALIAN
Women

KAY SAUNDERS

ABC
Books

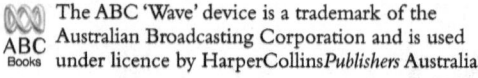 The ABC 'Wave' device is a trademark of the Australian Broadcasting Corporation and is used under licence by HarperCollins*Publishers* Australia.

First published in Australia in 2013
by HarperCollins*Publishers* Australia Pty Limited
ABN 36 009 913 517
harpercollins.com.au

Copyright © Kay Saunders 2013

The right of Kay Saunders to be identified as the author of this work has been asserted by her in accordance with the *Copyright Amendment (Moral Rights) Act 2000*.

This work is copyright. Apart from any use as permitted under the *Copyright Act 1968*, no part may be reproduced, copied, scanned, stored in a retrieval system, recorded, or transmitted, in any form or by any means, without the prior written permission of the publisher.

HarperCollins*Publishers*
Level 13, 201 Elizabeth Street, Sydney, NSW 2000, Australia
Unit D, 63 Apollo Drive, Rosedale, Auckland 0632, New Zealand
A 53, Sector 57, Noida, UP, India
1 London Bridge Street, London SE1 9GF, United Kingdom
2 Bloor Street East, 20th floor, Toronto, Ontario M4W 1A8, Canada
195 Broadway, New York, NY 10007, USA

National Library of Australia Cataloguing-in-Publication entry:

Saunders, Kay, 1947–
Deadly Australian women / Kay Saunders.
978 0 7333 3210 4 (pbk.)
978 0 7304 9375 4 (ebook)
Includes index.
Women murderers – Australia.
Female offenders – Australia.
Criminals – Australia
364.1523082

Cover design by Christa Moffitt, Christabella Designs
Cover images: Martha standing at the gate (MS 8296 Box 972/1 [b] Papers; Martha Needle. 1863–1894) courtesy State Library of Victoria; pattern by istockphoto.com
Typeset in 11.5/16pt Adobe Garamond Pro by Kirby Jones

To
Donald James,
a brave, lion-hearted man

Contents

Introduction	1
Chapter 1 Lethal Abortion in the Nineteenth Century	13
Chapter 2 Lethal Abortion in the Twentieth Century	39
Chapter 3 Baby Killers in the Nineteenth Century	65
Chapter 4 Baby Killers in the Twentieth Century	89
Chapter 5 A Baffling Case: Keli Lane	109
Chapter 6 The Deadly Baby Farmers	125
Chapter 7 Child Killers in the Nineteenth Century	151
Chapter 8 The Wicked Stepmother: Martha Rendall	167
Chapter 9 Child Killers in the Twentieth Century	179
Chapter 10 Poisoners of the Nineteenth Century	195
Chapter 11 The Thallium Killers	223
Chapter 12 Deadly Manoeuvres in the Nineteenth Century	241
Chapter 13 Killing of Partners in the Twentieth Century	258
Chapter 14 Eugenia Falleni, The 'Man–Woman' Killer	274
Chapter 15 Fighting Back	287
Chapter 16 Deadly Lovers' Pacts in the Nineteenth Century	303
Acknowledgments	323
Endnotes	325
Index	357
About the author	360

Introduction

In 1836 Charlotte Anley, a protégé of the prison reformer Elizabeth Fry, undertook a tour of the convict colonies of Australia to determine the condition of those transported and exiled. Her cousins William and Henry Dumaresq were prominent free settlers, with William initially serving as private secretary to New South Wales's Governor Ralph Darling and later appointed as a Legislative Councillor.[1] On her tour of the Parramatta Female Factory, which was used to incarcerate recidivists and women deemed too unruly to work as assigned servants on farms, Anley encountered two young prisoners who had been sentenced to life imprisonment for contributing to the death of their master, Captain Charles Waldon, a wealthy landholder and father of twelve children. They were, to the visitor, 'young and extremely pretty', though prison officials later told her they were 'both among the most refractory and violent' of the inmates. The encounter between Anley and Mary Maloney reveals many of the enduring Western cultural preconceptions concerning women and criminality, especially murder and killing. As Anley recounted:

> She and her companion [Sarah McGregor] were always pointed out as murderers, and they thought it hard that they could have no peace, but were 'hunted like wild beasts' for a crime they had never committed. I was afraid to irritate her by direct contradiction, but I ventured to say, that so serious a charge would hardly have been brought against them without some grounds. She repeated her denial of the deed, adding 'I

am not a murderer, for I never meant to kill the man. I was in liquor when we beat him as we did, but we couldn't help it that he died …'

I replied 'I could readily believe an act of murder to be of awful passion, and not a premeditated crime.' Here she interrupted me, looking up with an expression of deep emotion, such as I shall never forget, and exclaiming, 'Then you do believe that' – 'Yes' I replied, 'I could scarcely think otherwise of a woman.'[2]

Anley maintained the belief about the essential nature of women that, regardless of their status or class, they were inherently incapable of murder and premeditated violence. This was not simply the mistaken belief of an evangelical reformer; rather, Anley articulated far wider cultural patterns of gender differentiation and their inherent characteristics.

By the following year, with the ascension to the British throne of young Queen Victoria, those notions of women's essential passivity, goodness, virtue and empathy assumed far more power and scope. By 1854 these beliefs were enshrined in the term 'the angel in the house', taken from a poem by Coventry Patmore. The picture was of dutiful and devoted wifehood and self-sacrificing loving motherhood located within the security of marriage, where gender roles were rigidly delineated.[3] The separate spheres which had developed from the Industrial Revolution were now exclusive territories; men and women came together only within the patriarchal home. This construction of the ideal bourgeois family was an immense distance from the lives of countless poor women, who struggled to exist. Even for many privileged women within the confines of the home where servants undertook menial domestic labour, the ideal of a loving and beneficent husband was also altogether absent. Reality was reflected in the law, which provided only limited options to sever the marital bond and deprived married women of property rights and custody of their children.

INTRODUCTION

Despite its origins as mostly a series of convict colonies, these ideas flourished in colonial Australia, where notions of upward mobility and respectability took hold after the gold rushes of the 1850s. Thanks to the general level of comparative affluence, more settler women were located within the home. This development occurred despite other potent cultural and social forces. First, many women were poor and dependent upon arduous labour, often as domestic servants in the homes of other women. Second, without reliable female-controlled contraception until the advent of the oral contraceptive in the early 1960s, unwanted pregnancy and its consequences pervaded the lives of women of all classes.

Women's reproductive functions harboured the potential for calamity and ruin, especially for single women who found themselves pregnant. A network of underground entrepreneurs sprang up to address these individuals' adversities. Abortionists – often with little or no medical training – established lucrative practices, often under the guise of midwives. For backstreet women abortionists in particular, although the legal risks they ran were high, the remuneration and low overheads made up for it. Police attention to these illegal activities was largely concentrated upon those terminations that resulted in the patient's death, usually from blood poisoning. These illegal operations continued until the later twentieth century, when laws were changed to allow legal abortions under certain proscribed conditions.

Some desperate women who went through with an unwanted pregnancy later resorted to other drastic options. For the single young woman experiencing the stigma of unmarried motherhood and the inability to earn a living, infanticide could seem to be a viable option. It was not uncommon for domestic servants to be impregnated by the master or sons of the house and then left to face an uncertain future. Such illegitimate babies might be smothered or left unattended at birth, to be disposed of when the opportunity arose. As many of these births were unassisted and surrounded by secrecy, the possibility of discovery was diminished. One of the first cases in this book revolves around infanticide in Hobart in 1817. To bring the stories recounted in *Deadly Australian Women* full circle, the most recent major criminal trial examined in the narrative concerns Keli Lane, who in 2010 was found guilty of the murder of her newborn baby, Tegan Lane. This recent conviction harks back to nineteenth-century practices, when young unmarried women committed desperate acts that they hoped were invisible and undetectable.

For those vulnerable young colonial women who killed their babies and were caught out, should the law deem the act one of murder, the maximum penalty was execution. In reality this haphazardly occurred, and the lesser offence of 'concealing a birth' tended to be proscribed. Both the law and all-male juries often understood that the perpetrator was herself a victim of her circumstances.

By the later nineteenth century, the rise of a strong, organised feminist movement seeking to protect the rights of women and children ensured that public attention was directed to the plight of the young and unmarried filicide. The pronouncement of death sentences now caused public outrage as too harsh – especially when the absent father of the newborn escaped recriminations and prosecution. By the twentieth century, courts were taking into account biopsychiatric opinion about whether underlying medical issues contributed to the neonatal killing.

Before the introduction in the interwar years of legal adoption processes in Australian States, the practice of baby farming offered another solution to the unmarried mother who could not raise her baby. Many practitioners were caring married women who took in babies and small children to supplement their meagre household income. Others saw the opportunity to benefit financially from other women's misfortune. Babies and young children could be left in the care of a baby farmer, who would normally take a fee and a weekly subsistence allowance. That weekly stipend could be continued long after the baby had died either from gross neglect or from direct actions that resulted in death. Australia's most lethal multiple-killer, Alice

Mitchell from Perth, was responsible for the deaths of over thirty-five babies left in her care in the first decade of the twentieth century.

For mothers who killed older children, the law held no ambiguity. This was not infanticide – a category encompassing only babies. Killing one's own children, alongside killing parents, is the strongest taboo in Western culture. For a woman to kill her children defies every cultural notion of caring and nurturing responsibility. The image of the vengeful Medea, who murdered her children to take revenge on her husband, is a classic cultural depiction of the female monster who violates every notion of parental duty and accountability. Donna Fitchett, who was convicted of the murder of her two sons in Melbourne in 2005, gave a modern suburban twist to this archetypal portrayal. Recent research, however, suggests that many of these killers could not account for their motivation and described their actions as 'senseless'.[4] Their own traumatic childhoods, mental illness and substance abuse in many cases point to more complex explanations than evil or pure revenge. Since the mid-nineteenth century, firstly in the United Kingdom and subsequently in the Australian colonies, medico-legal expert opinion has been sought to determine the question of whether a convicted violent prisoner was mad or simply bad.

Other children have been killed by carers or babysitters entrusted with their welfare. Take sixteen-year-old convict nursemaid Mary Sullivan, who murdered an infant in her care in Hobart in 1852. The case was both repugnant and aberrant; Sullivan offered no explanation apart from her dislike of children. In 1980 Patricia Moore, an eighteen-year-old Sydney woman, was convicted of the murder of three children, including her own half-brother, and the attempted murder of two others.[5] After substantial if conflicting psychiatric evaluation was offered during her trial, the jurors decided she was simply bad, not mad.[6]

Husbands and domestic partners emerge as leading categories of victim, after infants and children. Reasons are varied. Before no-fault divorce was introduced in Australia in 1975, some individuals simply wanted to be rid of inconvenient spouses and inherit the marital property. Others, tired of their domestic situation and having met an attractive lover, conspired to kill the now redundant husband. The instance of Elizabeth Scott, the first woman executed in Victoria in 1863, concurred with this pattern.

Yet for other women in this book, the violence within their marriage coupled with the seeming impossibility of escaping their tormentor led to desperate acts. Despite the dramatic changes to women's legal, economic and political status from the late nineteenth century to the present day, the issue of domestic violence and what has come to be called the 'battered woman syndrome' persists. Power relations within the domestic unit have scarcely altered. Some women only escape when they eventually kill their domestic abuser. In 1991 this concept was first tested in an Australian jurisdiction in the Runjanjic and Kontinnen cases in South Australia.

The notion of women's essential goodness and innate nurturing capacity persists as a cultural image. Martha Clowers, in her entry on 'Women who Kill' in the *Encyclopaedia of Crime and Punishment*, concludes that 'women and murder are [terms seen as] mutually exclusive. Females are expected to be victims, not victimizers.' Women commit far fewer murders, manslaughters and other unlawful killings than men. Their patterns also do not conform to the male model of the accidental 'pub brawl' death, where the victim and the assailant are complete strangers. Women rarely kill strangers, historically or in the present day. They overwhelmingly kill intimates, and often within the direct family circle.

Women who kill use firearms or fists far less frequently than men do. They are typically portrayed as stealthy killers, more likely to use poison within the domestic setting to achieve their deadly purpose. Plato suggested that, by nature, all women were given to secrecy and stealth. What he may have identified is a response to the powerlessness of women's familial role, whether in fifth-century BCE or in twentieth-century Australia. As Melinda Page Wilkins proposes: '[The female killer] is deceitful, nearly invisible to her would-be victims and the surrounding culture, and cloaked in the raiment of her gender.'[7] Her invisibility in the home going about her domestic activities, her sheer ordinariness, often hides a darker reality.

Several high-profile legal cases in the nineteenth century resulted in the execution of women convicted of poisoning their spouses. Louisa Collins, executed in 1889, was the last woman hanged in New South Wales, while Elizabeth Woolcock was the only woman ever executed in South Australia.

Martha Rendall was executed for the murder by poisoning of her three stepchildren in Perth in 1908. She was accused and found guilty of administering poison while pretending to render treatment for serious illness. Serial poisoner, Caroline Grills, a motherly Sydney housewife, in the late 1940s and 1950s murdered three relatives and seriously harmed others by the use of thallium, which she dispensed in food and cups of tea. In the secrecy surrounding ordinary domestic rituals Grills killed over a number of years, her outward appearance of caring decency and motherly goodness belying her activities. She did not become rich from her crimes; she apparently simply enjoyed the power she had over her unsuspecting victims.

This book addresses the multiple ways in which women in Australia have killed others. *Deadly Australian Women* is not a book just about murder, which encompasses a legal definition of unlawful and wilful killing of another person with intent. The case of Audrey Jacob in Perth in 1925 shows the difference between killing and murder. On Wednesday 27 August 1925, with their fundraising ball at Government House in full swing, the organising committee of the St John Hospital was delighted with their social and financial success. Around 1am, in front of dozens of witnesses, Jacob shot and killed her sexually roaming fiancé. She did not deny killing Cyril Gidley, which would have been a rather difficult manoeuvre given the number of revellers who had watched her stride across the dance floor, pull out a revolver and shoot him. In her subsequent trial the jury found her not guilty of *wilful* murder and she was discharged. Her defence that this was an accident that she had neither planned nor intended was accepted by the all-male jury.

Rather than constituting a rarity, there are numerous instances where women in Australia have killed other people. I have canvassed cases from the earliest written records from the 1810s right up to the present day. As well as various historical periods, I have attempted a wide geographic coverage.

A vast array of primary sources is now available. Colonial newspapers from the earliest publication until 1954 are available online from the National Library of Australia's resource, Trove. Court proceedings were frequently reported almost verbatim and form an important depository of information. The case of Mabel Ambrose, whose body was discovered in a trunk in the Yarra River in 1899 – after she had been disposed of when her abortion proved fatal – was reported in detail not just in Melbourne but across the country. Some details were censored, however, as they were deemed not fit for public consumption.

The Macquarie University online series of colonial legal cases, while it repeats much newspaper coverage of earlier crimes, is another valuable resource. The Tasmanian State Archives provides an online service to researchers free of charge to investigate their files. Repositories like state archives hold many files open to researchers. I used the Queensland State Archives to read depositions and follow the progress of a number of significant legal cases.

In this book, the changing legal and judicial framework in which trials were conducted is an important factor. Criminal trials until 1839 were held with military juries, after which male property-holders were allowed to act as jurors. Only in the mid-1950s did women come to sit on juries in criminal cases. Until the late nineteenth century, few defendants could testify in their own defence, even for capital offences. Earlier, in 1830, convict Mary McLauchlan was tried and convicted of murdering her newborn son without the benefit of counsel or legal representative. Her military jury unsuccessfully recommended mercy.

Later, defendants relied upon the services of barristers appearing for them pro bono. Not until the early years of the twentieth century did the State provide public legal counsel for poor defendants. With generally fewer financial resources than men, women accused of serious crimes were doubly disadvantaged. For, as Kathy Laster reminds us, often women were treated more harshly simply because they had not lived up to the ideals of stereotypical womanhood. 'Precarious politics, not law, determined their fate.'[8]

While a considerable literature on female killers and murderers is concerned with well-known cases, such as those of Scotswoman Madeline Smith and Myra Hindley in England, Lizzie Borden and Aileen Wournos in the United States and Jean Lee and Martha Rendall in Australia, I have not confined my attention so narrowly to celebrity murderers. This canon, much of it constructed in the 'true crime' genre, is highly illuminating within the scope of its particular parameters. Notwithstanding these examples of deadly women, many of those convicted of killing or murder were ordinary women and girls caught up in desperate situations that seemed insoluble except through violent action. While criminologists have attempted to categorise them within analytical frameworks, such as Black Widows, Angels of Death, Thrill Killers, Child Killers, Revengers, Missionaries, Profiteers, Quiet Killers (mostly poisoners) and Team Killers (with a sub-genre the Couple Killer),[9] many fall into the category 'unexplained'. Killing is both a personal and a public act which does not readily fall into analytical categories.

Recent commentators Lindy Cameron and Ruth Wykes, in their book *Women Who Kill: Chilling Portraits of Australia's Worst Female Murderers* (2010), propose that 'Trying to understand why women kill is … well, it's pointless. Women kill for many of the same reasons that men do – and sometimes it can be explained, and sometimes it can't.'[10] Motives for killing are indeed varied. As this book proposes, the consequences of women's familial roles when they become distorted and extreme are the triggers for many lethal encounters. Killing unwanted babies, trying to cope with children while in a mentally precarious state and retaliating against violent domestic partners all appear explicable once the individual's circumstances are interrogated. But many others, such as thrill killing, poisoning family members just for the pleasure of watching them suffer or killing children in one's care, are less easy to interrogate for motive.

Unlike popular novels and television series would appear to suggest, those convicted of major crimes like murder do not willingly confess. Indeed, authors such as Judith Knelman argue that in the nineteenth century women convicted of murder in Britain were far less likely to repent or confess than male offenders.[11] Even on the gallows, convicted murderers such as Mary Sullivan and Mary McLauchlan did not repent; the prospect of being judged harshly in the next world did not elicit a response from them in their silent stoicism. The modern-day case of Keli Lane, who although convicted of murder has never confessed to any wrongdoing, is no different. Such cases remain bewildering and impenetrable. The common-law legal system, which we inherited from England, requires the prosecution to prove its case 'beyond all reasonable doubt', not for the defendant to prove her innocence. Even today, defendants are not obligated to testify in their own defence.

My own interest in women who kill goes back to 1981, when I was appointed as an official visitor and advocate for long-term women prisoners in the Women's Prison at Dutton Park in inner-city Brisbane. Ironically, the prison sat next to the Queensland State Archives, where I had spent several years undertaking research for my doctoral thesis. As a divorced young mother and academic, entry into the world of a prison was confronting. Nothing prepares a middle-class woman for the experience, albeit even as a visitor who leaves. I admire the courage of Charlotte Anley back in 1836.

One of the inmates was serving a sentence for infanticide. Her hopes of marriage with the baby's father had been sadly unfulfilled. Many of the long-term prisoners were in for drug-related offences

INTRODUCTION

and had been prostitutes who started taking illegal drugs then selling them to support their habit. To a woman, they all despised the filicide, whom they simply termed 'the baby-killer'. She was never referred to by her name and she was excluded from the bonds of friendship and camaraderie that characterised prison life. Unlike a male prison, where 'thuggery and buggery' dominate the internal culture, a women's prison is run along emotional lines of inclusion and exclusion. To be excluded and shunned made prison life even more unendurable. This woman never sought my company or advice, though she could have done so readily. Nor did she approach the two cheerful Sisters of Mercy who ministered to the inmates. I have often pondered this woman's sad desperation and wondered what happened to her.

The Queensland prison service also contained the so-called 'Lesbian Vampire Killers' in Brisbane, from 1991, and Valmae Beck, convicted of raping and murdering a young girl in tandem with her partner, Barry Watts. Cases like this are not included in this volume – they require another volume to examine their motives, exploits and trials.

Emerita Professor Kay Saunders AM,
Official Historian,
Bond University.

CHAPTER 1

Lethal Abortion in the Nineteenth Century

Sex has long been a lucrative business for entrepreneurial women, one way or another. Even during the supposedly puritanical decades of the Victorian era, courtesans and madams could earn fabulous sums selling sexual favours. But in the nineteenth century in England and the developing colonies of Australia, sex formed the basis of other more squalid business.

There has, of course, always been a flip side to the sex industry. Without reliable forms of contraception and with only a hazy idea of the reproductive cycle, unwanted pregnancies were not uncommon in the lives of nineteenth-century women of all classes. And the way of dealing with it depended also on class. An upper-class woman – or even one from the middle classes who had enough money and knew where to go – could, through the hushed network of whispered gossip, find a doctor who would be willing to help her. Acquiescent medical practitioners were able to offer more sanitary environments, the benefits of medical training and, later, anaesthetics such as ether or chloroform to dull the extreme pain of a termination.

But if a doctor refused to perform a termination, even affluent women had little recourse but to approach those nurses and midwives known to perform abortions, even though the risks of death were higher. Word of mouth or even carefully coded advertisements in newspapers could lead to these abortionists. Affluent women consulted the new 'male midwives', or accoucheurs – trained medical practitioners with more knowledge of anatomy and access to devices such as the speculum.

Poorer women, on the other hand, were forced to rely upon the age-old remedies of traditional midwives – the use of abortifacient herbs such as pennyroyal – or to run the risk of back-room poisons or implements of dubious safety to obtain abortions. Given the laws, practices and morals of the time, not only prostitutes but any woman who found herself pregnant had limited options open to her, particularly if she was unmarried. Unskilled wages were so low that it was often virtually impossible to raise a child as a single mother, let alone face the opprobrium attached to such a pregnancy. Terminating the pregnancy by some means or another was often the only answer to a desperate situation. Death was a frequent consequence of both childbirth and abortion.

In just one morning, a busy abortionist could earn the equivalent of several years of a domestic servant's wage. A working-class woman with little education or training and few skills could set herself up with almost no overheads. The risks were high, since the desperate women and girls who came to her might die from the effects of negligence, gross incompetence and filthy, unsterile instruments in dirty surroundings. Yet, despite the considerable hazards of this form of domestic entrepreneurship, the temptations to run an abortion business were great.

Procuring an abortion was initially not a common-law offence, and did not even enter the English statutes until 1803. Until the beginning of the nineteenth century, English cultural attitudes emphasised the importance of male reproduction. Anxiety passed from men's sexuality to women's reproduction. Whereas the law had no place in the bedroom to monitor the mechanical functioning of male ejaculations, suddenly women's reproductive capacity became the focus of harsh laws, repressive ideological imperatives and interventions because pregnancy provided a tangible physical and symbolic reality that sperm ultimately lacked.

Initially the new law against abortion did not receive widespread endorsement in legal or social practice. It took twenty years for the first case to be prosecuted in the Old Bailey.[1] The courts were not primarily concerned with the crime of procuring an abortion as such – instead, attention focused on whether the mother died following the procedure.

Then, in 1828, new legislation made the significant distinction between women who were 'quick' with discernible foetal movement – in which instance abortion was an offence – and those who were not. The House of Lords debate on the new Act was fully reported in New South Wales.[2]

Medical knowledge grew rapidly during the nineteenth century, and with it changes to relevant legal thinking, especially in the area of medical jurisprudence. For the first time the ethics of abortion – the harm to the foetus as well as to the woman – were taken into consideration. As early as 1823 Theodric Beck's *Elements of Medical Jurisprudence* addressed the issue, as did Alfred Swaine Taylor's 1836 *Manual of Medical Jurisprudence*, which contained sections not just on criminal abortion but also on concealment of birth. William Guy, Professor of Medicine at King's College, London, and a leading statistician, first referred to the term 'foeticide' (or criminal abortion) in his landmark and enduring treatise, *Principles of Forensic Medicine* (1844).

In 1861 the British Parliament enacted another *Offences Against the Person Act* whose provisions were followed in the Australian colonies (updating the Acts of 1828 and 1837), but the emphasis was on the use of poison and instruments to procure an abortion – both of which were far more dangerous, indeed lethal – rather than on the traditional swallowing of herbs. From this time, women who attempted to give themselves an abortion could now be prosecuted with a possible penalty of life imprisonment.

Despite these increased legal strictures, the justice system did not witness a sudden influx of cases under these provisions. The *British*

Medical Journal launched a spirited campaign against criminal abortion in 1868 to no avail.[3] The following year, Pope Pius IX issued his *Apostolicae Sedis Moderationi*, in which abortion was equated with murder. This had been an early Christian belief, but it had been reversed from the fifth century when St Augustine argued that an unborn child could not have a soul. Pius IX's 1869 papal bull radically changed over a thousand years of official Church thought. Even then, this represented a moral and theological conceptualisation and not a legal proscription in common-law jurisdictions such as the Australian colonies.

After 1828, with the enactment of the *Australian Courts Act*, all the laws of the United Kingdom were upheld before the tribunals and courts of the young Australian colonies. From the mid-nineteenth century, as self-government and elected representation began in the colonies, greater autonomy in the interpretation of the laws was accepted. This explains why penalties for performing an illegal abortion in the Australian colonies could be more severe than in England and Wales.

The first notable case to appear before the Australian courts relating to abortion with death as a result of negligence occurred in December 1882 when Elizabeth Taylor, a widowed abortionist from Richmond in Melbourne, was named in the inquest into the suspicious death of Mrs Margaret Robertson of West Melbourne. Initially, Mrs Robertson had visited Dr James Beaney. Known for not removing his diamond rings when performing terminations, 'Champagne Jimmy', as Beaney was also known, had been charged twice with the murder of a young woman in 1866 caused by an inept abortion. Though acquitted, Beaney's reputation as an abortionist persisted.[4] When Beaney refused to become involved in Margaret Robertson's case, Robertson consulted Taylor, whose abortion business was thriving.

On the day that Robertson sought her services, Taylor's house was full of patients, each paying some £20 for a termination; this fee was a domestic servant's wage for ten months. On returning home, Robertson was seriously ill. Dr Samuel Peacock was urgently summoned for a consultation. He was a noted wealthy abortionist who also charged £20 or more, depending on the financial circumstances of the client,[5] conducting his own women's hospital in East Melbourne. But there was little he could do for this patient, who was dying of gangrene.

In an obvious attempt to disguise the illegality of the situation before her death, Robertson told Peacock she had suffered a miscarriage, and that 'Mrs Smith' (the name she used for Taylor) was her nurse. Robertson's common-law husband cooperated with police, however, and identified Taylor as the abortionist who had caused his wife's death.

In her testimony at the inquest Taylor said she had run into Robertson, an acquaintance, in the Royal Arcade – off Collins Street in Melbourne – and Robertson had mentioned seeing Taylor's advertisement offering her services as a nurse and midwife: 'Elizabeth Taylor, Practical Midwife, Ladies' Nurse, consulted 10 to 4, 1 Waxman's Cottages, Bridge Street, RICHMOND.'

The inquest jury decided that Taylor was guilty of manslaughter and should stand trial. They also recommended that doctors submit accurate death certificates.[6] Despite the verdict at the inquest, at her trial in February 1883 – with no witnesses, no confession and a practice conducted in secret – Taylor was found not guilty of manslaughter after attempting to procure an abortion.

Mrs Taylor was again in the national news in 1886 with the coverage of her trial following the death of twenty-one-year-old Julia Warburton. Warburton, an actress, had recently finished an engagement at St George's Hall in Bourke Street. She and her siblings were orphans and her late father, Percival Warburton, a well-known theatrical manager, had left the family in straitened circumstances. The three younger children had been sent to the Home of Hope, a private institution for destitute children in Collingwood, and their stepmother worked as a nurse and companion to an invalid in Royal Park. With her stepmother's approval, Julia rented a room in a 'small and ancient cottage' in Young Street, Fitzroy, in preparation for her termination. The owner, Rose Calloway – known as Mrs Hamilton[7] – supplemented her meagre income by cooperating with Taylor in her illegal abortion business. Hamilton's compensation was low for she believed that she took very few risks.

Julia Warburton underwent an abortion on 20 July 1886. Within six days she was seriously ill, and on 27 July she died without having seen a doctor.

Mrs Taylor, when she went to check on Julia at Mrs Hamilton's house, claimed that the girl had died from blood poisoning after extensive drug-taking. Her immediate problem was how to obtain a legal death certificate signed by a consulting medical practitioner. Dr Samuel Peacock had been summoned but refused to produce the certificate – for an enlarged liver – that Mrs Taylor requested from him.[8] When notified of the young woman's death, police immediately became suspicious of the circumstances and arrested Taylor within twenty-four hours.

Taylor's solicitor was Samuel Gillott, later Lord Mayor of Melbourne and Victoria's Attorney-General. With a large police court practice, he was also solicitor to Caroline Hodgson, 'Madame Brussels', the proprietor of two of the city's exclusive brothels on Lonsdale Street.[9] It is a testament to Taylor's earning capacity as an abortionist that she could enlist Gillott's services.

Professor Allen of the University of Melbourne conducted the autopsy on the now blackened corpse and declared that Warburton had succumbed to blood poisoning after an 'illegal operation'. When she heard the report of the autopsy, Taylor became desperate. She declared to her neighbours: 'I'm innocent. I knew of nothing wrong.'[10]

Taylor's protestations of innocence were rejected. Melbourne's coroner, Dr Richard Youl, hastily convened an inquest at Pepper's Victoria Parade Hotel. Born in Van Diemen's Land in 1821, he had trained in London and Paris, becoming Melbourne's coroner in 1854.[11]

At the inquest, details of the operation of Taylor's lucrative abortion network emerged.[12] Mrs Hamilton (aka Rose Callaway), the resident of the cottage in Young Street, feigned ignorance of Taylor's business and said that she regretted having rented out a room to Taylor for her clients' use. She testified that Taylor had asked her not to reveal anything when Dr Peacock was called in to attend her 'patients'. Taylor had told her that she would ask Dr Peacock to certify Warburton's death as rupture of the liver, paying him £50 for his services. He refused.

The inquest also heard that Taylor had tried to enlist the support of Dr Peacock, declaring that 'the girl is just dead. She has actually poisoned herself with drugs.' This was hardly feasible when Warburton died from gangrene. Peacock had warned her not to attempt to bribe him, which raises the question: had this occurred in the past? Peacock would certainly not have wanted to get involved with a midwife whose 'patient' had just died from an abortion. He had his own lucrative business to protect.

For her part, Taylor claimed that Warburton had gone to Hamilton's house in Richmond simply for a consultation with her as a nurse. As Warburton had never trained through the hospital system, this was unlikely; nor was she recommended by a doctor.

A neighbour, Annie Walton, told the inquest that on the day of Warburton's death Taylor had asked her to run a message, explaining: 'I am in trouble.'

After deliberations the jury decided that the injuries Warburton had suffered were not self-inflicted. Furthermore, Elizabeth Taylor had performed an illegal operation, the result of which caused the young woman's death. She was committed for trial after the inquest declared that she was guilty of murder.

Taylor was indicted for murder and the case was heard in September 1886 before Justice Edward Dundas Holroyd, who had trained at Trinity College, Cambridge, and at Gray's Inn, and was recognised as a jurist for his fairness and impartiality.[13] She was found guilty of murder, a crime that carried the death sentence.

In an appeal in late November to the Full Court, consisting of Justices Holroyd, Thomas à Beckett – nephew of former Chief

Justice William à Beckett – and Hartley Williams,[14] the case revolved around the distinction between murder and manslaughter. Taylor was represented by James Liddell Purves QC, who had studied both medicine and law in London,[15] and who, with instruction from Sir Samuel Gillott, formed an enormously expensive legal team.[16]

After considerable deliberation, Taylor was found guilty of manslaughter. With the jury's recommendation for mercy taken into consideration, she was sentenced to two years' hard labour. This was a light punishment, given that this was a case where death had resulted from gross negligence, which could have attracted life imprisonment or even the death penalty.[17]

It appears that despite her punishment, Taylor was undeterred on release. The profits from her enterprise must have been too high to be dismissed because of any moral qualms or fears of conviction. In June 1891 she again appeared in the Supreme Court – before Mr Justice à Beckett, who had heard her earlier appeal. She was indicted for the murder of Mrs Eliza Carter from Ballan, a small settlement 80 kilometres from Melbourne, following an abortion in May 1891. By word of mouth, Taylor's reputation as an abortionist had reached far beyond the boundaries of urban Melbourne into the rural districts.

In his testimony before the Royal Commission to Enquire into the Fall in the Birth Rate in 1903, pharmacist George Stevens testified that not only did women frequently consult him in search of abortifacients, but he was aware of the informal women's networks in rural areas that spread the identity and location of urban abortionists.[18]

The jury again found Taylor guilty, their recommendation of mercy no doubt reflecting an understanding of the desperation that drove women to call on her services during the decade-long Depression in the 1890s, when banks and businesses collapsed and unemployment was high, and even those who still had a job were forced to accept lower wages. Despite this recommendation, Taylor was convicted and sentenced to death.[19] On appeal, the sentence was reduced to fifteen years' hard labour.[20] Taylor was allowed early release.

In September 1898 she was arraigned once more on charges, this time before Justice Holroyd, concerning the death of a young woman named Mathews. Whether struck by remorse or guilt after her termination, this daughter of a local schoolteacher had committed suicide by hanging herself in the family home. Her mother, Mrs Walters, was now chronically depressed as a result. Taylor was found not guilty of the various offences pertaining to Mathews' death.

Justice Holroyd remarked with some sarcasm: 'You are an exceedingly unfortunate and very indiscreet woman. You know what I mean. You can go.'[21]

Taylor never again appeared in court. Perhaps the prospect of finding herself on the end of a noose was an incentive to close her once-lucrative enterprise.

Every capital city in the colonies contained a network of well-known abortionists. Some businesses were highly organised. In Sydney, for instance, an outfit in Elizabeth Street calling itself the British Medical Institute was the front for an elaborate termination clinic in the 1890s. None of the male and female abortionists had any medical knowledge or training.[22] On 3 October 1892 a detailed advertisement appeared in the *South Australian Register* alerting readers to the practice of Madame Melissa Harpur, a 'Lady Doctor' with extensive training and professional experience in England, Wales, Ireland, France, Germany, Scotland and America, as well as in New South Wales 'where no doctor has set foot'. At her consultation rooms, the advertisement continued, at North Terrace in Adelaide, she specialised in 'diseases of women' and could supply 'corrective pills' (code for supplying drugs to produce abortion). She also treated 'palpitations of the heart, restlessness at night, despair of recovery, anxiety, fear of death, nervous irritability, sluggish liver, epilepsy, coated tongue, varicose veins and consumption'.

Madame Harpur was not a registered medical practitioner in the colony and her long list of supposed areas of expertise was simply

'Madame Harpur' was just one of many aliases used by abortionist Melissa Harper. She became well-known to the justice system because over the years several of her patients died. Image: *Barrier Miner*, 6 March 1897.

part of her cover as an abortionist. She went under various other names: Melissia Fairburn, May Freebairn and Melissa Fairbairn. She was assisted in her practice by her untrained daughter, Elsie. Her husband, Dr Brierley Fairburn, *was*, however, a registered medical practitioner and on occasion collaborated in her practice. Additionally, he had had considerable legal training so he knew how to evade any police prosecutions.[23] He was regarded by his peers as unscrupulous and disreputable. He conducted abortions with Harpur on several occasions that came to police attention.[24]

Harpur made an excellent living out of her practice, often performing five abortions in a morning.[25] Five years passed without her attracting official notice. In March 1897, however, 'May Fairbairn, known professionally as Madame Harpur', was charged with the murder of Mrs Frances Blain from blood poisoning following a late-stage abortion. Blain was a married woman of thirty-four whose husband had gone to seek his fortune in the Western Australian goldfields. She sought assistance from Fairbairn when she was advanced in an adulterous pregnancy. Blain had suffered a wound in her uterus which became infected.

The accused was represented by the distinguished and expensive barrister and parliamentarian Sir John Downer QC, a notable conservative who nevertheless was a strong advocate of women's rights.[26] The Crown case acknowledged that murder had not been the intent but rather the death was the consequence of illegal procedures. Discrepancies in the evidence of Fairbairn's servants, even about the date of Mrs Blair's consultation, substantially aided her case.[27]

Expert testimony was given by Dr William Ramsay Smith, a Scottish physician and forensic medical specialist who came to South Australia as a pathologist and in 1899 was appointed city coroner.[28] He suggested that the deceased had died as a result of a wound from an incorrectly inserted catheter.

Presided over by Chief Justice and Privy Councillor Samuel Way, the trial was notable for Downer's expert cross-examination of the prosecution's witnesses. The court was overflowing with eager and curious visitors in the gallery, including many well-dressed women, some of whom spilled out into the wide corridors.

Way's explanation to the all-male jury of the distinction between murder and manslaughter was concise and erudite. After twenty-five minutes' deliberation, the jury returned a verdict of guilty of manslaughter. Mr Justice Way pointedly told the prisoner that she had escaped the penalty of a capital offence. He made particular mention of the fact that Fairbairn had not 'brought in a medical man' when the patient was obviously infected. Nevertheless, Fairbairn received a lenient sentence: three years' hard labour.[29]

In April 1903 Fairbairn was again committed for trial in the South Australian Supreme Court after an inquest into the death of a hotel cook, Annie Holmes, the mother of a six-year-old child who lived in Victoria. The coroner, again Dr William Ramsay Smith, was aided in his deliberations by the presence of the attorney-general, J. M.

Stuart KC. In the nineteenth century, attorneys-general were active participants in cases before the courts.

The first witness was horse trainer Alexander Miller, a friend of the deceased. His testimony was somewhat contradictory. He said that Holmes had told him she had used this particular service several times previously. Madame Harpur's business had run for the previous two years from a house in Flinders Street; a prominent notice in the window advertised her services. Even though Miller advised Holmes not to 'have anything to do with Madame Harpur', he did, however, make inquiries on Holmes's behalf and, in fact, went to see Harpur.

Holmes was weak and ailing soon after her termination when she and Miller met at the Globe Hotel in Glenelg, where she worked and he resided. During their conversation Holmes admitted she had bled profusely although 'everything has come away'. Fairbairn had used an instrument which, for some unknown reason, Holmes took home with her and thus could later be used as evidence in the trial.

Nurse Bertha Stacey testified that she looked after Holmes at the hotel before taking her to the Adelaide Hospital in an ambulance. Local practitioner Dr A. P. T. O'Leary attended Holmes, who by then was haemorrhaging and suffering a high temperature. Further testimony from Dr A. E. Shepherd, the honorary gynaecologist at the Adelaide Hospital, confirmed her parlous condition, which had required more surgery.[30] But in the absence of antibiotics, there was little he could do for his patient.

Fairbairn was arrested on 19 March 1903 while Holmes was still alive in hospital. On the order of Mr Justice William Bundey, a former parliamentarian with a successful practice in criminal law, Fairbairn was escorted to the dying woman's bedside for a positive identification. Holmes died soon after. The inquest jury returned a verdict of death from septic peritonitis, caused by an abortion during which a catheter had been used by Melissa Fairbairn (sic), otherwise known as Madame Harpur.

Judicial action was challenged by the prisoner's defence counsel, Rupert Ingleby, on several grounds. In the first instance, he argued, a hospital was not a site within the justice system; further, the prisoner did not have to incriminate herself; plus, the identification visit occurred on the Lord's Day, Sunday, 22 March 1903. In a hearing in banco – that is, with the full bench – consisting of the chief justice, Mr Justice James Boucaut, and Mr Justice Bundey, the matter was reviewed. The picture that emerged was one of judicial and administrative bungling.

Mr Justice Bundey made the revelation that he had been ill in bed when he was visited by the crown solicitor, who urged him regardless to issue an order on the grave matter of Holmes's botched termination and impending death. This in itself was an extraordinary action, suggesting how keen the Crown was to prosecute. The crown solicitor filed the required affidavits. The learned judge remarked that he had doubted even at the time of the crown solicitor's visit whether it would be to good effect, since Sunday was not a day set aside for court business.

Dr Helen Mayo, the University of Adelaide's first female medical graduate, was a young intern in the Adelaide Hospital and charged with the care of Holmes. When the police rang her requesting she permit a 'visit' from the prisoner, she informed them that her patient was critically ill and declined the request. Dr Mayo's concerns were overruled; the police took Fairbairn to the hospital for a positive identification.

As a result of the legal technicalities raised by Ingleby, the matter against Madame Harpur did not proceed to trial, despite the inquest's findings and recommendations.

In spite of her narrow escape from formal prosecution in 1903, Melissa Fairburn (aka May Fairbairn) was the centre of another coronial inquiry in April 1908, once more headed by Ramsay Smith. Laura Tucker, a poverty-stricken twenty-three-year-old woman, died following a termination at the hands of Madame Harpur. Tucker's mother had been dead for many years and her blind father resided in a benevolent institution for the impoverished, so she had been self-sufficient from an early age, working as a domestic at the Adelaide Hospital. She had a young, illegitimate child, who was boarded out with a Mrs Harriet Markham.

The last time Markham saw her alive was on 7 April 1908, when she took an obviously unwell Tucker to the Wright Street residence of a Mrs Billingham, presumably Tucker's landlady. Miss Jean Mills, the supervisor of the Lady Victoria Buxton Girls' Club, an Anglican charity, was consulted for advice since she was an authoritative middle-class woman. She advised that Tucker was in urgent need of medical attention.

In her testimony at the inquest, Miss Mills said that she had asked the other women to leave the room so she might speak to Tucker in private. The stereotype of innocent spinster certainly did not apply to Mills, who showed herself determined and knowledgeable about the 'troubles' that beset women who became unwillingly pregnant. No doubt other such cases passed through her club. Tucker only admitted to having fallen heavily and denied being 'in a certain way'. Mills knew this to be a lie. Seeing that Tucker was desperately ill, Mills summoned a district nurse to attend her, and also made urgent inquiries for further medical attention.

As she was being readied to go to hospital, Tucker confided in the nurse, Theodora Sweetapple, that Madame Harpur had performed an abortion by using an instrument 'which she left in for a few days'. She had charged five guineas for the service, although the inquest revealed Tucker had only paid £3/3/-. When Tucker first became seriously ill she had stayed with Harpur and her daughter, Elsie, for several days before she was turned out, literally onto the street. Harpur warned her not to say anything about what had happened to her, and her parting words were: 'You go to your lodgings and you will get along all right.' Unlike Elizabeth Taylor, who attended to clients who became ill as a result of their abortions, Fairburn took care not to be directly implicated.

At the inquest the police stated that when they interviewed Tucker on her deathbed she was rambling from the effects of her fever. Inspector Edward Priest testified that the dying woman admitted she had been pregnant and had sought a termination at 'a certain place' where a woman and her daughter 'helped her'. She maintained that 'Madame' and her daughter had 'been kind to me', despite forcing her to leave the house and abandoning her near the cemetery. Tucker told the police that Cyril Jackson was the father but she had no idea where he lived or how to contact him.[31]

Immediately, a warrant was obtained for the arrest of Melissa and Elsie Fairburn. Inspector Priest returned to the hospital later in the evening with James Gordon, a stipendiary magistrate, and William Hall, the clerk of the Adelaide Police Court, who were there to record Tucker's testimony in the presence of medical staff. Tucker stated that she had procured an abortion at Madame Harpur's place, adding that they 'tried to burn my eyes out'. As her fever intensified, Tucker's narrative became even more confused and rambling and the doctor in attendance, Edgar Wells, stopped the proceedings. Elsie and Melissa Fairburn were arrested soon after, but both strenuously denied having any knowledge or acquaintance with Laura Tucker.

Dr Wells testified that he knew Laura Tucker because she was a maid on the wards at the hospital. He had questioned her when she was admitted and she told him she had been to see Madame Harpur. Tucker told him that she hoped to 'get well soon'. And she sang him a song. When the coroner questioned Dr Wells, he testified that he thought the deceased had very little idea of the court proceedings at her bedside, but that she had positively identified Madame Harpur.

The coroner reported the jury's decision that Melissa Fairburn and Elsie Fairburn were guilty of wilful murder, and both were committed for trial. At the conclusion of the inquest, the defendants' counsel, Rupert Ingleby, identified certain inconsistencies in the bedside vigil. Clearly, the deceased's accusations that her eyes were burned out indicated some level of confusion.[32]

The trial was set for 1 June 1908 in the Supreme Court presided over by Justice Robert Homburg, who had studied under Sir James Boucaut and Sir John Downer. However, in preparing their case, the police concluded that the prosecution did not have sufficient direct evidence to substantiate a charge of murder and so the trial was abandoned. This was the last time that Madame Harpur – under any of her names – appeared in the judicial system.[33]

In the week before Christmas 1898, the body of a young woman was found at South Richmond floating in a trunk in the Yarra River. Three boys out boating sounded the alarm after they opened the box, which had been tied up with rope and weighted down with a large stone. A decomposing body, 'quite nude' and with a shaven head, had been shoved downwards into the trunk.[34] The 'Body in a Trunk' was an immediate public sensation. The government offered a reward of £50 for information leading to identification of the corpse and a further £500 for information leading to a conviction of the killer(s).[35] A free pardon was offered to any accomplice deciding to provide queen's evidence.

The police decided to take the unusual step of decapitating the corpse and preserving the head in spirits to offer for inspection. Several dozen families ventured to the morgue to determine whether this was the remains of missing daughters. In addition, thousands of people, including parents with small children, also visited the morgue eager to view the gruesome spectacle.[36] A local satirical magazine, *Melbourne Punch*, published a photograph of the woman's pickled head and an accompanying article on 12 January 1899, a decision of poor taste and judgment unrivalled in the annals of Australian journalism.

That same day, Olga Radalyski, Travice Tod and Thekla Dubberke were arraigned in the Melbourne City Court in connection with the suspicious death of Mabel Ambrose, the girl in the trunk, whose mother had identified her head. Mabel had been just seventeen years old and had lived in South Yarra. A large crowd milled around Russell Street court during the arraignment, anxious to hear any salacious revelations about the mystery that had gripped the city over the summer. Three police officers had to be stationed to prevent the public galleries overflowing. Seven honorary magistrates sat on the bench, a mark of the importance of the case.

Thekla Dubberke, described as a pale young woman in a simple black frock with a gold cross at her throat, was the star witness; she had provided the police with vital evidence, denying that her motive was to obtain a reward. Constable Organ in South Yarra had made local inquiries, which led to Dubberke's involvement in the investigation. She was remanded for a week. Next, an older woman, 'Madame Olga', who was both deaf and nearly blind and looked 'wretchedly ill', and Tod, a young man in his twenties, were remanded in custody. Dubberke was taken under police escort to 73 Osborne Street, South Yarra, to assist the police with further inquiries.[37] The alleged perpetrators of the crime had been foolish enough to leave a card with this address in the box with the body. It was where Thekla Dubberke and Madame Olga lived.

That same day, 12 January 1897, a medical practitioner with rooms in the Prell Building in Collins Street was mentioned in the confession Tod supplied to police. Dr William Gaze MD LSA LMCP London MRCS was a principal in the Polypathic Medical Institute. Dubberke (or Beatrice Jamison, as Gaze knew her), he first alleged, asked him in mid-December to accompany her to a house in Osborne Street, South Yarra, where her 'step half-sister ... Madame something or other', was caring for a girl who was 'very ill'. He told her he never made home visits. Further conversation with his visitor revealed why the girl was dying. Gaze stated to police that he '... never had anything to do with cases of this sort'.

After consulting with an unnamed colleague, Dr Gaze visited the house in South Yarra, by which time the 'patient' was dead. Dubberke told him a local doctor had issued a death certificate. Gaze also told police that Tod, the deceased's lover, who had been present during his visit, had arranged to pay for the funeral expenses.[38]

The following day Gaze supplied another statement, in which he said he had had a conversation with Dr James Neild, a medical colleague he had never previously met, on the subject of the crime. This in itself was odd, since James Neild was a distinguished forensic pathologist lecturing on the subject at the University of Melbourne since 1864.[39] It was then that Gaze admitted that the 'patient' was not simply dead when he went to the house in South Yarra but already decomposing. The body lay on a bed covered in blankets and hot water bottles. He saw that she had been dead for at least a day and he believed that the ruse to keep her warm was to make him think the girl had just died.[40]

The police further interviewed Gaze, who now claimed he visited the premises in South Yarra merely as 'a personal favour to Dubberke' – this despite previously denying that he knew her well. He then elaborated to say that he had met her when she accompanied Madame Olga to his consulting rooms. Gaze further stated he did not consider these circumstances 'suspicious'. The *Argus* on 16 January noted that Gaze had opened his practice in Melbourne only two years previously, after moving from New Zealand, and had taken over the rooms of the former coroner, Dr Youl, a close colleague of Dr Neild. The police discovered that Gaze, reportedly, had been a notorious abortionist in Westport, New Zealand, where he also 'kept' a number of women.[41]

The Radalyski house in Osborne Street was soon a destination for thousands of curious onlookers, who crowded onto the street and footpath. Some went to look at the real-estate agency – located in the same street – where Tod was employed, as well as the home of Mabel Ambrose's mother, Mrs Ambrose (or Dissratia, as she was also known), in Grosvenor Grove. The public was so gripped by the case that the *Argus* continued to report on events occurring even 'within the last 2½ hours', especially as statements made by Dr Gaze showed him increasingly drawn into the web of accomplices.

On 16 January, Gaze finally admitted that he had indeed known Dubberke 'for some time' and that she had brought Mabel Ambrose to him for a consultation to determine whether she was 'in a certain condition'. This seems to suggest that such a visit was a regular occurrence, thus implicating Gaze in Madame Olga's abortion racket, although perhaps not as a surgical abortionist.

In a press statement issued on 16 January 1899, Gaze confirmed that Ambrose was pregnant when she consulted him the first time, but said he only saw her again when she was dead.[42] Gaze now admitted that in retrospect it was 'foolish not to have reported the matter to the police'.

Dubberke's testimony at the inquest further alleged the doctor had supplied an abortifacient and recommended the internal injection of Condy's crystals.[43]

The officer in charge of the investigations, Superintendent Brown, was keen to obtain a conviction. Police had had Madame Olga primarily in mind when they began their investigations after the corpse was discovered on 17 December 1898. She was already a well-known palm reader and fortune-teller in Melbourne, and women in this line of work were often a source of information for clients who wanted to obtain an abortion.

Madame Olga's Russian pseudonym belied her origins as Elizabeth Elburn, the daughter of the licensee of the National Hotel in Essendon. She had married a career criminal, Charles Boswell, who – on release from prison – established himself in August 1894 in Launceston as a masseuse and 'medical electrician' – another euphemism for abortionist – under the improbable name of Carlo Adolph de la Lebedur. He was in fact an abortionist, with Madame Olga acting as his 'nurse'. Neither had any medical training or knowledge. They relocated to Dunedin in southern New Zealand and set up as abortionists again, but Madame Olga returned to Melbourne in December 1896 with her daughter, Mary, after her husband went off with another woman.[44] At the time of her indictment in January 1899, Madame Olga had never been implicated in performing abortions in Victoria, although the police had had their suspicions.

On 20 January, Dubberke accompanied the police to the city morgue, where she identified the trunk in which Ambrose's body had been abandoned and the handwriting on the card bearing the address as hers.[45] This was the vital piece of evidence the police needed to link the body to the perpetrators. That the handwritten card had accidentally been left in the trunk was remarkable, but that it had then somehow survived the immersion was extraordinary.

Events moved swiftly as the inquest was convened on 25 January 1899 under the watchful and experienced eye of coroner Dr G. C. Morrison. It was a comprehensive inquest, with crown prosecutor C. A. Smyth, Dr Neild as the forensic pathologist for the Crown, and barristers representing the three key witnesses. The *Argus* continued to relate proceedings in immense detail for the entire case. According to the report of 26 January 1899, 'Madame Olga ... was the only one who looked the part in the drama that was to be enacted'. She appeared depressed, staring into space, while her co-accused Alexander Tod, the father of Ambrose's unborn child, appeared not to realise that this grave matter concerned him. Dubberke, on the other hand, smiled and seemed insensitive to the situation, 'an interested observer rather than the central figure in the case'.[46]

The deceased's mother, Mrs Dissratia, as she was now known to be, testified that her daughter had met Tod, their house agent, through her. Tod's counsel, H. S. Cole, immediately attacked Dissratia, who admitted that Mabel had been wayward and often absent from home. Later testimony revealed that her daughter was known as 'Dirty Mabel' and was a habitué of inner-city hotels – with the implication that she was a young woman of loose sexual morals. Worse was to come when Dissratia's younger daughter, only ten years of age, told the inquest that Tod had given Mabel a card on which were printed the words '73 Osborne Street'. This was the card in Dubberke's handwriting that had been found in the trunk. The girl gave her testimony with no understanding of the importance of this evidence.

The Crown now had the sequence of evidence to link the three suspected perpetrators, although it was not explained how Tod had contacted Dubberke, the chief instigator of the tragic events.

Undoubtedly local knowledge had been readily available on the whereabouts of abortionists.

Thekla Dubberke was next called to the witness box. The *Argus* dramatically reported that 'a strained silence which had prevailed from the first was, if possible, deepened and interest was intensified'.[47] Dubberke was only twenty years of age, yet, as the report continued, 'she demeaned herself as if she were twice that age'. She was favourably compared to experienced expert witnesses: 'calm, self-possessed, decided, keen to grasp the purpose and direction of every question, with a well-modulated voice, a correct and even refined articulation, a ready command of well-chosen words … She might easily have been taken for a well-educated lady.' It turned out that she was an uneducated woman from rural Victoria, born to immigrant German parents.

Unfortunately, the newspaper did not print her direct evidence, as it was deemed to be too 'gruesome'. At the time, there was no such thing as a court reporter to take down the proceedings in shorthand as a court record. Thus, newspaper accounts were the most comprehensive public record of trials.

As the drama unfolded there was clearly going to be someone defined as an ogre and someone who would seem to be an almost innocent bystander, although, as events revealed, the persona changed. Dubberke portrayed herself as an upright citizen who waived her right to remain silent during police interrogations, anxious only to assist. The thought of the £550 reward and immunity from prosecution of course did not enter her head. Her composure in court remained 'unruffled', calm and persuasive.

Readers were assured that Dubberke had indeed identified the sequence of events undertaken by young Mabel Ambrose with such fatal consequences. Once more assuming the role of bystander, Dubberke described how she heard 'terrible screams which drew her to the room in time to see the dying girl laid back on the bed. Tod had left the house an hour before.' Her role, she claimed at first, was passive and at a distance.

Dubberke provided damning evidence against Tod, who she alleged had purchased two chains with which he intended to weigh down the trunk destined for the river. Several days later, 'Thekla' as she was now dubbed in the papers, had taken an emotional Madame Olga 'to the spot on the river bank where the trunk was despatched, hopefully never to emerge'. She went further and identified Dr Gaze of the Polypathic Institute as an accomplice.

According to Dubberke, 'Madame Olga' took up residence at 73 Osborne Street on 22 November 1898 when she leased the house from a builder, William Dixon. His later testimony at the inquest was that Madame had been accompanied by 'a young girl', whom he identified as Thekla Dubberke. Another 'girl' he could not identify had stayed there for around three weeks. This was undoubtedly Mabel Ambrose, who had been asked to perform household duties while undergoing procedures to effect an abortion. Another male acquaintance of both Radalyski and Dubberke could not positively identify Ambrose as the third woman he had seen them with.

When Dubberke (or Vera Orloff or Beatrice Jamison, as she variously called herself) returned to the witness box, she continued her role as the star of the proceedings. She said that she was a domestic servant who had known 'Madame Olga', then a palm reader, for only six months. Ambrose had come to see the palm reader seeking treatment for 'her certain condition'. Dubberke stated that Ambrose told her that Alexander Tod was the father. He had promised to marry her, even though he was engaged to be married to a respectable young lady. Tod also supplied 'dangerous' drugs which caused Ambrose 'great pain' and uncontrollable retching. Dubberke, under cross-examination later, told the inquest she had advised Ambrose to consult an unnamed, well-known abortionist who was a medical practitioner, but Ambrose refused.[48]

Dubberke also attempted to obtain drugs from a pharmacist – initially unnamed – at the Royal Alfred Hospital to ensure an abortion for Ambrose. The pharmacist was familiar with the operations of 'Madame Olga'.[49] This implies that the latter had been practising as an abortionist, but until now no one had died as a result and thus she was unknown to the courts.

When the inquest reconvened on 2 February 1899, Edward Fisher, the dispenser at the Royal Alfred Hospital, stated that Dubberke had come to see him saying she had infected gums and needed drugs. He told her to consult a dentist.[50] He denied supplying ergot, a well-known purgative used to assist abortions.

Another witness, Robert Gabriel, an assistant at a 'Eucalyptus Oil Depot' in Chapel Street, Prahran, also testified that Tod had come to the business asking for ergot, admitting that it was to procure an abortion. 'Madame Olga was going to do the trick with a battery,' he confided, but this was the backup. Gabriel purchased ergot from Felton Grimwade and Co., a firm that manufactured chemicals. Tod returned several days later saying that 'it has not worked'. But all was well, he informed Gabriel, as Ambrose had run off with an unnamed man from South Australia.[51]

With no results after three weeks, 'Madame Olga' asked Dubberke to take Ambrose to consult Dr Gaze in order to get 'more drugs'. Gaze originally said he had refused, advising Ambrose to stop her 'treatments' with 'Madame Olga'. After this Ambrose was subject to an operation with the electric battery 'which caused her great pain'. When she died on 13 December, the ruse to obtain a medical certificate the following day from Dr Gaze was perpetrated. Clearly, Tod was desperate to get rid of his problem with Ambrose, using as many methods as possible to effect his desired outcome.

When no death certificate was forthcoming, the accomplices decided to dispose of Ambrose's body. Tod offered to bury it in the bush, but had to abandon the plan when he encountered difficulties hiring a suitable buggy. He then decided to dump it in the river. Dubberke and Tod placed the body in the trunk and then disposed of it in the river without realising that it would float to the surface. Concerned, Dubberke visited Dr Gaze the following day, under the name Vera Orloff, and told him what had happened. He told her that gases in the body would probably make it rise to the surface.

Under cross-examination from Gaze's barrister, Dubberke was forced to admit she was 'kept' by a man whose identity she refused to reveal. He did, however, have an office in the Prell Building, the same building in which Dr Gaze's rooms were located. It was delicately implied that the star witness might be a prostitute. Her positive portrayal in the press came to an abrupt end as more was revealed of her life and circumstances.

Dubberke was actually kept by three different men, each of whom thought he was her sole protector. She also admitted that she had sexual intercourse with other men. Gaze may have been a client since she revealed he sometimes 'gave me money'. Laughter broke out at the inquest when Dubberke then added: 'He said he might have me taught dispensing and typewriting.' She also stated he had given her unspecified 'medicine' (presumably an abortifacient) on one occasion.

Returning to the issue of the disposal of the body, Dubberke reluctantly revealed to the inquest that she had 'contemplated' cutting off Ambrose's hair and had suggested knocking out her teeth to prevent further identification. The body had had several lower teeth knocked out and had been shaven.

'Madame Olga's' defence counsel, Mr Levy, with a certain desperation after these revelations, suggested that Ambrose may have succumbed to an epileptic fit, which explained the use of the battery. Why it would have been deployed for epilepsy in Ambrose's uterus was left unanswered.

At the conclusion of the inquest Dr McInerney, William Gaze's counsel, added that his client had indeed supplied a 'harmless remedy in the case of a slight irregularity'.[52] This was the term used in abortionists' advertisements – they did not perform abortions, rather they simply relieved menstrual irregularities. The evidence pointed to Gaze as an unethical medical practitioner involved in the lucrative abortion business.

The jury retired to consider its verdict for just seven minutes. Ambrose had died of 'suffocation' at the hands of 'Madame Olga

Radalyski', with Dubberke, Gaze and Tod accessories before the fact. They were all committed for trial at the Victorian Supreme Court. This was despite Dubberke's cooperation with police inquiries and her belief that she was therefore protected from prosecution. The police were commended for their strenuous efforts. Senior Constable Davison was praised for his foresight in preserving the decapitated head in spirits.[53]

The trial before Chief Justice Sir John Madden (1844–1918) began on 22 February 1899, with the gallery packed with well-dressed women fanning themselves in the heat. Radalyski was charged with wilful murder, and Tod and Gaze as accessories. Dubberke was the star witness for the Crown. Her evidence reiterated that given at the inquest and was again described as 'unrepeatable' for public broadcast.[54] No new testimony or evidence was supplied after the comprehensiveness of the inquest. Dubberke, however, asserted that she did not want 'Madame Olga' imprisoned for 'concealing a body' if Tod escaped prosecution. This had been her motive for turning queen's evidence.[55]

At the conclusion of the trial Gaze was acquitted, although his medical practice was now ruined. He had hired Sir Frank Gavan Duffy,[56] who was to be appointed in 1913 as Justice and in 1931 as Chief Justice of the High Court. He was an outstanding orator in the courtroom, a service for which his clients paid dearly. Radalyski and Tod were found guilty of murder, with a recommendation from the jury for mercy since the defendants had not intended to kill Ambrose. Chief Justice Madden was not a sentimental man. He ignored the jury's plea for mercy and sentenced the defendants to death.[57] A week later Dubberke, now living with a Lutheran pastor's family, claimed the reward of £500. Constable Organ of the South Yarra Police Station also contemplated applying for the reward.[58] The matter was referred to the Colonial Secretary.

In the end it was Mr C. S. Pratt from the Prell Building in Collins Street who received the generous reward. He initially gave information to the police that led to their identification of Dubberke. No details regarding Pratt's source of information were forthcoming.[59] There was speculation that he was one of the unnamed men who 'kept' Dubberke. On 13 April 1899, the *Argus* reported that Charles Seymour Pratt had vacated his office and left the colony.

On 26 April 1900, the marriage of Thekla Regina Dubberke to an unnamed 'old admirer' was conducted in an unnamed Church of England parish. According to the newspaper account, dressed all in brown, Dubberke had two Anglican deaconesses as witnesses. The only other members of the congregation were 'two girlfriends and an elderly man'. Dubberke had sought refuge in the 'Deaconesses Home' and was now, as the Reverend Canon Charles Godby, rector of St George's, Malvern, revealed, 'truly penitent'.[60] What was not reported was that Dubberke had been admitted to the Anglican nuns' House of Mercy in Cheltenham, which had begun life as a home for wayward girls in Lonsdale Street.

For Tod and Radalyski, life did not proceed so promisingly. Radalyski wrote to her father on 27 February 1899: 'I may never see you again in life. Better had it been last year than I should have lived through this disgrace and horror. God comfort you my father and pray for your unfortunate girl and forgive me …'[61] The disgrace she referred to was clearly the death of Ambrose and the subsequent inquest and trial rather than her occupation as an abortionist. Radalyski's parents petitioned the governor to extend mercy, blaming her marriage to her criminal husband for all her misfortunes.

The Victorian cabinet considered the capital sentences on 19 March 1899. After extensive debate a recommendation was forwarded to the Executive Council asking that Radalyski's sentence be commuted to ten years' hard labour and Tod's to six years' imprisonment. Both condemned prisoners were told their good news as they sat in their cells awaiting the dawn on the day they were to be executed. Radalsyki heard the news through an ear trumpet into which the prison governor shouted loudly. From that moment onwards, she disappeared from the public gaze.

CHAPTER 2

Lethal Abortion in the Twentieth Century

Australia entered the twentieth century a society obsessed by sex – or at least the results of it. Influenced by the Depression of the 1890s, there was a dramatic decline in the birth rate in Australia from 1891 – when married women typically gave birth to seven or more babies – to 1901 – when the number had fallen to five, a fact that prompted intense debate. Politicians, clergymen, journalists and medical practitioners fumed about 'racial decay' and 'race suicide' as they envisaged scenarios of a thinly populated bastion of British civilisation 'swamped' by the 'hordes from the north'. In cartoons and illustrations of the day, the new nation was frequently depicted as a nubile if modest young woman whose virtue was under siege from nefarious Asian interlopers intent upon rape and plunder. This collective anxiety reached its crescendo in 1903 when the New South Wales government established a Royal Commission to inquire into the decline in the birth rate.

Australian women were the targets of the commission's criticisms: it argued they were selfish in their desire to limit their families, initially by the use of contraception. The often hidden spectre of abortion and maternal death also moved from the shadows into the full light of public inspection and discussion.

In 1905 two sensational cases brought the issue into widespread public scrutiny again. In the Hobart Police Court on 30 August 1905, Dr Bingham Crowther, the scion of one of Tasmania's most illustrious scientific and medical dynasties,[1] was charged with the murder of Winifred Luttrell. His colleagues, Dr P. J. Godfrey and nurse Sarah Knight, also stood condemned. The postmortem revealed Luttrell had undergone an abortion a few days before her unexpected death. In the Supreme Court trial, heard before Tasmania's Chief Justice, Sir John Dodds (1848–1914), in September 1905, all the plaintiffs were found not guilty after the jury deliberated for just twenty minutes.[2] Given Crowther's background (his father, Dr W. L. Crowther, was well known as a surgeon and parliamentarian in Tasmania, and had briefly – in 1879 – been the premier), the finest and most expensive legal counsel represented the trio.

In the second notable case, the defendant was *not* a well-connected medical practitioner. Margaret Jackson, an elderly unqualified 'nurse', was arraigned on the charge of the murder of a young woman, Sidney Hanlon, who died of peritonitis after undergoing an abortion in Sydney. William Hanlon, the husband of the deceased, was found guilty of manslaughter for supplying the fee for the procedure, and sentenced to two and a half years' imprisonment and a self-recognisance of £100 upon release.[3]

At her trial the police produced evidence of extensive advertising by Jackson, with hundreds of pamphlets and cards offering abortifacients as well as other 'midwifery' services for 'irregularity'.[4] Margaret Jackson was found guilty of manslaughter and sentenced to six years in prison – with 'light labour', a concession to her advanced age.

When Jackson appealed her sentence, justices Henry Cohen, Sir William Owen and Robert Pring, all of whom were considered fair and humane jurists, quashed her sentence on technical argument.[5] At a time when public and official concern was focused on maternal deaths and the falling birth rate,[6] this was an unpopular decision. The Crown in turn appealed, taking the case to the new High Court of Australia, even though this august institution had primarily been established to determine constitutional issues. This appeal was heard by Chief Justice Sir Samuel Griffith and justices Edmund Barton and Richard

LADIES!

The Special Diseases incidental to young, middle-aged, and old ladies.

IRREGULARITIES treated with entire confidence and success.

FEMALE PILLS,

for Irregularities and Obstructions. 10s. and 20s. per Box (extra strong). Guaranteed.

29 York-st, Wynyard-sq.;
Box 920 G.P.O., SYDNEY.

Dr. CARTWRIGHT'S
FEMALE TABLETS

Nothing causes Girls and Women so much Worry and Distress as Irregularities and Delays. These Newly-Discovered Tablets are a Positive Cure, even in the most obstinate cases of Obstruction.

Price 10s and £1 per Box (extra strong). Call or Write.

29 York Street, Wynyard Square, Sydney.

Bulletin, 7 November 1896.

Advertisements for so-called cures for menstrual irregularities – the 'cures' were really abortifacients – offered hope for women dealing with unwanted pregnancies.

O'Connor, and the original conviction against Jackson was upheld.[7] In his opening remarks, Griffith did observe that criminal appeals from the Crown were unsuitable for his court's jurisdiction.

The matter did not end there, however. Jackson's counsel, Wilfred Blacket, moved for a *rule nisi* on the grounds of habeas corpus due to the defendant's re-confinement in Darlinghurst jail.[8] Subsequently, the Full Court of New South Wales ruled that she could be released, even though the Chief Justice had declared that Jackson had indeed been fortunate in the first instance not to be found guilty of murder as charged.[9] This was not in any way a precedent for lenient treatment of cases where a death occurred after an illegal abortion; rather, it was a ruling based on points of law.

In 1906 the New South Wales government established an inquiry into the operation of private and unregulated 'lying-in' hospitals, where so many illegal abortions were conducted. That year Octavius Beale, a commissioner on the 1903 birth-rate inquiry, funded a federal commission into the sale of secret cures, drugs and foods; abortifacients were clearly a target.[10] Undeterred by what he perceived as official hesitation, Beale continued his campaign, publishing an alarmist polemic, *Racial Decay*, in 1910.

Such admonitions from community and government leaders hardly deterred the lucrative abortion industry. The *Adelaide Register* of 4 December 1908 featured an article entitled 'Women and Tragedies', which dealt with one case of a lethal abortion and another of infanticide and domestic violence.

Florence Hope, 'a fashionably dressed woman of about forty years of age', was taken to the Melbourne watch house at midnight on 3 July 1908. She had been arrested in connection with the death of Bertha Whitford, a twenty-seven-year-old domestic servant, at The Hospital for Women in Melbourne on the previous 30 November. The daughter of farmers in rural Victoria, Whitford had gone to see Hope at her home in the expensive bayside suburb of Sandringham several days before her death.[11]

The inquest conducted at the city morgue was presided over by an experienced coroner, Dr Robert Cole. The famed pathologist Crawford Mollison had conducted the postmortem and he testified that Whitford had died from blood poisoning. Represented by Percy Ridgeway, a solicitor with nefarious connections and reputation, Hope was released on bail to appear in the Supreme Court in February 1909.[12]

The crucial evidence in the trial heard before Justice (later Sir) Leo Cussen concerned testimony taken by police at Whitford's bedside when she knew she had no hope of recovery. Apart from testimony from Whitford's sister, this constituted the only substantive evidence for the prosecution. Dying declarations in the case of homicide have a special place in English law and were (and still can be) regarded as the equivalent of a sworn oath. This exception to hearsay evidence law rested on the unfairness of secret offences going unpunished.

Hope was found guilty and sentenced to death despite the jury's recommendation for mercy. She appealed immediately with the Full Court of Victoria, which upheld the original sentence. Still determined, Hope appealed to the High Court on the grounds that the dying statement of the deceased was inadmissible evidence. The case was heard in the High Court of Australia by Chief Justice Griffith and justices Barton, O'Connor, Isaac Isaacs and Henry Higgins in March 1909. Hope was represented by William Schutt, who had been an associate of Isaacs and was later appointed to the bench of the Supreme Court of Victoria.[13] A majority indicated that the appeal should be denied.[14] Hope's only chance to avoid the noose lay with the Victorian Executive Council, which deliberated on 19 March 1909. The Chief Justice, Sir John Madden, in his role as lieutenant-governor of the state, presided at the meeting; the outcome was a recommendation that Hope's sentence be reduced to ten years' hard labour.[15]

On 7 May 1910 police discovered the body of a 'neatly dressed girl' in O'Connell Street, North Melbourne. Isabel McCallum was not a girl but a domestic servant from Geelong, aged in her early twenties, who had died from haemorrhage, shock and peritonitis following an abortion. At the inquest conducted on 22 May, her fiancé, a blacksmith named James McCarthy, testified that he had wanted to marry McCallum and had pleaded with her not to undergo an 'illegal operation'. He said that, despite this, he had accompanied her to a house in Stanley Street, Collingwood, on 4 May. There he met Minnie Yee Lee, a herbalist from Ballarat, who assured him his fiancée was 'in good hands'. Present also was a 'heavily veiled', disguised woman, later revealed to be Clara Pennington. When he visited the house again on 7 May he was informed Isabel was dead and that he should 'keep his mouth shut or it will cause terrible trouble'. The abortion had cost £10/10/-. McCarthy was distressed not just by his fiancée's death but also by the apparent theft of her engagement ring.

Although they did not perform the lethal operations, Yee Lee and Pennington were sisters and both involved in an abortion business that clearly operated through regional centres and was linked into Melbourne. Yee Lee stated that she had given McCallum herbs at her practice in Ballarat[16] and, when questioned by police, both women admitted they had taken McCallum to the house of 'nurse' Elizabeth Downey on 4 May, and had then gone back to Pennington's home to have 'a cup of cocoa' before returning to Downey's later in the evening. They alleged that the deceased had asked them to return her engagement ring to her 'sweetheart'.

The coroner found Yee Lee, Pennington and Downey guilty of murder and committed them for trial. Clara Pennington's husband, Henry Pennington, was arrested as an accessory. Police Magistrate Cresswell granted the defendants bail.

Charges were dropped against Henry Pennington but Yee Lee, Downey and Clara Pennington stood trial on 20 June 1910 before Justice Sir Joseph Hood. He was the first Melbourne-born and educated justice in Victoria, appointed in 1890 to the bench, and regarded highly as fair and logical in his judgments.[17]

Downey was represented by George Maxwell, considered the foremost advocate of the criminal bar in Victoria, whose fee matched his reputation and expertise.[18] James Purves KC and L. B. Cussen appeared for the sisters. Both were highly experienced, able and expensive counsel.

The Crown rejected arguments that Downey should be tried separately. Indeed, the prosecutor, Mr Woinarski KC (later Judge Woinarski), informed the jury that this was not a case of wilful murder where malice or revenge was involved.

Downey stated she had not performed an illegal operation and had merely taken McCallum into her home as 'an act of charity'. But McCarthy's testimony revealed how the unfortunate series of events occurred. He had written to Yee Lee at 6 William Street, Ballarat, although he did not explain how he knew she was an abortionist who could 'bring things right'. The 'medicine' was ineffective, so he inquired about 'an operation', which he was informed would cost £10/10/-. When he replied that he did not favour this action, Yee Lee wrote back that 'this was a great injustice to the girl'. McCarthy accompanied his fiancée to Pennington's home in Melbourne. Here he was reassured that Yee Lee had 'dealt with thousands of cases like this and had a doctor behind her'. Yee Lee telegrammed him initially that all went well. The use of letters and telegrams – albeit that they could be later used as tangible evidence – suggests that the abortionists were confident and highly experienced. When McCarthy returned to Melbourne, however, Clara Pennington informed him that 'your young lady's dead. She took a bad turn at nine o'clock, and died at eleven.' Some time later, McCallum's engagement ring was actually returned to him.

Justice Hood pointed out to the jury that while the operation was performed by Downey, the other two defendants were equally involved as accomplices. The jury found all guilty of murder, with a recommendation for mercy for Pennington. All received the death sentence and were admonished for 'carrying on an abominable trade for some time'. Many women in the gallery burst into tears when they heard the sentence, some even becoming hysterical.

It turned out that Downey had been in court on abortion charges eight times previously. On one occasion she had been found guilty and sentenced to death; the sentence was later overturned on a technical point on appeal to the full bench.[19]

Eventually, cabinet recommended that Downey serve life imprisonment, with Yee Lee given fifteen years' hard labour and Pennington ten years.[20] Downey died in prison in April 1912 after a stroke.

On Saturday, 13 January 1923, newspapers contained a tiny item about thirty-one-year-old Frank Bonfiglio, who had been shot in the left arm and the back at 2 Burnley Street, Richmond, in Melbourne. The police discovered other bullet marks in the wall of the house. Bonfiglio was admitted to St Vincent's Hospital, where he was questioned by police.[21] His former wife, Hannah Elizabeth Mitchell, aged forty-five, had shot him, he alleged. Police arrested her.

These were the only details initially released. That a woman shot a man with a pistol was an unusual event in Australia at the time since women rarely used firearms here or elsewhere. Despite this, the tone of the article was very matter-of-fact. According to later newspaper reports, an unnamed woman had rung the Richmond police saying: 'I have just shot a man.' In Burnley Street they found Frank Bonfiglio, who had crawled to the next-door neighbour's house, from where Nurse Ilma Walters called the police.[22]

Walters was not the assailant. When Detective Frederick Piggott interviewed him as he lay in St Vincent's Hospital, Bonfiglio revealed that 'Nurse Mitchell' had shot him. Subsequently, Hannah Mitchell was arrested for attempted murder and then released on bail.

The lead-up to the story was complicated. It seemed that Bonfiglio and Mitchell had planned to remarry on November 1922, but Bonfiglio decided instead to go to Western Australia to re-establish himself as a marble cutter. While he was in Perth, Bonfiglio admitted, he had tried to extort money from Mitchell. Then, when he returned to Melbourne on 12 January 1923, he had 'come to her and asked for £500',[23] an exorbitant amount.

Aspects of the story seemed strange to the investigating police. Why would Mitchell be so eager to marry for what would be her fourth time? By law, however, spouses could not be forced to testify against each other in court proceedings. Exactly what Bonfiglio had over his former wife was not revealed …

Then the national newspapers of the weekend of 3 February 1923 were dominated by a story that was both gruesome and fascinating. In a feature entitled 'Body Thrown from Bridge', the *Sydney Morning Herald* carried the eyewitness account of Harold Sharkey-Boyd of West Melbourne, who had seen what he believed to be a body dumped into the Yarra River at 11pm the previous Thursday. A car stopped at Anderson Street Bridge, and 'two figures … emerged from the shadows, carrying a heavy object'. After apparently satisfying themselves that no one was watching, or so they thought, the pair dumped their cargo in the water and the car then sped away towards Richmond. Sharkey-Boyd was unable to recall the number plate. Within hours police were dredging the river, and eventually a heavy bag was discovered.

By this time hundreds of spectators had lined the bridge to watch. Their curiosity was rewarded: inside the bag Detective Sydney McGuffie and Detective Sergeant Taylor found the putrefying corpse of a young woman. Police reported that 'the legs were bent up' to fit into the corn sack. Inside there was another smaller bag, with the logo 'Victorian Portland Cement Company, Cave Hill, Lilydale'. Upon opening this, the police found a woman's skull, its brown hair slimy and entangled with ferns. This suggested that initially the body had been buried, then later thrown into the river.

Brisbane's *Courier Mail* that weekend emphasised that the body was naked as well as headless. Comparisons were drawn to the case of Mabel Ambrose (see pages 28–38) some twelve years before: could this be another instance of a lethal abortion?

On 2 February forensic pathologist Dr C. H. Mollison conducted the autopsy on the headless corpse, announcing it was impossible to ascertain the cause of death due to the severe decomposition of the body. Pupa casings caught in the dead woman's hair were an important finding. He noted, too, that the skull had no teeth.

This gave police an important lead in identifying the victim. A woman previously reported missing, Bertha Coughlan, had had all her teeth extracted by a dentist three years earlier, in 1920.

Based on the findings of the forensic examination, the police suspected that the woman's body had first been dumped in a gully in Coldstream, near Healesville.

Swiftly, Hannah Mitchell, a nurse from Richmond, was charged with Coughlan's death. The shooting of Frank Bonfiglio and the discovery of the young woman's body now began to seem connected. Newspapers ran the two items concerning Nurse Mitchell as one feature, even though reporters were yet to unravel the relationships and violent actions surrounding her.

From then on events moved rapidly. On Saturday, 3 February 1923, Melbourne's city police court was crowded with spectators eager to follow the arraignment of Nurse Mitchell, her daughter Margaret (known as 'Queenie'), and Mitchell's sister, Margaret Milward, for the murder of Bertha Coughlan on or about 18 November 1922. It was Bonfiglio's allegations while in hospital the previous month that had ultimately led to the arrest of the three women; he was granted immunity from prosecution.

Detective Piggott submitted to the court that on or about 17 November, Coughlan had gone to Mitchell's house in Burnley

Street, Richmond. The following day, Mitchell and 'a man named Bonfiglio' went to Carlton to obtain a car. Two days later the car was driven to Coldstream in the Yarra Valley.

'The accused were smartly dressed and composed in their demeanour during the proceedings,' major newspapers reported. The local *Richmond Times* went even further, giving fashion details: 'Mrs Mitchell wore a frock of biscuit-coloured *crepe de chine* with a smart grey fur and a small hat decorated with oriental colours.'[24]

Despite their smart clothes and property in Carlton and St Kilda, the Mitchell women were aggressive and coarse. It was reported that Hannah Mitchell's daughter, Queenie, a nineteen-year-old student, threatened to shoot Bonfiglio – 'if you do any harm to my mother … and I will shoot your son' – when he suddenly appeared on their doorstep on 12 January 1923. He returned later that night and joined Nurse Mitchell in bed for the evening. She shot him the following morning when he attempted to blackmail her. Journalists also noted that longtime residents of Richmond were standing across the road from the courthouse to watch Mitchell's appearance in court.[25]

Police had located the car, in which bloodstained carpet was found. It was owned by one of Mitchell's sons-in-law, although this individual was not implicated in any wrongdoing.

Mrs Milward admitted that she had been in the car when the body was dumped and had assisted her sister and Bonfiglio. At this point in the proceedings, Mitchell's solicitor, the notorious Percy Ridgeway, demanded to know if Milward was the police informant. This was overruled by the police magistrate.

Mitchell was remanded in custody while her accomplices were each released on £500 bail, guaranteed by Ridgeway.[26]

By Monday the Melbourne *Argus* of 5 February was able to fill in some gaps in the story, confirming that the corpse belonged to Bertha Coughlan, for whom police had been searching since 13 January 1923. (She had in fact been missing since 18 November 1922.) Coughlan was the twenty-eight-year-old unmarried daughter of a farmer, John

Coughlan of Hinnomunjie near Omeo. Her engagement to the local grocer had recently ended – the break-up triggered by the revelation that she was pregnant to a married farmer.[27] Relatives reported that Bertha had taken her broken engagement badly. She shredded her wedding dress and hid the remains in a drawer. Her former fiancé had left the tiny township suddenly.

Detective Piggott along with his team, including Dan and Warry, two black trackers, were searching bushland to try to match the ferns found in the sack. They were also trying to locate a gold brooch with the word 'Coughlan' engraved upon it. This was a treasured keepsake given to Bertha by the residents of Omeo in memory of her elder brother, James, who had died in the Great War. Bertha always wore this brooch.

The lengthy inquest into the death of Bertha Evelyn Coughlan, held in the Melbourne morgue under the direction of coroner Dr Robert Cole, began on 1 March 1923. Detectives Piggott and Edmund Ethell were key witnesses for the prosecution of the case. Piggott refused to divulge his informant's identity, although it could only be Bonfiglio and/or Milward. He told the court he had been informed that the body of the deceased had been moved several times, with the head removed from the body at a time unknown. The accidental finding of the headless body in the bag off the Anderson Street Bridge was 'a complete fluke', thanks to Harold Sharkey-Boyd.

Frank Bonfiglio was the star witness at the inquest. He recounted how his former wife, Hannah Mitchell, had come to visit him unexpectedly at Palamara's Richmond fruit shop on 18 November the previous year, asking him to accompany her to Caulfield racetrack. He reported he was not entirely comfortable about going with her since Mitchell had falsely charged him with 'cruelty' during their marriage. Her lover and solicitor, Percy Ridgeway, had collaborated on the charge, and Bonfiglio was convicted and imprisoned.[28]

Nevertheless, he did go to the races with Mitchell that afternoon – and she won £600, a considerable sum. He later returned to Mitchell's town house in Richmond, at around 9.30pm.

As usual, the downstairs bedrooms were filled with women, often four to a bed, crying and moaning – all Mitchell's patients who had undergone abortions. Unlike many abortionists, Mitchell provided accommodation and care after any procedure. In the sitting room, Bonfiglio got into conversation with a man, Horace Solly, whose wife was a patient. They simply could not afford a sixth child, he confided, saying Nurse Mitchell was their only hope.[29]

Suddenly Mitchell appeared, demanding Bonfiglio assist her to get a patient 'who has taken very bad' to the bathroom. In an upstairs bedroom a young woman lay in a pool of blood on a bed. With some difficulty, he and Milward got the seriously ill woman ready for another procedure. Mitchell performed a dilation and curettage on her without any painkillers or anaesthetic. Milward's son was asked to fetch the girl some brandy after forty-five minutes. Mitchell continued her work. Her next-door neighbour, Nurse Walters, came in at some time during the proceedings, the inquest revealed, and heard a 'glug of blood forming in the girl's womb'. The patient began to haemorrhage and was put back to bed. Mitchell was so exhausted that she retired to bed, telling Bonfiglio to keep her sister company.

At the inquest Bonfiglio stated that he asked Mitchell why she did not call a doctor. 'A doctor can do no more than I did to her,' she responded.

Milward continued giving the patient brandy, although it was clear she was dying. She told Milward she belonged to the Church of England and her name was 'Coug…' before she died. She was distressed that 'her boy' was not present. Her last words were: 'I feel so cold. Could you rub my hands, please? You are kind; you are so good to me … I am dying.' Milward then went into the kitchen and had a cup of coffee with her friend, Mrs Florence Spicer.

Bonfiglio claimed he tried to wake Mitchell from her slumbers when he learned of the death. When she asked him later to help dispose of the body, Mitchell made it clear to Bonfiglio that she had successfully disposed of dead patients in the past with the assistance of unnamed accomplices with cars.[30]

Throughout the inquest, more came to light about the series of events that led to this terrible death. John Coughlan said he had reported his daughter missing in November and was not surprised to learn she had died. He could not remember her birthday but thought she was 'about twenty-seven or twenty-eight'; nor could he give a good description of her appearance. All he could really say was: 'She had not a baby face.'

Bertha had travelled to Melbourne seeking treatment for persistent earaches, and had stayed with her aunt. She learned of Mitchell's services through a network of men from her own district, including the local train driver and another, who paid for her confinement. This man was presumably the unnamed father.

It was startling how Bertha had learned of Mitchell since in other cases it was generally a tight women's network of information that was at work. Evidently men had their own network when needed.

The morning after Coughlan died, the inquest heard, Mitchell went to Nurse Laura Gidley's private hospital next door and spoke to Nurse Walters. On occasions, Mitchell passed on her clients. She told Walters that a patient with a *placenta praevia* (where the placenta expels before the foetus) had died. This was untrue – both Milward and Queenie Mitchell had seen the evidence on the blood-soaked bed. This was Mitchell's ruse to deflect any suggestions of incompetence or a failure to call a doctor.

When Mitchell returned home, she asked Mrs Spicer to locate a particular man she knew to be a 'fixer', who would dispose of the body for £300 or £400. The task proved fruitless since the unnamed man refused on this occasion to engage in any illegal activities.[31]

It was later that Mitchell borrowed her son-in-law's car and dumped the body at Coldstream, with the assistance of Milward, Bonfiglio and her daughter. They covered the stiff corpse with leaves and ferns but made no attempt at burial. Mitchell's only comment, as reported in the press, was that 'she will be eaten by some animal in a few days, and it will not be known who she is when they find her'.[32] At dawn they returned to Richmond and set about destroying all traces of Coughlan's presence, trying to decide what to do with her gold brooch and her engagement ring. Mr Solly was still waiting for his wife in the sitting room, unaware of the drama that had unfolded.[33]

A Mrs Lillian Mueller, described at the inquest as the person who had originally brought Coughlan to Mitchell's place, suddenly turned up to take Coughlan back to her home. She did not persist when told Bertha had already departed. It would appear that Mueller was acting as an agent for abortionists.

Another crucial witness, Mrs Emily Tucker of Prahran, told the inquest that Bertha Coughlan had stayed with her before going to Mitchell's place. Mitchell had turned up on her doorstep asking her to say that Bertha had been at her home on 20 November. As an incentive to change her story Mitchell offered her £500 as the 'other two would try to lay the blame on me'. Tucker refused.[34]

More sensationally, Margaret Milward's testimony confirmed Frank Bonfiglio's. Her chief point of difference was to emphasise that Coughlan had suffered a 'premature confinement', not an abortion. She also testified that she told her sister she felt guilty and would tell the police what had happened. It was after this that Mitchell arranged for three unnamed men to pick up the body from the gully and dump it into the Yarra River.[35]

Young Alfred Milward also testified at the inquest, reiterating his mother's account of the events that led to the death of Bertha Coughlan. Florence Spicer gave damning evidence, testifying that Mitchell had told her: 'Keep your mouth shut. You know people who talk can be silenced.' That was the last time she spoke to Mitchell, who was well connected in the Melbourne underworld.

On Friday 9 March, the coroner concluded the hearings, stating first that there was no possible doubt the body was that of Bertha Coughlan and, second, that Hannah Mitchell was guilty of murder, with Margaret Mitchell and Margaret Milward accessories to murder.[36] Within a few days, though, all charges against Margaret

Milward and Margaret Mitchell were withdrawn after they fully cooperated with the police.[37]

Despite this, in the hearing at the city police court on 12 March, all three women stood accused. R. Knight acted as police magistrate, with a bench of six justices of the peace. The police restated their willingness to withdraw the charges against the accessories. Hannah Mitchell was ordered to appear before the Supreme Court of Victoria on 22 March.

The Supreme Court case was heard before Justice Frederick Mann, who in 1935 became Chief Justice of Victoria. He was noted for his scholarly knowledge of the law and his sense of justice.[38] Mitchell was represented by L. B. Cussen, instructed by Percy Ridgeway. Cussen's defence was canny; he called Dr Richard O'Sullivan to testify that, given Coughlan's persistent poor health, she might have died 'from a natural mishap'. Precisely how ear infections were relevant to her death was not explained. Nurse Mitchell, in this scenario, was merely assisting a patient in difficulties.

Mitchell elected not to testify under oath but took the extraordinary measure of addressing the jury from the dock for over an hour.[39] Even with three participants giving evidence for the prosecution, she was found not guilty – a surprise, given the finding at the inquest that she was guilty of wilful murder.

Undeterred by her narrow escape from a possible death sentence or life imprisonment, Mitchell continued her lucrative business. She appeared in court again in September 1923, charged with performing an illegal operation on a single woman, Beryl Moreno. The case did not proceed.[40] In early November that year she was in court once more, charged this time with the murder of Mabel Hodgkinson, a married woman with three children, who died after an abortion on 28 October 1923. Ridgeway again appeared for her defence in the police court. Senior Detective Davey informed the court that he had interviewed Mrs Hodgkinson in the Women's Hospital. He had been accompanied by Mitchell, who was identified as the person who had performed the abortion that had turned septic. Mitchell was allowed bail of £1000 as well as a personal surety of £500.

At the inquest, Owen Hodgkinson, a house painter from Brighton, testified that he had not been in favour of his wife's course of action, although he had accompanied her to Nurse Mitchell's place in Burnley Street. Mitchell said she would help and would charge £15 as 'he is a poor man'. This amount was still more than a male worker's pay for a month. After the procedure Mabel Hodgkinson went to her sister's house. When her condition deteriorated, a medical practitioner was consulted and she was admitted to hospital. The coroner found Mitchell guilty of wilful murder and committed her for trial in the Supreme Court of Victoria on 15 February 1924.[41] At the trial, yet again she was found not guilty.[42]

A year later, Mitchell was once more charged with wilful murder. Eva Pitt, a married woman with a family, died after undergoing a procedure. She had provided the police with a statement identifying Mitchell as the person who had conducted her abortion. By then, Hannah Mitchell had become well known to readers across the nation. The *Brisbane Courier* on 10 March 1925 announced: 'Hannah Mitchell Again In Trouble'. At the inquest heard before the city coroner, Frederick Pitt testified that his wife, Eva Pitt, the mother of six children – the youngest of whom was only seventeen months old – had undergone an abortion performed by Mitchell on 29 January. The coroner pronounced Mitchell guilty of murder but allowed her bail of £500.[43] By 25 March, the crown prosecutor had dropped all charges for this offence.[44]

On 11 January 1928, George Rosser, a young draper from Cowra in New South Wales, reported his wife, Inez Rosser, missing. He told the police he had accompanied her to a house in Richmond, where she had undergone an illegal operation. They had married on Boxing Day, even though she was pregnant to another man. In relation to this matter, Hannah Mitchell was arrested for 'using an instrument'. She denied the charge, although she did admit that she had met George Rosser.[45]

Rosser further told police that he last saw his wife on 2 January at Mitchell's house and she was 'seriously ill'. When he returned three days later, he was informed his wife had left after lunch and she was 'all right'. When he demanded to know what had happened to Inez, Mitchell simply told Rosser to go to the police if his wife was missing.[46] The police announced they would drag the river near Richmond.[47] Despite rigorous efforts, nothing was discovered.

After Rosser made his missing person's report, the police also searched the house in Burnley Street. No trace of Inez Rosser was found. A full description of the missing woman and the clothes she was last seen in was released. A week after that, the Victorian government offered a reward of £250 for information leading to the whereabouts of Inez Ada Rosser, 'dead or alive'.[48]

Initially, newspaper accounts of Rosser's disappearance were vague, referring to a missing woman 'with foul play suspected'. Soon, though, Nurse Mitchell's name was in the news[49] when, by February 1928, reporters discovered that Mitchell was again under suspicion for the death of a young married woman.

In the hearing before the Richmond Court, Mitchell was ordered to appear in the Supreme Court on charges of malpractice.[50]

The case was heard in November 1928 before Judge Williams, in a courtroom packed with enthusiastic spectators. Mitchell was represented by a former journalist, the successful and expensive barrister Thomas Brennan, only that year appointed as a KC. This time she chose not to use Ridgeway as her instructing solicitor but rather J. Barnett. It was a hard case to prosecute successfully with no eyewitnesses to the procedure and with no body. The jury deliberated for only an hour and found Mitchell not guilty as charged.[51] This proved to be her last appearance in the Supreme Court.

It can only be speculation that Inez Rosser died on the premises at Burley Street and that her body was disposed of more efficiently than that of Bertha Coughlan. It was clear she had not joined her former lover, a naval officer. A year after the trial, police investigated reports that a young woman's body had been dumped in a mine at Korumburra in the Gippsland district; they got nowhere.[52] The whereabouts of Inez Rosser were never discovered.

By the late 1920s, attitudes to sex, at least to marital sex, were undergoing significant transformation. Dr Marie Stopes's publications *Married Love* and *Wise Parenthood*, both published in 1918, commended a new frankness. A palaeobotanist by training, Stopes was part of the movement that favoured planned parenthood and marital sexual compatibility, not simply for the benefit of the individual family but for the wider eugenic health of Western society. The eugenics movement, which was popular in the early decades of the twentieth century, believed that planned reproduction would ensure that preferred characteristics were strengthened in the human population, while less desirable ones were bred out. Followers believed that the poor simply bred too many sickly, malnourished children – as enlistments in the armed services had so starkly revealed during the recent global war. Although Stopes's books were initially banned by Australian Customs,[53] during 1928 the film of *Married Love* was shown across the nation. In Brisbane it played at the Lyceum Cinema on a double bill with Charlie Chaplin's *The Circus*.[54]

The first indications that such ideas might have an effect on the liberalisation of legal attitudes to abortion were evident in the United Kingdom when Justice Sir Henry McCardie applauded a grand jury at the Leeds Assizes in December 1931 for throwing out a case against a woman who had performed a lethal abortion. The deceased had three children already. The judge said that he could not 'think that any woman should bear children against her will'. This was a revolutionary concept for the times. He then proceeded to criticise the law that prosecuted lethal abortion with a charge of murder.[55] This 'era of savagery' should end, he concluded. McCardie was a prominent member of the Eugenics Society in the United Kingdom.[56]

Even though Australia's laws were still influenced by those of Britain, McCardie's rebellious opinion was not immediately echoed in the Australian judiciary or statutes.

In 1933 the Racial Hygiene Association of New South Wales opened its first family planning clinic in Sydney, designed to cater to women with a family history of hereditary medical problems and those in poverty. Its founder, Lillie Goodisson, had been married to a syphilitic man later confined to a lunatic asylum.[57] The society upheld eugenicist principles of racial fitness and national vitality, which – it believed – were diminished by the evils of syphilis, 'mental retardation' and 'inferior stock'.

The clinic of course could hardly prevent all Sydney's unwanted pregnancies. This was a service performed from the mid-1940s onwards by Dr Reginald Jones, a Macquarie Street gynaecologist, reputedly with a lucrative abortion practice. A well-known racetrack identity, he also owned the Four Hundred Club, where many underworld figures gathered. Attempts to prosecute him proved fruitless.[58] Medical practitioners had long been preferred for such services by those who could afford their fees. Only doctors could legally use chloroform, a bonus during such a traumatic and dangerous procedure.*[59]

The birth rate fell dramatically during the 1930s with the impact of the Depression, during which there were fewer marriages and more abortions. To mark King George V's silver jubilee, in 1935 a subscription fund was set up by the federal government, with an initial £50,000 government grant announced by William Morris (Billy) Hughes, the federal Minister for Health, who regarded maternal welfare as a national priority.[60] The King's Jubilee Gift Fund for Maternal Welfare supported reforms to improve child and maternal welfare along the lines of the provisions that had already been instituted in Queensland since 1922.

---

*   In 1915 Dr Thomas Hodgson in Brunswick Street, Fitzroy charged £35 for a procedure conducted under chloroform and £15 with none in 1915. He was prosecuted in 1915.

That year the distinguished gynaecologist, obstetrician and lecturer at the University of Sydney Dame Constance D'Arcy delivered the Anne MacKenzie Oration at the Institute of Anatomy in Canberra, where she addressed Australia's alarmingly high maternal mortality rate: one in 180 women died in childbirth and it was estimated that up to 20 per cent of women who obtained illegal abortions died as a direct result of the procedure. As a young medical practitioner, she had been called to give evidence in a lethal abortion inquest, and the experience confirmed her antagonism to this procedure.[61]

Dame Constance was not the only influential person who campaigned against abortions and their perpetrators. Tragedy hit the family of W. M. Hughes, the federal Health Minister, when in 1937 his daughter, twenty-one-year-old Helen Hughes, died from an illegal abortion in London. She had attended the coronation of King George VI with her parents.[62] The details of Helen's death were kept secret but no doubt fuelled Hughes's campaigns against abortion and its often lethal consequences. And rumours had circulated in Victoria in the 1920s that the police commissioner, Thomas Blamey, was hard on abortionists because a former girlfriend had died at the hands of Dr Albert Bretherton.[63] Death from a mishap during an abortion could strike women from all classes, not just those who consulted unqualified local women trying to earn a living.

In 1938 Professor Marshall Allen, an academic and obstetrician from Melbourne, followed up his earlier groundbreaking, empirical research into the incidence of maternal mortality, claiming that one-third of maternal deaths were due to abortions.[64] That same year, Dr H. H. McClelland, a senior gynaecologist at the Women's Hospital in Brisbane, also publicly decried the incidence of lethal abortion, blaming 'degenerate doctors and nurses' as well as 'the decay of chivalry'.[65]

Despite a landmark case in England in 1938 that changed the principle of British law for almost the next thirty years – *R vs Bourne*, in which gynaecologist Dr Aleck Bourne was acquitted after prosecution under the 1861 *Offences Against the Person Act* for performing a therapeutic abortion on a fourteen-year-old rape victim – and a 1929 amendment that allowed for 'preserving the life of the mother' when done in good faith, such defences of lethal abortion did not immediately follow to Australia, where earlier strict precepts were maintained.[66]

World War II saw a spate of prosecutions for illegal abortions where death resulted. The influx of a million young American servicemen into Queensland, Sydney and Melbourne challenged more traditional moral values. Sexual behaviour for many young Australian women changed dramatically.

In February 1943, Vera Humphries stood trial before Chief Justice Sir William Webb in the Queensland Supreme Court on the charge of murder. On 6 January that year, Detective Inspector Frank Bischof had accompanied Humphries to the Brisbane General Hospital, where Laura Mowat lay dying from toxaemia and gangrene of the uterus; she died five days later. A clerk at the GPO in Brisbane, Mowat had become pregnant to Corporal Patrick Hill, a soldier in the 2nd Australian Imperial Force, who she thought would marry her. But – it emerged at the trial – he was already married, and Mowat was not his only lover.[67] So, instead, he located an abortionist for her. Hill stated that: 'Somebody gave me the number J 3914 … And I told [Humphries] I had a girl in trouble and she said she would fix her for £12/10/-'.[68] Humphries visited Mowat at home when she became ill, reminding her and Hill: 'If you get a doctor, mention no names, nor anything that has happened.'

Humphries was an unusual abortionist. She was well educated and had been a governess on a property before her marriage in 1920 to a farmer in Cairns. She ended the marriage after seven years of domestic violence. Later she worked at the Goodna Mental Hospital and had been an abortionist for a number of years when she married Petty Officer Thomas Humphries of the Royal Australian Navy in 1942.[69]

The jury deliberated for some time before finally delivering a verdict of guilty. She was sentenced to life imprisonment with hard labour, upheld on appeal.[70]

Concern for the falling birth rate was again expressed in public policy when the federal Labor government in 1944 established another inquiry to investigate this 'national decay'. The federal parliamentary Labor Party now contained many more Roman Catholics than previously, leading to a renewed hardening of attitudes towards any form of birth control. Arthur Calwell, the Immigration Minister in Chifley's government from 1945, suggested in a parliamentary debate that Australian laws should be similar to those of Nazi Germany and Italy.[71] In 1943, providing an abortion to an Aryan woman became a capital offence, and Mussolini not only outlawed abortion but banned contraception. That Australia had been at war with these nations seemed to escape Calwell's notice. Australian attitudes to illegal abortion were also reinforced. In South Australia three justices of the Supreme Court in 1944 proclaimed their dismay about this 'dangerous modern trend against the natural increase of the population' as well as criminal abortion.[72]

Several post-war cases exemplified the renewed determination to punish lethal abortionists. In February 1946, a housewife in inner-city Brisbane, Amelia Dow, was charged with the murder of Mrs Freda Bevan. Dow had no medical training – she simply 'wanted to help all these girls'. Bevan had left her war-time job and marriage in Sydney, relocating to Brisbane in 1943, where she engaged in sexual affairs with American servicemen. She obtained work at the Oriental Café in Fortitude Valley, close to the city centre, and with another woman set up in a flat in the nearby inner suburb of New Farm in March 1945. Her friend Sheila Malone stated that Bevan had '… kept company with a US serviceman', who had returned home. Pregnant and alone, Bevan had arranged to have an abortion with Amelia Dow for the sum of £16. Dow also cared for six state-fostered children, a fact which no doubt made her more aware of the fate of unwanted children.

Bevan came to seek her help via the networks that surrounded abortion practices. She arrived at Dow's inner-city home in Brisbane at a time when Dow's husband was working an extended shift on the tramways. Initially, Dow told Bevan that she was 'tired of doing this sort of thing'. She relented, unfortunately for Bevan. Dow admitted performing an abortion, stating that Bevan got up and left after the procedure. Mrs Bevan was found the next morning fully dressed and dead in Plunkett Street, Paddington, with £16/17/3½ in her purse and ants crawling all over her body. The trial revealed that Dow's adult son, Jim Dow, had arrived home at 9pm when Bevan was already dead. He took her body and dumped it in a nearby street.

Dow's main concern was not the fate of her deceased client but for her husband, who she said, '... knows nothing about all this business ... This will kill poor old Dad.' Despite the case being heard before Mr Justice Benjamin Matthews, a judge particularly sympathetic to ordinary people,[73] the jury had no hesitation in finding Dow guilty, with a recommendation for mercy. Nevertheless, she received a life sentence.[74] On appeal before the Full Court, her sentence was reduced to five years' imprisonment, largely because the trial judge had not sufficiently explained to the jury the distinction between murder and manslaughter.[75]

In Melbourne in March 1949, Gladys Brown and Kathleen Brian were convicted of the murder of Brian's sister, Mrs Joan Brady, on 8 December 1948. She died from suffocation when hands were held over her mouth to prevent the noise of her screams being heard, her counsel alleged. The postmortem revealed Brady died from heart failure when an instrument was plunged into her uterus. There was no suggestion that Brown had any medical training. Brian, an unskilled process worker from West Brunswick, had taken her sister to Brown for the procedure.

Brian was defended by the leading criminal barrister of the day, Jack Cullity KC. The case was heard before Mr Justice Duffy, who condemned Brown for conducting 'a horrible trade' but also lamented the harshness of the law concerning this sort of case.[76] The defendants were found guilty and sentenced to death, despite a recommendation for mercy from the jury.[77]

In dramatic circumstances, the Full Court of Victoria upheld the original decision, with a reduction in the sentence to three years' hard labour. The appeal rested on the point that the trial judge had taken the jury away from a general verdict by the direction of his remarks. The jury should have been able to return another verdict, such as manslaughter. Their Honours Justice Martin, (Sir) Charles Lowe and (Sir) John Barry also pointed out that this harsh legal regime had not been in force in England for fifty years. In that country, juries were allowed to distinguish between murder and manslaughter, for which there was no anticipation of death. Justice Barry was also less than happy that Kathleen Brian's confession might have been made under police duress.[78] For the prisoners, this was a reprieve beyond anything they could have imagined as they sat in the cells in Pentridge Prison awaiting imminent execution.[79]

Another sensational case in Melbourne occurred when Edna McDonald, aged twenty, died following an abortion. Her partly clad body was found dumped in a rubbish tip. George Cowen, Fred Cranella and Harold Plummer were charged with illegally disposing of a dead body.[80] Varna Patterson, the mother of six children, and Lillian Cohen were charged with McDonald's murder. Patterson had urged McDonald not to undergo the procedure, even offering to adopt the child herself.[81] Both judge and jury took note of this offer and she was released on a bond, while Cowen was sentenced to eighteen months' imprisonment for manslaughter.

In 1948, Ruth Park's prizewinning novel *The Harp in the South* was criticised for including a scenario in which a character, Rowena Darcy, contemplates having an abortion, although her Catholicism prevents her undertaking the procedure. Though newspapers had for decades reported on the underworld of abortionists and those who died at their hands, the subject had not yet entered the realms of literature. Park's novel is set in poverty-stricken Surry Hills in Sydney, and in many ways depicted a disappearing world.

By the 1950s, medical practitioners with access to the new drug penicillin, as well as to painkillers, were favoured as abortionists. The female 'backyard' abortionists had by no means disappeared, but the days when those convicted for murder after a lethal abortion were given sentences of death or life imprisonment were over.

CHAPTER 3

Baby Killers in the Nineteenth Century

Life for the newborn, as Charles Dickens wrote in *Oliver Twist* in 1838, was all too often '... unequally poised between this world and the next'. In some cases their mothers assisted their journey. Without effective contraception, British women had long resorted not only to abortion but also to infanticide to deal with unwanted pregnancies. In the years from 1803 to 1828, 107 women were publicly executed in Great Britain and Ireland. Seventeen were hanged for 'murdering a bastard child' and another nine for murdering an older child – more than 25 per cent.[1] But by the twentieth century infanticide and child murder had become the most common crimes for which English and Welsh women were sentenced to death. In the years 1900 to 1950, 102 female prisoners were given a capital sentence out of a total of 130 for baby and child murder.[2] In New South Wales at the end of the nineteenth century 80 per cent of women charged with murder were indicted for killing their newborn baby.[3]

Three sensational infanticide cases occurred in Van Diemen's Land (later Tasmania) in the earliest years of the colony, and each demonstrated an extraordinary range of responses and outcomes for the perpetrators of this desperate crime.

In 1817 Lily Mackellar, a single woman who lived in Hobart with her sister and affluent brother-in-law, gave birth to an illegitimate baby, an 'almost perfect child' later found buried with his umbilical cord tied around the neck. Dr Edward Luttrell (1756–1824), the aristocratic and reportedly negligent principal surgeon of the colony, declared the boy had bled to death.[4] He should have been more suspicious since Mackellar had previously asked him for calomel, a product used at that time to produce an abortion. A request he'd refused.[5]

At the inquest another surgeon was asked if the baby had been born alive or stillborn. His answer was that 'it [sic] may have died at birth'. He was unlikely to have known any better. In 1817 the disciplines of forensic science and jurisprudence were in their infancy. A paper entitled 'On the Uncertainty of the Signs of Murder in the Case of Bastard Children' by a surgeon and 'male midwife', the late William Hunter, was presented to the Medical Society in London in 1784. Hunter's research was only preliminary but he had identified the presence of air in the lungs as a sign of life, although he had conceded that a newborn could die soon after.[6] His approach was sympathetic to desperate mothers driven to commit infanticide, laying the blame upon their seducers.[7] This short treatise was not printed, however, until 1818.

The imprecise nature of forensic principles at the time, therefore aided Mackellar's case. At the inquest a servant told the court that she had never seen 'Miss Mackellar making baby linen', an indication that Lily had never intended keeping the baby alive. Mackellar never admitted she was pregnant until the evidence of the dead baby appeared. She did, however, make a confession in which she admitted that 'at 5.30 the child was born. I took the child up and laid it in my arms. It was a male child, [and] it was alive. I fainted and when I came to myself it was dead ... '[8] Her position as a middle-class woman clearly helped Mackellar evade legal penalty. Her reputation, however, was irredeemably damaged.

The case of Mary McLauchlan thirteen years later could not have been more different in its progress and outcome. Born in the ancient fishing village of Saltcoats, near Glasgow, she was a twenty-six-year-old worker from Glasgow who had been convicted of 'theft by housebreaking' in April 1828 at the west circuit of the High Court of Justiciary. Many items had been stolen, suggesting that more than one person was involved in the robbery.[9] There is evidence that she protected her husband, William Sutherland, from the forces of the harsh law. In the original investigation he had been the primary suspect. A respectable relative of her father also provided her with a credible alibi. Sutherland worked at home as a weaver, an old occupation under significant threat from the Industrial Revolution. Mary McLauchlan was employed from dawn to dusk as the supervisor of ten children who worked in William Dunlop's cotton mill in the Barrowfield Road as cotton pickers.[10] This area, near the Clyde Iron Works established in 1786 by James Dunlop at Tollcross, formed the heartland of the new industrial economy.

McLauchlan had no previous convictions before her transportation to Van Diemen's Land for fourteen years. This was a severe sentence given that Scottish Roman-based law was generally more liberal than its counterpart in English common law. The goalkeeper at Tollbooth prison wrote of her: 'Connexions respectable and former course of life good.'[11] This suggested that the economic downturn of the late 1820s, which had hit Scotland hard, affected normally law-abiding people such as McLauchlan and her family. Mary McLauchlan was transported on the *Harmony* from a southern English port, arriving in Van Diemen's Land in January 1829 after a voyage of nine months.

On disembarkation in Hobart, the women from this voyage of the *Harmony* became the first group to be sent to the new Female Factory at the Cascades in south Hobart rather than to the original Factory beside Hobart Town jail. Female Factories were a form of workhouse, where production such as spinning took place, as well as a temporary residence for female convicts who were kept there before being assigned to an employer. The Factory at the Cascades held the women away from the more populous areas of Hobart and, as a purpose-built structure, made sure the women were contained; there had been frequent escapes from the Hobart Town Factory. The group from the *Harmony* disembarked at 4am to prevent any commotion likely to be caused by the presence of 100 women in a male-dominated convict settlement.

There, Principal Superintendent of Convicts James Gordon and the Convict Muster Master Josiah Spode took down details of the newly arrived felons in order to record their details for Governor George Arthur's Black Book, and to assess their prospects for work with settlers. McLauchlan was described as 5 foot 3½ inches (161 centimetres) tall, with an oval face, dark hair and complexion, and hazel eyes. She had one missing tooth in her lower jaw.[12] The women in the group were also examined by surgeon James Scott, a Scotsman who had trained at the University of Edinburgh. He was also permitted to conduct a lucrative private medical practice and was given extensive land grants.[13] In this small community he was a powerful man.

After eight days of assessment each woman was given a fresh set of clothing, consisting of a brown serge jacket, a petticoat, a linen shift, a pair of worsted stockings, a pair of shoes, and a neck scarf. McLauchlan was assigned to a merchant, Charles Ross Nairne, who lived with his sickly wife, Katherine Stirling, and their young son on a farm on the Coal River near Hobart.[14] The Nairnes, from Paisley in Scotland, had arrived in the colony on 1 March 1822.[15] McLauchlan was intended as a domestic servant, an occupation quite unlike her previous industrial employment.

Within two months of her assignment McLauchlan was pregnant, a not uncommon situation for female convicts. Sexual services all too often comprised part of the duties expected of assigned domestics. Most of the convict women sent to the Female Factory at the Cascades returned from service pregnant or with a baby.[16] McLauchlan never revealed the identity of the father although many suspected her employer whose wife was then eight months pregnant. The marriage was turbulent and not destined to survive the scandal of McLauchlan's fate.

When McLauchlan was five months' pregnant Nairne sent her back to Hobart, charging her with unspecified forms of 'misconduct'. Unrepentant, McLauchlan told Spode, now the Principal

Superintendent of Convicts, that she had not been given her new clothing allowance. She was despatched to the House of Correction (the Female Factory) while Spode then made inquiries about the matter. The official record stated that he requested Katherine Nairne to provide further evidence concerning McLauchlan's allegations. Mrs Nairne refused. This was unusual since employers invariably gave at least the appearance of cooperating with the authorities to ensure a continued supply of convict workers. Katherine Nairne's refusal was possibly connected to her knowledge of the parentage of McLaughlan's child. McLauchlan was placed in a cell on a diet of bread and water for six days awaiting further investigation.[17] Governor Arthur had published the rigid new regulations concerning offending convicts in the *Hobart Town Gazette* on 3 October 1829.

At the House of Correction, McLauchlan was placed in C class – for criminal women – along with her former shipboard companions, Mary Cameron and Sarah Bromley. Another woman, Mary O'Donnell, had recently been found 'not guilty' for infanticide at her trial in the Supreme Court. The work and diet regime in the House of Correction was thought harsh even by colonial standards. McLauchlan gave birth to a baby boy on 1 December 1829. His body was found in the privies. Mary Cameron had given assistance while other women stood outside. One of the inmates, however, reported the matter to Superintendent Esh Lovell and Matron Anne Lovell.

An inquest was ordered. Court records of this proceeding and for the Supreme Court trial that followed were not kept. Court reporters in Australian jurisdictions did not exist until the 1920s; Pittman's shorthand was not invented until 1837. Any information to be found comes, as it mostly did during this period in Australian history, from accounts in local newspapers. Such trial reports tend to give broad outlines of proceedings rather than minute accounts of testimony; moreover, many events such as the murder of a baby or a spouse were deemed simply too gruesome and unsavoury for extensive reportage in the press.

Joseph Hone (1784–1861), formerly a barrister at Gray's Inn in London, was appointed as the coroner to the inquest. He had arrived in the settlement in 1824, taking on the role of Commissioner of the Court of Requests and Master of the Supreme Court, as well as Commissioner of the Quarter Sessions for the island. He was conscientious, although 'universally looked upon as only a few degrees removed from an idiot'.[18] The facial twitch he suffered made him seem even worse. Even more detrimental to McLauchlan's case was that Hone had business interests in the Derwent Steamship Navigation Company with Charles Nairne. These fellow businessmen and respectable settlers had strong bonds of loyalty and self-interest.

On 15 April 1830, Mary McLauchlan's trial in the Van Diemen's Land Supreme Court began. Established in 1823, this was the first superior court in Australia. Chief Justice Sir John Pedder (1793–1859), who had trained at Cambridge and Middle Temple, presided. Given the difficulty at the time of finding enough suitable free men to make up a jury, the legal system allowed for military juries to act in this capacity. In McLauchlan's trial the jury consisted of six officers and one ensign of the 63rd Foot Regiment, two of whom had already served at Mary O'Donnell's trial. Captain Pery Baylee, commandant of convicts at the feared Macquarie Harbour penal station,[19] headed the jury. He was considered to be severe but fair.

The legal system in this brutal outpost of the Empire was particularly vicious – runaway outlaws and bushrangers were decapitated on capture and their heads displayed on pikes around what is now Salamanca Place in Hobart. There were over 200 offences deemed as capital, which meant the number of public executions for such a tiny population was high. Most were for the theft of sheep and cattle. Some 103 men were executed in the year 1826–27, their bodies often left for the carrion to feed upon as a reminder to everyone who saw them to obey the law. Twenty-two prisoners were executed in a single day, on 3 May 1830.[20]

McLauchlan was not represented by counsel at her trial. This was not uncommon, given how few barristers and solicitors there were at the time – and even fewer rights for felons. Nor were prisoners able to speak on their own behalf until the late 1890s. The basis of law was for the prosecution to prove its case rather than the defence to demonstrate innocence. Trials were generally short in duration, even in capital offence hearings, but in McLauchlan's case a large number of witnesses were called. Surgeon James Bryant was the most important witness. He was described in the newspapers as a gentleman,[21] no doubt to distinguish him from 'barber–surgeons' and apothecaries who were also able to act as medical practitioners before the profession was regulated in 1844. He had arrived in Van Diemen's Land in November 1828 along with the new attorney-general and later Supreme Court judge, Algernon Montagu (1802–80), the illegitimate grandson of the Earl of Sandwich.

Bryant already knew McLauchlan since his duties included the inspection of inmates at the House of Correction and other government facilities. He was young and inexperienced, and in constant conflict with his superior Dr James Scott. The older man was better qualified, but had not been born a gentleman – and such distinctions counted. Scott, however, had the advantage of training at the University of Edinburgh in the new discipline of medical jurisprudence, which had been formally established in 1807.[22] This had greatly aided the outcome of Mary O'Donnell's trial for which he had been the principal medical and forensic witness.[23]

Despite the growing body of forensic knowledge, an autopsy was not carried out on the dead infant to determine whether air had entered his lungs. This was highly detrimental to McLauchlan's case since evidence from an autopsy was vital in cases of infanticide where there could be doubt as to the cause of death. McLauchlan was found guilty and ordered to be publicly executed and her body dissected after her death. The court did not charge her for the lesser offence of 'concealing a birth', even though the particular circumstances warranted such an indictment.

Just two years later, in 1832, the eminent Scottish legal commentator Sir Archibald Alison provided a sympathetic analysis of the plight of unmarried pregnant women, who, he argued, should be pitied and helped rather than being given the death sentence:

> Their distress of mind and body deprives them of all judgement, and they are delivered by themselves ... and sometimes destroying their offspring without being conscious of what they are doing. Accordingly, it is a principle of law, that mere appearance of violence on the child's body are not *per se* sufficient, unless some circumstances of evidence exist to indicate that the violence was knowingly and intentionally committed.[24]

The secrecy and lack of expert assistance that surrounded illegitimate births like McLauchlan's always made the investigation and judgment of neonatal deaths problematic. But, given her circumstances, McLauchlan was never going to be granted the benefit of doubt or any sympathy. She was a convict in a pitiless prison system. In England, women who killed their newborns might find themselves incarcerated in a lunatic asylum, such as Bethlem in south London, or one of the many private 'madhouses' for the more affluent. These institutions did not exist in the convict settlements in Australia.[25]

McLauchlan's was the first female capital sentence in the settlement, although women convicts had been executed in Sydney for crimes such as armed robbery. The Executive Council, chaired by Governor Arthur and including Chief Justice Pedder, Colonial Secretary John Burnett and Colonial Treasurer Jocelyn Thomas, reconsidered her punishment. Thomas was a well-born Irishman who had arrived in Van Diemen's Land in 1824, driven to leave his native Ireland after the failure of a land reclamation venture; the Scotsman, Burnett, was the first colonial secretary of the settlement but was soon recognised to be a man of limited ability and vision.[26] Pedder and Burnett actively disliked each other, disagreeing on all matters.[27] Governor Arthur was not clear where his authority exactly lay within the Executive Council and yielded 'in every *doubtful* matter'.[28] The Executive Council met on the Saturday following the trial and then again on the Sunday. Clearly, there was dissent. Thomas and Burnett were inclined to leniency, believing McLauchlan could have been forced into her actions by pressure from the well-to-do father, Charles Nairne. Pedder, on the other hand, stood by his sentence.

While her fate was being decided, McLauchlan was visited by the Reverend William Bedford (1781–1852), the Anglican chaplain who had worked diligently on behalf of prisoners since his arrival in Hobart Town in 1821.[29] The governor of the Hobart jail, John Bisdee (1796–1862), was also regarded as a 'just and humane man'.[30] His wife Ann attended McLauchlan with considerable devotion.[31] Despite their ministrations, McLauchlan did not immediately confess to her crime, nor did she reveal the father of the baby. Reverend Bedford suspected McLauchlan might denounce her 'seducer' on the gallows where prisoners were permitted final words. It is telling that her master Charles Nairne did not make entreaties for mercy on her behalf to the governor, a common practice in capital cases. McLauchlan did, however, reveal his identity to Mary Cameron, her fellow felon, who aided her at her confinement.

An extraordinary event occurred on the Monday, the day before her scheduled execution and dissection. A letter arrived from Captain Baylee, the jury foreman, who revealed that all the jurors believed that McLauchlan had been '… driven to commit the crime by a sense of degradation and shame from the fear the birth of her child would become known to her relatives at home'.[32] As a married woman with children this was far more shameful than had she been single. All members of the military jury had been impressed by her demeanour and courage during her trial. Governor Arthur immediately asked Joseph Hone to speak to McLauchlan to determine her motive and the identity of the father. She had no reason to confide in this powerful man: not only was he an ally of Nairne, but he was also the coroner who should have demanded a proper autopsy at the inquest, and the master of the Supreme Court. She said nothing to save herself.

The *Tasmanian and Austral–Asiatic Review* provided the most extensive coverage of the execution on Monday, 19 April 1830, noting that McLauchlan wore a long white gown 'and appropriate underclothing'. She was composed and silent as the Reverend Bedford, Bible in hand, assisted her on her last walk. On the previous evening she had finally confessed her story and the identity of the father of her child to him. The Presbyterian minister, Mr McArthur, also attended the young Scotswoman. A newspaper later printed Nairne's name in capital letters to remind readers of the name of her employer and implied 'seducer'. McLauchlan refused to confess in public and did not beg for forgiveness for the crime of murdering her baby. Her last words on Earth were a poignant 'Oh, My God!' as the hangman, John Dogherty, kicked aside the peg on the scaffold and the drop opened.

The press took up McLauchlan's case with some degree of fervour, particularly after her execution. The *Tasmanian and Austral–Asiatic Review* of 23 April 1830 denounced her 'seducer' and his escape from justice, reminding readers that in England such a case would more likely have been prosecuted under the lesser charge of 'concealing a birth'. The penalty for that was two years' imprisonment. The *Colonial Times* was uneasy about the execution and subsequent dissection given the ambiguity about whether the baby had been stillborn. The *Hobart Town Courier* was not quite so favourable to McLauchlan's case.

In the Tasmanian State Archives there is a bizarre final mention of the case, composed by Edward Cook, the convict clerk of records, who drew a little gallows with a hanging figure in a dress alongside his incorrectly dated entry: 'Executed for the Murder of her Infant'. This was Mary McLauchlan's last entry in the official record.

Yet McLauchlan's punishment did not end in death. Under Imperial legalisation dating from 1752, those executed for murder were given to medical practitioners and surgeons to 'anatomise'. These procedures in hospitals and mortuaries were frequently public events. Prisoners often feared this additional penalty far more than death itself. Even for those not religiously inclined, the thought of not being able to mount intact into heaven on the Day of Judgment, as foretold in the New Testament, was terrifying beyond measure.

The dissection of murderers was banned in England in 1832 under the *Anatomy Act* which instead allowed unclaimed bodies, particularly deceased inmates of workhouses or prisons, to be 'anatomised' by surgeons. This legislation was widely reported in the Australian press.[33] Regardless, Tasmania maintained dissection for murderers until 1857 when Alex Cullen was despatched to St Mary's Hospital in Hobart after his execution for the murder of Elizabeth Ross.[34] Three murderers were dissected in Melbourne as late as 1864 when Professor George Halford wished to examine their brains for signs of congenital insanity.[35]

Dr James Scott conducted McLauchlan's dissection in the Hobart Town Hospital, which was likely to have been witnessed by notable but unnamed men of the colony as well as medical students. The convict surgeon Francis Hartwell, John Dawson, a surgical instrument-maker, and artist Thomas Bock, who drew other dissected felons, were probably in attendance.[36] Surgeon Edward Bedford, the son of the Reverend Bedford, would have been present since he was a student of Scott. The colonial auditor, George Boyes, who kept records of his impressions of the colony, had previously attended medical dissections and private anatomy lessons in London, and may also have been present.[37] McLauchlan would have been laid naked on the table since the hangman was permitted to keep the clothing of those executed. The dissection of a healthy young woman was a rare event, an invaluable lesson for medical practitioners and students who in that era were not permitted to examine the bodies of living women.

After the surgeon and students had completed their task no one bothered to record what happened to the remains of Mary McLauchlan.

Just five years later another extraordinary case of infanticide occurred in Van Diemen's Land. We know far less about the case of Sarah

Following Mary McLaughlan's execution for the murder of her newborn son, her burial was duly recorded in the Parish of Hobart Town's register. Image: Tasmanian State Archives and Library, RGD34-1.

Masters since she was found not guilty, and therefore no execution – with its attendant records, publicity and public discussion – took place. On Friday, 8 May 1835, Mrs Sarah Masters appeared in the Supreme Court before Justice Algernon Montagu, indicted on the charges of 'bringing forth a male child alive, and afterwards making an assault upon the body of the said child, by smothering it in a blanket, by which act of the mother the child instantly died … '. The military jury was sworn to secrecy and reconvened the following day.[38]

Masters pleaded not guilty on all counts. Her circumstances differed greatly from those of Mary McLauchlan. First, she was a free woman, not a felon, and lived with her husband most of the time. Joseph Masters had gone away for some six months in search of work. While he was away she became pregnant to another man. The deceased baby was the product of this union. The boy was '… not entirely of European origin … from the appearance of the face, the width of the nostrils, and the thickness of the nose and lips; the hair was jet black, and thick; much thicker than children's hair normally is; the face was very dark; there was a woolly appearance on both sides of the face …' reported Surgeon F. J. Park, the medical practitioner who conducted the autopsy on the dead boy. Joseph Masters, Park assured the court, was certainly not black. The father was likely to have been an Indigenous Palawa man, who remained unnamed. This was a scandal of the highest order in colonial society, breaching every rule of propriety. How Sarah Masters met this man and how they conceived a child together was not discussed in the trial.[39]

One witness, Catherine Fenwick, who had been serving four days in Oatlands' jail for misbehaviour, told the court that she was released to assist with the birth. The labour was prolonged, Fenwick recounted. Sarah Masters returned to bed, telling her husband to go out all day with the children and 'let her not be disturbed'. She took some gruel and went to sleep. After several hours, Masters asked for Fenwick to help her again, saying 'she was very bad'. Fenwick claimed she did not know what was wrong, thus contradicting herself. After making the children's bed and attending to Masters' soiled bed linen, Fenwick gave her half a pint of brandy, a remedy to alleviate pain in the absence of anaesthetics, which were not discovered until 1847. After this Masters declared she had given birth to a stillborn baby but insisted that her husband was not to be told. Instead, he was to be informed his wife had suffered a painful miscarriage.

Fenwick claimed the baby was stillborn with the 'natal string round its neck'. The dead infant was placed in a box and covered by a blanket, Fenwick continued. Masters suddenly laughed, declaring the baby was not her husband's and that it was conceived during his absence. She was anxious the truth not be revealed to her husband as it would be 'the cause of [their] parting and she loved her husband and two children, as she loved her life'. Masters also revealed that 'it was the first time she had been guilty of such a crime [adultery] since her marriage'. When Joseph Masters returned, Fenwick informed him his wife had suffered a miscarriage and was feeling very ill.

A few days later Fenwick removed the body in secret with the help of Henry Soby, the cook at the local public house. There was no imputation that he was the father. He testified he had been given '… a bucket with Mrs Masters' miscarriage and threw it into the lagoon'. Why he undertook this unpleasant task and what his relationship was to the two women was not revealed in the testimony. A few days later he returned with another man named Salmon and retrieved the body. During this recovery he noticed a baby's leg protruding from the bundle. Evidently his conscience had been bothering him and he wanted a witness to his actions.

When Salmon was asked to give evidence, he testified that what was wrapped in the quilt was a dark, fully formed baby 'with very large features'. Surgeon Park was present at the discovery of the body, dissecting the remains afterwards. In his testimony Dr Park stated that the results of his autopsy led him to believe the boy had been born alive since the lungs and liver were buoyant when placed in a bowl of water. He further gave his opinion that the baby had been strangled and the umbilical cord had not been cut and tied properly. At this point newspaper reports state that no more of the doctor's extensive and detailed evidence would be published given its graphic and offensive nature. Dr Edward Bedford, now highly qualified after studying in London, gave expert opinion that in some rare instances respiration could occur during birth, with a resultant death.[40] Dr James Scott told the court that he could offer no opinion apart from the observation the child could have died from natural causes. Neither Scott nor Bedford was present at the autopsy, but this opinion from the colonial surgeon would certainly have helped Masters's defence.

Several important legal points were made by the judge concerning provisions within the 1828 *Offences against the Person Act*. First, in the case of 'concealing a birth' and 'disposing of a dead body', the concealment of the birth had to be undertaken by the mother herself. The attorney-general pointed out that the concealment of a birth by the mother could be regarded as evidence of murder, the penalty for which was death. But in this case others had disposed of the body and they had not been charged with the offence. The jury, no doubt swayed by the opinion of Dr Scott, came back with a verdict of 'not guilty'. Justice Montagu was not altogether pleased with this verdict, clearly believing that Masters had killed her baby and got others to dispose of the body. He closed the court by remarking that the defendant could have been charged with manslaughter in the first instance, a point dismissed by the attorney-general. Sarah Masters was discharged from the proceedings, her life and marriage ruined by the revelations of the case.

With the emergence of medical specialisation and professional training in British hospitals from the 1820s, new textbooks became available. Gynaecology and obstetrics emerged as a new discipline for male medical practitioners rendering traditional female midwives less qualified and authoritative. Edinburgh-trained Dr Robert Gooch (1784–1830), a pioneering 'man-midwife' and lecturer in midwifery at St Bartholomew's Hospital in London from 1812, produced the influential text *On Some of the Most Important Diseases Peculiar to Women* in 1829 and, posthumously, the following year, *Observations on Puerperal Insanity* in which he coined the term 'puerperal insanity' to describe postpartum psychosis, a serious affliction that could cause a newly delivered mother to kill her baby. This was the commencement of biopsychiatric understanding of the disease.[41]

In 1861 the British parliament passed a new *Offences Against the Person Act*, which provided clauses to extend legal penalty to males assisting in infanticide or in concealing the body of a newborn baby. The Royal Commission inquiring into capital punishment in 1864 reviewed these penalties. As the distinguished jurist Baron Bramwell suggested, it is difficult to secure a conviction against a person who does not have to testify against herself: if a birth is conducted in secret, there are often no witnesses; and when does birth in fact occur – before or after the separation of the umbilical cord?[42] The penalty for the conviction of the wilful murder of an older child remained the same – death by hanging.

These more liberal views did not immediately translate into practice in the Australian colonies. In New South Wales, the Bathurst Circuit Court on 23 October 1867 heard two separate cases of infanticide. In one, Elizabeth Coppock was found not guilty of the murder of her infant daughter. The second case was far more convoluted and profound in its effects. Harriet Short and her mother, Mary Williams, were indicted for the murder of Short's illegitimate three-week-old daughter in Bathurst on 11 September 1867. They were defended by Edward Lee, a court-appointed barrister. Senior Sergeant Waters testified how he had recovered the body of a baby in a well near Williams's restaurant. He removed the body, dressed in a frock, chemise, and flannel bandages, and took it to the local hospital for a postmortem.

William Wells, a carpenter from Bathurst, told the court that his children played near the well. One day he saw the lid was not secured correctly, and on investigation he noticed what he first thought was a child's doll in the water, until he realised it was a baby. The most damaging testimony came from a neighbour, Ellinor Johnson, who reported that Mrs Williams, whom she hardly knew, came to her house and started lamenting the fate of the 'baby in the well', declaring: 'Oh, the wretch of a mother, whoever she is, wants to be hanged.' She continued: 'It's no odds; it will never see God, for it never was christened.' As an Irish Roman Catholic, Williams was implying that the infant would stay for eternity in limbo. The following evening she returned late to again decry what had happened. She suddenly blurted out: 'It's a pretty mess that Harriet has got herself into … she couldn't keep it; she has nothing to keep it with, as she has nothing to maintain the ones she has.' When Johnson asked her why she had not given the child into care, Williams replied that '… she wants to hide her shame as much as she can'. Williams then admitted she had urged her daughter to 'chuck it into the well'. When she was unable to, Williams told Johnson, she had said to her daughter: 'Then give it to me and I will.' When probed further Williams admitted that she had 'indeed chucked it in the well'. Johnson immediately informed the police.

The putative father, Charles Atkins, swore under oath that 'I am not the father of Mrs Short's infant' and that he hardly knew her, even as a casual acquaintance. Other evidence, however, did in fact suggest he was indeed the father. Without the support of Charles Atkins, Harriet Short's options were very limited, as her mother had told Ellinor Johnson. At the time there were no foundling hospitals in the colonies and church orphanages tended to admit children rather than babies.

The case received widespread publicity especially when both women were found guilty and sentenced to death for wilful murder. The final public execution for infanticide in England had occurred in 1849 when Rebecca Smith was executed outside the Devizes House of Correction in Wiltshire. She had killed seven of her eleven children by arsenic poisoning. Since the colonies tended to follow metropolitan precedents, it was unlikely that the death sentence would occur in this particular case. To date, only Mary McLauchlan in Hobart in 1830 had been executed for this type of murder.

Mary Williams appeared to be brutal and pragmatic in her treatment of her little granddaughter, whom she regarded as simply a thing to be disposed of after some initial delay. But this was not an uncommon response to illegitimate babies at the time – although it was usually the mother who killed the baby and hid the body. Williams herself had had a fraught life as an abandoned infant sent to a foundling hospital in her native Ireland. She had survived against the odds for such children and had arrived in New South Wales in 1835 on the *Duchess of Northumberland.*

The judge had also had a troubled and chaotic life that impinged upon his judgments. John Fletcher Hargrave (1815–85) came from a modest merchant family in London and was educated at Trinity College, Cambridge, and Lincoln's Inn. He was unstable and volatile to such an extent this wife had him committed to a private mental asylum in 1849. He arrived in Sydney eight years later, and became a foundation judge of the new district court. Driven by resentment for his wife, he determinedly decided against female defendants and plaintiffs. The local bar boycotted his swearing-in as a Supreme Court judge in 1865 because he was erratic in his behaviour and judgments. He spent much of his time on the regional circuits of the court before he was overwhelmed by permanent insanity.[43]

Hargrave did not recommend mercy in his correspondence with the colonial governor about the trial. This was unusual in a case of infanticide. He pointed out that the act had been premeditated and designed for concealment. He was particularly concerned with what seemed to be a spate of infant and child murders in Bathurst and pressed for execution for all 'domestic crimes of aggravated guilt'. The governor, however, chose to ignore Hargrave's suggestion and extended mercy to Harriet Short, who served ten years' imprisonment, while her mother was given a life sentence.

The story of Harriet Short had one final twist in the tale. A month after her initial capital sentence was announced the history of her marriage was revealed. A Dr Hayley, who had a practice in Queanbeyan, New South Wales, told newspaper reporters of the death of one his patients, Alfred Short. A brief account had already appeared in the local newspaper in July 1867 concerning the death of 'a stranger' from consumption (tuberculosis). He had come into the township looking for work as a private tutor. Unlike most rural itinerants, Short was a highly educated man whose father was a wealthy solicitor residing in the exclusive area of Regent's Park in London. In Short's pockets Dr Hayley found a letter from a firm of solicitors informing Short that he had been left a considerable inheritance. Further investigation revealed that Short had married Harriet Williams in the Church of St Michael and St John in Bathurst on 28 December 1859. How such an educated man came to marry a poor unschooled woman was not revealed. The couple had two children before they separated. The drowned infant was not his child.[44] As his wife, Harriet Short and her legitimate offspring would have inherited his estate had circumstances not brought her to the killing of her illegitimate baby.

The colonial courts dealt harshly with sane married women indicted and found guilty of killing an unwanted newborn. A former domestic servant, Annie Magann Judge, had been married for three months and was living in a 'humpy' at Sandy Creek near the mining settlement of Clermont in Queensland. Her husband Michael Judge could barely earn a living. Jane Brown, a neighbour, testified before the preliminary hearing in the Police Magistrate's Court in Clermont that on 15 December 1884 around 7am Judge had complained she had sore eyes and 'a bad cold'. She was agitated that she was unable to meet the train to get meat for her husband's meal that evening. She also said that she had taken a fall and that she was bleeding. Brown fetched the local midwife, Mrs Parson, from Clermont as she had already noticed that Judge 'was in the family way'. Dr Apiridion Candiotti testified that he was summoned by the police to examine Judge two days later and confirmed she had recently given birth. He also found the body of a newborn boy wrapped in a silk handkerchief and a towel in a box. Working under a gum tree he conducted a postmortem investigation that revealed the boy had been born alive and died of suffocation. His testimony was detailed, although it was not published in the newspapers. When he returned to the humpy Judge was 'composed but crying'.

Mary Anne Parsons, the midwife, an illiterate but highly articulate witness, informed the proceedings that Judge told her she had suffered a miscarriage and thrown away the child. Pressing further, Parsons insisted the baby be found. A trail of ants leading to a box eventually led her to the body. Still Judge refused to admit she had just given birth. When her husband returned later she also refused to confide in him saying simply that she 'would tell Mrs Parsons what happened'. Parsons refused to identify the father of the baby.

Judge was indicted on 15 December 1884 in the Queensland Supreme Court in Rockhampton before Justice George Harding (1838–95) on the charge of wilfully murdering her newborn son with malice aforethought. Educated at Magdalene College, Cambridge, Harding was far more comfortable in the lofty heights of equity cases rather than in sordid criminal matters.[45] Even though this was a capital case, Judge was undefended during her trial because 'she is too poor to procure counsel'. No solicitor or barrister oversaw the case to protect her interest, which was not unusual in this type of trial. The crown prosecutor, Patrick Real, was a highly able barrister who later became a judge of the Queensland Supreme Court. He had risen from humble circumstances in the mining town of Ipswich and was noted for his sympathy for the poor.[46] Yet in this instance it was notably absent.[47] The jury, however, recommended mercy given her youth and a suspicion that she had been insane at the time of the killing. Under these circumstances Annie Judge could have been judged guilty but insane and sent to the lunatic asylum near Ipswich. But she was given the death sentence.[48]

Despite being a married woman who had killed her illegitimate baby and clearly tricked her husband into marriage when she knew she was pregnant to someone else, the Queensland public was sympathetic to Judge's plight and outraged that the death sentence had been passed. Petitions to plead for clemency, signed mostly by men, were assembled in Brisbane and Rockhampton.[49] Although there is nothing to confirm this in the records, it is probable that Judge was able to mount an appeal thanks to public generosity. For the appeal to the Full Court, Judge was represented by a barrister, Edward Mansfield, who came from a distinguished English legal family. He was later appointed as a District Court judge as well as an Acting Justice of the Supreme Court. His peers believed he always acted with 'fairness and common sense'.[50] Mansfield argued that the prosecution had not established its case, although an impartial reading of the evidence confirms it had. The court then went off at a tangent about what constituted 'legitimate issue', given that the baby was born in wedlock. In the final point, Mansfield emphasised that the appellant had been undefended in her original trial.[51] This constituted a far more reasonable argument, especially in a capital case. Her sentence was commuted to penal servitude for ten years.

The later 1880s and 1890s witnessed a period of intense concern over the falling birth rate and national vitality. Members of a select committee that convened in New South Wales in 1886 to investigate the registration of births and deaths expressed their alarm at the irregularities that surrounded illegitimacy and stillbirth. It was known, for example, that some mothers forged the signature of a midwife to register the death of a child they had killed.[52] The New South Wales Coroner's Annual Report for 1891–1892 listed a depressing catalogue of abandoned dead babies – some starved, and others drowned, mutilated or otherwise subjected to violence.[53] Dead babies were found in privies, in parks, mineshafts, secluded streets, rivers, beaches, gardens and dumps, with no indication who they were – they were simply unwanted refuse to be disposed of in secret. The *Argus* newspaper editorialised that there was 'a very army of murderesses within our midst'.[54] Only a small number of these cases ever went to court. Often no mother was found to prosecute.

When Maggie Heffernan, an unmarried domestic servant from Gundowring in rural Victoria, fell pregnant to her longtime boyfriend, she anticipated he would marry her. When he refused she went to Melbourne – the big city allowing her to escape the opprobrium she would have been forced to endure if she had remained in her small community. She gave birth on 29 December 1899 in the hotel where she worked before being transferred to the Melbourne Women's Hospital. After six days she went to a church refuge run by Mrs Cameron in Armadale. A week later Heffernan unsuccessfully tried to find accommodation in several boarding houses. Desperate, with nowhere to go, Heffernan wandered around the Treasury Gardens. A Mrs Taylor asked her if she needed assistance, clearly concerned by Heffernan's appearance and agitated manner. She took Heffernan and the baby to two institutions in search of accommodation, only to be told they did not admit women with babies. Heffernan eventually found a room above a coffee shop for 1/6-. The next morning the landlady gave her a cup of tea and a slice of toast, the only food she had consumed for over twenty-four hours. But as she didn't have enough money, Heffernan had to leave.

Heffernan then purchased a newspaper to look for employment where she could take a baby. There was none. After tramping the streets for hours, tired and increasingly desperate, Heffernan discovered her milk had dried up. Walking down to the river, she again tried to feed the baby but when this proved unsuccessful she threw him into the Yarra, where he drowned. As she walked back to Flinders Street Station she noticed she still had baby clothes on her arm, and she began crying: 'Oh God! What have I done to my baby?' No one came to her assistance or asked why she was so upset.

Soon after, Heffernan found work as a wet nurse in Hawthorn, but she was dismissed because her work was unsatisfactory, presumably because she had no milk. Heffernan was arrested for wilful murder on 20 January 1900, but was not cautioned by police. A lady, presumably her employer, visited her in jail and secured a leading barrister to represent her. When the sheriff suggested she accept Sir Bryan O'Loghlen, she did so thinking he was the person arranged for her. Irish-born O'Loghlen (1828–1905) trained at Trinity College, Dublin, and was called to the Victorian bar in 1862. He became a QC and practised criminal law for fifteen years before going into parliament in Victoria, where he was known for his liberal views.[55] During his political career, O'Loghlen was premier for one term and attorney-general three times. When he took on Heffernan's case he was seventy-two and had retired from politics.

The trial was a disaster. Heffernan's parents were not informed until just a few days before proceedings began, and could not attend. Her weak intellect,[56] former good character and her attempts to support her child were not used as mitigating evidence. Nor was the story of her absconding lover who'd left a bogus forwarding address. The trial judge, Justice Sir Henry Hodges (1844–1919), while known to be capable of humane sentencing, was considered sarcastic and temperamental.[57] When medical witness Dr (later Sir) Richard Stawell, who had trained in paediatrics at the Great Ormond Street Hospital for Children in London, was asked whether Heffernan suffered from puerperal fever, he simply replied 'no', and both Hodges and O'Loghlen left it at that.[58] In such a case, a gynaecologist conversant with puerperal fever and problems of newly delivered mothers would have given supportive expert testimony. Stawell, however, had specialised in paediatrics at Great Ormond Hospital for Children in London. But unlike medical experts in other Victorian cases, he believed that a woman suffering from puerperal fever would be 'unable to give a distinct account of her actions'.[59] Unlike Maggie Heffernan.

Heffernan was found guilty and sentenced to death.

Public opinion and feminist organisations swung behind her, since her sentence was so manifestly unfair under the circumstances.

The influential Sydney feminist Rose Scott worked tirelessly on her behalf alongside women's organisations in Melbourne. Huge public protests were held in Sydney and Melbourne, arguing the Crown had spent little on her defence and allowed the father of the child to go unpunished. A petition with some 15,000 signatures was forwarded to the Executive Council. The citizens of her hometown and district sent a long petition begging for mercy. The *Argus* newspaper on 22 January 1900 pleaded for justice for this young woman who was 'in the shadow of the gallows'. After consideration, the Victorian cabinet commuted Heffernan's sentence to four years' imprisonment. She was finally released on the signature of the solicitor-general, Agar Wynne, in December 1901.[60]

CHAPTER 4

Baby Killers in the Twentieth Century

On a Monday morning in March 2009 the crew assigned to the water treatment plant at Pinkenba in Brisbane was confronted by an operational disaster. Among the human waste they found the decomposing body of a newborn baby girl.[1] This was by no means a singular event; in 2008 workers at the Jacks Gully Waste Disposal Centre at Narellan in New South Wales found the body of a newborn baby boy who had been placed in a rubbish bin near Camden.[2] These events could just as easily have been played out a hundred years earlier, when unwanted babies were routinely abandoned. It wasn't until the 1920s, when adoption legalisation was introduced, that the children of single mothers could be given up to a new family, creating a way out other than taking drastic measures. In 1973 the federal government introduced the supporting mother's pension, which provided a basic allowance for single women to care for their children, somewhat reducing the level of economic hardship. Yet despite shifts in legalisation, public opinion and more liberal social attitudes the stigma of unwanted pregnancy and birth has endured.

Despite the pro-natalist fervour of the early twentieth century, the courts could sometimes deal sympathetically with mothers who killed their unwanted babies. Sydney resident Emily McDonald was charged with the wilful murder of her eighteen-month-old daughter, Thelma, by crushing a box and a half of phosphorus match heads into a drink of water in January 1901. She had afterwards tried to kill herself by also ingesting the poisonous match heads then throwing herself from a window. McDonald's husband and sister-in-law attested that she had been depressed since Thelma's birth. The jury at her trial in February delivered a verdict of not guilty, adding that they believed she had not been of sound mind when the acts were committed. She was held under observation in an asylum at the governor's pleasure.[3]

Agnes Ferry, described as a 'young, unmarried girl', was charged with the wilful murder of her daughter in the sittings of the Supreme Court of Victoria at Horsham on 4 March 1913. Born into a poor family in the rural district of Dimboola, Ferry had little education and few skills. The baby, already in an advanced state of decomposition, was found in an outhouse (toilet) located in a laneway in the township. A lace from a corset was wound tightly around the baby's neck. Ferry told the court that she had no memory of the birth, or of killing the baby or disposing of her body. Her testimony was consistent with a newly delivered woman suffering from severe postpartum anxiety disorder where the mother is confused, dissociated from her actions and often suicidal.[4] With the additional factors of an undisclosed and unwanted pregnancy, and an unassisted birth, the factors leading to neonatal killing are high.[5] Medical research as early as 1830 had identified this syndrome, although it was not referred to in Ferry's case.[6]

Ferry was represented by the leading criminal barrister in Victoria at the time, George Arnot Maxwell (1859–1935).[7] A man of strong Presbyterian convictions he was also sympathetic and devoted to the legal causes of the poor, especially those like Agnes Ferry. Sir Thomas à Beckett (1836–1919), the scion of Victoria's leading legal dynasty, presided over proceedings. His forte was equity, although he was calm, resolved and patient in criminal cases.[8] The jury returned a verdict of guilty but recommended mercy. His Honour had no alternative but to sentence Ferry to death as demanded by law. On hearing this Ferry collapsed and required medical attention. No appeal was heard. When the Executive Council reviewed the capital sentence it recommended that she be detained at the governor's pleasure thus setting no limits for release.[9]

In 1915 Emma Lonsdale was arraigned in the Supreme Court of Victoria for the murder of her newborn son George. She was a seventeen-year-old unmarried mother who had given birth in a nursing home in Carlton. On 20 March 1915 a nurse went to Lonsdale's room to check on the baby, only to find him unconscious on the bed. She immediately called for the local doctor. George had been poisoned with Lysol, a strong disinfectant, and later died in agony in the Children's Hospital. Lonsdale told the court she did not know 'what came over her' nor did she realise the consequences of her act – she merely wanted him to stop crying. She was also distraught that her parents had abandoned her. Her defence team, again led by George Arnot Maxwell, argued that she was suffering from puerperal mania. The jury was not convinced, returning a guilty verdict.[10] In sentencing her to death, the chief justice, Sir John Madden (1844–1918), took into consideration her youth and circumstances, although he admonished her for the terrible way she had killed George. He added that he would recommend mercy to the governor on her behalf. Her sentence was duly commuted to 'the pleasure of the governor', something that could mean life imprisonment.[11] Emma Lonsdale's was the last case of neonatal murder in Australia where the death sentence was recorded.

Nellie Spiers, a domestic servant living in the exclusive suburb of Clayfield in Brisbane, appeared in court in June 1924 on the charge of 'concealing a birth'. The gardener, Arthur Clarke, testified that he found the decomposing body of a baby boy in a paper bag in the garden where he was digging. His employer, retired bank manager Arthur Noyes, called the police around 7pm on 10 May 1924. He testified he did not notice that Spiers was pregnant and nor did she complain of being ill at any time. He added that he left all the management of the servants and the house to his wife, Susan Noyes.

As soon as the body was discovered Susan Noyes questioned Spiers, who readily admitted that she had given birth in secret and buried the baby. Spiers, twenty-six, made a long statement to the police in which she revealed that she was from Charleville and had come to work in Brisbane thirteen years before, after her parents had died. She had been employed by the Noyes family for over ten years. During the war, she said, she 'kept company with soldiers but nothing happened to [her] then' and that she had 'much misconducted [sic] [herself] with them'. Later she 'kept company' for nearly a year with a returned serviceman, Jack Williams, a scrub cutter from Nanango. She was distressed that he left for Melbourne without telling her of his intended departure.

Spiers also admitted she was 'keeping company with two other men ... and used to meet them different nights during the week'. She only knew them as 'Ernie' and 'Bill'. They never went out on dates; rather, they simply had sexual encounters in secluded but public places. When she realised she was pregnant, Spiers could not identify who the father might be. Not that such knowledge was likely to have led to a proposal of marriage.

With no other choice, Spiers kept working despite illness and nausea. She stated that the baby was suddenly born in the lavatory: 'I was half silly at the time but the baby was not alive as it did not move ...' After wrapping the body in paper she then buried it. Later in her statement Spiers referred to 'her miscarriage', although the baby was full term. She outlined the shame, fear and confusion about what she should do, and the secrecy that she felt had to surround the birth even though her parents were dead and she did not live in her hometown. Spiers was at pains to inform the police that she had never taken any 'medicine to get a miscarriage'.[12]

The trial was heard before Justice Lionel Lukin (1868–1944), the first Queenslander to be appointed to the bench, and the autopsy conducted by the distinguished physician Dr Espie Dods (1875–

1930), who had served in the Boer War and at Gallipoli.[13] He reported that there were no signs of violence upon the body to which the umbilical cord was still attached. With the decomposition he could not say whether the baby had been stillborn or born alive. With this medical testimony Spiers was found guilty of the lesser offence of 'concealing a birth'. Lukin dealt sympathetically with Spiers in his sentence of twelve months' imprisonment, suspended on the payment of a £100 good behaviour bond. As this sum was far beyond her limited means, no doubt her employers paid it. Whether she remained in their employment was not recorded.

Legal adoption had been well embedded into social policy and law in the states since the 1920s, but an article in January 1952 on the Berry Street Foundling Hospital (the former Victorian Infant Asylum and Foundling Hospital, established in 1877) revealed that babies were still abandoned in Melbourne in 'rubbish bins, hedges and somebody's front lawn'. A baby boy had been found in Royal Park wrapped in a newspaper. Matron Elizabeth Fry pointed out that the centre provided 'a sanctuary' for 'unmarried girls' who found themselves pregnant and alone. Care was extended for three months.[14] For those mothers who concealed their pregnancy and gave birth in secret, the public acknowledgment of their 'shame' by taking their baby to the foundling home was too dreadful to contemplate. This type of response continued right into the twenty-first century. Lauren Curnow, a seventeen-year-old student from Ballarat, gave birth in her bedroom unassisted in August 2004, having managed to conceal the pregnancy from her parents. Curnow punched the boy soon after birth, resulting in his death. After extensive forensic psychiatric evidence and testimony she was sentenced to five years' imprisonment, immediately suspended by Justice Bernard Bongiorno in the Victorian Supreme Court.[15]

Many cases of neonatal killing defy any suggestion of broad categorisation. The arrest in October 1951 of Alwyn Atkinson, a farmer from Kimba in South Australia, throws light on an issue rarely discussed in public. The father of twelve children, Atkinson had committed incest with one of his daughters for three years. She became pregnant in October 1950, giving birth to a baby boy in June 1951. No one knew that the child was the result of an incestuous union. Somewhere between Port Augusta and Buckleboo the infant was smothered and then buried in the bush.[16] At the trial before Justice Sir George Coutts Ligertwood (1888–1967) in the Supreme Court of South Australia only Alwyn Atkinson was arraigned. He received a light sentence of four years' imprisonment for each of the offences of manslaughter and incest.[17] Since he pleaded guilty, the full circumstances of the case remain undisclosed. However, this highlights the possibility in other cases that infanticidal young mothers may be victims of incest but remain silent to avoid the shame and notoriety.

Other cases of neonatal killing have occurred within domestic settings that appeared outwardly normal and suburban. One of the most complex and disturbing cases of serial murder in modern Australia involved infanticide that went undetected until four infants had died at the hands of their mother, Kathleen Megan Folbigg. Her own early life, full of trauma and abuse, had an impact on her ability to nurture her four babies. The full extent of the horror she had herself experienced as an infant only came to public light when she was sentenced in the Supreme Court of New South Wales in October 2003.[18]

When Folbigg was just eighteen months old, her father killed her mother, stabbing her more than twenty times. Folbigg entered the foster system. In 1970, when she was three, she was fostered by Neville and Deidre Marlborough and led an apparently unremarkable childhood. She left school at fifteen and went to work as a cash register operator in a local service station. Kathleen Marlborough found out some details of her early life and adoption two years later when she met her half-sister. The following year she met Craig Folbigg, a worker from the local BHP Steelworks. They married in 1987 and set up home in the suburb of Mayfield, becoming more financially secure with Craig Folbigg's change of career to car sales.

Caleb Gibson Folbigg was born on 1 February 1989, a healthy baby except for a 'floppy larynx', a minor condition that caused some difficulties in feeding. Folbigg underwent an epidural delivery with forceps that precluded stable walking for a month, a trying situation for a vain young woman proud of her figure and appearance. She decided not to breastfeed since it made her feel uncomfortable. When he was two weeks old Caleb was taken to see Dr Barry Springthorpe, a leading paediatrician at the Royal Newcastle Hospital, to investigate the feeding problems that were connected to difficulties breathing through his nose. Two days later Craig and Kathleen Folbigg took Caleb with them to a family barbeque. That night Caleb ate well and went to sleep without difficulty.

Caleb took his early morning feed at 2am on 20 February 1989 without any difficulties and went to sleep straight away. Kathleen Folbigg attended to Caleb some hours later, although he was not due for another feed and did not wake her crying. When she entered his semi-lit room, she recalled: '… you can hear babies breathing. They are very definite in how they take a breath. So I when I … didn't hear that, that's when I thought, what have you done? Have you rolled over or something? … And I just placed my hand on his chest and didn't feel it … rise … I don't remember exactly what happened next … I was just callin' out to Craig, which I had to do three times as he is a sound sleeper … and back then we didn't know about CPR … So it was a case of us both pretty much panicking on what we were supposed to be doing … and we just rang the ambulance.'[19]

Craig Folbigg's version differed in some details concerning whether Caleb was in his bassinette. He stated that he grabbed the still-warm baby from the bassinette, noting that his lips were blue. He attempted CPR until the ambulance arrived. Ambulance officers David Hopkins and Richard Baines, who arrived at one minute before 3am, were unable to resuscitate the boy, and Hopkins recorded 'Sudden Infant

Kathleen Megan Folbigg, pictured leaving court in 2003, supported by Salvation Army chaplain Major Joyce Harmer. Photo: Fairfax Media FXJ 125429.

Death Syndrome' (SIDS) in his case notes. Kathleen Folbigg had kept a diary of her activities as a young mother, almost obsessively. The last entry, at 2am on 20 February, noted: 'Finally asleep!!' The following day the couple were offered counselling from social workers on SIDS. The autopsy did not provide any conclusive findings, and a case of SIDS was recorded. Dr Springthorpe also took time to talk to the Folbiggs about their loss. Their reactions to Caleb's death contrasted markedly. Craig was depressed and in mourning, while his wife was seemingly cheerful, going back to work at the restaurant where she had been employed before Caleb's birth, and resuming an active social life nightclubbing with friends.

To make sure such a tragedy never happened again, the Folbiggs renovated their house to eliminate any drafts. Craig also agreed never to smoke in the house. When Kathleen fell pregnant again she appeared happy. Patrick Allen David Folbigg was born on 3 June 1990. His mother recorded in her diary: 'I had mixed feelings this day [of Patrick's birth] whether or not I was going to cope as a mother and whether I was going to get stressed out like I did last time. I often regret Caleb and Patrick only because your life changes so much and maybe I'm not the sort of person who likes change, but we will see.'[20] Kathleen Folbigg did not adjust to her maternal role, often appearing angry and resentful, to such an extent that she would growl like an animal, as her husband testified at her trial.

Craig Folbigg dedicated himself to his family, realising that work had to take second place. Patrick was given a newly renovated bedroom. He settled easily into routines, and fed and slept well. After some weeks at home Craig Folbigg began work at a new car dealership. Three days later trouble struck again when Kathleen Folbigg awoke suddenly in the night and went to check on Patrick only to find him not breathing. When Craig Folbigg heard his wife screaming, he ran to Patrick's room to investigate, and called the ambulance. Officer Hopkins returned again, performing CPR on the little boy, who was struggling for breath. Hopkins noticed pressure marks on the baby's neck.

Patrick was taken to hospital, where multiple tests were conducted that showed he had an abnormal amount of glucose in his urine. He was now epileptic and blind. The additional work required to care for a severely disabled infant proved too much for Kathleen Folbigg. She became depressed and resentful again, although she had a lot of support. Craig's sister, Carole Hewitt, a registered nurse and an experienced mother with a large family, offered a lot of assistance. Around this time, Craig Folbigg read his wife's diary to try to understand her mood swings. He was shocked to find out how deeply resentful she was.

Patrick returned from hospital to Caleb's old room, in retrospect a sign that his days were numbered. On the morning of 13 February 1991, after Craig Folbigg had gone to work, Patrick apparently had another fit, and Kathleen Folbigg believed she then went into 'a trance' as a result. She rang Carole Hewitt, who came to the house to find the little boy dead. Kathleen Folbigg rang her husband at work at 10.30am, saying: 'It's happened again.' The ambulance was summoned and Patrick was taken to hospital even though his lips were blue. Doctors informed his parents that the baby died from asphyxiation. Once again the parents' reactions were completely different: Craig was inconsolable; he lost his job, retreating to his shed and playing a lot with a neighbour's little boy. Kathleen Folbigg, on the other hand, was ready to change jobs and make new friends.

They moved house to Thornton, near Maitland, and Kathleen announced she wanted another baby. Whatever suspicions Craig Folbigg might have had about the deaths of his sons he suppressed for the time being. Sarah Kathleen Folbigg was born on 14 October 1992. The couple installed a sleep apnoea machine to monitor the little girl's breathing through the night but discarded it when it beeped with false alarms. The new baby was a fitful sleeper. Kathleen Folbigg fell back into the patterns laid down in the past: she began growling in anger and frustration. With her husband forced to spend long hours commuting to a new job she was left alone with 'one grouchy little bugger'.[21] The broken sleep patterns of the baby and Folbigg's need for strict routine added to her growing anger and instability. The baby had to be put to bed at 8.30 each night no matter what, an example of Folbigg's rigidity that was the cause of constant arguments between the couple.

Events following a family outing on 29 August 1993 repeated the previous tragedies. When they returned home from a day at the beach, Kathleen Folbigg was tired and frustrated. She accused her husband of 'revvin'' up' Sarah, who was too excited and unwilling to go to bed. Craig was disturbed to hear loud growling come from the child's bedroom, a now-familiar warning. 'You fucking deal with her!' he was told as Sarah cried loudly. Later that night he heard screams from the baby's room and discovered an agitated Kathleen there. Sarah was showing no signs of life at 1.34am. Later, a calendar was discovered with 'Sarah left us at 1am' written across the date of 30 November. At this time, by Kathleen Folbigg's account, Sarah had been asleep.

On this occasion, two detectives and a police photographer from Maitland Police Station investigated. There was some discrepancy in the times recorded by the police as to when Sarah had been alive and well. The autopsy revealed no obvious cause of death and SIDS was identified again. It seemed statistically unlikely that three children in one family should perish in this way but the Folbiggs were informed it was 'just bad luck'.

Craig Folbigg suffered such extreme depression and inconsolable grief that his wife ordered him in writing to seek grief counselling. They moved house again; Craig spent a lot of his spare time alone in the garage. When his grief did not abate, Kathleen Folbigg left him 'to get on with it on his own'. She returned to Newcastle, enjoying the parties and nightclubs there as much as when she was a child-free, single woman. It wasn't until Kathleen's foster family moved to Darwin that the Folbiggs resumed their marriage. Kathleen Folbigg felt as abandoned as she had been as a toddler.

Craig and Kathleen Folbigg contemplated having another child. They consulted Dr Christopher Seton at the sleep unit at Westmead Children's Hospital for advice. She confided in her diary on 18 June 1996: 'I am ready this time and I know I'll have help and support this time. When I think I am going to lose control like last time I'll just hand the baby over to someone else. Not feel totally alone ... I have learned my lesson this time.'[22] Kathleen Folbigg learned she was pregnant again in November 1996. Yet an entry recorded on 30 October was ominous: 'I pray I'm prepared and ready, mind wise, for this next one. Maybe nature has decided I never will be and it will never happen.' Her feelings of incompetence had not abated, as she revealed in her diary on 4 December 1996: 'I'm ready this time, but have already decided if I get feelings of jealousy or anger too much I will leave Craig and baby rather than being as before ... I know that battling wills and sleep deprivation were the causes last time.' But the causes of *what* was left unexplained in her written thoughts. Hindsight reveals that she meant the death of Sarah. Another diary entry on 1 January 1997 was chilling to contemplate: 'I am going to call for help this time and not attempt to do everything myself anymore. I know that was the main reason for all my stress before, and stress made me do terrible things ...'[23] What these 'terrible things' were was not defined.

Laura Folbigg was born on 7 August 1997. Kathleen Folbigg felt that the nurses forced her to breastfeed, a practice she stopped as soon as she returned home. She did, however, make a seemingly positive move to engage with Sydney researcher Dr Christopher Seton's program on sleep disorders and SIDS. Help was also provided by the David Reed Sleep Unit at the Westmead Children's Hospital. Staff advised the use of a sleep apnoea machine once more to monitor breathing. But all was not well. Folbigg confided again to her diary: 'Sleep? Who needs it? Yes, I am getting a little bit irritable now. This is my punishment for the others, to be continually woken up, because this time we know we have a child with a sleeping disorder ... and I'm getting stressed as I cannot rely on Craig for any real support or help ...' During the day, when Craig Folbigg was away at work, Folbigg turned the monitoring machine off, a source of argument at home and concern at the sleep unit. Within five months, further diary entries revealed her thoughts of running away to rediscover the joys of a single, unencumbered life. That motherhood entailed substituting a 2am departure from a nightclub with a 2am feed never seemed to occur to her, nor that it was something experienced by every parent.

By early 1998 Folbigg's mood had worsened, as she wrote in her diary: '... I've done it. I lost it with her. I yelled at her so angry that it scared her. She hasn't stopped crying ... I knew I was short-tempered and cruel to her [Sarah] and she'd left with a bit of help. I don't want it ever to happen again. I actually seem to have a bond with Laura ... Her moaning, bored, whingey sound drives me up the wall ... '[24] Nightclubbing and going to the gym was her response to her frustrations. Finally, Folbigg wrote to her husband, even though they lived in the same house, that she wished to leave him due to his 'oppression'. More disturbing was that Laura would leave with her when she terminated the marriage. Almost inexplicably Craig Folbigg continued to love his wife, despite the trauma they had endured and the strains on their relationship. The marriage held tenuously together.

By this time Laura was afraid of her mother and reluctant to stay with her. On 29 February 1999, following a fierce argument at breakfast, during which Folbigg growled and became abusive, Craig Folbigg was summoned from work to learn that their daughter had suddenly stopped breathing. By the time he reached the hospital Laura was dead. Kathleen Folbigg told him that after a morning at the gym – with Laura in childcare – she had put Laura to bed for a nap. She heard the monitor go off but did not go to investigate for around ten minutes. When she got to the bedroom, she discovered Laura had turned blue and did not respond to CPR.

When Craig Folbigg came home, Laura's sandals were on the futon and not in the hallway as Kathleen Folbigg had told him on the telephone. Also the monitor could not be heard from the clothesline, where she reported she had heard it ringing. The police were suspicious, as the likelihood of another SIDS death, especially with a nineteen-month-old child in the daytime, was remote. Detective Senior Constable Bernie Ryan thought it was more than suspicious but lacked evidence to prove otherwise. As he told *Australian Story* on ABC Television: 'Singleton is a small country town. It's not a place that one would go searching for major crime. March 1 1999 was a day that changed my life. It was a very dark day for Singleton that day.' His search of the house revealed anomalies such as the sandals being on the futon rather than in the bedroom. 'Why? Because what Kathleen said didn't happen.'

At the funeral Kathleen Folbigg seemed calm and sedate. In the car going home with her husband, her foster sister, Lea Brown, and her brother-in-law, Michael Folbigg, all she could say was: 'Well, thank fuck that's over. Now I can get on with things.' Even at the wake she was composed and chatting amiably with her gym buddies. One week later, she was back at the gym as if nothing had happened. She returned to work quickly and seemed undisturbed by the tragedy that had engulfed her husband and his family. Rather than showing sympathy for her grieving husband, Folbigg accused him of 'moping'. The marriage ended soon afterwards.

When Craig was sorting through those things of hers remaining in the marital home, he discovered another of her diaries with more chilling entries. One written on 14 October 1996 particularly intrigued him: 'Obviously I am my father's daughter.'[25] His suppressed suspicions were confirmed – his wife had cold-bloodedly killed their four children and there seemed to be evidence of it in her diary. The Crown's case rested upon the entries in the diary, although Folbigg's defence claimed they were mere 'babble books'.[26]

Dr Quang Tuan Au, who conducted Laura's autopsy, informed Detective Ryan that he believed that it was not a SIDS death: her death resulted from murder. Further investigation with Dr Allan Cala at the New South Wales Institute of Forensic Medicine was undertaken. He detected myocarditis (inflammation around the heart) but indicated that this was not the cause of Laura's death. Like Sarah, her lungs were collapsed, although this did not prove suffocation. He left his findings as 'undetermined causes of death'. He did point out, however, that usually SIDS deaths are found in the morning on waking whereas the first three Folbigg children were found with the mother in the early hours of the morning. He contacted Detective Ryan, suggesting a medical review of the four deaths. Only one Folbigg infant had been under six months at death, the customary age by which death by SIDS abates.

Soon after, Craig Folbigg told Detective Ryan that he had read his wife's disturbing diary. From the moment he saw the diary, Ryan decided that it was now a murder investigation. Folbigg spent many hours going over his memories of events with the detective. That same night Kathleen Folbigg went to a ball and brought home a businessman, whom she kissed on her doorstep before undressing in the lounge room, quite visible through the thin curtains. Craig Folbigg confronted her after waiting outside to talk to her. All she could say was: 'You're an arsehole!' She then proceeded to scream at him as she chased him down the driveway, shouting: 'Are you accusing me of Laura's death?' Then she found out the police were investigating all the deaths. He also told her he had read her diary and given it to the police. Kathleen Folbigg's mood changed abruptly as she cajoled and soothed Craig's fears. Despite all that had happened, he agreed to resume their marriage.[27]

To an outsider, the success of Folbigg's emotional manipulation seems unbelievable. Yet it convinced Craig Folbigg to attempt to retract his statement to police. This meant that Detective Ryan could not continue to pursue his investigations with the vigour he required. So he embarked on his own extraordinary quest for justice for Laura and the other three babies.[28] Ryan met with leading international SIDS researchers, such as Dr Susan Beal at the Women's and Children's Hospital in Adelaide, Dr Janice Ophoven in Minneapolis, and pathologists Professor Peter Berry at the Bristol Royal Hospital for Sick Children and Dr Peter Herdson, senior pathologist at the Canberra Hospital, as well as psychological profilers with the FBI and Israel's Mossad.[29] Ryan also investigated Münchausen's Syndrome by proxy, a behaviour pattern in which a parent (usually a mother) injures a child in order to get attention and support for herself.

On his return from his extensive research, Detective Ryan arranged for the installation of listening devices in the Folbigg house in July 1999. On 23 July he went to the house and requested that Kathleen Folbigg accompany him to the local police station. The interview was long and detailed, although he did not point out the multiple discrepancies in her stories. This was not a cross-examination. Its purpose was to unnerve her so she would say things at home that could be recorded. He also confronted her with the exact meanings of various suspicious diary entries, all of which she brushed off as if they were of no importance. Her response to the entry about 'stress makes me do terrible things' was merely to indicate she got angry and shouted.[30] After eight hours Folbigg was released and informed that her house would be searched. Police attempted to locate more diaries.

Life for the Folbiggs was tense; Craig was constantly worried he would trigger explosions of rage and abuse if he pressed his wife too hard with his nagging worries about their children's deaths. Alone, Kathleen Folbigg began acting out courtroom scenarios with herself as both defendant and prosecutor, adopting a strange American accent.

Detective Ryan continued to analyse new evidence found in the diaries. Folbigg wrote just before Laura's birth: 'Maybe then he will see when stress of it all is getting to be too much, and save me from feeling like I did before during my dark moods. Hopefully preparing myself will be the end of my dark moods ... That will be the key to this baby's survival. It surely will. But enough of dwelling. Things are different this time. It will all work out for sure.'[31]

On 9 November 1997, when Kathleen Folbigg was angry with her husband for getting drunk, she laid out her frustrations in her diary. Her focus was foremost on Laura's crying, a normal part of early infancy, recalling that, 'with Sarah all I wanted was for her to shut up and one day she did'. Ryan continued his research in Canberra as he prepared his brief. The director of public prosecutions at this time believed there was insufficient evidence to proceed.

By mid-2000, the Folbiggs' marriage was finally over, which allowed police to pursue inquiries in more depth. Craig Folbigg was re-interviewed on 19 April 2001; he was now scared when he was arrested for 'hindering an investigation'. Kathleen Folbigg was charged with four counts of murder on 20 April 2001. She was refused bail. Her new partner had no idea that she had had four children let alone what had happened to them. On 18 May 2001 she successfully applied for bail before Justice Robert Hulme of the New South Wales Supreme Court. In the meantime, Detective Ryan went to Melbourne in an attempt to get Folbigg's foster sister, Lea Brown, to act as a witness for the prosecution. She began taping all her conversations with her sister. Brown later told a newspaper that 'if the death penalty was reintroduced she would be the first in line with the injection syringe'.[32]

On 13 February 2003, Folbigg, through her counsel, sought to have each of the four counts of murder be dealt with separately rather than concurrently. The New South Wales Court of Appeal dismissed the application.[33] Her barrister took the matter to the High Court of Australia where Justice McHugh in a hearing in chambers dismissed the application for a stay of proceedings.[34] This decision was later examined thoroughly by forensic investigators who argued that it allowed for a Crown argument of similarity and coincidence, as SIDS is a difficult area to diagnose.[35] The trial was conducted in the New South Wales Supreme Court presided over by Justice Graham Barr, with eminent QC Mark Tedeschi, who had prosecuted the case against serial killer Ivan Milat and the killers of Dr Victor Chang, leading for the Crown. Folbigg was defended by Peter Zahra SC. After outlining the circumstances of each of the four deaths, Tedeschi concluded his opening remarks to the jury on 13 May 2003 by reading an excerpt from the defendant's diary of 31 December 1997: 'Getting Laura to be [one] next year ought to be fun. She'll realise a party is going on and that will be it. Wonder if the battle of wills will start with her and I then? We'll actually get to see. She is a fairly good-natured baby. Thank goodness. It will save her from the fate of her siblings, I think she was warned.'

It was alleged that the defendant did not suffer from symptoms of postpartum depression but that this was cold-blooded, premeditated murder. When a video recording of her interview with Detective Ryan was played, as well as another of Laura on the day before she died, Folbigg became hysterical and nearly fell out of the dock. The trial was adjourned while she received medical treatment at nearby St Vincent's Hospital.[36]

When the trial resumed the following day, forensic psychiatrist Dr Rod Milton testified that Folbigg had a narcissistic personality, although she was not insane, an opinion with which other specialists concurred. Folbigg decide not to testify, which common-law systems allow. Justice Barr pointed out to the jury that this is not an admission of guilt since it is up to the prosecution to prove a case beyond reasonable doubt. The jury retired to consider its verdict on the multiple charges. Folbigg was found guilty of the manslaughter of Caleb, the murder of Patrick, Sarah and Laura, as well as inflicting grievous bodily harm upon Patrick. Folbigg was so distressed she could hardly walk past the holding cells below the courtroom to the waiting police van. Craig Folbigg read a short statement to the waiting crowd and media outside, thanking the jury and Detective Bernie Ryan.

In prison, Folbigg received many death threats; even among murderers, killing your own children is unthinkable. In prison she maintained her anger, believing that the Folbigg family were making a fortune by selling the story. On 23 August 2003 Folbigg, dishevelled and unkempt, appeared for sentencing. Detective Ryan, now an expert on child murder, watched from the public gallery. Peter Zahra called psychiatrist Dr Bruce Westmore, who testified that his client was suffering from some deep, unspecified personality disorder and from the effects of her early abuse. Justice Barr attempted to understand the long-term factors that led to Folbigg's convictions, and delivered his statement calmly and methodically.

Kathleen Megan Donovan was born on 14 June 1967. Her Welsh father, Thomas Britton, was a violent man who worked as an enforcer, hit man and debt collector for Sydney underworld crime figure Robert Trimbole. In 1952 he cut his first wife's throat, a crime for which he served just eight months' imprisonment. He fathered several children by different mothers. Britton met Kathleen Donovan in 1965, and spent three years with her before she left him because of his violence. Every morning he would hold a knife to her throat and whisper: 'Will I or won't I?' She abandoned baby Kathleen with him in Balmain, then a rough inner-city suburb. Encountering her out walking one day, Britton begged her to rejoin him. Donovan refused, so he punched her in the face when she took refuge in a butchers shop. He then stabbed her twenty-five times with a carving knife. She died on the footpath. Britton leaned over and pronounced his final words to her: 'I'm sorry, I had to do it.' He was found guilty of her murder in May 1969 and sentenced to fourteen years' imprisonment. He was later deported to Wales.

As an infant Kathleen Donovan endured prolonged abuse. As a toddler, after the death of her mother and imprisonment of her father, she had first been taken in by an aunt and uncle, but was subsequently sent into care at Bidura Children's Home where she was reportedly a severely troubled and disruptive child. At the age of three she went to live with the Marlboroughs. Her development had been so stunted it was initially feared that she was intellectually handicapped. Under the Marlboroughs' strict care, Kathleen began a calm and stable period of her life. But her adolescence was shattered by constant arguments with her mother. Justice Barr noted that during this time there was 'some minor offending but no pattern of violence'.[37] Her husband Craig Folbigg found out some of her past during their marriage when she sought to become reconciled with her natural extended family. Under the circumstances, her potential for good parenting was remote.

But her upbringing, no matter how violent and traumatic, was not a mitigating factor in her sentence. Forensic psychiatrist Dr Michael Giuffrida, who visited her on five occasions during the trial, reported that Folbigg was not psychotic but a deeply troubled and tormented woman who constantly felt abandoned and alone. Her emotional detachment from her own actions and the deaths of her children characterised her demeanour. She had suffered irreparable impairment to her emotional development that manifested itself in lethal consequences. He stated that her attachment to her children was 'a practical and mechanical kind devoid of any sense of loving and passion'. Justice Barr also noted that Folbigg had not physically neglected her children; rather, she was simply incapable of nurturing or caring for them. He sentenced her to forty years' imprisonment with eligibility for parole in 2033.

Represented by David Jackson QC, one of the nation's most eminent lawyers, Folbigg unsuccessfully appealed her conviction on 17 February 2005.[38] Her sentence was, however, reduced to thirty years with parole hearings available in 2029. Folbigg then sought leave to appeal to the High Court of Australia on May 2005 on the grounds that errors in judgment had been made at her trial. She was unsuccessful.[39] On 16 May 2007 she was granted leave to appeal again on the grounds that jurors had access to information from the internet about her mother's murder and also that the jury had been misled about body temperature after infant death. The appeal was heard in the New South Wales Court of Criminal Appeal in November 2007 by Justice Peter McClellan, Justice Carolyn Simpson and Justice Virginia Bell.[40] It was dismissed.

Folbigg has now exercised all her rights to appeal her sentence. Her trials have been lengthy and numerous. But she determinedly maintains her innocence and is convinced of the unfairness of the legal system towards her. In a letter to Lea Brown, Folbigg laid out her case: 'Try to imagine your life spread out, ripped to pieces, examined, opinions cast, character assassinated, your every action, word, thought, doubted, and you're told that you do not know yourself. Add to that, because of all of the above, the most HATED woman alive … You can't. I live with this every day. I endure all of this knowing that vindication will be mine. This is the last time I'll state – I did not kill my children.'[41]

Folbigg will spend her sentence in isolation for her own protection. This is in stark contrast to Kathy Knight who murdered, skinned and cooked her partner, and was sentenced to life imprisonment 'never to be released' in 2001. Like Folbigg, Knight is incarcerated in Silverwater Women's Correctional Centre (formerly Mulawa Detention Centre), but unlike Folbigg she is able to spend her time sewing amicably with other inmates. Knight is frequently so involved with her craft activities she does not see visiting family members.[42]

CHAPTER 5

A Baffling Case: Keli Lane

There are persistent stereotypes of the type of women who commit infanticide. There's the poverty-stricken, desperate woman with little education and few skills, or the young, frightened single teenager. Such stereotypes are as predictable as they are frequently true. However, neonatal killing can also be driven by severe postpartum depression or psychosis. So how to interpret the actions of a 'golden girl',[1] in the words of Justice Anthony Whealy, who was accused and found guilty of killing her newborn daughter and hiding the body, which was never found? Keli Lane came from a well-respected family in Manly in Sydney. She was an elite sportswoman with Olympic aspirations who taught at a prestigious private girls' school, and yet in December 2010 she stood convicted of murder.

Born on 21 March 1975, Keli Lane lived in the northern beachside suburb of Manly in Sydney from the time she was four years old. Her father, Robert Lane, was a highly regarded police sergeant and rugby union player and coach. Even though he later switched to rugby league, he remained a core member of the Manly Rugby Union Football Club. Keli's mother, Sandra, was also involved with local sports clubs and was, as well, manager for travelling women's water polo teams. Keli was a keen swimmer who, by adolescence, was a champion water polo player representing the state and the national teams at a junior level.[2] She attended Manly Vale High School (now MacKellar Girls High School), where she excelled in water sports. Not academically inclined, Lane was more prominent as a noted sportswoman, well connected to the social and sporting culture of the area, which in Manly conferred prestige.

Her first boyfriend, Aaron Tyack, a surf lifesaver intent upon undertaking trade training, knew the competitiveness of Manly's local culture well: 'Manly can be a very cliquey place. It's like a small town.'[3] In this hierarchical environment, Keli Lane was a star – beautiful, athletic, popular and outwardly charming – from a high-profile local family. At seventeen, though, while she was still a school student, Lane became pregnant and underwent a termination. She told her boyfriend of the pregnancy but not her parents. She had another termination, this time a late-term abortion, again without informing her parents, whom she suspected would be disapproving and unsupportive. And this time she didn't tell Tyack. Her relationship with him, which had been strong and committed, fell apart soon afterwards.[4]

In 1993 Lane was selected for the Under 20s squad to represent New South Wales at the national water polo championships. The team did well, auguring more national and perhaps even international success, although it was not yet an Olympic sport. Yet Keli's teammates Lisa Berry and Taryn Woods were considered more suitable for continuing elite participation.[5]

The following year Lane met Duncan Gillies, whose family included several professional rugby league players. Their mutual commitment to high-level sport, competition and partying were important elements of their relationship. Gillies often spent the night with Lane at her parents' home, where she resided. Robert and Sandra Lane did not entirely approve, though they realised that this was the modern trend and they respected their daughter's choice of boyfriend. Lane began an Arts degree at the University of Newcastle but dropped out fairly quickly.

That year she was deeply disappointed when she was not selected for the Australian women's water polo team, especially when friends and teammates were fortunate in this regard. It spurred her ambitions even more fervently to join the big league of competition. Lane also had a clandestine affair with an older married man in 1994, by whom she became pregnant. This was another secret pregnancy, even though she continued her relationship with Gillies. Rumours circulated about her expanding belly. Witness Allison Cratchley testified at a coronial inquiry in 1995 that 'Manly can be a very toxic place. If you put on a little bit of weight, the next thing you're accused of being pregnant. That's something that happened to me in the past, so I dismissed those rumours.' Barrister David Woods asked the New South Wales head coach Les Kay whether he had broached the subject of pregnancy with Lane at the time. 'It's not a good place to go,' he replied.[6]

On 18 March 1995 Lane and her team from the Balmain Water Polo Club played Sydney University Water Polo Club. Almost unbelievably she gave birth that night at Balmain Hospital after first attending a post-match party at the Bridge Hotel, also in Balmain. Even Gillies' mother, Julie Gillies, an experienced nurse, had no idea that Lane was about to give birth. Incredible as this seems, other contemporary cases show that Lane was not alone in concealing multiple pregnancies. French nurse Dominique Cottrez was accused of murdering eight of her babies in 2010. Her husband had no idea about any of the pregnancies until he found the bodies in their garden.[7]

Lane's newborn daughter was immediately placed for adoption. Social worker Deborah Habib recalled later at the coronial hearing that she advised Lane about the adoption procedures. Lane was emotionally overwrought and sad. As she explained to Habib, she wanted to compete in the Olympics and wouldn't be able to if '... she continued to parent a baby'.[8] On 3 April 1995 Lane swore an affidavit in the adoption proceedings that falsely claimed that Duncan Gillies was willing for his child to be adopted. False, since he knew nothing about the pregnancy and nor was he the father. In a further affidavit Lane swore that Gillies maintained he wanted nothing to do with his daughter and had refused to sign consent forms.[9] Insufficient inquiries were made into her deception.

Lane resumed her life without seeming to miss a beat, representing Australia for a silver medal in the World Championships in Canada. In early 1996 Lane was selected to compete in the New South Wales women's water polo team, which she believed would get her into a future Olympic spot. She was also accepted for study at the Australian College of Physical Education. By this time, Gillies had purchased a home in Gladesville, making their time together even more sporadic.

Yet in December 1995, just nine months after her daughter's birth, Lane became pregnant once again. The father of the baby is unknown.[10] For her twenty-first birthday in April 1996, her parents threw an impressive party. Persistent rumours at this time suggested that Lane and Gillies, now a professional football player, were no longer involved. Gillies had been painfully honest with Lane, telling her about a sexual encounter with a teammate and friend of Keli.[11] His straightforwardness was something she didn't reciprocate.

Other areas of Lane's life progressed. Her career began to take off in 1996 when she became a sports mistress at the prestigious Ravenswood School for Girls on Sydney's North Shore. By this time she was visibly pregnant, although again in secret – or so she thought. Allisa Warren, one of Lane's former students, and later employed as a reporter for Channel Nine News, stated that the students all knew 'Miss Lane was pregnant' in 1996. 'There wasn't much gossip about Miss Lane – but as her belly grew, so did the judging glances and snide remarks between parents. Miss Lane was obviously young, obviously pregnant and not married.'[12]

Her water polo teammates were also highly suspicious that Lane was pregnant. Stacey Gaylard, who had boarded with the Lane family for eight months in 1994, recalled that in 40°C heat at the Sydney International Aquatic Centre at Homebush in 1996 Lane turned up in a heavy tracksuit when everyone else wore shorts and singlet tops. 'I saw her take her towel off and my eyes nearly popped out of my head. I thought, "Oh, my God, there can only be one possible reason for her stomach being so big."' She was so astounded that she and Taryn Woods decided to view Lane from an underwater perspective. She continued: 'We started swimming laps and as we passed her, we looked. She was just so obviously pregnant. How could she think no one would notice? We assumed it was Duncan's baby and that they handled the situation together – maybe arranged for adoption.'

In the past, teammates thought Lane was a 'Keg on Legs', a solidly built woman who partied hard and enjoyed drinking. Coach Les Kay wondered if her weight had been caused by too much 'winter grazing'. He later said that he had heard rumours that Lane was pregnant in 1996 '... but I stay well away from that'.[13] That no one confronted Lane about the pregnancy or even inquired about the possibility indicates that for all her popularity she was emotionally closed and secretive, with no close friends or confidants. In fact, Lane had managed to conceal her pregnancy with her firstborn child not just from her family but also from Gaylard, who had shared a bedroom with her at the time.

On Thursday, 12 September 1996, after an induced labour, Lane gave birth to her daughter Tegan at Auburn Hospital in western Sydney. She admitted herself, telling nursing staff that her family was currently away and that her scheduled midwife, 'Julie Melville', could not be located, thus ensuring that staff would be unable to check her medical records. She spun an elaborately concocted story about a desired homebirth, telling the nursing staff that her partner, Duncan Gillies, a professional footballer, was also away. Unlike other new mothers, she had no visitors, no excited relatives, flowers or cards. Even in her hospital room she drew the curtain around her and did not engage in conversation with her fellow new mothers.

At some point a telephone call came from Ryde Hospital inquiring whether a Keli Lane had been admitted since she had presented at Ryde requesting an induced birth.

As it was later revealed, Lane had needed to give birth on the Thursday so she could go to a wedding with Gillies the following Saturday.[14] Lane did allow a hospital social worker to take down case notes: she 'admitted' that Duncan Gillies was her boyfriend, 'currently overseas' before their permanent move to London in a few months.

Lane requested a discharge on Saturday, 14 September, and was supplied with Medicare forms that she was pressed to complete. Other medical records were left for her to post back to the hospital. On the form Lane named the newborn Tegan Lee Lane, thus leaving an official paper trail of the baby's existence. When medical staff agreed that both mother and baby were fit for release, Lane left surreptitiously, possibly by the fire exit. Tegan did not have the usual baby capsule or bassinette and was simply carried out in her mother's arms around midday. The nurse on duty recorded in the case notes that Lane's private midwife needed to be contacted to ensure the Guthrie test for congenital illnesses was conducted. By 3pm Lane had arrived home alone seemingly composed and perfectly normal. She and Gillies dressed for the wedding and neither he nor her parents noticed anything different about her appearance. At 4pm she went to the wedding with Gillies, but she seemed a little tired and not as exuberant as usual; she left the festivities unexpectedly early.[15]

On Monday, 16 September, Lane rang the Auburn maternity ward informing the duty nurse that she wanted to cancel the standard home visit as she planned to have Tegan's tests and medical procedures done by her homebirth nurse. Lane resumed her normal life as if nothing unusual had happened. Later in the year she was invited to Ben Gillies' wedding and accompanied Duncan as his partner.

The following year Lane faced a series of disappointments. She was not selected for the state women's water polo team and therefore could not participate in the FINA World Cup. The sport was then selected as an Olympic event, raising her hopes for inclusion even though she was not invited to attend the official announcement. When the Australian Institute of Sport released its selection her name was not included. Then in February 1999 she was not selected at the trials in Noosa, and from then any realistic hopes for Olympic glory were gone. Duncan Gillies' career, on the other hand, although not brilliant, was progressing to international level in competitions against Scotland and Fiji. In early 1998 he ended his relationship with Lane. Despite the setbacks, her enthusiasm for her sport did not diminish and she kept alive her hopes that she could be selected to represent her country for the 2000 Summer Olympics in Sydney.

Keli Lane has never been able to adequately explain what happened to her baby Tegan. Photo: Fairfax Media FXJ 40197.

Alarmingly, Keli Lane discovered that she was pregnant again; her attempt to secure a late-term abortion this time was rejected. The father was entirely unaware of this pregnancy, believing Lane was taking contraceptives. As before, Lane informed no one and concealed her pregnancy. She gave birth to a son in Ryde Hospital on 31 May 1999. Again there were no flowers, family or friends to celebrate with her in the maternity ward. And again she indicated to the admission officer that her family and her partner, Duncan Gillies, lived in London, and that she was only back in Australia briefly. When queries about Tegan were made she said that she was in Sydney. Who was minding Tegan while Lane was a maternity patient was not discussed. The little boy was adopted through Anglicare. The adoption officer, Virginia Fung, immediately contacted Lane to sort out the now-complicated procedure for adoption, which had been designed to protect vulnerable women who were relinquishing their babies.

Lane insisted that her baby's father had abandoned her when he found out she was pregnant and that she intended returning to London soon, adding to the confusing web of lies and conflicting stories she had told to different officials and hospital employees. A social worker interviewed Lane, reassuring her that adoption was a discreet process that eliminated as much stigma as humanly possible. Lane left the hospital without the baby and without informing the nursing staff of her departure. The baby had simply been a problem to be solved and then swiftly forgotten about. When the Ryde Hospital postpartum midwife went to Gillies' house in Gladesville to check up on Lane she was informed that Duncan Gillies had not lived there for over eighteen months and that Lane had never been a resident. From that point on Lane made sure she was hard to contact, turning off her mobile telephone. When eventually Virginia Fung caught up with her, she spun another story – that Duncan was emotionally remote and uncaring.

Keli Lane's infant son was initially fostered for a month, and at the end June his long-term future needed to be decided. With Lane remaining elusive, he became an abandoned baby with no real legal status. And this provoked exactly the kind of attention Lane had wanted to avoid. Her unusual behaviour alerted care workers that here was a complicated and potentially unresolved case. On top of that, Ryde Hospital also had a copy of Tegan's birth records.

At this point Virginia Fung was not yet aware of Tegan's birth or that there was any mystery regarding her whereabouts. She was a thorough and sympathetic adoption officer who, when Lane continued to be elusive, next attempted to contact Duncan Gillies through the Manly Rugby League Club. When Gillies received the correspondence he was perplexed that anything involving Lane would now concern him, especially since he was engaged to be married. When Gillies spoke to Fung he confirmed he did not live with Lane and he had never been in London with her. Lane's subsequent discussion with him about pregnancies and babies was confused, contradictory and disturbing for him and his fiancée Karen. Tracking down the fax numbers, Fung realised that some had come from Ravenswood School, proving that the story about living in London was a fabrication.

Fung persisted in her hunt for the truth. Lane was deemed to be in no fit state to continue with the adoption process and Fung advised her to seek psychological assistance. Her newborn baby became a ward of the state. A meeting near Ravenswood in mid-1999 proved unsatisfactory, so a few days after that Fung went to visit Lane at the school. Lane told her the name of the father was Aaron Williams, a merchant banker in London with whom she had no further contact. When asked whether her son had any siblings Lane said no, this was her first baby. She requested an access visit with her baby and seemed perfectly happy to be with him. Adoption procedures were resumed. The day that Lane picked potential new parents for the little boy, John Borovnik, a Department of Community Services officer, tracked down the files on Tegan's birth and discovered her absence from any official records.

When confronted by Fung with the fact that she had given birth before, Lane told her that she felt no one would help her if it was revealed she had already been through it previously. The first baby had been adopted, but what of the second, Tegan Lee Lane?

When Borovnik first asked her about Tegan's birth in 1996 Lane denied the baby's existence. On 4 November 1999 Borovnik contacted police in Katoomba, the nearest area to Auburn Hospital.[16] Aaron Williams could not be traced and Julie Melville, although a nurse, did not practise as a midwife.

In late 1999 the Lane file arrived at Manly Police Station and landed on the desk of Matt Kehoe, who was already well regarded for his detective work in the case of Louise Sullivan, the Sydney nanny who had been accused of killing a baby in London. But this new case presented difficulties from the start. Unsuccessfully, Kehoe requested a transfer from the case. In the end it took him more than eighteen months to interview Lane; in that time he did not contact Fung or Borovnik. He did, however, interview Julie Gillies – whose professional name is Julie Melville. Duncan Gillies was as perplexed as his mother to learn about the birth of a baby girl to Keli Lane in 1996.

In late 2000, Keli Lane became pregnant to a young family friend, who had been staying with the Lanes.[17] In February 2001, Kehoe finally interviewed Lane about Tegan's whereabouts. She told him that the baby's father was a man called Andrew Morris, who lived in Balmain with his partner, and that Tegan lived with them. She had lost contact with them years ago. But in her formal interview at Manly Police Station on 13 February 2001, Lane still had Tegan's Medicare card in her possession, hardly likely if the girl lived with her father.[18] Yet, when Kehoe could not locate a birth certificate for Tegan, for another three months nothing was done.

The delays and false starts are understandable, especially since Manly Police Station was under investigation as part of the wider corruption inquiry known as Operation Florida. Kehoe, an officer with an exemplary record, was transferred to another station. In October 2001, Detective Richard Gaut, a new officer to the station, took over the Tegan Lane case.

At first Gaut was concerned to rectify Tegan's legal status and provide her with registration of her birth. Part of this process involved locating her father, Andrew Morris – a frustrating and fruitless task. His interview with Keli Lane was difficult, the interviewee uncooperative. Even the name of Tegan's father was changed – perhaps it was Andrew Norris, who knew? For a woman now with a toddler, from a respected local family and with a position at a prestigious girls' school, Lane hardly appeared on the surface to be a woman who had rather carelessly abandoned an ex-nuptial baby to a man whose name she was not certain of. Inquiries with Medicare revealed that no services had been requested or processed, again unbelievable for a five-year-old urban child. Gaut also contacted Lane's old water polo teammates, who confirmed that Lane had looked pregnant in 1996.

When questioned again in late 2003, Lane admitted she had lied on numerous occasions to social workers and nursing staff regarding her family situation and residence. What is surprising is that she identified real people, like Julie Gilmore and Duncan Gillies, with whom facts could be later verified or refuted.

Detective Gaut was not about to give up his inquiries concerning what appeared to be a missing child case. He informed Lane the matter would be forwarded to the coroner's office for further investigations.

Rental records did not find an 'Andrew Morris' or 'Andrew Norris' renting in Balmain on the dates Lane had given. On 4 January 2004, Gaut received permission to tap Lane's telephone.

Four days later, Lane was interviewed at Manly Police Station again. By now she had realised that a coroner's inquiry would be a public proceeding and that her parents would find out about the concealed births and the three babies. Lane was distressed and alarmed by the tone of Gaut's questions when he asked why she had wanted Tegan's birth to be induced. An expert psychiatric evaluation of this interview, conducted by Dr Michael Diamond, commented that these questions '… were very close to revealing her true distress at the time when [Lane] was pregnant with Tegan, had kept the pregnancy secret, had no plan for what she might do with Tegan after the birth'.[19] The story that Tegan was given to her father somewhere between Auburn Hospital and Lane's home in Manly was unbelievable.

Lane and her boyfriend intended to marry in February 2004, so she told him about Tegan. She also decided she had better tell her mother.

On 14 March 2004, Tegan's case was referred to the coroner's office as a possible murder. Lane was intensively interviewed again in November 2004, a situation that she found stressful. She was 'in a mess and she was scared', the Supreme Court was later told; this was quite unlike her calm demeanour the day she left Auburn Hospital with Tegan and attended a wedding later that afternoon. Her GP, Dr Jeremy Thompson, treating her at the time, reported that Lane was 'in a distraught state' as she felt she was 'being given a hard time' both by the police investigation team and the journalists who 'hovered around her'. Lane confided in him about the 'compulsions and unhappiness that underlay her prior destructive behaviour' although she strenuously denied having harmed Tegan.[20]

Lane's parents hired a QC to represent her, something far beyond their financial resources. She was advised to say as little as possible, which frustrated the proceedings. With no leads, the court opened up the intriguing case for public scrutiny in newspapers and other forms of media. In June 2005, Coroner John Abernethy, assisted by Sergeant Rebbecca Becroft, began the official public inquiry beset by myriad difficulties, given how much time had passed and the inadequate initial police investigations. Gaut, Fung and Borovnik all testified. Robert Lane took the stand, affirming that he could not believe that his daughter would harm a child, regardless of the circumstances of the secret birth. Duncan Gillies and Julie Gillies and a range of friends provided testimony to the coroner. During the proceedings, Sandra Lane did not attend court. She was, however, summoned to appear to answer close questioning about her views on abortion and ex-nuptial birth. She stated that she would have supported her daughter regardless of local negative opinion, contrary to what Lane had assumed.

Keli Lane initially declined to take the witness stand. Coroner Abernethy and her barrister discussed whether she was worried that she could incriminate herself under oath. Eventually she reluctantly took the stand, reminded from the bench that she did not have to answer questions that would incriminate her. When asked about Tegan's birth, she declined to answer. The media outside the court smelt blood and a scoop. From now on Keli Lane was a sensational news item.

On 15 February the coroner's report was released. It canvassed several core questions: that no body had been discovered; that there was no forensic evidence to examine; that Keli Lane had put up her first and third child for adoption; and that Lane may have released Tegan to the care of her natural father in the car park, and that he declined to come forward. However, the coroner concluded by saying that he believed Tegan was dead and that all details of the hearings were to be forwarded to the homicide squad of the New South Wales Police.[21] Lane was admonished for wasting so much police time. When he retired in 2007 after seven years in the Coroner's Court, Abernethy said that 'Tegan Lane was arguably the most frustrating case I did. It was a case I simply could not solve.'[22]

In late 2006, ten years after Tegan's disappearance, the homicide squad assembled a task force with two detectives plus fifteen other police and intelligence officers. Their first task was to check all birth registrations for the relevant period as well as to check records of some 9000 primary schools with white female pupils aged ten. Many parents enrol their children without producing a birth certificate as proof of age, a factor that increased the task force's workload as records were meticulously checked across the nation. DNA samples were taken from over a thousand girls. Men with the name of Andrew Morris or Andrew Norris were also investigated.

Keli Lane's marriage ended in 2007. The strain of the coroner's investigation and her husband's knowledge of the previous three children were no doubt contributing factors. Her employment at Ravenswood School was also terminated.

One by one, Lane's secrets were uncovered. Her medical records revealed that the second pregnancy had been terminated when she was five months pregnant. Apparently, she had been willing to go through a late-term abortion and might have done so for the other pregnancies had she been able to at the time. Her sexual history exposed other secrets: her friends realised that the mystery father of her firstborn child had attended the wedding on the day that Tegan disappeared, and yet Lane remained untroubled.[23]

In August 2008, the police decided to search and excavate Duncan Gillies' Gladesville property in the hope of finding Tegan's remains. None were found. This was a distressing event for the entire Gillies family, which was reeling not only from the knowledge of Lane's secret births but from the fact that these children had been fathered by other men at a time when Lane was regarded as Duncan Gillies' partner.

In late 2009, after several years of intense police investigation, Keli Lane was arraigned for the murder of Tegan Lane. At her initial hearing on 4 December 2009 before Justice Roderick Howie, Lane – accompanied by her father – was granted bail. On 9 August 2010 she was charged in the New South Wales Supreme Court before Justice Anthony Whealy of three counts of false swearing and one of murder.

The crown prosecutor, Mark Tedeschi QC, was the most experienced criminal barrister in the state, known for his successful prosecutions of serial killers Ivan Milat and Kathleen Folbigg. Having depleted her financial resources, Lane was represented by an experienced Legal Aid-appointed barrister, Keith Chapple SC.

Tedeschi presented the jury with a withering and damning assessment of Lane's character, revealing that in the five years between 1992 and 1999 she underwent two abortions and had three ex-nuptial babies, one of whom is now missing. He questioned whether her heavy drinking and partying at pubs, where she kept up with the boys in alcohol consumption, rendered the oral contraceptive she was taking ineffective. The various fathers of her children and her deception towards Gillies were also canvassed, throwing a negative light on her morals. He alleged that the motivations for her callous and in one instance lethal actions were her desire to compete in the Olympics; her desire to maintain an active social and sex life; and her fear of rejection from her family and friends if knowledge of her pregnancies was discovered.

The question of why Tegan was not adopted like the two other children Keli Lane gave birth to remained a vexed one. Attending her friends' wedding several days after Tegan's birth seemed to be imperative to Lane. She could have requested leave of absence from the maternity ward for the evening.

Tedeschi continued his attack: 'Ladies and gentlemen, there is not the slightest suggestion that the accused was suffering from postnatal depression or other mental disturbance after Tegan's birth. Quite the contrary. At 3pm she had an appointment to meet her boyfriend Duncan Gillies at her parents' home so they could get dressed and go to a wedding … The accused was observed having a perfectly good time socialising, drinking, dancing. She was her normal self.' His address took two days to deliver.

Lane's counsel then attempted to dismiss the Crown's contentions. Justice Whealy reminded the jury that telling lies was not evidence of murder.

Various friends, from whom Lane was now estranged, gave evidence, all expressing disbelief as the revelations of secrecy, adoption and the charge of murder rolled out. Listening to their evidence and that of Virginia Fung reduced Lane to tears and despair. Her parents had initially appeared before Justice Whealy without the jury, although they established they were willing to testify in open court. Sandra Lane was confronted with all the information about Tegan and her disappearance. Robert Lane appeared equally uncomfortable in the face of the evidence of his beloved daughter's secret life.

The trial was conducted over four months, much of it consumed with police and forensic evidence. Several men with the name of Andrew Morris or Andrew Norris were called, but none knew Lane. The jury began their deliberations on 6 December 2010 amid intense media coverage and speculation. They took a week to deliver their verdict. The foreman informed the court that they were unanimous in their verdict on the lesser charges of false swearing connected with the two adoptions but divided on the question of murder. Justice Whealy pointed out that a decision of eleven of the twelve was sufficient. When the jury returned after lunch, the foreman informed the court that they had reached a decision and found the accused guilty of murder as charged. Lane was so overcome she collapsed in the dock, requiring medical attention.

Sentencing took place three months later. Unlike many other prisoners guilty of serious criminal acts, and despite the fact that she had been in custody since her conviction, Lane was well dressed and well groomed at her sentencing hearing. *Sydney Morning Herald* journalist Jane Cadzow reported that '[s]he looks so wholesome and outdoorsy – so uncomplicated'.[24] With these words Cadzow captured the sentiments of many who had followed and pondered this intriguing case over the years.

Justice Whealy delivered his long and comprehensive sentencing statement on 15 April 2011. Dr Diamond's assessments of Lane's taped interviews with Detective Gaut gave crucial insights into her character and motivations. Lane, he believed, did not have a psychiatric illness but he did describe her behaviour between 1992 and 1999 as 'very destructive [and] repetitive', that of a person with a disordered personality. His Honour addressed the question of premeditation and found that there had been a degree of premeditation, if 'for only a short time', given that Lane had made no provision for Tegan after leaving the hospital. Her history of concealing her pregnancies and births, her multiple deceptions, and her lack of remorse inclined him to a sentence with a non-parole period of thirteen years, to expire on 12 May 2024, after which she was to serve her sentence for the three counts of false swearing: 'A balance of the sentence is to commence on 13 May 2024 and to expire on 12 December 2028.' Justice Whealy expressed his deep regret for the impact this case and sentence would have on the life of the daughter from Lane's marriage, to whom she had been an exemplary mother.

Even at the end of this long trial, despite all the testimony, despite all the press coverage and interviews and speculation, the motives and intentions of the 'golden girl' remained elusive.

Taryn Woods won a gold medal in the 2000 Sydney Summer Olympics.

CHAPTER 6

The Deadly Baby Farmers

'Baby farmer' is a now-forgotten term referring to a long-ago industry in which illegitimate babies were minded – frequently by unscrupulous paid carers who made money at the cost of an infant's welfare and often, too tragically, its survival. In Gilbert and Sullivan's HMS *Pinafore* (1878), the comic figure of Mrs Cripps (Little Butterfly) refers to the practice, a scandal of the day:

> *A many years ago*
> *When I was young and charming*
> *As some of you may know*
> *I practiced baby-farming.*

Where unqualified abortionists might 'help out' girls 'in trouble' at the beginning of an illicit pregnancy, baby farmers helped out at the end of it. Often they were the only way a single woman with a dependent child could manage to work and afford to keep herself in the days before social welfare or even legal adoption. Baby farmers acted in a variety of capacities: as permanent baby carers who were paid an initial lump sum plus a weekly allowance by the mother, as day carers, or even as informal adoption agencies. For the more unscrupulous, though, the temptation to take the money and let the infant die was sometimes too lucrative to resist.

In late nineteenth-century England and Wales, six baby farmers were executed for their crimes. English criminologist H. L. Adam characterised a baby farmer as possessing a 'complete lack of maternal feeling'.[1] Yet this was just the point – a baby farmer ran a business, something that depended on cash not sentiment. As the medical journal *The Lancet* affirmed on 24 January 1903: 'The people who relieve parents of their offspring act from sordid and not benevolent motives.'

In the Australian colonies, baby farmers were largely concentrated in the larger urban areas where anonymity prevailed.

For many married working-class women, becoming genuine foster mothers had the benefit of being home-based work.[2] Yet even in such genuine situations, babies still died at alarming rates, particularly those who were bottle-fed since the absence of proper teats on feed bottles and impure milk created significant nutritional and health problems. 'Boarded-out' babies, as they were called, represented a high proportion of all neonatal deaths at the turn of the century. The English magazine *Pall Mall Gazette* noted: 'There is no human creature ... so defenceless as an illegitimate child.'[3]

There had been attempts to regulate the boarding-out trade in the various Australian colonies. In 1873 the New South Wales premier, Henry Parkes, established a Royal Commission to inquire into charities and social welfare. Barrister and later Justice William Windeyer acted as chairman. Educated at The King's School, Parramatta, and the University of Sydney, Windeyer was a liberal thinker with profound Christian sentiments. His wife, Mary Thorley Windeyer (1837–1912), was the daughter of an Anglican priest and was also committed to social justice. In 1874 she supported the establishment of a foundling hospital in Sydney, 'to remove temptation to infanticide' for destitute and single mothers. She also took an active interest in boarded-out children, orphans in church and state institutions and basic education for the poor.

Despite these reforms and institutions, the worst aspects of boarding-out and baby farming persisted. The most lethal and gruesome aspects of baby farming emerged in 1893 in Sydney. Sarah Makin (1845–1918) and John Makin (1845–93) ran a grisly business killing illegitimate babies for profit.

Born to lower middle-class parents in Wollongong, John Makin had established a successful small business as a drayman, carter and butcher. Despite this, Makin served a term of three months' imprisonment in 1881 for stealing a sheep when he killed a lamb he was supposed to be delivering to a customer at Darling Harbour in Sydney.[4] By this time he already had eight children, whose lives were now thrown into extreme poverty by his incarceration and lack of income.

Sarah Makin's past was far less respectable – her father had been transported to Van Diemen's Land from Leeds in 1833, convicted of stealing worsted cloth. He died in Liverpool Asylum for the Destitute and Infirm (New South Wales) in 1885. Her mother was buried in a pauper's grave in Rookwood Cemetery, Sydney, in 1890. At the age of twenty-one and described as a barmaid, midwife and nurse, Sarah Makin married a Scottish sailor, Captain Charles Edwards, in a Presbyterian church in Sydney before marrying again as 'Sarah Edwards, Spinster' five years later to Makin in a Church of England ceremony. She had been neither divorced nor widowed, making her a bigamist. They had ten children, of which seven survived, then a common occurrence because the infant mortality rates were so high.

When John Makin was injured and unable to continue his trade, the couple decided to run a baby farm. The *Infants Protection Act* of 1891 required that all baby farmers, foster parents and lying-in facilities be registered, but this could be sidestepped by categorising the activity as informal adoption over which the Act had no jurisdiction. John Makin would answer newspaper advertisements placed by women seeking care for their babies, and offer bogus adoption agreements, frequently under one of a number of pseudonyms: John Burt, John Maclaughlin or McLaughlan. The prospect of a caring home would have appeared attractive to these desperate mothers, who paid a small fee for the service. Sometimes Makin offered to arrange external adoption for illegitimate babies, also for a fee.[5] These infants never found other homes, instead ending up dead in various gardens around inner Sydney.

A drainer and plumber, James Hanoney, and his offsider, Frances Cooney, were called to a premises at 25 Burren Street, Macdonaldtown, Sydney, on 11 October 1892 to fix some blocked drains. Initially, he thought some foul-smelling baby clothing was the problem until, constructing some trenches, they discovered the decomposing corpses of two babies. The tenants had been John and Sarah Makin and their children, Florence, Clarice, Blanche, Cecil (Tommy) and Daisy, who had lived there from June to late August 1892. They now lived in Botany Street, Redfern. The bodies were removed to the South Sydney Morgue, where government analyst William Hamlet conducted preliminary investigations. He noted in his report the presence of black calico dressing one of the little corpses, a fabric he had seen on one of the Makin daughters.

Two inquests conducted by the Sydney City coroner, J. C. Woore, inquiring into the deaths of the two bodies found in Macdonaldtown, began on 13 October and adjourned for further police investigation.

On 20 October, Sarah Makin allegedly confronted a former neighbour, Mrs Elizabeth Hill, outside the Coroners Court in Chancery Square, screaming at her: 'I have a good mind to ribbon you, bitch. How dare you give evidence against me? You don't know me; you never spoke to me. The child is yours. You took drugs and you put it there.' She raised her umbrella in anger.[6] Hill was the agent for the owner of 25 Burren Street. The Makins strenuously denied any wrongdoing in their testimony, yet when they answered questions, they were evasive, contradictory and confused.

A second inquest opened on 28 October 1892 to assess the circumstances of the death of the second male. Blanche Makin testified that there was only one newborn baby – a girl – in her mother's care. The jury was unable to decide how the baby had died.

During an adjournment in the first inquest, the police continued their grisly business. On 3 November 1892, while digging in 25 Burren Street, constables Thomas Conan and Alexander Brown found another corpse in a shallow grave. Their search was hindered by the large number of spectators who swarmed the street and nearby houses. An hour later they found a further bundle containing the body of a baby; the total by the end of the day came to seven. That afternoon, Sarah, Blanche, Florence and John Makin were taken to Newtown Police Station for further questioning. Protesting, Florence argued that she rarely stayed with her parents as she was in domestic service elsewhere.

The discovery of these small corpses demanded further investigations and inquests, so the previous addresses of the Makins were searched. Three more infant bodies were found at 109 George Street, Redfern, although none were located at 55 Botany Street. On 11 November 1892, the police found two more bodies at 11 Anderson Street, Redfern, where the Makins lived from 7 November 1891 to 28 January 1892. A neighbour, Mrs Williams, told police that she had never seen baby clothes on the washing line. The next day police unearthed the skeleton of a baby at 28 Levey Street, Chippendale.[7] By this time news of the police finds had spread through the community. Despite an unseasonable cold and wet day, a large crowd gathered in Levey and Abercrombie streets in Chippendale, where a tiny body was found buried in the garden. As digging proceeded, another corpse, that of a baby around twelve months of age, was found.

The postmortems carried out by Dr Frederick Milford the following day ascertained they had been dead for between nine and fourteen months. No cause of death could be ascertained after such a long time.

The police began intensive interviewing. The neighbours of the Makins in Levey Street complained of offensive odours and believed babies were buried under the floorboards. At one time the child of these neighbours brought home a bloodstained baby dress and five rusty needles, all wrapped in calico. Senior Constable James Joyce believed those needles had been used to pierce the hearts of the victims. When the floorboards were raised, only dead rats were discovered.[8] The backyards of Kettle Street, Redfern; 6 Wells Street, Redfern; Bay Street in Glebe; Cook's River Road at St Peter's; and Harbour Street near Darling Harbour failed to discover more bodies. A body of a baby was found at Zamia Street, Redfern, wrapped in clothing identified by a mother who left her child in the Makins' care.

Jurors at the various inquests were unable to determine the times or causes of these deaths. The police became frustrated and angry as the proceedings continued. Another inquest began on 12 November 1892, again before the coroner, Mr J. C. Woore. Some of the Makins' older children cooperated with the police, who determined that the parents had been conducting their business for around two years. Clarice Makin, aged fourteen, testified that her mother fed babies in her care with condensed milk. They went from healthy to ill in a short time. She recalled a Mr Bottomley coming to the house in Burren Street to inquire about a baby, but which one she was not certain. She could not recall what her mother said about the disappearance of the various babies. Even though her testimony had been terse and vague, Sarah Makin cursed her daughter loudly for cooperating with the proceedings, unlike Florence and Blanche, who stood condemned with their parents.[9] Clarice identified baby clothing that her mother had pawned.

The coroner condemned the Makins for their many confusing and contradictory statements as well as their outright lies. There was a 'chain of circumstances' that connected the multiple deaths on various properties, all where the Makin family had lived. And it was inconceivable that Sarah Makin, who had reared so many of her own children, was ignorant of infant care. After fourteen days, this inquest concluded, with the jury returning a verdict of guilty of manslaughter for John and Sarah Makin and guilty knowledge for daughters Florence and Blanche.

The way the Makins moved constantly meant that mothers, and in one case a father, could not keep track of their boarded child for whom they paid an allowance, collected regularly by John Makin. Coroner Woore turned his attention to the case of baby Mignonetta Lavinia Davis. Her story was unusual since her unmarried parents, Mignonetta (Minnie) Davis and Horace Bottomly, a proofreader at the *Daily Telegraph*, visited her weekly. When she suddenly died, the Makins took money supposedly for the undertaker and said they would arrange the funeral. They simply pocketed the money and buried the little girl in the garden at Burren Street.* The coroner also raised the question of death certificates, which John Makin would fabricate. Pawning the clothes of the dead babies was a particularly repellent aspect of this deliberate trade.

Another inquest was conducted in December 1892, investigating the circumstances of the death of the baby found in Alderson Street, Redfern. Dr Milford and Dr Marano conducted the autopsy and stated that the baby, aged two to six weeks old, had been dead perhaps six to twelve months. They could not determine the sex or cause of death. The Makins refused to testify and the jury returned an open verdict. Inquests into the deaths of the babies found in George Street, Redfern, were opened. Clara Risby, a single domestic servant, testified that she had placed her daughter with the Makins (who called themselves McLachlan) for the cost of £5 in early May 1892. She identified clothing presented in court as belonging to her baby. Joseph Lopez, a pawnbroker in Waterloo, testified that he had received these items from Daisy Makin on 8 August 1892.

Another single mother, Amber Murray, gave birth to her ex-nuptial son, Horace Amber Murray, in June 1892, arranging for the Makins, then living at 139 George Street in Redfern, to organise his adoption. She was prepared to pay the sum of 10/- per week for his upkeep. This was a considerable amount for an eighteen-year-old domestic servant. It was to be a fateful decision for both Murray and the Makins. Amber Murray gave evidence about the circumstances of the adoption of Horace by a Mrs John Hill (Sarah Makin). Blanche Makin had collected Horace Murray from his mother on 27 June 1892, thus indicating her complicity with the family business. By now there had been fourteen inquests in total. On the order of the coroner, John

---

* Davis and Bottomly married in 1894 and had a son, Harold, born the following year.

and Sarah Makin were ordered to stand trial on 20 February 1893 for the murder of Horace Murray and another baby, name unknown, on 29 June 1892 at 109 George Street, Redfern.

In March 1893 John Makin and Sarah Makin faced proceedings in the New South Wales Supreme Court for the murder of Horace Murray. The trial was heard by Justice Matthew Stephen, the distinguished son of the former chief justice, Sir Alfred Stephen. Williamson again acted as counsel for the accused, receiving £61 for his services and £70 in expenses, some of which was paid by Makin's brother, Thomas.[10] Amber Murray, the first witness, testified that she wanted a 'kind, motherly woman to adopt her fine baby'. Answering her advertisement in the newspaper, John Makin replied that he and his wife could provide little Horace with such a home for the fee of £3 and a weekly payment of 10/-. She handed over Horace, dressed in a long white gown and a shirt, to their daughter, Blanche Makin. She added that she had made the clothes herself and identified exhibits as Horace's outfit.

Other witnesses confirmed the baby was strong and healthy before he left his mother's care. After the testimony of Senior Constable Joyce, counsel for the defendants objected to the further line of questioning which took evidence from premises beyond Burren Street and upon which the Makins were not charged. Justice Stephen, however, ruled that he would allow the scope of the evidence to range wider than Burren Street.[11] Agnes Ward testified that she had entrusted her son aged three months to the Makins, then in Kettle Street, Redfern, in April 1892. She could not locate them when they moved. The next witness, Clara Risby, repeated her evidence from the inquest that she had given £5 to Sarah and John Makin, then living in East Street, Redfern. She sent three baby gowns with the baby. When she went to visit him Sarah Makin told her he was out with her children. After that they moved, and she could not find them. Mary Stacey, another domestic servant, reported that she gave birth to an illegitimate baby in April 1892, whom she gave away in adoption to a 'Mr Ray of 109

George Street, Redfern'. 'Sarah Ray' said they were soon moving to Marrickville and the new address would be forwarded. It never was. Stacey identified the Makins as the Rays. She clearly identified some clothing, which she had made herself with various embellishments.

The Makins' trial is one of the most famous in Australian legal history, for it enshrined the principle of 'similar fact' – meaning in this case that the evidence surrounding the bodies of unidentified babies was allowed alongside that of Horace Murray.[12] This judgment was applied in the British case in 1896 for which Amelia Dyer, Britain's most notorious baby farmer, was executed at Newgate Prison.[13] It was also used as a precedent in the famous 1992 case of serial killer Rodney Cameron, the so-called 'Lonely Hearts Killer', who was convicted in the New South Wales Central Criminal Court.

Neither John nor Sarah Makin testified. They provided no evidence in their defence nor did they call for witnesses.[14] The testimony of their daughter Clarice for the Crown case helped convict them. Both were found guilty of wilful murder. The jury recommended mercy for Sarah Makin. The Makins promptly appealed their sentence on the grounds of the inadmissibility of 'similar facts' evidence. They were represented by a leading Sydney barrister, Sir Julian Salomons (1835–1909), who had stepped down from the bench in 1886 due to the extreme anti-Semitism he experienced from William Windeyer, a progressive on other social issues. The following year Salomons was appointed to the Legislative Council as a Liberal supporter of Sir Henry Parkes.[15]

The Full Court consisting of Justice Windeyer, Justice Innes and Justice William Foster heard the appeal premised upon the question that testimony from other mothers whose babies disappeared in the care of the Makins was not evidence in the death of Horace Murray. It had only served to establish their reputations as disreputable baby farmers and mass murderers. Windeyer, however, got to the heart of the matter when he stated: 'A family might be unfortunate enough to take a house in the backyard of which babies had been buried by a former tenant; but no one could believe that it was a mere coincidence that a person took three houses in the backyards of which former tenants had secretly buried babies.'[16]

The Makins lost their appeal. They reappeared before Justice Stephen to hear their sentences on 30 March 1893. When asked whether they had anything to say before sentence was passed, Sarah Makin remained silent while her husband proclaimed their innocence. Both were sentenced to death, although Justice Stephen stated he would recommend mercy for Sarah Makin to the Executive Council. He concluded: 'You took money from the mother of this child [Horace Murray]: you beguiled her with promises you never meant to perform, having already determined the death of this child ... you buried the child in the yard, I say, like you would bury the carcass of a dog ... carrying on this nefarious and hellish trade ...'[17] The editorial of the *Sydney Morning Herald* for 31 March 1983 praised the decision of the appeal judges, who allowed the evidence of 'similar fact'.

John Makin's family in Wollongong – brothers George, Thomas and Daniel – were devastated by the sentence and refused to believe that he had conducted a career as a deadly baby farmer. They wanted the appeal process to continue and unwisely took it to the Privy Council in London. This would mean a considerable delay in carrying out the sentence if the appeal was lost. Edmund Barton QC, later the new Commonwealth's inaugural prime minister, was then the Attorney-General of New South Wales and it was in his hands the appeal was forwarded. On 17 July 1893 the case was heard in the Privy Council funded by the Makin brothers. The appeal was lost. A deputation of citizens from Wollongong met with the premier, to no avail.[18] The Makin family then appealed to Premier Sir George Dibbs for clemency. A large petition from the people of the Illawarra was despatched to the government for consideration. One of John Makin's sisters-in-law took up the cudgels, claiming that Sarah Makin was a violent woman who had struck down her own blind mother in a fit of rage, and that if John 'had got a good woman, he would never have been in the position he was'.[19] The Executive Council reconsidered the appeal for clemency on 14 August. Makin was hanged on 15 August 1893, going to the gallows affirming his innocence and that of his wife.

The Executive Council ruled that Sarah Makin should serve a life sentence. She first went to Bathurst jail, established in 1830, and then to Long Bay State Reformatory for Women in Sydney. Her daughter, Minnie Helby, petitioned for her release in 1907, as did Florence Anderson in 1911. On 11 April 1911, Sarah was released into the care of Florence Anderson, dying in 1918 and buried with the benefit of Anglican rites. Clarice Makin, who had testified against her parents, died in 1951 and was buried in Rookwood Cemetery, far away from her mother's grave.[20] Horace Murray was also buried in this cemetery. The boys all changed their surnames.

On 8 November 1949, a curious little item appeared in the *Sydney Morning Herald* announcing that the threatened railway extension between Redfern and Erskineville would demolish the house where the body of Horace Murray was found. No one protested.

In January 1894, a young married mother of two children, Frances Knorr, convicted of murdering babies in her care, was executed. She was an unregistered baby farmer operating in desperate and chaotic circumstances. How she came to stand on the gallows reveals much about the more vicious aspects of the trade. Evidence of her activities came about by chance, when the new tenants of a modest house in Moreland Road, Brunswick, commercial travellers named William and Francis Clay, decided to make a garden on 4 September 1893. William Clay found the body of a baby some thirty centimetres under the grass. Melbourne's newspaper, the *Argus*, the following day issued an extensive editorial about this 'Traffic in Babies'. In this instance the nude body showed a fractured skull 'almost broken into pieces' and other evidence of violence. The police ascertained that an unnamed woman had occupied the house for a short time in April before moving to Davis Street. While at Moreland Road she borrowed a heavy spade from a neighbour, returning it an hour later. The police, readers were informed, had this woman in their sights for baby farming. She remained elusive, changing address with alarming frequency. The police at this time believed that under various aliases she conducted her trade in Middle Brighton, Coburg, Brunswick, Carlton and Prahran. Former residences were examined in an attempt to locate more bodies of infants after three remains were located in Brunswick at Moreland Road and Davis Street.

At the height of the 1890s Depression, the rate of infanticide in Melbourne had increased. As police and coroners averred, inquiries into the fate of dead babies were a regular and saddening feature of their daily working lives. Most distressing were the babies left alive and abandoned in parks, public gardens and on the doorsteps, many to die slowly. Before the passing of the *Infant Life Protection Act* of 1890, many more would be deliberately killed by poor feeding and neglect. The suburban courts were filled with the cases of neglected babies. In the first eight months of 1893, sixty-seven inquests were held in Melbourne to investigate the deaths of abandoned dead infants. In twenty-five cases the court recorded a finding of 'murder by person or persons unknown'.[21] Yet what the *Argus* editorial failed to grasp was the underground trade in babies that often led to death. The unnamed woman from Moreland Road was soon to capture the country's attention by her lethal exploits.

The police eventually tracked down Frances Knorr, who often went by her birth name, Minnie Thwaites, or by Minnie Knorr, even though she had fled to Sydney with her husband. She was about to give birth quite literally. When Detective Edward Keating informed her as she lay in bed that he was from the Melbourne CIB she immediately said: 'All right, Mr Keating. I know why you have come for. You will not arrest him. Whatever I have done my husband knows nothing about this.' Her young daughter, Gladys Knorr, was left with the Sydney Benevolent Asylum since she had measles and was unfit for the sea journey back to Melbourne.[22]

As the arrest was made public, Knorr was dubbed the 'female Herod'.[23] By 9 September, she was described in the press by Detective

Sergeant Nixon, the investigating officer, as a woman of '… very loose habits, immoral character and hardened nature'.[24] The public was primed for a scandal that promised a catalogue of sexual intrigue, murder and the elimination of unwanted babies. These elements established the basis for a riveting few months of reading.

A month after the discovery of the body in Moreland Road, Coroner Samuel Candler (1827–1911) began inquest proceedings. By now an elderly man, Candler had studied as an apprentice apothecary – the precursors to medical practitioners – before his time as a digger on the goldfields in the 1850s. He was regarded highly by colleagues in his role as a coroner, considered to be 'exacting and austere'.[25] Minnie Knorr (alias Thwaites) and Rudolph Knorr were held in custody over the offence and represented by separate legal counsel. The first witness was Dr James Neild, who had conducted the autopsy on Isaac Marks, the infant found at Moreland Road. He told the court that the skull had fractured due to decay rather than overt violence in the first instance. The baby was about one month old when he died, and had been buried for around three months. The landlady of the premises, Ellen Wood, stated that she had rented the house to a dressmaker, 'Mrs Thwaites', who had explained that her husband was a miner in Broken Hill. Her tenant had then asked if Wood would board her daughter Gladys for several months at the rate of 8s 6d per week. That very evening Thwaites had brought a baby into her new home, but did not divulge his origins. Mrs Thwaites left the premises soon after, moving to Davis Street. Mrs Wood denied that she had cared for the newborn, which she described as 'healthy'. A neighbour, Elizabeth Mullery, recalled that she had seen Mrs Thwaites and Gladys, but saw the baby only once.

Another witness, Mary Drummond of Coburg, testified that Mrs Thwaites had engaged her young daughter Harriet as a nursemaid. Harriet Drummond remembered that Mrs Thwaites had borrowed a spade from a neighbour, but she did not know for what purpose. It was returned with the comment that a pick was required for the heavy digging. Harriet had once also asked her to mind another unnamed newborn baby, who Mrs Thwaites had collected from a young woman at the Melbourne Meat Markets.

This testimony demonstrates the workings of the networks conducted by women to look after babies born to single or deserted mothers who could not care for their child themselves. There was a careless informality to all the proceedings, and it was this outsourcing of maternal attention and its consequences that lay at the heart of the problems with baby farming. Knorr's business was so chaotic that she could not keep track of the various infants in her care and, it was later revealed, sometimes substituted one baby for another when anxious mothers came to visit their boarded infant.[26] At the end of proceedings Coroner Candler ordered that Minnie Knorr stand trial for wilful murder.

Frances Knorr was arraigned in the Supreme Court of Victoria before Justice Sir Edward Dundas Holroyd (1828–1916) in October 1893. Prosecutor Walsh opened the Crown case by detailing Knorr's constant change of address, and her deceptions about her life and the babies placed into her care. The evidence in the backyard and the testimony of the nursery maid were crucial to pointing to the babies' murders. Under oath Knorr revealed the circumstances that had brought her to the dock of the Supreme Court.

She was born to William Thwaites, a respectable and devout hat-maker of Chelsea, London, and his wife Frances in 1867. When her teenage affair with a soldier was discovered, her parents sent her to a reformatory for wayward girls.[27] The superintendent urged her parents to take her back, as Minnie, as she was then called, was not a suitable resident for his institution. Her parents did so, on the proviso that she emigrate to save the family further shame.

At the age of nineteen she arrived in Sydney where she was soon in jail for three months for theft. She married a German waiter – and petty criminal – named Rudolph Knorr at St Philip's Church of England on 2 November 1889. They then moved to Richmond in Melbourne where Rudolph Knorr found work as a waiter at the Oriental Hotel, and then at Parer's Crystal Cafe in Bourke Street. But with hard economic times and few restaurant patrons, he lost his job. To make ends meet Knorr turned to selling furniture he had obtained on hire purchase. The couple fled to Adelaide to evade prosecution but they were found and Rudolph was jailed for eighteen months in Pentridge jail. Frances Knorr took on work as a parlour maid at the Exeter Hotel in Port Adelaide. She also attempted to establish a business as a dressmaker but it failed in the economic climate of the Depression, made worse by her decision to relocate to the small settlement of Quorn, over three hundred kilometres from Adelaide. She stole from one of her employees to pay for her fare back to Melbourne.[28]

In 1892 Frances Knorr gave birth to her daughter Gladys in the Melbourne Women's Hospital. At the time she lived with Mrs Sarah Walkerden, with whom she was soon entangled in a bitter dispute. They argued over a little boy she had decided to take in to wet-nurse along with her own child. Walkerden wanted to orchestrate a lucrative baby-farming business, which Knorr decided would be her financial saviour – but not with Walkerden. She left owing her landlady the large sum of £10 and took to squatting illegally in vacant houses. As she moved from house to house, Walkerden pursued her, telling neighbours that Knorr was the wife of a convict and a thief and an immoral woman 'living in sin'. Knorr had found another means of survival when she entered into a relationship with the local fish hawker, Ted Thompson, who supported her and Gladys at a number of residences in York Street, South Melbourne, and George Street, Fitzroy. They set up house together at Canning Street until his parents intervened and forced him home.

Knorr left Gladys in the care of Ted's mother, Ann Thompson, a seemingly strange choice in her chaotic and increasingly desperate life, and she and Thompson went to Adelaide together. The lovers parted after quarrelling, and Knorr went to retrieve Gladys. She begged Ann Thompson for money but when none was forthcoming she and the little girl spent the night on the streets. Knorr eventually obtained work as a dressmaker with a Mrs Gresham in Cardigan Street, Carlton. To make ends meet she also took in Lillian Crichton's baby. Ted Thompson continued to offer 'a few shillings now and again'.

Then in April 1893 she relocated to Brunswick. By the time Knorr arrived in the house in Moreland Road she was exhausted and defeated. She was now only twenty-five, with a small child of her own and one on the way, another child to mind, a husband in jail, a lover who had abandoned her, and a failing business.

She took to her bed with the two children, both of whom were malnourished and crying. As Knorr testified: 'I found the milk had turned quite sour and it was impossible to give either of the children. I had no barley in the house and could not make barley water ... the two children continued screaming until morning and at about quarter to four the child Crichton died. It went black in the face and was shaking all over ... It died from convulsions ... I swear I did it no harm. I thought of going to the police first but got frightened. Then I thought, "I will bury it".' She buried the baby naked, aware that clothing had identified various remains leading to the conviction of the Makins. She said that a man she knew called Wilson helped her bury the body, after which she moved to Davis Street.

Rudolph Knorr rejoined the family in May 1893. His chances of finding gainful employment – as a former convict during a Depression – were slight, forcing Frances Knorr to be the sole breadwinner. Frances Knorr told the court she took in a baby from another young woman, whose name she did not even know. The 'baby was in a dirty filthy state' when she received him, she recalled. 'It died that day and I buried it in the backyard' without her husband's knowledge. This baby, found with a knot around its neck, was, she hinted, murdered by Thompson, although what motive he might have had was never explained, other than on one occasion he had gone to get a baby from its mother for her. Another man, by the name of William Wilson, also assisted her, although he was to remain elusive. She took in another unnamed baby, who also died and was buried without ceremony.[29]

On the witness stand Thompson produced a letter written to him by Knorr during the inquest in October, attempting to establish an alibi for herself. The letter had several passages blacked out, no doubt of an intimate nature. Thompson had showed his mother the letter and on her instigation it was now used as evidence for the prosecution. The contents were frantic attempts to establish false dates for the acceptance of boarded-out babies. On the other hand, the letter could have been dictated by Thompson to clear his own limited involvement in Knorr's business. He may have been what was at the time called a 'fizgig' or police informer.[30]

After a five-day trial Frances Knorr was found guilty of wilful murder and was sentenced to death, the execution to take place on 15 January 1894. Before she collapsed, Knorr shouted out to Ted Thompson, sitting in the public gallery: 'God forgive you your sins, Ted.' The particular sins were not enumerated. It was highly unusual for a woman, particularly the mother of a toddler and a very young baby, to be given a capital sentence. No woman had been executed in Victoria since Elizabeth Scott in 1863. Public opinion was outraged, despite the prurient interest taken in the revelations of adultery, illicit sex and murder heard in the court.

A petition from the 'Women of Victoria' pleaded for mercy, arguing that 'the killing of a woman by any body of men did not accord with the moral sense of the community'.[31] Even the trial judge, Justice Holroyd, said that the evidence was circumstantial, although 'exceedingly strong'.[32] And Sarah Makin, who had killed more babies than Frances Knorr, had been given a commuted life sentence. Over 200 people held a vigil in Russell Street and marched to nearby Government House to ask for mercy for this young mother. The governor, the seventh Earl of Hopetoun, informed the deputation that, on the advice of the Executive Council, he did not intend to issue a reprieve. Rudolph Knorr begged for clemency, telling the government his wife was an epileptic given to strange irrational behaviour.[33] Her behaviour was at times irrational but whether this was from any mental infirmity or caused by her desperate poverty and circumstances remains open to debate.

While she awaited execution, Knorr became zealously religious, taking to hymn singing day and night at the top of her voice. In this mood of repentance as she sought absolution of her sins, Knorr confessed to killing the three babies and hoped 'that my fate will be a warning for others ... and act as a deterrent to those who are perhaps carrying on the same practice'. The confession appears to have been dictated, as the language does not match that used in her letter to Thompson.[34]

Rudolph Knorr brought Gladys to say goodbye. The *Weekly Times* of 20 January 1894 reported that 'the sight of the mother clinging to the baby was particularly painful ... She heaped kisses on the poor little mite, and prayed she should never know'. Rita Daisy Knorr, the baby she had had with Thompson, ended up in police custody as a neglected child even before her mother's execution. Her chances of survival were slim. Neither Rudolph Knorr nor the Thompsons were willing to take charge of her welfare.[35] Knorr had been correct when she cried out in court at the end of the hearing: 'God help my poor babies!' for she realised Rita might have as short a life as those babies she had killed.

Outside the prison large crowds singing hymns gathered to protest against the proceedings inside. Frances Knorr went to the gallows singing 'Abide with Me' and 'Safe in the Arms of Jesus'. She was calm and dignified. The prison matron collapsed in a fit of hysterical sobbing. Dr Shields, the prison's resident medical officer, was in attendance for the entire ordeal. Usually a member of the clergy or nuns gave comfort to a condemned prisoner but in this case it was Dr Shields who supported the condemned woman.[36] Knorr's last words on this earth were: 'The Lord is with me. I do not fear what men can do unto me, for I have peace, perfect peace.' Chief Warder Long remarked that she died as 'plucky ... as brave as Ned Kelly'. What more fitting tribute could such a hardened man give to this woman of only twenty-six?[37]

Frances Knorr was convicted of three child murders but there was speculation that she was responsible for more deaths. Photo: Public Records office, Victoria, VPS 5900. Photograph of prisoners sentenced to death and coroner's inquest sheets, PO, Unit 1.

After Knorr's execution many women came forward to police telling them sad stories of babies entrusted to her care, now missing and presumed dead. Knorr may have killed thirteen in all.[38] Along with those of the other three women executed in the Old Melbourne Gaol in Russell Street, now a museum, her death mask is on public display. Her skull is also an exhibit, although it has been wrongly labelled 'Martha Knorr', confusing her with notorious serial poisoner Martha Needle.[39]

In 1907, an even more appalling case of murderous baby farming occurred in Perth. Alice Mitchell was suspected of killing by starvation and neglect up to thirty-seven babies in her care. Her methods were not so much acts of wilful murder like those carried out by Sarah Makin or Frances Knorr, but slow death by negligence.

Despite British settlement since 1829, Western Australia had only attained self-government in 1890. This coincided with the discovery of gold in remote Kalgoorlie (1893) and Coolgardie (1892), substantially aiding the colony's economic development. Yet in the wake of this sudden prosperity came myriad social problems. Government agencies could not provide the public infrastructure and health services required to accommodate the rapidly expanding population. Like Brisbane and Sydney, Perth endured episodes of bubonic plague. The eastern fringes of the city in particular contained noxious industries and places where those who could not find work or success on the goldfields took advantage of cheap accommodation. Alice Mitchell established her business as a baby farmer at various addresses in this area, at Wellington Street, Cavendish Street, Peterson Terrace, Lord Street and Edward Street.[40] Like the Makins and Frances Knorr, she moved constantly, trying to keep one step ahead of any investigation into her deadly trade.

The new colony passed legislation modelled on the English *Infant Life Protection Act* of 1897, which had been enacted in the wake of the Amelia Dyer revelations the previous year. Persons taking in boarded-out children and babies in particular had to be registered and their activities monitored by public health officials. Mitchell, a married woman with a grown family and a husband who kept out of the house from early morning until late at night, registered as an infant carer in January 1901. Every one of the first thirteen children she took in for care died. But no investigation was undertaken even though this was such a suspiciously high number. Between 16 December 1902 and 18 July 1906, Mitchell took in twenty-one infants, and another five from September 1906 to January 1907.[41] Various undertakers at her trial testified that they had taken from her houses thirty-four babies to be buried. More alarming was the fact that, although a medical certificate signed by Dr Officer accompanied each case, there were no inquests into these sudden deaths.[42] Their testimony also indicated that they were not in fact aware that an inquest report was needed before burial.

Alice Mitchell was a greedy woman. When one of her clients, Maud Brown, fell behind in her payments for the upkeep of her infant, Mitchell summoned the police to pursue the debt. Sergeant Patrick

O'Halloran went to visit Mitchell's business, which operated not just as a boarding-out facility but also as a boarding house. He was alarmed by what met his eyes. In his report he said: '[One] child was in an appalling condition. Pus was coming from its eyes, it was fly-specked, extremely wasted, and giving off an offensive odour.' When he summoned a government medical officer, Dr T. G. Davy, the baby was found to be near death and was taken to hospital. This child was Ethel Booth.[43] The death of this previously healthy, thriving baby on 12 February 1907 drew concentrated attention to Nurse Mitchell's activities.

Ethel's mother, Elizabeth Booth, told the Coroners Court in April 1907 that:

> I am a single mum and a general servant. I get 15/- per week. On 29 September 1906 I was delivered of a female child at the [Catholic] House of Mercy, Highgate Hill. It [sic] was a healthy baby ... I stayed three months ... and then took the baby to Alice Mitchell, who is now in court. I arranged to pay her 10/- per week and doctor's fees ... I continued to visit the child twice a week ... the father gave me 7/6 per week all along ... I gave her 5/- to have the child vaccinated ... [Mitchell] did not have the child vaccinated ... [After] three weeks I was not allowed to see the child. Mrs Mitchell always said it was asleep ... When I did see her I hardly knew her. She had sores all over her head, sore eyes, and she was very thin. Mrs Mitchell said she was suffering from her teeth ... the next night I was going to examine her but she smelt so horribly that I put the cover back over ... I told Mrs Mitchell I did not think she was getting on well and she replied, 'Yes, she is getting on and Dr Officer is very pleased with it.' ... I told her the child was very ill ... and I would take it to Perth Hospital ... I got the notice of its death on Tuesday around two o'clock. I was present when the coroner and the jury viewed the body of the child. It was the body of my child, Ethel Booth.[44]

Under these circumstances, the police intervened because medical staff were alarmed by Ethel's condition on admission and her subsequent death.

When the news of Ethel Booth's death – unlike those of the other thirty-six babies who had been buried quietly, unnoticed – reached the newspapers, public attention focused on the various establishments run by Alice Mitchell. The *Western Australian* of 15 February 1907 was confident that 'these rumours … if found to be accurate, will create one of the greatest sensations known in this state and will result in a unanimous demand for more stringent regulations regarding the care of boarded-out infants'. Indeed, this appraisal was prescient; the inquiries surrounding the death of Ethel Booth brought to an end the era of lethal baby farming across the new nation.

The Children's Protection Society, modelled after the Royal Society for the Protection of Children in Great Britain, had been formed only six months previously to address the issues of boarded-out and abandoned children. Confinement for poor women was onerous right from the start – at this time there was no proper midwifery or paediatric training available in Perth. The Fremantle Midwifery Training Centre did not open until 1910 and the King Edward Memorial Hospital in Perth, which catered for confinements, did not open until 1916.[45] Other private concerns – such as the homes run by the Anglican Sisters of the Church, the Catholic House of Mercy, the Salvation Army's Golden Gate, and the Good Shepherd Sisters, as well as the Waifs' Home and the Poor Women's House – could only for a short time assist desperate women with dependent babies and few resources.[46] This is what drove the demand for services like those offered by Alice Mitchell.

On 16 February 1907, the day after the press exposé, Mitchell was arrested and charged with the unlawful killing of Ethel Booth on 12 February 1907. Mitchell was described as being forty-six years of age, 'married, a nurse, able to read and write'. Dr Officer, who Elizabeth Booth had paid for consultations for Ethel, made a public statement defending Mitchell:

[She] had called him in on several occasions to attend to infants who were ailing. Some of them recovered but others died ... he instructed Mrs Mitchell on their feeding and attention. To the best of my knowledge, his instructions were always carried [out]. In the majority of cases death was due to bowel complaints following summer diarrhoea.[47]

Diarrhoea was a prolific killer of infants, with Western Australia having the highest infant mortality rate in the new Commonwealth.[48] Sanitation in the burgeoning townships of Kalgoorlie and Coolgardie and in the capital was primitive and too overstretched to cope with the expanding populations. Babies that were not breastfed immediately found themselves in a life-threatening environment. They were frequently given condensed milk, which was full of sugar, or barley water or, the best alternative, Nestlé powdered formula, which had been available in the Australian colonies since the 1870s. It was, however, extremely expensive and far beyond the means of poor women. Even with the best intentions and level of care, bottlefed babies were vulnerable to disease, starvation and death. But Alice Mitchell had no such good intentions.

The inquest into the death of Ethel Booth opened in Perth on 4 March 1907. Registrar and Master of the Supreme Court of Western Australia James Cowan presided over the proceedings with a jury of three. He and his wife Edith Cowan were prominent advocates of children's rights.[49] Inspector Sellenger prosecuted on behalf of the Crown, with barrister R. W. Pennefather KC and N. W. Cowan appearing for the Children's Protection Society. At this stage Mitchell did not have a barrister, but a Jesuit-trained criminal law specialist, Michael G. Lavan (later appointed a KC), watched on her behalf. He did so actively, as evidence from the inquest revealed. On the second day of proceedings, Pennefather for the Children's Protection Society pointed out that baby Brown had died of starvation and that it should be admitted as evidence based on the argument of 'similar facts'. Lavan objected, arguing that only the issue at hand, the death of Ethel Booth, was relevant.

Keith Robertson, an officer with the Perth Local Board of Health, was next called. He stated that Mitchell was registered under requirements of the 1898 *Health Act* to care for babies and infants less than two years of age. Her original licence had been granted for her premises in Wellington Street. He then charted her movements as she set up across various establishments. Her record-keeping was slovenly and inadequate, leading to confusion not just about the name of new arrivals but when they arrived or anything about their history. Elizabeth Booth then gave moving testimony about what she believed had happened to Ethel. Matron Catherine Patterson and the laundress Alice Skinner both confirmed that Ethel was in peak health when she left the House of Mercy to go to Mitchell.[50]

Some thirty-six witnesses were called. The accused did not provide evidence or witnesses for her defence. The inquest concluded on 11 March, with Acting Coroner Cowan declaring that there was sufficient evidence of 'culpable negligence' to go to trial. This commenced on 8 April 1907 before Justice Robert Furse McMillan (later Sir Robert and chief justice) (1858–1931).[51] Mitchell was defended by R. D. Beresford, and the distinguished Scottish-born crown solicitor, Alexander E. Barker, led the Crown case. Mitchell was charged with wilful murder, an offence that carried the death penalty if convicted. Sergeant O'Halloran gave more details about his examination of the premises where he discovered the condition of Ethel Booth. Maud Brown's baby was similarly emaciated and in a filthy condition. Dr Davy challenged Mitchell's account of her care of the babies.

Two medical staff at the Perth Hospital provided testimony of the state of Ethel Booth on admittance. The chief medical officer, Dr Herbert Tymms, stated that 'she was in a dying condition, extremely emaciated with sunken eyes, and the skin on the body was in folds'. Ethel died the following day, from chronic starvation. He also recalled the similar case of the baby of Susie Turvey, a servant of Mitchell. Dr Saw, another doctor in the Perth Hospital, also confirmed that he saw other starving babies admitted after living with Mitchell. Evidence was submitted that Dr Taaffe had refused to provide further services and home visits as early as 1902 when he saw the state of the premises and the babies. Dr Frederick Hitch also refused further treatment and reported the matter to the police, who did not proceed as Mitchell claimed that she used Dr Officer as her medical practitioner. Dr Hitch had been threatened by legal action for his report.[52]

When Dr Officer took the witness stand he was at pains to establish the difficulties faced by non-breastfed babies. He denied noticing any neglect or filth at Mitchell's home. Justice McMillan was highly sympathetic to this witness, allowing him every opportunity to duck and weave to avoid any taint of negligence on his part. The crown solicitor also attached no blame to his woeful laxity. Officer frequently attended to the infants boarded with Mitchell at the cost of 5/- per visit and yet baby after baby died of malnutrition and neglect. The health inspector of the Perth City Council, Miss Lenehan, was equally negligent in her duties, testifying that she deferred to Dr Officer's expertise.

Yet other witnesses were not so reticent or willing to hide behind professional formality. Carl and Marion Roux had at one time boarded with Mitchell, and testified that the house was filthy and the babies neglected. Carl Roux stated that Susie Turvey's baby was sadly neglected. He catalogued the vast array of filth on the premises, with babies crawling into the henhouse, babies in soiled nappies covered with flies left in rooms to suffer from starvation. But why didn't they take their concerns to the police or the Board of Health at the time?

The jury found Mitchell guilty of the manslaughter of Ethel Booth after only an hour's deliberation. She was sentenced to five years' hard labour.

In the wake of this judgment, far-reaching reforms into infant welfare and health were enacted in Western Australia. What is surprising is that Mitchell got off so lightly. At least thirty-three babies had died under her negligent care. Although not caused by acts of wilful murder, slow and painful death by starvation and disease was possibly more excruciating. From some perspectives, Alice Mitchell rivals mass killer Martin Bryant, who slaughtered thirty-five people at Port Arthur in 1996. He killed with a gun; Mitchell killed by calculated neglect and a wilful cruelty towards those entrusted to her care.

CHAPTER 7

Child Killers in the Nineteenth Century

In early 1842, hundreds of Sydney residents gathered on the foreshore of Circular Quay awaiting the arrival of the latest ship from England. Since 1840 they had followed the tale of Little Nell Trent and her grandfather published in instalments as part of Charles Dickens's weekly periodical, *Master Humphrey's Clock*. The plot of *The Old Curiosity Shop* was full of pathos as young Nell attempted to aid her ailing and decrepit grandfather. But her struggle to render good made her ill with fatigue. In part seventy-two of the eighty-eight instalments the fate of Little Nell was to be revealed. Would she live? Or, as many eager devotees of Dickens's work secretly feared, would she succumb to exhaustion and die? As the ship docked and the boxes of periodicals came down the gangway, eager readers tore the packaging to find out what had happened. Well-dressed gentlemen cried aloud: 'No! No! She is dead! Little Nell is dead.' Across the wharves and then throughout the city, tears and lamentations were heard as the tragic news spread. Copies of the weekly were auctioned at Moore and Heydon's premises in Pitt Street on Good Friday in 1842, attracting keen bidding.[1]

In this work of fiction the self-sacrificing child dies after a heroic crusade. But the reality of children's deaths in the nineteenth century was far more sombre. The continuing high mortality rate from disease – from measles, influenza, diphtheria, scarlet fever and chicken pox – was lamentable, but there were also those children who were killed by human hand, and their passing was recorded in the clinical reports of autopsies conducted in morgues, and coronial inquests and trials.

A recurring theme in the nineteenth century, particularly in the 1890s when the world was deeply affected by the economic Depression, is the desperation of impoverished women and particularly those who were mothers. Whether they were unmarried or not, poor women had a hard lot in the Australian colonies. Conditions were so difficult and money so hard to come by that many were forced to live in appalling circumstances of filth and hunger and disease, frequently abandoned by their men, or the recipients of their husband's excessive drinking and violence.

Mary Sullivan was a sixteen-year-old Irish nursemaid sentenced in County Cork to seven years' transportation to Van Diemen's Land for stealing quilts. This was her third offence, with previous convictions for stealing clothes and robbing a workhouse. County Cork was particularly hard hit by the potato blight, which triggered the Irish famine that so devastated the country and was responsible for 1.5 million deaths (almost 20 per cent of the population) between 1845 and 1849. To rob a workhouse where the most destitute of people were sent indicates a desperation that only someone who had lived through the famine could share. What Sullivan had suffered in her early teenage years and whether she lost most of her family to starvation was not recorded in the official records of her crimes.

Sullivan arrived on the *John William Dare* on 22 May 1852 with 171 other female felons. Her stature even for those impoverished times was tiny – she was only 139 centimetres (4 foot 7 inches) in height. Sullivan was described as a 'stout, rough-looking girl of forbidding appearance, and a sullen disposition'.[2] Though her behaviour on board ship had been exemplary, Sullivan was so unruly on arrival that she stayed only four days with her assigned employer. She was returned to the Cascades Female Factory for reprocessing.

Assigned felons had no say in who was to be their employer or the duties they would be expected to perform. Sullivan was next sent to Mrs Emma Langley in Campbell Street, Hobart, to work as a nursery maid. Larret Langley had died in September 1849 leaving his widow with three small children to rear alone. To survive she took in other children as boarders. On 7 July, after just one week in Langley's employ, Sullivan killed Adeline Blackburn Frazer, a two-year-old girl entrusted to her care.[3]

It was not just impoverished single mothers who were forced to give up their children into the care of other women to survive (see Chapter 3). Circumstances could make it necessary for even those who were more affluent. Adeline's father, John Frazer, had formerly served as the assistant superintendent of convicts at Jerusalem, Tasmania, from 6 October 1846 to 12 November 1848, after which he first took up the licence of the Royal Oak Hotel in Macquarie Street and then the Old Commodore Hotel in Brisbane Street.[4] He then left for the goldfields in Victoria, leaving Adeline, aged two, and her brother John, aged four, in the care of Langley because his wife, Elspeth Frazer, was seriously ill in St Mary's Hospital at the time of his departure. Such a disruption to family life was common in the colonies as men ventured to the diggings to make their fortunes – or so they hoped.

On the morning of the killing, described in the *Hobart Town Courier* of 10 July 1852 as 'a cold-blooded and diabolical murder', Sullivan absconded, leaving her fellow convict servant, Mary Ann Farmer, who was employed as a needlewoman, to explain her absence and do her chores. Sullivan had stolen a bonnet, a pair of boots owned by Master Dean, one of Mrs Langley's former boarders, and some tea and sugar. She left behind her government-issued convict garb. Farmer lit the fires and went to wake the children for their breakfast only to find Adeline missing. The boy reported that Sullivan had taken his sister out of her cot into another room. She had not been crying or restless that night. After a search, Farmer discovered Adeline's body, strangled by a strip of calico and hidden in a water-storage unit in the backyard. Dr William Huxtable was called in, but too late for the child had been dead for some time. When District Constable Simpson arrived to investigate he suspected Farmer of the deed and took her into custody.

The inquest into the little girl's murder was held before the coroner and a jury on 14 July in the York Hotel in Brisbane Street. Farmer testified that she had called a neighbour, a Mr Piesse, to assist her before calling for Dr Huxtable. Another boarder at Langley's house, a Miss Hurton, who was blind, reported that even though the children slept in the same room as she did, she did not hear Adeline removed from her cot. Constable Chandler testified that he apprehended Mary Sullivan the next day in Murray Street. As he approached her she said: 'I did not murder the child.' Sullivan also told him that she did 'not care to mind children'. She did not testify at the inquest and was committed for trial in the Supreme Court.[5]

The case with nine counts against Sullivan opened in the criminal sittings of the Supreme Court of Van Diemen's Land on 21 July 1852. The jury was chaired by the wealthy merchant and director of the Van Diemen's Land Bank, George Salier (1813–92).[6] The solicitor-general acted for the Crown and, as was common at the time, the defendant was unrepresented. Sullivan was, however, allowed to question witnesses herself. This opportunity was taken up with invective, accusing Farmer of the deed. Sullivan asked for no witnesses in her own defence and offered no explanation of her actions. Proceedings were lengthy and much of the evidence tendered followed that already heard at the inquest. The jury took only a short time to deliver their verdict. Sullivan was found guilty of wilful murder and was given the mandatory sentence of death and dissection.

Yet the case was puzzling. Constable Chandler was at a loss to understand why Sullivan had acted in such a way towards a vulnerable child placed in her care, however unwillingly: 'The motives which could have prompted the girl to such an exercise of her destructive faculty are as yet incomprehensible.'[7] A large petition assembled on her behalf tried to justify her actions as compelled by madness. A medical board examined the prisoner to decide whether or not she was sane but was satisfied that she was merely evil, consumed by an 'utter callousness'. By this time, medical practitioners had increased their professional reputations as expert witnesses able to determine the inner workings of the mind, and therefore going far beyond the primary legal concept of intent. A whole genre of medico-legal literature concerned with women's reproduction, and social and biological functions, had matured in the 1840s and 1850s, influencing procedures even in far-distant Van Diemen's Land.

On 2 August 1852 a warrant was issued by the sheriff for the execution of Mary Sullivan, who 'hitherto manifested an unrelenting obduracy, and nothing seems calculated to bring her to a sense of her enormous guilt'.[8] A large crowd, consisting mainly of women and children, gathered to watch the public execution, which was held in front of the Hobart Town jail in Murray Street three days later. They had waited for hours to get a good viewing spot to watch the terrible spectacle. This was an unusual execution since very few women were hanged in comparison to the large numbers of men in this colony or elsewhere. Moreover, Sullivan was very young. Yet the brutality of her crime and the lack of motive mitigated any real sympathy for her. As Sullivan stood on the scaffold she did not make her confession and nor did she seek forgiveness for her crime. The Roman Catholic vicar-general, the Reverend Dr William Hall (1807–66) attended to her to the last moment of her life. She did pray silently moments before the cap was placed on her head to cover her eyes and then she dropped quickly to her death.[9] After her execution her body was given to the colonial surgeons to dissect under the gaze of various medical staff and apothecaries, as well as assorted gentlemen of the colony.

Emma Courtenay was born into poverty in Launceston in 1873. Until she became pregnant at the age of fourteen, she lived with her mother,

Ann Ross, at 117 Margaret Street. With a degree of unwillingness, Courtney married twenty-seven-year-old Frederick Williams. Theirs was a 'short and miserable married life',[10] turbulent from the start, exacerbated by her early parenthood and poverty. Their little daughter was at first cared for by Emma's mother. The couple then moved to Melbourne where the child was sent to foster parents who were friends of Frederick Williams. For Emma Williams was now pregnant again. This was disastrous, especially given the long Depression still virulent in 1893. Not only could he not find work or support his family, but Frederick Williams caught typhus from the unsanitary conditions and died in the Melbourne Hospital.[11]

Emma Williams had no skills or resources. Unlike most children born in the 1870s, she was illiterate. With no government benefits even for widows available at the time, she went to live with a man in Port Melbourne. Annoyed by the presence of her little boy, John, who was now about two, the man told Williams to leave and fend for herself. Her only alternative was to engage in prostitution, a heavily crowded industry in this time of severe economic crisis. Constable John Asker of the South Melbourne Police Station commented that: 'I regarded her as a woman of ill fame, having often seen her in the streets at late hours and generally in the company of other women of ill repute. My impression was that she partly, if not wholly, lived on the proceeds of money obtained by illicit means.' This opinion showed no understanding of the series of forces that had propelled the young widow into this desperate way of life. She lived briefly with several men, one called 'Penguin' and another named 'Blizzard'.

At first Williams attempted to care for John. The local fishmonger, Frederick Foster, noticed that she 'took good care of the child'. This was when he was a baby; but as he grew older and learned to walk he proved an impediment to the way she earned a living. Clients not surprisingly objected to his presence. Her solution was to foster him with a baby farmer, Mary Wilson of 105 Ingles Street, Port Melbourne, who took him for the sum of 5/- per week. At Williams's trial, Wilson testified that she ' … appeared fond of the child. She was trying to get work and could not get it. She took the child away because I could not keep it [without payment] any longer.' Williams later brought him back to Wilson and simply left him there for six weeks without notice or payment. When she returned, Wilson forced Williams to take her son back.

With few clients, in early 1895 Williams went to live with a labourer, William Martin, an unsuccessful petty criminal working under various aliases such as Frederick Matthews and William May. He had already served several incarcerations for his crimes including housebreaking, possession of housebreaking tools and vagrancy. His next career move was to act as pimp for Williams. They shared the cottage with John Brown and Mary Costello. Williams's career as a prostitute continued to languish, forcing them to move frequently through the slums of Port Melbourne and South Melbourne without paying their debts or the rent they owed. Williams's life was spiralling further into chaos and desperation. Once, she left the little boy with a stranger for three days after saying she had to run an urgent errand.

In early August 1895, Williams, the child and William Martin moved to 24 Little Park Street in South Melbourne. The place was sparsely furnished – the boy slept in a wooden crate. On 11 August Williams told Martin she had had enough and intended to take her son to a 'Salvation Army woman at the barracks'. This wasn't actually the case for Williams took the child to the Port Melbourne lagoon, placed a bluestone around his neck with part of her petticoat and threw him into the stagnant water, where he drowned. The following day, council worker Neil Oberg found the body. Dr John Brett, who conducted the autopsy, reported the child had died from drowning. He was well fed and well nourished.[12] The news was taken up by the *Herald–Standard*, which featured it on the front page the following day. Martin reported the story to Williams, asking her if it was her son. She said she could not read so she had not heard. He later stated

The brief life of Emma Williams was blighted by poverty and chaos. Photo: Public Records office, Victoria, VPS 5900. Photograph of prisoners sentenced to death and coroner's inquest sheets, PO, Unit 1.

that he tried to get her to go to the police; but all she replied was 'I am innocent and I won't go ... I will sell the furniture and go to Sydney if you want to go with me ... They can't take us in another colony ...'[13] In this, though, she was misinformed since baby farmer Frances Knorr had been extradited from Sydney to stand trial in Melbourne the previous year.

The police were sure, however, that Emma Williams was the mother of the dead boy. She was arrested and sensational newspaper accounts followed the case. The *Herald–Standard* of 14 August proclaimed 'HEARTLESS MURDER OF A LITTLE CHILD. A CRUEL DEED' next to a drawing of Williams dressed in a hat and a high-collared blouse. She protested her innocence, although when she was in custody she tried to dispose of her petticoat up the police station chimney. William Martin told the police of her actions, no doubt in an attempt to distance himself from the crime. Confronted with the remnants of her petticoat, Williams confessed to killing her son.

Her trial before Justice Sir Henry Hodges (1844–1919), a stern disciplinarian and fervent Christian, took place on 24 September 1895. Williams was defended by William Forlonge, a distinguished barrister from a wealthy pastoral family. He and Alfred Deakin had represented the international serial killer Frederick Deeming in 1892 before Justice Hodges. Williams testified in her own defence. She reported that she had tried to lodge her son with a Catholic home but was refused because they were not Catholics. She then went to Sulina Sutherland, a noted philanthropist, but with no success. Sutherland (1839–1909) was a lay 'lady missionary' to the urban poor in Melbourne where her particular concern was with destitute children. Unfortunately, in the two years before this trial there had been dissent in the Melbourne Presbyterian community over the extent of her activities, which were then curtailed.[14] Williams had begged her mother in Launceston to take in the boy, another plea that was refused. She also detailed the various baby farmers who cared for the boy, but without sufficient funds to support him this strategy also failed.

Williams's lover William Martin provided testimony for the prosecution. He had earlier told the police about the hidden petticoat. He also recounted a conversation in which Williams admitted that she had killed John. The court was told there had been arguments in the joint household about John's crying, and that Williams had said she intended giving John to the Salvation Army to care for. Mrs Costello was also unsympathetic to the defence case. Forlonge let matters slip in his cross-examination, as if he already knew he was going to lose.

In his address to the jury William Forlonge asked its members to consider that this had been an act of desperation committed without premeditation, done 'on the impulse of the moment'. In his directions to the jury, however, Justice Hodges was not so inclined to this view. Having sat on the case of serial poisoner Martha Needle the previous year, he believed that society had no responsibility to care for the children of immoral women. He continued by saying that 'all the facts pointed to the one conclusion that the prisoner intentionally took the child's life, when she threw it [sic] into the water with the fixed determination that it should not rise to the surface ... There was not one single question that could be put to the jury on the other side.' The jury took heed of his directions, finding Williams guilty of wilful murder after a deliberation of just twenty minutes. She was sentenced to death by hanging.

Williams claimed she was pregnant and therefore could not be executed. When Dr Andrew Shields, the prison visiting medical officer, examined her he was not certain whether she was pregnant or not. She was brought before Justice Hodges once more on 18 October 1895. Forlonge again represented her, most likely pro bono since she could not afford his fee or that of his junior, H. S. Cole. She was examined under chloroform in a room adjacent to the courtroom by a team of doctors including the eminent gynaecologist Dr Walter Balls-Headley, J. W. Dunbar Hooper, a fellow of the Royal College of Physicians, and the prison surgeon.[15] This was a unique occurrence in the Australian legal system. Under the law, a woman who was 'quick with child' (that is, more than twenty weeks pregnant) could not be executed; one under that could be. No impediment to her execution had been found. The jury was informed of this development immediately.

The public was not quite so eager to see a young woman executed even if she had earned a living as a prostitute. Two journalists, Henry Hyde Champion (1859–1928) and Marshall Lyle, took up her case. Champion was an unusual advocate: he had attended Marlborough College and the Royal Military Academy in England, and had seen action in the Afghan War. Although he seemed to be a member of the Establishment, his strong social conscience compelled him to take radical stances. He visited Melbourne in August 1892 before taking up a position in England as the editor of the prestigious literary journal *Nineteenth Century*. But he returned to Melbourne in April 1894 after standing unsuccessfully for the seat of Aberdeen in Scotland. Champion joined the Women's Suffrage League and was a co-founder of the Victorian Social Democratic Federation. In June 1895 he established his own journal, entitled *Champion*, from whose pages he sought support for Emma Williams.[16] The issue dated 26 October 1895 proclaimed that Williams's intended execution 'would exhibit Victoria to the world as the very lowest and most degraded of all civilised communities'. The force of his pen won more sympathy and petitions for the condemned woman.

Another radical advocate, Dr Charles Strong (1844–1942), a founder of the freethinking Australian Church, also sought her reprieve. A well-educated Scotsman with a Calvinist upbringing, Strong originally served as minster to the prestigious Scots Church, Melbourne, from 1875 to 1882. His increasingly radical stance alarmed both the elders and the congregation of this conservative bastion of Presbyterian worship. His new church was determined to change the social system that produced poverty as well as to give more immediate support to its victims.[17] From his pulpit in Flinders Street he urged his congregation to help Emma Williams's cause by petitioning the government for mercy. Three days later a substantial petition was forwarded to the new governor, Lord Brassey (1836–1918), for his consideration.[18] The government decided to determine once more if Williams was pregnant. She was re-examined by the three experts who had already seen her and once again they declared she was not pregnant. The execution was to go ahead. The chaplain at Melbourne jail, the Reverend H. Scott, acted as her spiritual adviser, urging her to become penitent and ask God's forgiveness.

Newspapers carried reports of her last hours. She slept soundly the night before her execution, suggesting she had been administered sedatives, then ate a light breakfast and received counsel from the Reverend Scott. She left a message for Mrs Costello, the landlady who had testified against her at her trial, saying: 'I forgive her.' When the sheriff – the officer of the Supreme Court entrusted with overseeing executions – 'demanded her body in the usual form', Williams was composed, walking 'calmly to the scaffold, on which she maintained her calm demeanour'. When the white cap was drawn over her face, she called out: 'O Lamb of God, I come.' But as the lever of the trapdoor adjusted to her weight she screamed out in fear. She died instantly, or so newspapers reported.[19] This had been the third execution of a woman in Melbourne in two years: Frances Knorr, Martha Needle and now the filicide Emma Williams all died by the noose. The public hounded Sullivan's executioner, Constable Robert Gibbon, to such an extent that he begged the government to allow him to carry firearms for his own protection. His mental health deteriorated under the strain and he was committed to Yarra Bend Asylum as 'a raving lunatic' two years later.[20]

In November 1896, a unique case was heard before the Supreme Court of Queensland. Forty-year-old Marie Christensen, the acting matron at the non-denominational Myora Mission (1891–1942) on Stradbroke Island, stood in the dock accused of the manslaughter of one of the inmates, a five-year-old girl called Cassey.

An earlier mission experiment on Stradbroke Island, conducted by the Italian Passionist fathers in 1825, just a year after the Moreton Bay penal settlement was established, had failed. This new initiative, Myora, had been the brainchild of a group of Brisbane philanthropists who wished to establish a reformatory for Aboriginal children. Under the *Industrial and Reformatory Schools Act* of 1865, magistrates had the power to remove children from neglectful parents. This included any Indigenous children. Children could be sent to missions such as Yarrabah near Cairns, or to this new establishment. Stradbroke Island already housed the state-funded Dunwich Benevolent Asylum where the destitute of the colony – the infirm, the incapacitated and the alcoholic – lived in prison-like conditions.

Myora Mission also contained a state-funded primary school under the leadership of teacher Atkinson Dunnington. With no family, Cassey had been sent to Myora in June 1896. Her health was poor; she was tiny for her age and malnourished. On the morning of

14 September 1896, Christensen took the children down to the sea to bathe. Cassey found the walk from the cottages difficult and resisted entering the water, which suggests she might have come from inland. Christensen forced her into the water anyway, after which Cassey collapsed. She was then forced to walk up the sand dunes. When the little girl lagged and found herself unable to continue, Christensen beat her savagely with a switch, a flogging that went on for several minutes. Cassey was unable to move so the matron roughly dragged her along by the arms. The girl begged a fellow inmate, Jackie Gowrie, to help her and Christensen responded by finding another switch and beating the little girl again. She then retrieved her cane from her quarters and continued the flogging in earnest. Several older Indigenous people saw the commotion, including seventeen-year-old Topsy McLeod from the kitchen where she worked. One older resident, Budlo Lefu, rushed out of her humpy, gathered Cassey into her arms and went to walk off with her. But Christensen intervened and insisted she put the child down. Lefu reluctantly did so, aware that the power dynamics on the island favoured the acting matron.[21]

Budlo Lefu and her family were not part of the mission but lived a more independent existence. They were not local people but may have been Melanesian islanders brought to Queensland to work in the sugar industry. There were other Melanesians living on the island with the Indigenous people. Lefu's two children attended the mission school but she was concerned by the degree of punishment inflicted on the children by Christensen.[22]

After the acting matron retrieved Cassey, she took her into the dormitory and began to flog her again. Afterwards, Cassey became seriously ill and was unable to eat. Atkinson Dunnington advised Christensen to send for Dr Patrick Mahoney from the Benevolent Asylum, which she did the following day. He prescribed some whisky as a stimulant. The following day Cassey died. Dr Mahoney notified the justice of the peace, arguing he could not issue a death certificate as he had only seen the deceased once.

The justice of the peace, W. R. North, decided to convene a magisterial inquest into Cassey's death, which was held on 19 and 20 September.[23] This was unusual: of the 469 inquests held in Queensland in 1896 very few were conducted into the death of any Indigenous people. Even more unusually for the period, North allowed the sworn testimony of non-Europeans, even though he did not correctly record Budlo Lefu's evidence in the records. Dr Mahoney testified to the thirty contusions on Cassey's buttocks, but he believed these had been insufficient to *cause* death. However, given her weakened and anaemic condition these injuries would have contributed to her death. North filed his report stating 'Suspect: Marie Christensen. Suspicious circumstances. Flogging child in weak state of health.'[24]

The report of the inquest was forwarded to the attorney-general's office on 25 September, and then to the commissioner of police for his opinion as to whether the matter should go to the crown prosecutor's office. Sub-inspector James Coathcote and Constable Michael Toomey investigated the case. Toomey went to Stradbroke Island on the government launch *Lucinda*, the vessel on which only five years previously the distinguished members of the Constitutional Convention had worked on the first draft of the Australian Constitution.

On questioning witnesses, Toomey found that North had not recorded the evidence of Christensen's cane. When he spoke to her, she denied owning a cane, although she admitted to using a small switch. Constable Toomey then examined her room and found a cane but Christensen denied using it on Cassey, saying she 'reserved it for the big ones'. Problematically, when he first approached Christensen for questioning, Toomey had not identified himself as a police officer nor did he caution her, issues that were later important at the trial.

A hearing before Philip Pinnock began on 29 September. He was a highly respected old settler who had been appointed police magistrate even before the colony was formed in 1859. Pinnock was considered a fair man ruled by evidence. Christensen was represented by counsel.

The hearing went on for five days with the Crown alone calling twelve witnesses. Constable Toomey had returned to Myora to check the veracity of witness testimony by conducting re-enactments to see, for example, whether Topsy McLeod had indeed been able to see the events from her kitchen window. Evidently, Philip Pinnock was convinced that Christensen had a case to answer and ensured that the proceedings were rigorous.

The case came before the Supreme Court where Christensen pleaded guilty before Justice Patrick Real (1846–1928), a man who had come from the most humble origins to rise to great professional heights. He was considered to be a jurist who favoured the plight of the poor and unfortunate. The Crown case was led by Attorney-General Sir Arthur Rutledge (1843–1917), a former Liberal acting premier with progressive views. Christensen did not have counsel at her trial.[25] Free legal representation for defendants was not available in Queensland until 1903. In her own defence, though, Christensen testified that '[she had] meant no harm to the child'. Dr Maloney also stated that Cassey had not died from her beatings alone but rather from a series of contributing factors. The Home Secretary presented a report stating that the defendant was a 'woman of good character' but 'not a very strong mind'. None of the material in the proceedings gave any indication of how Christensen came to this point in her life or even what her age was. The position of matron on a poorly funded Aboriginal mission was hardly likely to attract the services of a competent, intelligent person. In such circumstances, employees were often substandard and desperate for work of any sort.

Christensen was given a sentence of two years' imprisonment, which was immediately suspended on payment of a good behaviour bond of £100 for the period of her probation. After the Crown divulged that the Salvation Army had offered to care for Christensen, Justice Real advised that he was willing to apply the new provisions relating to first offenders in the *Offenders' Probation Act 1886*, one of the first such Acts in the world. Whether it was lenient or an appropriate sentence cannot be determined since this was a unique legal case. What the case did reveal was the extreme brutality meted out to Indigenous children in institutions supposedly set up for their care and protection. The fate of removed or 'stolen' children is revealed in this rare and early documented case. Given the racial ideology of that period in Queensland, it is also remarkable that the case ever came to light and was pursued to the highest court in the colony.

CHAPTER 8

The Wicked Stepmother: Martha Rendall

Stepmothers get a bad press; the term 'wicked' is frequently added automatically. Euripides set the stereotype for the next 2500 years when in his play *Alcestis*, written in 483 BC, he declared 'better a serpent than a stepmother'. European folktales are replete with 'wicked stepmothers': they are there in Snow Drop (Snow White), Cinderella, Hansel and Gretel, as well as in the English tale, the Rose Tree. Stepmothers are always jealous of the husbands' children and will do anything to make sure their own get ahead. So say the stereotypes.

Australia had its own notorious stepmother – Martha Rendall – who was executed for the murder of her stepson and the suspected murder of his two sisters in Perth in 1909. In 1932 a feature in the *Western Australian* on 12 May described her as a 'torturer', the perpetrator of 'diabolical cruelty'. She was accused of being 'undoubtedly a sadist who obtained sexual pleasure from inflicting pain on others. She was the most inhumane fiend who ever stood in the dock of the Criminal Court, Perth.' Former Perth CIB Detective Aubrey Lamond, who conducted the police investigations into the murders, described Rendall as 'a sadist of the worst kind. Seeing someone in great agony appeared to give her sexual gratification. A queer woman if ever there was one.'[1]

Crime writer Paul B. Kidd describes Rendall as going 'down in history as being among the most sadistic serial killers the world has ever known …'. He compares her reputation to that of Moors murderers Myra Hindley and Ian Brady, and to American child killer and cannibal Albert Fish.² More recently, historian Professor Anna Haebich has re-evaluated the extensive evidence to present a far more complex understanding of the deaths of the three children, and the conviction of their stepmother for their murder.³

Contemporary assessment of her character debated whether or not Martha Rendall had been born a criminal. From the perspective of pioneer criminologist Cesare Lombroso (1835–1909) and eugenicist Francis Galton (1822–1911), who actually coined the term 'eugenics' as well as the expression 'nature versus nurture', this would certainly have been the case. Five weeks after the inquest into the deaths of the three Morris children, Perth's *Sunday Times* on 19 September 1909 sought answers to this perplexing question. At the outset the journalist pointed out that 'Rendall is her maiden name and is the only one to which she is legally entitled'. This pulled away the facade that she and her de facto husband Thomas Morris had so carefully cultivated – that they were a respectable if poor married couple with a large brood of children.

The article revealed that Martha Rendall's father was an English immigrant to South Australia in the 1840s, a respectable man who died when she was twelve years old. Her mother, it was said, then married a man called Moreton who made life 'irksome to the young girl and she soon left home to earn her own living as a domestic servant'. This, the journalist implied, befitted her status as 'an illiterate, uneducated woman, hardly able to write and certainly unable to spell properly'. Rendall met Morris while working as a maid in a hotel in Magill, South Australia, although the year was unknown. Morris and Rendall travelled together to Western Australia in 1905, where she went into service under the name of Mrs Moreton. She had several employers during this period. At the end of the article it was disclosed that she had left two ex-nuptial children back in South Australia. These revelations were published before the trial, creating negative impressions about Rendall's origins and morals. *Truth*, a newspaper devoted to presenting sexual scandal in as many lurid details as possible, also canvassed the outline of Rendall's life and morals. Such exposés of an accused person's life would not be permitted under current media guidelines, but in 1909 sexual innuendo was enough to utterly condemn a woman's reputation and was no impediment to legal proceedings.

Martha Rendall's parents, Thomas and Mary Ann Rendall, arrived in South Australia in 1849 as children, marrying in 1860. He worked as a labourer in the Adelaide foothills. There were thirteen children to the marriage with seven infant deaths. Martha was born in 1871. After her father's death and mother's remarriage Rendall developed an intense and enduring hatred of her stepfather. She went to work as a domestic servant at the age of fifteen and had a son at the age of sixteen. Whether her stepfather strongly disapproved and forced her out, or could indeed have been the father, remains conjecture. The child's father remained anonymous and what happened to it remains a mystery. Rendall entered into a bogus marriage with Alfred Roberts. He was presumably the father of her further two children, Albert who died at the age of three months and Alice, born in 1891.[4] Rendall's life was hard as she continued to work as a servant, barmaid and invalids' nurse. From this evidence we can deduce that she did not rear the children herself since the demands of unskilled manual employment would have prevented her from regular and consistent parenting. Having three illegitimate children by the age of twenty clearly marked Rendall as a 'fallen woman' in the language and sentiments of the era.

Through Alfred Roberts, Martha Rendall met the man who was to control her life and destiny for the next thirteen years, until her execution. Roberts was a cousin to Thomas Morris, born in Melbourne from South Australian parents. Morris was then a married man with a family of seven children, and he was to have two more with his wife before he abandoned her in favour of Rendall. During their early relationship, which commenced around 1896 while he was still living with his wife, Rendall suffered several miscarriages. No doubt these were Morris's children. Rendall followed Roberts to Western Australia in 1900 (not 1905 as stated during her arraignment), although he did not leave his wife for another six years. Morris had family already in the west, who secured him work.[5] His wife had urged the move to get him away from his attractive and persistent lover.

Clearly, Rendall was not a woman who cared about the conventions of marriage and motherhood. She already had two living illegitimate children to a man she pretended was her legal husband, another to a different man, and she abandoned them all to follow her married lover to a distant city. There is no evidence that Rendall ever saw them again after she left for Perth in 1900. Although technically 'Miss Rendall', when she sought employment as a domestic servant she called herself 'Mrs Moreton', her mother's name and title. Perhaps she portrayed herself as a young widow.

Or perhaps when Morris and his wife finally parted in April 1906 the opportunity to establish a home with all the appearance of conventionality presented itself. Divorce was expensive and therefore out of the question. Morris was given guardianship of the five younger children, which, since the enacting of the various legislations concerning infant and child custody in the 1890s, was no longer the most usual outcome. After Morris threw his wife Sarah out of their house because of acrimonious arguments over his liaison with Rendall, she was unable to earn a good living and was forced to take in washing and mending to scrape a meagre existence.[6] In retrospect Rendall would have been better to continue her affair with Morris and leave his wife to care for the family. At first Rendall presented herself to the children as the 'housekeeper', but after she moved to share Morris's bed, she insisted the children – William, Olive, Annie, Arthur and George – call her 'Mother', a term they resisted fiercely. William worked for a living but the other four children were dependent.

Any dreams she may have harboured about domestic felicity and comfort were shattered by their actual location at 23 Robinson Street,

THE WICKED STEPMOTHER: MARTHA RENDALL

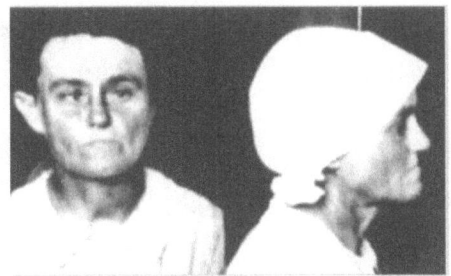

Does Martha Rendall deserve her description as a sadistic serial killer? Photo: Western Australian Police Museum.

in the poorer area of East Perth. To have waited for so long and then to live in a poverty-stricken and dirty neighbourhood along with a brood of resentful children and teenagers was hardly an anticipated romantic outcome. By all accounts, Rendall was a harsh and abusive carer, constantly beating five-year-old Olive and seven-year-old Annie, although this was not uncommon in an era when the rod was never spared, even for minor infractions of discipline. Neighbours such as Lena Carr reported hearing Rendall screeching and screaming at the children for hours on end. This information was used against Rendall in her trial. When he was at home after his long hours at manual labour, Morris apparently chose not to notice.

In April 1907, George, Arthur, Olive and Annie contracted diphtheria, a deadly infectious disease then in epidemic proportions in Perth. Known as the 'strangling angel of children', the disease was easily transmitted. It could reach anyone, no matter how well-born or protected: Princess Alice, the third child of Queen Victoria, died when she contracted the infection as an adult. There was no vaccine until 1913.[7] Treatments before this relied on keeping the throat open and neutralising the toxins that gathered at the base of the throat. Various patent remedies were available, such as the dangerous use of quinine and prussic acid (hydrogen cyanide) with emetics. Other home treatments recommended the application to the inside of the throat of sodium benzoate, now used as a food preservative.[8] Before stringent legislation in the 1920s, many patent medicines were deadly. Godfrey's Cordial, which was made for babies, contained lethal doses of laudanum (a by-product of opium) if used incorrectly.[9]

Rendall cared for and nursed the seriously ill children, hampered by the lack of effective treatments. Further care was provided by a Miss Copley from the Silver Chain nursing organisation. The Perth Children's Hospital was not established until 1909 so no residential care was available. Dr James Cuthbert was called in on numerous occasions to provide medical attention. He used the new anti-toxin developed in 1895 as well as strong painkillers. Then Olive, Arthur and George contracted typhus, an often-lethal infection spread in squalid and unhygienic surroundings. Again Dr Cuthbert attended the patients.

Annie was not so fortunate; she died in agony on 27 July 1907. Later evidence revealed that behind closed doors Rendall applied a lotion to her throat that caused her to scream in agony. This was not as suspicious as it might seem; the disease was highly contagious and barriers were necessary to prevent its spread. George Morris later claimed that his stepmother was cruel and heartless, telling him to watch Annie try to get out of bed as Rendall laughed out loud. She was also accused of beating Annie on several occasions when she lay dying.[10] Dr Cuthbert was not alarmed, however, and he provided a death certificate stating that she died of epilepsy and cardiac weakness.

Olive Morris died on 16 October 1907, with Cuthbert certifying death from typhoid and convulsions. At this time the Morris family regularly attended the local Methodist church. The congregation provided considerable support in the wake of the double tragedy. Rendall was also debilitated and constantly ill. During Easter 1908 the family went to Bunbury, where Thomas Morris obtained work.[11] No doubt the temporary relocation was to take advantage of a healthier environment that held no memories of the two dead girls. By this stage, with the revelations of the lethal baby-farming enterprise run by Alice Mitchell documented in all its sordidness, an escape from East Perth was also a flight from the moral contamination of the area. The family returned to Robinson Street on 10 June 1908. When Arthur came home from school one day complaining of a sore throat – the first symptom of diphtheria – he was sent to bed immediately and Dr Cuthbert summoned. Swabbing the patient's throat with a tincture of diluted sulphurous acid in glycerine was ordered. Unlike his sisters, at times the boy appeared to recover before again relapsing.

At the time, Dr Cuthbert had no suspicion that this might be anything but a mysterious ailment that had afflicted children already debilitated by diphtheria and then typhoid fever. He consulted other colleagues for advice. Dr (later Sir) John Cleland (1878–1971) had been trained in tropical medicine in London, arriving in Perth in 1905 to take up the post of government bacteriologist and pathologist. His biographer, R. V. Southcott, notes that the Rendall case made his early reputation.[12] Cuthbert's other distinguished colleague, Dr John Cumptson (1880–1954) had trained in Melbourne and London, becoming an early expert on scarlet fever and diphtheria. He arrived in Western Australia in December 1907.[13] Again the sensational Rendall case helped establish his reputation. At the time they visited Arthur Morris they were unable to detect what ailed him and were as puzzled as Dr Cuthbert.[14] Rendall was suspected of suffering from syphilis and the boy was tested in the belief he was her natural son. No results were forthcoming.

The next-door neighbour, Lena Carr, had come to live in the street after the deaths of the two girls. The sound of Arthur screaming alarmed her. She advised sending him to hospital, advice Rendall rejected. Carr claimed at the inquest that she had heard Arthur on several occasions call out 'Murder! Police! Mrs Carr, save me!' Carr did in fact go into the house to investigate. She claimed that she was disturbed by the use of spirit of salts (hydrochloric acid) that Rendall diluted to treat his throat. However, in diluted forms it *was* sometimes used as a home remedy. On one occasion after inhaling the greenish-yellow swabbing liquid that made her eyes sting, Carr said to Rendall, who she believed was the boy's mother: 'Good God, woman! You are not using that for the boy's throat; it is enough to kill a horse.' Carr was also disturbed when Rendall laughed at Arthur's attempts to get out of bed in a weakened condition. As well she alleged that Rendall yanked Arthur out of his bed and threw him onto a couch saying: 'There! Lie there and die!' Another day when Arthur refused treatment Rendall flogged him. Carr did not inform the police because she believed that Rendall was following the regimen ordered by the local doctor.[15] It provided damning testimony at the inquest and trial. On 8 October 1908, Arthur died.

The neighbours were alarmed by the deaths of three children who only two years ago had been so healthy. The Morris household was the talk of East Perth. But the talk did not take into account that they had been afflicted by the deadly infectious diseases diphtheria and typhus. Florence Feakes sent an anonymous letter to Dr Cuthbert expressing her concerns.[16] This may have been what provoked him to test Rendall for syphilis. An autopsy was conducted on Arthur by Cleland, Cumpston and a thoracic specialist, Dr Crouch. Very unusually, Rendall insisted on sitting in on the procedure – relatives never wanted to see their kin dissected and discussed in clinical detail by pathologists. Yet here was a woman, supposedly the child's mother, watching calmly and intently. When the team came to open the chest and throat, she objected and demanded the termination of the autopsy. Since this was not yet a legal case they had no alternative but to acquiesce to her strange request. Dr Cumpston suspected poison, although hydrochloric acid did not occur to him. This is not surprising since poisoners at the time tended to use arsenic, antimony or strychnine. The matter was closed for the time being and no official report was submitted or even kept.

The Morris–Rendall household moved to Edward Street in East Perth. Around April 1909, George, then aged thirteen, alleged that he had been given bitter tea, which burned his throat. Rendall apparently said to him: 'You'll be the next to go.' He later told the inquest that he had heard his father and Rendall quarrelling over the deaths of the children. When Rendall accused Morris of believing she had deliberately murdered his children, he retorted 'So, it is.' This hearsay evidence by a hostile witness was used at the inquest and the trial.

George took flight without telling his father. Neighbours who had heard of the deaths of the three children were alarmed when George disappeared, fearing he had been murdered. One male neighbour went to CIB headquarters to discuss the matter with Sergeant Harry Mann. The commissioner of police requested that Thomas Morris be brought in for questioning. Disturbed by the interview, police went to the house in Edward Street to question Rendall, whom they believed to be Morris's wife. There, William Morris also said that he did not know where George had gone.

The day after the police visit, William went to CIB headquarters to speak to detectives away from his father and Rendall. Now he revealed that George had gone to Subiaco to stay with their mother. When asked why George had run away, William told police: 'Mrs Rendall was trying to poison him. She poisoned my two sisters and one of my brothers.' When located and questioned by detectives, George reiterated William's story. The boys' allegation presented the opportunity for further investigations. To divert attention away from her, Rendall said she had had the same symptoms as the dead children had suffered. The distinguished local ear, nose and throat specialist Dr Macaulay reported treating Rendall for a severe sore throat but determined she did not have diphtheria. He suspected she had used a chemical irritant to produce her symptoms.

With the authority of police magistrate Augustus Roe, the police disinterred the bodies of the three Morris children in July 1909. Doctors were present at the exhumation, as were their parents, Sarah and Thomas Morris. Mrs Morris fainted during the grisly proceedings. The remains of the children were tested by a government analyst. Dr Edward Mann conducted the initial investigation, followed by an autopsy by Dr Tymms, the principal medical officer of the Perth Hospital. During the autopsy of Arthur Morris, Tymms found intestinal irritants he believed could have been caused by a poison of some sort. Forensic science was still primitive in Western Australia at the time, so in terms of evidence this was insubstantial and indefinite.

Roe still concluded, however, that a coronial inquest was appropriate.

The inquest was followed widely in Perth. Rendall's elaborate fabrication of respectability fell apart as she was revealed to be a woman of questionable morals with illegitimate children; an adulterer who broke up the marriage of a man with nine children and held him in some strange sexual sway. Since the forensic evidence of the prosecution was weak and lacked the rigour usually required in coronial inquiries, the case largely rested on the evidence of Lena Carr and, more importantly, George Morris, who acknowledged he had never seen Rendall use spirit of salt (hydrochloric acid) on any of his siblings, although he had heard them scream because of the gargle they were given for diphtheria. The *Sunday Times* in Perth had to admit that the evidence was 'circumstantial'.[17] Rendall did not help her own case: she remained defiant, unmoved and stoic. A woman in her position was expected to show distress; that she did not seemed to confirm a callous nature that could have easily killed three children.[18] The jury at the inquest was convinced by the flimsy evidence, and found Martha Rendall and Thomas Morris guilty of wilful murder. On 16 August 1909, Augustus Roe ordered they stand trial for wilful murder.

The trial in the Supreme Court of Western Australia opened on 8 October 1909. Acting Chief Justice Robert Macmillan (1858–1931), who had presided over the Alice Mitchell case two years earlier, conducted the proceedings. The defendants pleaded not guilty. Crown solicitor Alexander Barker, who had prosecuted the Mitchell case, appeared for the Crown. Morris was represented by F. J. Shaw, while Rendall was represented by James Clydesdale, a University of Glasgow graduate of high calibre. Clydesdale was substantially hindered because his client did not have the resources to obtain her own expert witnesses or request independent forensic tests. Moreover, criminal trials in this era were stacked in favour of the prosecution, given the strength of its resources over those of the much poorer defence. Much of the evidence presented to the coronial inquiry into the death of Arthur Morris was repeated at the five-day hearing. Considerable latitude was given to the admission of hearsay evidence. The prosecution's case was notably weak given that there was no proper forensic evidence, and that various reputable medical men had signed death certificates without demur and had made no official complaints after the first, partial autopsy conducted on Arthur. Still, the Crown had the resources to bring Dr John Cleland back from Sydney where he had taken up a senior position at the Bureau of Microbiology.

Rendall mostly stood condemned as a liar and an adulterer, a heartless mother who had abandoned her own children to run after Thomas Morris.[19] Although Morris was also an adulterer who had abandoned his family, little dirt was cast against his character. He appeared as a shadowy figure in this drama in which Rendall was the protagonist and driver of the fatal events that had befallen the Morris children.

Justice McMillan was clearly convinced of Rendall's guilt as he presented his summation to the jury. She represented a 'moral deformity', although whether lack of morals could be said to lead to mass murder remained unexplained. The jury took less than four hours to reach their verdict: Rendall was found guilty and Morris was found not guilty. Rendall protested her innocence before she was taken away to await execution. In Western Australia at the time there was no court of appeal that could reinvestigate the case. In other states, where this Full Court review existed, the weak prosecuting case should have been sufficient to warrant further examination. McMillan's emotive and biased address to the jury alone would have constituted grounds for appeal. The Court of Criminal Appeal in Western Australia was established in 1911, two years after Rendall's trial. In 1913 the Supreme Court was able to overrule a jury verdict if it was contrary to the facts presented in the case.[20] These reforms were too late to help Martha Rendall.

Her case caused considerable controversy across the state. Few, however, were concerned with Thomas Morris and his role in his children's demise. On 3 October 1909, the *Sunday Times* issued a long feature entitled 'Should We Hang Martha Rendall?' Surprisingly, the paper, having canvassed most of the legal fraternity in the city, decided that she should not be hanged. The prosecution case in her trial was torn into shreds, revealing its essentially flimsy nature. The article concluded that Rendall stood condemned because leading doctors and other specialists could not discover what had actually killed the children, and therefore they made the assumption that they had been killed by human hand. Unlike cases in Victoria in which women condemned to death for infanticide had been reprieved after public outcry, the incipient feminist moment in Western Australia did not come to Rendall's defence.[21]

Rendall's primary public advocate was a Methodist minister, the Reverend Tom Allan, who had a parish in Fremantle. Reverend Allen was her spiritual adviser from the time of her sentencing on 15 September to her execution on 6 October 1909. He was convinced of her innocence and organised a petition to the attorney-general on her behalf.[22] The radical Labor MLA for the seat of Kanowna, Thomas Walker, himself no stranger to scandal, also spoke in her defence in parliament – to no avail.[23] Thomas Morris visited his longtime lover to say his final farewell. Rendall was executed at 8am on 6 October 1906, protesting her innocence to the last. The attorney-general had ruled that the press could not witness the execution, much to its collective chagrin. Outside the prison gates a large crowd gathered, many protesting the execution of a woman on dubious forensic evidence.[24] She was buried in an unmarked grave in Fremantle Prison.[25]

CHAPTER 9

Child Killers in the Twentieth Century

On 25 October 1994, Susan Smith drove her two young sons, aged three and fourteen, into a river in South Carolina and left them to drown. Her initial account was heartrending and tragic: she claimed that she had been carjacked by a black man. Yet as Smith wept in front of an international television audience begging for the return of her boys, the police were investigating the unthinkable – Smith had cold-bloodedly murdered them, leaving them abandoned and trapped in her car to drown. She had disposed of her children believing it would win her the affection and commitment of a well-born and wealthy lover who had told her that the boys stood in the way of any union. Smith sacrificed the lives of her two sons to follow a romantic chimera. She was sentenced to a minimum of thirty years' imprisonment.

Sixty years before this event, Australia too had its own terrible drama in which a young mother killed her son to gain the acceptance of a suitor. On 25 March 1935 Mary Stevens was found guilty in the Supreme Court of Victoria of wilfully murdering her thirteen-month-old son, Leslie. She was sentenced to death.

Stevens was a young domestic servant living in Albury, who, in November 1932, gave birth to a baby out of wedlock. She relocated to Melbourne in order to find work and a place that could care full-time for Leslie. In January 1934 she asked the Children's Welfare Department to arrange for him to be 'boarded-out'. He went to the City Mission Home in Brunswick, where she paid 10/- a week for his maintenance. This non-sectarian organisation provided residential care for single mothers from 1900 onwards, and had recently taken on the care of toddlers like Leslie Stevens. Later that year Mary Stevens became engaged to Eugene Rollings, a truck driver, also from Albury. At first she was overjoyed that, despite the false step she had taken in life, she seemed assured of a home and financial security. Stevens's happiness was short-lived when Rollings told her that he was unwilling to rear another man's child. Their marriage would only nurture their own children, not, in the colloquial expression of the time, 'someone else's bastard'.

Despite her affection for him, Stevens attempted to have Leslie permanently adopted. This was a hard time to arrange for adoption: marriage and birth rates had plummeted to record lows because of the Depression. As unemployment, evictions and homelessness soared, the possibility of placing a toddler was remote. Leslie's father had taken no responsibility for his welfare and baulked at even the slightest payment for his upkeep. On 21 December 1934, Stevens called at the children's home and took Leslie out with her, saying that she intended going to see her family in Albury for the Christmas celebrations. The following morning Leslie was found in the Yarra River, floating face down. Stevens had dressed him in a new blue jumper. Her desire to dress him in new clothes suggests that her initial intention had not been to kill him but indeed take him to Albury with her.

When the police arrested her in Albury, Stevens at first denied having thrown Leslie into the river, concocting a story about a woman who was willing to adopt him. She told Detective F. W. Sickerdick that the woman lived in Lal Lal, near Ballarat, but that she didn't know her name. When pressed further, Stevens admitted that she had murdered her son because he stood in the way of her forthcoming marriage.[1] She told him she had sat on the bank of the river for several hours wondering what she should do. Her only solution, she believed, was to get rid of Leslie for good. How she imagined this would solve her problems when so many people – from her fiancé and parents to people from the children's home and state welfare services – would ask about him is hard to fathom.

Her trial was held before the recently appointed justice to the Supreme Court, Fred Martin (1887–1981), with C. H. Book KC leading the Crown case. Book was a highly experienced and able prosecutor, later appointed to the County Court of Victoria. Stevens was defended by J. M. Cullity. In his testimony Eugene Rollings stated that he had asked Stevens what had become of her son when he saw her in Albury for Christmas. She told him what she told Detective Sickerdick: that Leslie had been adopted but she did not know the woman's name. A labourer, William Henwood from Footscray, testified that he had seen Stevens walking on the north bank of the river near Richmond holding a baby. Later he had seen her alone.

When Stevens entered the witness box she told the court that she loved her son and had done nothing to harm him, a fact clearly at variance with the evidence and her confession to police. The jury deliberated for five and a half hours, returning a guilty verdict, with a strong recommendation for mercy. She was given the statutory death sentence for murder.

The day after her conviction Rollings applied to the governor of Pentridge Prison for permission to visit Stevens. He said he still wished to marry her. He told reporters that he would 'marry her now if they will let me. She has suffered enough already, and my only desire is to give her peace and safety for the rest of her life.'[2] The Executive Council of Victoria considered her sentence in April and commuted her sentence of execution to three years' imprisonment.[3]

The records do not disclose whether Rollings kept his promise and finally married Stevens.

Unaccountably, there was a series of lethal attacks by Australian women armed with axes and knives during the 1930s. Alma Richter of Moonee Ponds killed her nine-year-old son, Allen, with an axe in March 1935. She was found guilty but insane, and was thereafter confined to a psychiatric hospital. In July 1934, Mrs Dominica Guizzardi murdered her neighbour Livia Pinti, the mother of three children, plus her own two-year-old son, William, and five-year-old Alma Giovinazzo, who just happened to be at Mrs Pinti's house delivering a message for her father. There had been no disputes or ill feeling between Guizzardi and Pinti before the attacks with a kitchen knife in Pinti's kitchen. Guizzardi then committed suicide by slashing her own throat. This was one of the worst multiple killings by a woman in Australian history. Police reported that the perpetrator had been treated for 'mental troubles' and was seen just before the murders walking around her neighbourhood of Redcliffe in Perth 'in a very disturbed state of mind'. No one thought to call in a doctor or police at the time.[4] Three years later, at Mount Molloy, near Cairns in Queensland, Isabel Scott West murdered her son George, aged twenty-two; another son, Neil, aged nineteen; and her daughter Ivy, aged fourteen. All were asleep at the time of the attacks by axe. She could offer no explanation for her unprovoked killings.[5] These killings were regarded as particularly traumatic and inexplicable because they had been perpetrated by mothers who had killed their own children.

One of the most intriguing cases of Australian filicide – killing a son or daughter – occurred in Carnegie, a suburb of Melbourne, in 1950. A middle-aged mother, Ivy Cogdon, got out of bed on the night of 11 August, took an axe, and killed her nineteen-year-old daughter, Patricia, as she lay asleep. When arrested by Detective W. W. Mooney, she told him she was 'receiving treatment for a nervous complaint'.[6] In the Coroner's Court on 23 October, Cogdon told Magistrate Burke that she suffered from nightmares. Three medical specialists all presented expert testimony stating that she was 'suffering neurotic troubles and nightmares' and that she had 'not known what she was doing the night her daughter was killed'.[7] Arthur Cogdon revealed that their daughter, Patricia, had been treated for a mental illness and her mother was afraid to the point of obsession that she would never recover.

Sidney Miller, Ivy Cogdon's brother-in-law, testified that she had come to his door, crying hysterically, on the night of 11 August, saying: 'I've had another terrible nightmare. The place was full of soldiers and I was fighting them. Go and see if Pat is all right.' He found his niece dead with dreadful head wounds. Cogdon did not say at the time that she had killed Patricia.

Psychiatrist Dr Henry Stephens of the Prince Alfred Hospital confirmed that Cogdon was troubled by depression and hysteria. 'She is liable to perform certain automatic actions, such as walking in her sleep, and, in such a condition, would have no knowledge of what she was doing and might injure herself or others,' he explained to both the coronial inquest and the criminal trial. Dr John Hurt believed that, while she was not legally insane, Cogdon had no memory of what she did under the blackouts from which she had suffered for twenty years.[8]

The trial for wilful murder was heard in the Supreme Court of Victoria with recently appointed Justice Thomas Sweetman Smith presiding. Her defence team was lead by R. V. Monahan KC, who had secured his considerable reputation when he successfully defended Victorian Premier Robert Cosgrove in the 1947 inquiry into corruption. Mr M. Cussen, the son of the distinguished jurist Justice Sir Leo Cussen, appeared for the Crown.

The testimony relied upon expert witnesses. Psychologist Edward Campbell believed Cogdon was the 'hysterical type', who could not deal with ordinary life and suffered a low frustration level. Stephens agreed with this diagnosis, adding more details concerning her somnambulism and amnesia. Hysteria and brutal murder, however, are not generally connected in the pattern of mental disorders. Her previous diagnoses and treatment were revealed to be woefully inadequate and inappropriate.

Cogdon's specific fears and delusions manifested themselves in her reaction to current events. She dreamed that Korean Communist soldiers had invaded her suburb and were intent upon 'polluting' her daughter. The Korean War had commenced on 25 June 1950, and Australia readily joined the strong US Allied offensive. Liberal politicians and many citizens believed that this military engagement would be the prelude to a third world war. Australia had not been invaded by the enemy in World War II, but many now believed that a new enemy would realise their long-held fears. Intense anti-Communist feelings heightened this sense of imminent incursion. Cogdon gave no indication of her political beliefs during her trial, although clearly these international developments preyed on her.

The trial concluded on 19 December 1950. The jury acquitted her without even hearing the summation by the Crown and the defence, an event extraordinary in itself. The case was a landmark in common-law jurisdictions, for it was the first time that sleepwalking had been allowed as a defence in an indictment for a capital offence.[9] Cogdon collapsed when she learned she had been found not guilty of wilful murder due to mental impairment. The records do not indicate whether she was confined to a psychiatric hospital.

On 5 December 1980, Helen Moore was sentenced to life imprisonment for the murder of three children. She first suffocated her cousin, sixteen-month-old Susan McIntosh, whom she was babysitting. Nine months later she suffocated another child she was minding, twelve-month-old Vaughan Nicholson, and a month after that she attempted to kill Aaron Crocker, who survived the attack but was left blind and disabled. Within two months Moore had struck again, this time killing her seven-year-old half-brother, Peter Moore. When taken into questioning at the local Sydney police station, Moore readily confessed to Peter's murder. She was just seventeen years old.[10]

Helen Moore was born in 1962 and raised in poor circumstances in western Sydney. Her mother Jesse Moore reported that even as a young child her daughter was violent and destructive, tearing her toys apart. At the age of five she was molested by a group of boys at her school. Soon after, a psychiatric patient frightened her with sexual behaviour as she sat on the school bus. Already quite cold and distant in her emotional responses, Moore became more destructive and uncontrollable. Her parents' divorce when she was seven traumatised her further. At the age of thirteen, after she had attacked her brother and nearly tore his hair out by the scalp, Moore was taken to consult a psychiatrist. Rather than addressing the issue of her daughter's violence and anger, Jesse Moore was prescribed Valium to help her cope with her domestic and familial disorders. The implication was that Jesse's mothering and coping skills were at fault, rather than that Helen Moore was a deeply disturbed and possibly psychotic individual.

Five years later Jesse Moore remarried and had two more sons, Peter and Andrew. On 1 March 1979, when he was fourteen months old, Andrew died, apparently from cot death. Helen Moore later said: 'My life started to go wrong when Andrew died. I loved my brother Andrew. I don't know why he was taken away from me but when he was, something happened. Everything in my life went wrong and everything I did went wrong.'[11] She was, however, later charged with his murder before John Hiatt SM on 9 April 1980.[12]

Less than two months later Moore killed Susan McIntosh by holding her hand over the toddler's mouth. Her death was first thought to have also been caused by cot death, even though the syndrome most commonly occurs in infants under six months old. Later at her trial Moore bluntly told the court that 'she [Susan] didn't put up much of a struggle'. She also alleged that her uncle William McIntosh, Susan's father, had sexually abused her regularly from the age of eight until the time of his daughter's death and this was her revenge. He strenuously denied the allegation.

Moore's attempt to suffocate Vaughan Nicholson was not as successful. After her attempt to kill the one-year-old, Moore went back to watching television, only to hear him crying. Alarmed by this unplanned event, she called in a neighbour. Vaughan was admitted to Campbelltown Hospital where he was resuscitated. After these two incidents it is astonishing that anyone could still want Moore's babysitting services. But they did. Two-year-old Aaron Crocker was suffocated in the same manner as Vaughan. Even though he survived the brutal attack, tragically he was in a coma for two weeks and was left blind and crippled. Moore visited him at his bedside. He remained frail and died several years later.

Vaughan Nicholson survived a second attack while Moore was babysitting. By this time, though, people were becoming suspicious. Vaughan's parents started to wonder what pattern was emerging. Yet the thought that a local teenager was deliberately killing children was so unthinkable they put their qualms aside. On 24 February 1980, two-year-old Rachel Hay died suddenly while in Helen Moore's care. The Nicholsons now knew there was 'something very, very wrong going on'.[13] But they still didn't call the police. Five weeks later, on 31 March 1980, Moore rang her mother at work screaming that Peter had fallen down the stairs and killed himself. As soon as she got home, Jesse Moore went straight to the Nicholsons' house across the road in order to call the police. She too had harboured grave concerns about all the sudden and unexplained deaths of previously healthy children. In the police car with Helen after identifying Peter's body, Mrs Moore noticed all the scratches on her daughter's hands confirming her suspicions there had been a struggle before Peter died. She later said: 'Finally, I knew she had done it – she had killed them. I had been facing the terrible truth for so long and finally I knew.'[14]

Moore admitted killing her half-brother immediately. She told the police that she had grabbed him from behind while he was watching his favourite cartoon on television and attempted to suffocate him. He did not die quite as quickly or easily as the infants. It took a determined struggle over four minutes to suffocate him before she threw him down the stairs. Moore then went and had a shower before calling her mother and an ambulance, as investigating officer Sergeant D. Worsley testified.[15] The previous day she had taken Peter to the zoo, an event they both enjoyed. She also confessed to the other two murders and two attempted murders.

Her trial was held in the Supreme Court at Parramatta before Justice Adrian Roden in November 1980. Her counsel, John Marsden, was a highly respected and senior barrister. He argued that his client was insane and therefore not responsible for her actions. The eminent forensic psychiatrist Dr William Barclay diagnosed a borderline personality, suggesting that Moore was aware of what she was doing but unaware it was wrong. Dr Greta Goldberg, an experienced clinical and forensic psychologist, offered the opinion that the sexual abuse Moore suffered as a child and teenager had destroyed her normal development.[16]

The prosecution refuted these assessments. Forensic psychiatrist Dr Oscar Schmalzbach OBE, the founder of the Australian Academy of Forensic Sciences, told the court that Moore knew what she was doing and was not mentally ill. Her actions were deliberate, planned – if opportunistic – and persistent.[17] It took the jury just two hours to return a guilty verdict on all three counts of wilful murder and two counts of attempted murder. Helen Moore was sentenced to life imprisonment on each of the three murder counts and ten years for each of the attempted murder counts. After serving only twelve years Moore applied for a sentence review under new 'truth in sentencing' legislation. Justice Loveday reviewed her sentence on 4 September 1992, handing down a term of a minimum of thirteen years and nine months and a maximum of twenty-five years. She was released in 1993, and paroled until 2005 on the proviso she had no contact with any person under sixteen except under the most rigorous supervision. But two years after her release Moore gave birth to a daughter, which put the court in a quandary. Moore and her daughter were placed under twenty-four-hour supervision. There is now a complete media blackout on their current situation and whereabouts.

To contemplate killing one's own healthy, vibrant children with premeditation and deliberation is virtually unimaginable. But what if it is done for revenge? The story of Medea has long fascinated Western culture. The daughter of King Aeëtes of Colchis (modern-day Georgia), the granddaughter of Helios the sun god, she was later the wife of the hero Jason, famed for capturing the Golden Fleece with her wily help. In their decade-long marriage they had two children. They moved to Corinth, where Jason was convinced to abandon Medea for a younger woman, Glauce, King Creon's daughter. Medea not only murdered her rival but she killed her two children as revenge for Jason's betrayal.[18] The complete Medea story has many more elements of revenge, betrayal, murder and sadism, but at its heart is calculated filicide by an angry, vengeful woman who is prepared to go to unthinkable lengths – a story that continues to resonate in modern culture.

On 5 September 2005, Donna Fitchett made elaborate preparations to murder her two sons, Thomas, aged eleven, and Matthew, aged nine. At first she intended to take sedatives and jump with them off the cliffs at Sorrento in Victoria. Her next abandoned plan was to kill the boys with benzodiazepines and then commit suicide by decapitation with a chain saw. She wrote a long letter to her psychologist explaining what had led to these monstrous thoughts and plans. She posted the letter, and then Donna Fitchett came home and drugged her children. Thomas was then strangled with a sock and left in the marital bedroom, dressed only in a tee shirt. When Matthew woke up confused and groggy, crying because he had wet the bed, Fitchett changed his bed linen and clothes, and settled him down with his teddy bear. She then placed a pillow over his head to kill him. When the family pet, a Rottweiler named Gemma, tried to save his little companion, Fitchett took her outside, tied her up, and returned to the bedroom where she proceeded to strangle Matthew. She then took a non-fatal dose of benzodiazepine and wrote a letter to her husband, David Fitchett. When he returned home later he found his sons dead. Fitchett survived her ingestion of sleeping tablets.[19]

This horror happened in a middle-class suburb of Melbourne; those involved the most unlikely candidates for such calculated destruction and revenge.

Donna Fitchett was born in the outer Melbourne suburb of Doveton, near Dandenong, in 1959. She attended a Catholic school, leaving in Year 11 to undertake nursing training at St Vincent's Hospital in Melbourne from 1976 to 1978. By the time she met David Fitchett in 1990 she was an experienced and capable nurse. They married in 1993 and had Thomas in 1994 and then Matthew two years later. At first Fitchett continued to work. In 2002 she lost her job at a health clinic in Canterbury and retrained as an options trader. The start-up cost of $150,000 for this risky venture was secured as a loan against equity in the Fitchetts' house in Balwyn North. David Fitchett encouraged his wife's new career move.

After each of her children was born, Fitchett had suffered undiagnosed postnatal depression.[20] Later she was diagnosed with Hashimoto's thyroiditis and an early menopausal hormonal depression. These conditions led to depression, mood swings, tiredness and feelings of confusion. She was prescribed treatment by her local general practitioner, who did not think that psychiatric care was appropriate.[21] The Fitchetts' marriage deteriorated as Fitchett's health and judgment increasingly worsened. Donna Fitchett became obsessed with the relationship her husband had with their sons; she was convinced that he was a lax, uncaring and largely absent father. She blamed his long hours at work and his commitment to playing golf. There was no substantive evidence to support this perception, but the debt on their house was a pressing and constant concern.

In June 2004, Fitchett decided to deal with her problems by consulting psychologist Patra Antonis, which she did on thirty-seven occasions. During the course of her therapy Fitchett came to believe that her husband had a 'passive aggressive' personality and therefore would not change what she believed was selfish, procrastinating behaviour. From early 2005 her depression intensified to such an extent that she spent a lot of time under the blankets in bed. She was not treated for this escalation in her symptoms. David Fitchett was left to eat alone; their sexual life ceased, and they began living in separate bedrooms. On 30 August 2005 Fitchett decided to terminate this unhappy relationship. She told Antonis that she needed to engage in methodical planning, and by this Antonis assumed her client meant financial planning rather than the destructive course she undertook.

When Fitchett informed her husband of her intentions to leave him, their conversation was one-sided. She refused to listen to his point of view or take his feelings into account. When he told her it would be difficult for him to fund two homes, she reacted badly. She had no employment; her job as an options trader was dependent on the line of credit taken out on the marital home, a situation that would be terminated if divorce ensued and the property divided. David Fitchett told her in a moment of anger that 'it would have been better off you had never had the boys'.[22] Many separating couples vent their anger, hurt and disappointment, and what is said is often regretted when tempers cool and more rational judgment is restored, but could this have been the flash point that triggered the lethal attacks?

The next day was Father's Day and Fitchett told her husband that 'he had better ensure he enjoyed it because it would be the last he would have with them as the family'.

With her husband and the children out for the day, Fitchett cleaned the house 'obsessively, including putting some of the boys' clothing into garbage bags'.[23] It was as if the boys had somehow already disappeared and the vestiges of their presence needed to be removed. The following day, she kept the boys home from school to prepare, as they thought, for a wonderful trip. She visited her sister, Louise Mitchell, who described her behaviour as 'distraught' in the later court proceedings. She attributed this to the imminent marriage break-up. On the next morning, at 5.37am Fitchett emailed her other sister, Susan Buckley, declaring her love for her but making disparaging remarks about their father. Eight minutes later she contacted another sister, Marie Ryan, to apologise for not being able to attend their family Christmas lunch although no arrangements had yet been made. Later in the morning Fitchett dropped some things off at Louise Mitchell's house.[24]

Fitchett then wrote to Antonis saying that she 'was determined to lie, to cheat, be selfish and greedy in order to claim whatever I could in order to start a new life with Thomas and Matthew. Who was I kidding? ... I don't know how to be selfish or greedy ... Sadly I am too broken to go on. Today the boys will be given an overdose as I cannot and wouldn't ever abandon them ... They think they are going on an exciting trip today but I've told them they need to take some medicine so they won't get airsick. I'm not a coward – nor am I crazy. I see this as my greatest act of love. I am not punishing David. I pity him.'[25] She ended her letter 'Hugs and kisses, Donna'.

The letter she wrote to David Fitchett was composed after she had murdered their sons. It was equally callous and delusional. She told him: 'I didn't do it because I'm angry with you. I forgive you for whatever hurt you have caused me. You can't help it. I just couldn't abandon our beautiful boys. I have been dead for a few days and I just wanted peace. I overdosed the boys and when they were asleep I suffocated them and then strangled them in case they woke up, they put up a bit of a struggle but said nothing they didn't know it was me or what was happening to each other. They were happy this morning and said they loved you and had a great father's day ... please take care of the animals especially Gemma ...' Evidence provided at the trial reported that Fitchett had changed Matthew's soiled pyjamas and bed linen before she killed him as she was loath to think anyone would regard her as a 'bad mother'.

David Fitchett returned home on the evening of 6 September 2005 to find his sons dead. He unsuccessfully tried to resuscitate them. Fitchett, who had also cut her arms, neck and groin, went and lay down in Thomas's room until she was taken to Box Hill Hospital under guard for psychiatric assessment. She was committed involuntarily to the Thomas Embling Hospital, where she was considered a high suicide risk. On 17 November, Fitchett was transferred to the women's maximum-security prison. Seven weeks later, Fitchett attempted suicide again and was readmitted to the psychiatric hospital. This pattern reoccurred, even though she was prescribed heavy antidepressants. Fitchett was victimised by the other prisoners and by

Chillingly, in 2005, on the verge of marital separation, Donna Fitchett warned her husband to make the most of Father's Day. It turned out to be the last time he saw his sons alive. Photo: Newspix NPX1101424.

the correctional staff in prison. Child killers and molesters rank on the lowest level in any prison's hierarchy; a woman who kills her own children is the lowest of the low.

In the trial held in the Supreme Court of Victoria in May 2008, Justice Geoffrey Nettle was on the bench, and Fitchett was defended by Graham Thomas SC, funded by Victorian Legal Aid. Often crying through his ordeal, David Fitchett testified about finding his sons cold and lifeless. He had last seen them happy and playful on Father's Day, a symbolic point that his wife had planned. For the rest of his life, Father's Day would cause him unimaginable pain and grief.

One of the key points of the trial concerned Fitchett's mental state at the time of the offences. The leading expert witness, Professor Paul Mullen, the emeritus professor of Forensic Psychiatry at Monash University, testified that Fitchett was suffering from a major depressive illness that rendered her incapable of understanding the consequences of her actions. Dr Daniel Sullivan, the Assistant Clinical Director of the Victorian Institute of Forensic Mental Health, argued that she was aware of the wrongfulness of her actions but considered that Fitchett was convinced she had acted in her sons' best interests. The expert testimony provided by Dr Yvonne Skinner, a consulting psychiatrist from New South Wales, on the other hand, argued that Fitchett was not seriously depressed at the time of the commission of the crimes – but that her depression had occurred when she realised the enormity and permanence of her crimes afterwards. She asserted that the prisoner fully understood her actions were wrong. The jury inclined towards this opinion in its verdict.

In his sentencing report, Justice Nettle was convinced that Fitchett was 'motivated by spousal revenge which [she] knew to be wrong'. He noted that at no time did the prisoner accept responsibility for her actions, relying totally upon a defence of mental impairment under the Victorian *Crimes (Mental Impairment and Unfitness to be Tried) Act* of 1997. Donna Fitchett was sentenced to seventeen years' imprisonment on each count of murder, with a seven-year sentence imposed on the second count to be served concurrently with count one, thereby reducing the total sentence of incarceration to twenty-four years. A non-parole period was set at eighteen years.[26] Nettle further ordered that Fitchett should be sent to a psychiatric hospital under a security order.

In April 2009, Fitchett appealed her sentence in the Supreme Court of Victoria Court of Appeal. Represented again by a Victorian Legal Aid-appointed barrister, Patrick Tehan QC, her appeal on the basis of her mental impairment was heard by justices Peter Buchanan, Frank Vincent AO and David Ashley. In the appeal, additional testimony emerged that Thomas had told other people that he wished to live with his father and not his mother, countering his mother's belief that her husband was an aloof and uncaring father. Whether Donna Fitchett was aware of her son's preference was not clear in the testimony.

The Court of Appeal found that the trial judge had erred in his instructions to the jury concerning the defence of mental impairment. A retrial was ordered.[27] The following year, Fitchett was retried before Justice Elizabeth Curtain in the Victorian Supreme Court, again represented by Patrick Tehan. The jury once more found her guilty on both counts of wilful murder. In her sentencing report, Justice Curtain emphasised how Fitchett had told the ambulance officers who came to the murder scene: 'I don't want to go to hospital. I've killed my boys. I just want to die.' While in prison, Fitchett tried to commit suicide four times and was on constant suicide watch. Her counsel reiterated that Fitchett was treated with 'disdain and absolute revulsion by the other prisoners'. She had been constantly bullied, belittled and assaulted. However, Justice Curtain also pointed to Fitchett's 'unfathomable selfishness', saying that her crimes were 'truly appalling and offensive to civilised society'.

Donna Fitchett was once again sentenced to thirty-four years' imprisonment, with a non-parole period of eighteen years. She will be nearly seventy when she is released.

CHAPTER 10

Poisoners of the Nineteenth Century

Rightly or wrongly, over the centuries women have been famed as poisoners – names such as Lucrezia Borgia have echoed through the ages. Poison has been used as a weapon when secrecy is paramount, often in a domestic setting, administered in food, drink and medicine. Family members were frequently the target.

But in nineteenth- and early twentieth-century Britain, the crime was peculiarly dominated by male medical practitioners such as Dr Thomas Cream, who murdered seven prostitutes; Dr Henry Lawson, a morphine addict who killed for financial gain using antinomy; Dr George Chapman, who murdered three women, each of whom believed she was his wife; and, most famously, Dr Hawley Crippen, who murdered his wife with hyoscin hydrobromide. Perhaps it wasn't so strange, given the easy and unquestioned access to drugs, poisons and narcotics that doctors have. In weighing the Hippocratic oath against financial gain or psychopathic tendencies, venality might just be the winner. In the late twentieth century, Dr Harold Shipman murdered many of his elderly patients with injections of narcotics. He was convicted of the murder of fifteen patients, although it is possible he murdered 200 more.

It was also not strange that few cases of poisoning were heard in the English courts in the eighteenth century. The symptoms of widespread diseases such as typhoid and cholera are similar to those of poisoning, and the sciences of toxicology and forensic pathology had not yet emerged.[1] This changed in 1803 under Lord Ellenborough's new *Offences against the Person Act*, which dealt with poisoning as well as proscriptions against induced abortions.[2] Early studies in toxicology had taken some time to appear: Samuel Farr's groundbreaking text, *A Short View of the Extent and Importance of Medical Jurisprudence*, was published in 1798; and George Male's textbook, *Treatise on Judicial or Forensic Medical Medicine; for the use of medical men, coroners and barristers*, first released in 1816, was the first creditable book in the discipline.[3] The isolation of the lethal poison strychnine from an Indian tree in 1819 gave impetus to further research into toxins and poisons.[4]

Two years later, in 1821, three important cases in England, in which the accused were each found guilty of murder by the use of arsenic, were examples of a marked increase in the prevalence of these trials. That year Dr J. G. Smith of the Westminster Hospital in London published a comprehensive textbook. There emerged expert witnesses in the form of chemists, apothecaries, and medical practitioners who had some training in forensic medicine.[5]

The first case of poisoning came not long after, in 1824, when Mary Ann Bradley was charged before the Supreme Court of New South Wales with poisoning her husband John Bradley. She was accused of using arsenic to kill him; but despite overwhelming evidence the military jury found her 'not guilty'. Arsenic had been first advertised in the colony in September 1823.[6] Fifty years later, a woman *did* go to the gallows, even though this time she may not have been guilty of poisoning her husband. Elizabeth Woolcock, hanged in Adelaide in 1873, was the only woman ever executed in South Australia, even though thirty-two executions had preceded hers.[7] Woolcock had been convicted of murdering her violent husband, Thomas Woolcock, by mercury poisoning. An examination of the documents suggests that her conviction for murder was tainted because the Woolcocks' drug-addicted medical practitioner, Dr Thomas Bull, may inadvertently have been at fault from incompetence.

Elizabeth Oliver was born to John and Elizabeth Oliver in 1848 in the rough South Australian mining settlement of Burra, 160 kilometres north of Adelaide. The Olivers had arrived in the new colony just five years earlier and lived in extreme poverty in rooms cut into the banks of the Kooringa Creek. Cornish-born John Oliver worked for 'the Monster Mine', one of the copper mines that had opened in 1845. When strikes and loss of production at the mine proved a disappointment for its owners and investors, workers such as Oliver, who had also lost all his possessions in a flash flood, decided they had better prospects when the Victorian goldfields opened in 1851. The family, which now included two other children, relocated to Ballarat, a town Elizabeth Oliver detested, describing it as 'this horrid, sin-stained colony of scoundrels and villains'.[8] The monthly mining licence of 30 shillings placed immense financial strain on unsuccessful prospectors like John Oliver. After infant daughter Catherine died from the prevalent dysentery, Elizabeth Oliver departed for Adelaide with another man, leaving her daughter Elizabeth to be raised by her father and neighbours. John Oliver moved to the Creswick diggings to try his luck in early 1853, and four-year-old Elizabeth was left on her own with only a kind neighbour, Bridget Darcy, to keep an eye on her.[9]

In the long confession she wrote just before she was executed, Woolcock outlined her chaotic childhood, during which she did not see her mother from the time she was four until she was eighteen. That she was even partially literate was unusual for a poor child living an itinerant life. Her father died from tuberculosis when she was nine, prompting her to earn a living as a maid to a pharmacist in Melbourne. What she did not disclose in her confession was that at just six years old she had witnessed the murder of her father's friend, Henry Powell, by police as an act of retaliation for taking part in the Eureka Rebellion in 1854. Arthur Akehurst, the clerk of the court at Ballarat, along with 'other persons unknown', was accused of murdering Powell by gunshot and sabre cuts. The persons unknown were mounted police who, in a show of the Crown's force, trampled Powell's body as he lay dying.[10]

The following year, when she was seven, Elizabeth Oliver was raped and left for dead by George Shaughshaw, an Indian itinerant. The criminal case was heard before the inaugural Chief Justice of the Supreme Court of Victoria, Sir William à Beckett (1806–69) in sittings in Geelong in January 1855. He described it as 'one of the most atrocious crimes to be brought before me'. The prisoner received the death sentence.[11] Elizabeth Oliver suffered serious and permanent gynaecological damage that rendered her infertile, and she was subject to constant pain for the rest of her life, for which doctors prescribed opium. Working for Mr Lees in his pharmacy since the age of nine, the girl had easy access to strong doses of opium, although it should be remembered that opium was a common ingredient in many patent medicines, as well as being readily available over the counter in Victorian chemist shops at the time.

At the age of fifteen Elizabeth moved back to Ballarat with a large stash of opium. She began working as a maid in a guesthouse, but also supplied opium to prostitutes intent upon robbing their clients. Despite her illegal activities, Elizabeth Oliver continued to attend the Wesleyan Chapel. With the help of William Goldsworthy, a visiting lay preacher who knew her mother in South Australia, she was reunited with her maternal family. Her mother wrote to her in 1865, expressing great sorrow about how she had treated her daughter and begging her to join her at Moonta Mine. Elizabeth Oliver wrote in her confession: 'I thought I should like to see my mother and have a home like other young girls so I gave up my situation and came to Adelaide. My mother and my stepfather received me very kindly and I had a good home for two years …'[12] She worked as a housekeeper, and taught Sunday school at the Wesleyan Church on the weekends.[13] For a while she weaned herself off her addiction since pure opium was far harder to obtain in South Australia than it had been in Victoria. In South Australia a doctor's prescription was required. Then, when her employers, Mary and Robert Slape, decided to engage a relative, she lost her job.

She met her husband, Cornish miner Thomas Woolcock, in 1866. His wife, Nanny Woolcock, and Francis, one of his sons, had died from fever the previous year and he engaged Oliver as his housekeeper. Hypocritically, given that he had run off with her married mother, Oliver's stepfather, William Williams, was outraged by this arrangement and insisted that Elizabeth and Woolcock marry. She revealed in her confession that he threatened to 'break both my legs. I was afraid he would keep his word as I never knew him to tell a wilful lie …'. This would imply that her stepfather was a violent and abusive man. Thomas Woolcock was also a violent man, addicted to drink and to beating his new wife and his child. Three years later, in 1869, Woolcock's mother and stepfather moved to Adelaide, leaving Elizabeth without a family network to rely upon.

In early 1870 Woolcock left her husband but returned when he promised to stop drinking. The promise was short-lived. Like many perpetrators of domestic violence he 'did not like to part with his money for anything else [but alcohol]'. Her subsequent attempts to leave him were defeated by parental pressure and lack of money. After three years of bad treatment, Woolcock's desperation was so acute she attempted to hang herself. The roof beam broke under the strain and she survived. Unable even to kill herself, Woolcock became still more frustrated and desperate, and started to rely on opium again, despite how difficult it was to obtain.

Thomas Woolcock was illiterate, like most other miners. He supplemented his earnings by diagnosing sick animals, although he left it to his wife to do the actual work. She was constantly at the local chemist obtaining medicines for the animals. Attending to ailing animals was still not sufficient to make ends meet so Thomas Woolcock decided to accept lodgers. A boarder named Thomas Pascoe took up residence in the small home, although the arrangement did not last after Thomas Woodcock became aggressive without provocation. Pascoe was appalled by how Elizabeth Woolcock and her little stepson were treated. Of course, Woolcock decided this was because his lodger had an interest in his young wife. Pascoe had to go. Soon after he left, the family dog was poisoned – believed to be from strychnine – and Pascoe was suspected of the cowardly act.

In her trial the alleged affair was proffered as her motive for eliminating her husband.[14] Despite it constituting no proof of an illicit relationship, the testimony of a neighbour, Frances Carpenter, that Pascoe visited Woolcock during the day when her husband was working at the mine was given credence.[15] That Carpenter was an extremely hostile witness against the young widow at the trial did not provoke concern.

On 23 July 1873, within a month of Pascoe's departure, Thomas Woolcock became seriously ill with severe stomach pains. Elizabeth Woolcock consulted three doctors, who all diagnosed different causes: Dr Thomas Bull prescribed a third of a grain of mercury for Woolcock's 'sore throat'; while Dr John Dickie recommended cream of tartar and rhubarb tablets for stomach problems. At the trial in December 1873, the third, Dr Lloyd Herbert, stated that when he visited Thomas Woolcock on 1 August, the ailing patient was suffering from severe thirst, excessive salivation and a sore throat. Herbert diagnosed 'salivation by mercury'. He continued treatment for thirteen days until Thomas Woolcock informed him that he could no longer afford him and would be returning to his Lodge practitioner, Dr Dickie, who treated him for nothing. (Miners at this time subscribed to medical and pharmaceutical benefits through organisations such as the Oddfellows Lodge.) Dr Herbert also said that Woolcock was already 'not a well man'; he had kidney disease, among other life-threatening complaints including tuberculosis. No doubt his excessive drinking undermined his health.

Elizabeth Woolcock decided to call in Dr Bull once more, despite the resistance of her husband, who said: 'I certainly don't want Dr Bull again, as it was his medicine that made me bad in the first place.' Neighbour Jane Nicholls testified that during his illness Woolcock's tongue became black and that he was vehemently opposed to any further consultation by Dr Bull.[16] This corroborates Dr Herbert's evidence that it was the ingestion of mercury – in other words, Bull's treatment – that had poisoned Thomas Woolcock.

The pharmacist in Moonta, John Opie, testified that he had frequently supplied Elizabeth Woolcock with morphine, which she initially pretended was to clean her curtains and linen. She also sent her young stepson, Thomas, along with notes to request more doses, as well as going herself in the company of a neighbour, Mrs Hannah Blight. Opie told the court that eventually he had to refuse. Then, under a false name, Woolcock sent for laudanum, a tincture of opium.[17] Such hopeless attempts at deceit in a small community where everyone knew everybody else demonstrate her desperation. Charles Rooke, the assistant manager of Birk's Chemist, also testified to her attempts to obtain narcotics. Other witnesses at her trial reported that it was well known that she was a drug addict who would use increasingly bizarre measures to ensure her supply. The testimony of expert witnesses such as these chemists had significant consequences for the outcome of her murder trial.

When Thomas Woolcock died on 4 September 1873, Dr Dickie provided a death certificate that stated he had died from 'pure exhaustion from prolonged vomiting and purging'. Thomas Woolcock's cousin, Elizabeth Snell, believed he had been poisoned and pressured for more investigations. Rumours saying that Elizabeth Woolcock was a drug addict who had poisoned her husband buzzed about the small mining settlement, but so did stories that he was known to be abusive and violent towards her.

An autopsy by doctors Dickie, Gosse and Herbert was conducted in the Woolcocks' house while Elizabeth Woolcock stood outside. Large quantities of mercury were detected in the remains. As well, it appeared that Woolcock had been suffering from tuberculosis and had dysentery at the time of his death. This would account for some of the symptoms he had presented to the three medical practitioners.

Fearful of losing his professional reputation, Dr Dickie ordered an inquest into the death, which was held at Moonta court house before a large panel of fourteen jurors, all of whom were hostile towards the deceased's wife. At the inquest the fact that Dr Bull had prescribed the mercury was completely overlooked. When proceedings concluded, Elizabeth Woolcock was placed under arrest for the wilful murder of her husband, and taken to Wallaroo jail in Adelaide.

The three-day trial in the Supreme Court of South Australia commenced on Wednesday, 3 December 1873, and was followed avidly by the public, with large crowds each day skirmishing to get a seat in the gallery. Those who did not, milled outside the courtroom waiting for developments to be relayed outside. The case was presided over by Justice William Wearing QC (1816–75). Prosecuting for the Crown was the solicitor-general, Richard Andrews QC (1823–84), who had served as attorney-general under Premier Sir Robert Torrens.[18] Woolcock was represented pro bono by London-trained barrister Dr James Cholmondeley Kaufmann, who ran a large criminal practice. The first witness was George Francis, an analytical chemist, who testified that he had examined specimens sent to him by Moonta police, and found large quantities of mercury. In a defence far more sophisticated and informed than that of the crown prosecutor, Dr Kaufmann attempted to refute Francis's claims by consulting the standard textbooks on forensic jurisprudence, *On Poisons in Relation to Medical Jurisprudence and Medicine* (1848) and *The Principles and Practices of Medical Jurisprudence* (1865), both by Alfred Swaine Taylor.

Much of the testimony from the residents of Moonta was highly critical of and antagonistic towards Elizabeth Woolcock, who was, in their eyes, an adulterer and a drug addict. Yet no one had witnessed Woolcock give her husband any mercury preparations other than those prescribed by Dr Bull. A letter to her family in Adelaide dated 10 April, in which Woolcock revealed all the abuse and ill treatment she had endured during her short marriage, was tendered in evidence against her.[19] It was believed to provide a motive for her actions. Until 1898 – twenty-five years into the future – an accused person could not testify in court to defend themselves, so often all a defence counsel could do was try to refute points made by the prosecution rather than presenting a coherent counter-case. In her meagre defence, her stepson testified that 'Mother', as he called her, had tended his father with great care.

It only took twenty minutes for the jury to find Elizabeth Woolcock guilty of the wilful murder of her husband. She was sentenced to death. The sentence caused considerable debate in the colony since no woman – especially one of only twenty-five – had ever been put to death there. Awaiting her execution in Adelaide jail, Woolcock was attended by the Reverend James Bickford (1816–95), a former missionary,[20] whose spiritual counsel and guidance were assiduous. Under his persuasion, Woolcock made her last statement and confession in which she wrote that 'Satan tempted me … I was so ill-treated that I was quite out of my mind and in an evil hour I yielded to the temptation …'. She gave Bickford the sealed letter as she walked calmly to the gallows on 30 December 1873. It was later published verbatim in the newspapers. She wore 'a plain white dress and carried in her hands a bunch of flowers'. The Reverend Bicknell walked to the gallows with her, comforting her with prayers and readings from the Bible.[21]

In her confession, Woolcock wrote that she had given her husband 'powder' that she believed contained poisons. She was most likely referring to a treatment for ringworm that had been procured for the dog, which contained small quantities of mercury. She elaborated that she took the powder herself to no ill effect. At the trial, expert evidence indicated this veterinary preparation was insufficient to kill a person.

At no other time, it appears, did Woolcock dose her husband with mercury drugs other than those prescribed by Thomas Bull. Later, whispers surfaced that the doctor was addicted to atropine, a drug used to treat eye diseases; that he had regularly overused various other drugs such as chloroform, opium and sulphuric ether. Dr John Dickie testified at the inquest into Bull's demise that the deceased had taken large quantities of belladonna and other narcotics.[22]

At the time he was visiting Woolcock, Bull was confused and muddled. He could certainly have prescribed an incorrect dosage of medication. Although he had studied at the University of Cambridge, Bull had undertaken his licensed medical studies as an apothecary, by then an old-fashioned route to professional qualification. He made up his own medicines for patients rather than providing them with prescriptions to be dispensed by a chemist.[23] Had a pharmacist checked and dispensed his prescription, any errors of dosage would have been noted and verified. Woolcock himself believed that Bull had been the cause of his rapid decline. Because of his addictions Bull was confined to a lunatic asylum after the trial and committed suicide soon afterwards.

Nor did Woolcock ever criticise or accuse his wife of attempting to kill him, even though he had had ample opportunity to do so in front of his family, workmates and neighbours. It is notable that Chief Justice Way wrote to relatives in England that the medical evidence in this capital case was 'unreliable' and even 'mistaken'.[24] Yet once she was found guilty, he had no other choice than to sentence her to death. John Dickie's professional reputation was ruined by the trial and he relocated in shame to Tasmania. Justice Wearing drowned in a shipwreck fifteen months after the trial.

In May 2004 a mock trial by students at the University of Adelaide's Law Week recreated the Woolcock prosecution – and unanimously found her 'not guilty'.[25]

By the 1880s, the expansion of insurance to cover working-class families provided another motive for murder by poison for the more ruthless and mercenary. Friendly societies and lodges began offering small weekly payments to relieve men's unemployment in England from the 1730s. They were slower to establish themselves in the new Australian colonies since there was little potential custom during the convict era. When free settlement began in earnest, however, the friendly societies soon followed. The first, the Oddfellows Lodge, was established in Sydney in 1836 by a far-sighted bookseller and engraver, William Moffitt.[26] Manchester Unity, a breakaway organisation, set up operations in Sydney in 1845. The successful draper David Jones was one of the founders of the Australian Mutual Provident Society in Sydney in 1849. In the absence of welfare benefits, government services, and hospital admission via subscription to the friendly societies and lodges, any severe illness, incapacity or unemployment affecting the breadwinner could plunge working families into dire poverty with alarming speed. At first only tradesmen could afford the premiums. But as relative affluence began to spread with the economic boom that had begun in the goldfields in the 1850s, and extended into the 1880s with a growth in manufacturing and a boom in investment and speculation, workers on more modest wages were able to afford premiums to cover illness, pharmaceuticals, unemployment and death. Life insurance did not simply cover the life of the breadwinner but could be taken out for all family members, including children.

Although it was hardly a novel epithet, Louisa Collins became known as the 'Botany Bay Borgia' when, motivated by passion and financial gain, she killed her two husbands in the late 1880s. In the United States in the 1860s and 1870s, there had been some other husband-murdering 'Borgias': Lydia Sherman progressively murdered three husbands, a stepdaughter and from six to eight of her own children, largely for insurance money. The press dubbed her the 'Borgia of Connecticut'. In the following decade Sarah Jane Robinson poisoned several of her children and relatives for insurance money. Robinson was popularly termed the 'Borgia of Massachusetts'. Like Sherman she died in prison serving a commuted capital sentence because the progressive north-eastern states baulked at executing women, no matter how terrible their crimes.[27] Judicial chivalry was not extended to Australia's own modern Lucrezia Borgia, for Louisa Collins was executed on 8 January 1889 after four separate and controversial trials.

Collins was born in 1849 to Henry and Catherine Hall. The couple worked on 'Belltrees', the profitable pastoral property near Scone in the Hunter Valley in New South Wales run by James White, who had leased the property the previous year from the prominent lawyer and parliamentarian, William Charles Wentworth.[28] The Hall family believed they were related to the 'gentleman bushranger' Ben Hall, who had been born in Maitland in 1837 to former convict parents.

Louisa Hall was a beautiful child with blonde curls and big alert eyes. From an early age she was aware of the attention her physical attractiveness brought her. She went into domestic service at nearby Merriwa, a small township to the west of nearby Scone. The men of the district soon noticed her and she was rumoured to be a provocative flirt. Indeed, rumours spread that she was far more than a flirt and offered more than a chaste kiss. Her good looks and teasing personality attracted the attentions of a thirty-six-year-old widower, Charles Andrews, who ran a successful butchering business. Her mother, no doubt fearful of scandal, especially if Louisa produced an illegitimate baby, pressured her to marry this quiet and industrious man with whom she had nothing in common. And so they married on 28 August 1865.

The couple moved to Waterloo in Sydney where Andrews had been raised. He found work initially as a carrier for Lord's Mill until it closed. They then moved into a small cottage at 10 Popple's Terrace in Botany, a rather desolate spot reached by crossing a wooden bridge spanning a fetid swamp. This whole area was deemed a 'noxious trade area', with its wool-scouring factories and tanneries that pumped out hazardous waste. With seven children and no close neighbours or family near her, life for Louisa Andrews became monotonous, lonely and alienating. As the belle of Merriwa she had expected far more, believing her good looks and sex appeal would elevate her from a life of domestic drudgery. She countered the monotony by frequently visiting the Pier Hotel on Botany Road, where she tried to relive her days as a sex siren. By now she was 'pleasantly plump, with bold good looks and a flighty disposition'.[29] But she was more than 'flighty' and flirtatious — she openly engaged in sexual liaisons with hotel patrons, causing gossip around the district. Charles Andrews apparently did nothing about her absences and behaviour, never criticising his wife in public.

Their income had fallen when Andrews left the butchering trade, but, with seven children to support, Louisa Andrews insisted they find ways to supplement the family's resources. The first option was to take in boarders. Rumours began to spread again that the landlady was engaging in sexual encounters while her husband was at work. Charles Andrews continued to maintain his silence, at least in public, wearing the humiliation of being a cuckold to a pretty and much younger wife with considerable dignity.[30]

When Louisa Andrews met labourer Michael (Mick) Collins in 1886 at the Pier Hotel she asked him to come and live at her house as a boarder. He was then twenty-two years old, fourteen years younger than Andrews, handsome and well built. She later described him in a letter to her mother as '… tall and handsome, he was good, loving, attentive, sober and honest … '.[31] He worked at a local wool-washing shed, earning a small wage. Collins settled in, and around the district became known as Louisa Andrew's accepted paramour. They were seen at the hotel, on the steam tram, and walking along the unpaved roads holding hands, embracing and kissing.[32]

Nine days before Christmas 1886, Charles Andrews reached the end of his tolerance and he vented years of resentment and humiliation when he got into a fight with his young boarder. After the altercation he evicted Collins, throwing all his belongings into the street. Louisa Andrews went straight to the local police station to report her husband's behaviour and seek their assistance. Given the current laws and prevailing attitudes towards the marital home in the 1880s, Constable Jeffs suggested that she calm down, go home and attempt to make peace with her outraged husband.

Louisa Andrews raged against her husband's lack of earning power, forgetting he could earn far more in his trade. He had worked hard to maintain her and their children, although by now the eldest son,

Herbert, lived in Maitland, and Rueben and Arthur were also self-supporting but still living at home.

Louisa Andrews decided to remedy her unhappy situation and forge a new life for herself while she still maintained a semblance of her looks. Around this time, she asked the local draper, a Mr Bullock, about the time lapse between death and an insurance claim.

On Friday 28 January, Charles Andrews told Bullock he would drop some good-quality pork around to him the following day. He failed to show up but the draper thought little of it. By Monday, Andrews was seriously ill, telling his local doctor, Thomas Martin, that he had terrible stomach pains. Gastric complaints and diarrhoea, however, were common in the squalid environment of the Frog's Hollow slum in hot summer. On top of that, his first trade of butchering was known to take place in a dangerous environment because of the poisonous chemicals it used.[33] And the local tanneries used oxalic acid, which was known to be deadly from 1829 when Robert Christison published his landmark textbook on toxicology, the *Treatise on Poisons: In Relation to Medical Jurisprudence, Physiology, and the Practice of Physic*. Arsenic was also used to produce the colour green in wallpapers, a device that Agatha Christie later employed to kill a victim in *The Blue Geranium* (1932). While the rough shanty of the Andrews family did not run to such bourgeois adornment as wallpaper, in his work Andrews dealt extensively with arsenic, and with lead.[34] Despite this combination of factors, Dr Martin did not think that poison was involved when he issued a death certificate for Charles Andrews, who died on Friday, 4 February 1887.

Louisa Andrews acted swiftly, catching the tram into the city centre, literally while her husband's body was still warm. With indecent haste, she was intent upon getting his insurance money – the considerable sum of £200 – from the Australian Widows' Fund.

The same lack of emotion was on display when a neighbour, a Mrs Price, asked how her husband was getting on. Andrews replied: 'Oh, he's dead. I'd like you to help me lay him out for the funeral.'[35] Even though it was normal to wear heavy black mourning clothes for at least a year in the late nineteenth century, her next move was to order some brightly coloured material from the draper. When he expressed his disapproval of this choice for a new widow, she dismissed his concerns, telling him: 'I can mourn Charlie in my heart without having to carry my grief in my clothes.' Three days later Louisa Andrews invited all her friends from the hotel to join her in a wild and noisy all-night party at her home. She had still not told her eldest son, Herbert, about his father's death and nor did she give him any of the insurance money.

Mick Collins moved in again soon after the funeral and became the acknowledged man of the house. On 9 April 1887 Collins and Louisa Andrews married at St Silas Church of England in Waterloo. The bride declared she was twenty-eight years of age instead of the actual thirty-eight. The couple then moved with her children to a small house at Johnson Lane, North Botany. Soon into the marriage, however, she realised she had made a disastrous choice; Collins, unlike her first husband, wasn't keen on working for a living, believing he was entitled to live off her insurance claim. Furthermore, he drank heavily and gambled at every opportunity. He went through her insurance claim with alarming rapidity. She produced a baby seven months into the legal union, presumably conceived while Andrews was still alive – Collins always acknowledged the boy as his child – but he died at the age of five months. Louisa Collins did not appear upset or concerned. She began drinking heavily again at the Pier Hotel and complaining to anyone who would listen that she had tied herself to a 'loafer' and a 'wastrel'. Mick Collins eventually roused himself to get a job, which paid 36/- per week.

A solution to Louisa Collins's disappointments was at hand. Once again poison would be the remedy. Her second husband was not insured, but he undoubtedly knew what had happened to her first husband and therefore she couldn't just leave him. Mick Collins began to suffer extremely painful abdominal seizures. He took to his bed, keeping his trousers on him at all times. Dr George Marshall was called in. He conferred with his colleague Dr Martin, who had treated Charles Andrews, and both attended to the now-dying man. Believing that to have two husbands fall ill with the same symptoms tested credibility, Dr Marshall took samples from the sick man, and the medicine by the bedside, for testing on 4 July 1888.[36] When the police were called in on the doctor's advice, Collins told them he didn't think he was being poisoned. Mick Collins died in agony on 8 July 1888.

This time, there were suspicions that he had not died naturally. The police found a glass containing a small amount of arsenic in the sickroom and, in a cupboard, the product 'Rough on Rats', a poison that could be found in any home at the time. Spurred by the information provided by Dr Martin, Dr Marshall refused to provide a death certificate.[37]

An inquest convened at the Sydney morgue before the city coroner Henry Shiell, and a jury of twelve men was concluded on 10 July 1888. Doctors Marshall and Martin were key witnesses. Marshall now argued that Charles Andrews might have died from arsenic poisoning. He also testified that Louisa Collins was an 'apathetic nurse', careless and constantly 'the worse for drink'. The government analyst, William Hamlet, testified he had found sufficient arsenic in Collins's stomach to cause death. Contrary evidence was produced that, during his short illness Collins had many visitors, some assisting Louisa Collins nurse her husband. No one saw anything untoward or improper. Collins argued that her husband had been depressed for some time due to a pain in the groin, and took medicine that may have contained poisons. Patent medicines to 'cure' syphilis contained arsenic so what she said may have been true. During the hearing she remained stoical, almost detached, which was used against her to prove she was callous and lacking in womanly feelings.[38]

On 14 July the coroner opened another inquiry, this time into the death of Charles Andrews. After exhumation his body was found to contain faint traces of arsenic. The body of the baby was also disinterred but was not found to contain any poison. Two weeks later the coroner ordered Louisa Collins to stand trial for the wilful murder of her two husbands.[39] She was taken into custody, although not under warrant, later that evening. She was drunk when the police arrived at her home at 6pm when she was feeding the children. With some prescience she told the children: 'I know I am not coming back.'[40]

Her first trial concerned the murder of Mick Collins and commenced on 6 August 1888 before Justice William Foster (1831–1909), a recent appointment to the bench, who had previously served as attorney-general under Henry Parkes. Evidence was presented by neighbours that Collins was often drunk and neglected her home and her children – something that counted against her at a time when gender roles were so rigidly defined. Dr Marshall was less hostile than he had been during the inquest, although he was clearly annoyed she had rejected his advice to admit her husband to hospital. The most damning testimony came from eleven-year-old May Andrews. She stated when asked about the box of 'Rough on Rats': 'I would know a box like it … I have seen it before … It was before my own father got sick – I saw the box first on the top shelf in the house, when we lived in [Popples] Paddock about a year ago.' This testimony linked the deaths of the two husbands together, however circumstantially. The jury could not agree on a verdict, making a second trial necessary. This one began on 5 November 1888 before Justice William Windeyer. The press speculated that Collins might have committed suicide due to illness and poor employment prospects. Perhaps toxic chemicals in wool washing were to blame, Louisa Collins's counsel suggested.[41] Again the jury was split and therefore dismissed.[42]

In the third trial, which opened on 19 November 1888 before Justice Sir Joseph Innes (1834–96), a former Minister of Justice in the New South Wales parliament, Louisa Collins was this time arraigned on the charge of murdering Charles Andrews. Her counsel argued that environmental and employment-related toxicity was to blame for Andrews's death. Again the jury could not agree and was discharged. For her fourth trial, she was again charged with the murder of her second husband, a highly irregular legal proceeding given that the two previous trials concerning Collins had been unsuccessful.[43] It was not until this trial, which commenced on 6 December 1888 before the Chief Justice Sir Frederick Darley (1830–1910), later lieutenant-governor of New South Wales during Federation, that she was found guilty of the wilful murder of Mick Collins. His Honour was savage in his remarks to the convicted prisoner: '... you watched his slow torture and painful death, and this apparently without a moment's remorse. You were indifferent to his pain, and gained his confidence by your simulated affection. There is too much reason to fear that your first husband Andrews also met his death at your hands.'[44] And with that, Louisa Collins was sentenced to death.

Despite her reputation as a drunken, slovenly adulterer there was a degree of sympathy for this mother of seven children now facing the awful finality of the noose. Controversial former undertaker Ninian Melville (1843–97), the member for Northumberland, told the New South Wales Legislative Assembly that the case against Collins was '... an unfortunate exhibition of what was called justice'.[45] Others, like fellow parliamentarian Thomas Walker, however, called her the 'Borgia of Botany Bay', a name that stuck for generations to follow. Premier Sir Henry Parkes canvassed the opinion of the chief justice on his opinion of the merits of the case, and reported to parliament on 19 December 1888 that the opinion was to proceed with the execution. During that debate there were insistent calls for an appeal.

After four trials an appeal seemed to be a remote possibility. However, it went ahead on 28 December 1888 before the full bench consisting of justices Windeyer and Foster and Chief Justice Darly. At this time judges could sit on appeals even when they had convened earlier proceedings and convictions. Collins again relied on a local lawyer, a Mr Lusk, to represent her pro bono, whereas the Crown had the finest legal minds in the colony at its disposal. Her appeal was rejected.[46] Her daughter May, in an interview with the governor, Lord Carrington, pleaded for her mother's life. He told her he was unable to intervene after the Executive Council confirmed its resolution to see the sentence carried out. He also received many petitions to extend clemency, generally argued on the issue of Collins's possible insanity and the fact that the three initial trials had been unable to convict her.[47] The governor was in a difficult position despite the generosity of spirit and largesse that characterised his term of office. The press was also consumed with opinions for and against the execution of Louisa Collins in early January 1889.

None of the public agitation was successful. Before her execution Collins wrote to Lord Carrington on the cheap blue-lined prison paper she was allotted. In it she begged him to consider that: 'Oh, my Lord. Pray have mercy and pity upon me and spare my life. I beg and implore you … have mercy on me for my child's [sic] sake. I have seven children … Spare me my Lord for their sake … Oh my Lord my life is in your hands.'[48] Supported by the sympathetic and compassionate prison chaplain, Canon C. H. Rich, who was attached to St Andrew's Church of England cathedral, she went to the gallows at Darlinghurst jail on 8 January 1889. Lord Carrington was castigated in the radical and nationalist press as an uncaring chinless wonder.[49] Louisa Collins the last woman executed in New South Wales.

If there is some measure of doubt in determining the guilt of Louisa Collins, there was none where Martha Needle was concerned. She was a psychopathic, ruthless mass murderer who killed her own children, her husband, and the brother of her naive besotted lover, all for financial gain. She was executed on 22 October 1894 in Melbourne jail.

Martha Needle's early life was chaotic and traumatic. Born Martha Charles in April 1863 to poor parents at Morgan, South Australia, on the Murray River, she was, of the six children born, one of only three children to survive. Despite his meagre existence in the colony, her father, Joseph Charles, was consumed with the fantasy that he was a wealthy heir to a large estate in England. This may have been a sign of mental instability. Her parents parted when May Charles accused her husband of attempting to poison her. He did not deny the accusation, replying that since 'they were living so unhappily she could expect nothing else'.

The couple reconciled and moved to Kapunda. But then May Charles alleged that he had tried to poison her again. She fled, relocating to North West Bend station where Martha was born some seven months later. Her parents reconciled yet again and moved to Port Lincoln with the other two children.[50] He again abandoned the family. Believing her husband to be dead, in March 1870 Mary Charles married a violent army deserter named Daniel Foran, who had arrived in the colony with the 2nd Somersetshire Regiment of Foot. He wore the detested letter D tattooed on him to indicate his status.

In 1876, Foran was jailed for two years with hard labour for indecently assaulting his twelve-year-old stepdaughter Martha Charles.[51] After the assault on her daughter, Mary Foran began to drink heavily and was constantly before the courts for being drunk in public, using indecent language and neglecting her children. After the attack Martha was sent into domestic service with a Mrs Drew in North Adelaide. That same year Mary Foran was jailed for a month for neglecting her two younger children, who were despatched to the Industrial Home for Neglected Children.[52] She was imprisoned again in 1877 for being a 'habitual drunkard'.[53]

In 1880, at the age of seventeen, Martha Charles married twenty-two-year-old English-born carpenter Henry Needle. The couple had three children: Mabel, born in May 1882, Elsie in October 1884, and lastly May in October 1886.[54] They decided to try their luck in Melbourne, with its booming economy fuelled by construction. At first they were happy together at Cubitt Street, Richmond, but soon the ambitious and beautiful Martha Needle began to resent her modest circumstances. She took to going out at night alone, fuelling domestic arguments. With the sudden death of three-year-old Mabel in December 1885, the marriage further deteriorated. Looking for more money to support his increasingly dissatisfied wife, Henry

Needle went to Sydney; he had little to show for his exertions when he returned.

During this time of stormy reunion, Henry Needle sought medical treatment from the Lodge doctor for severe stomach pains and nausea. Neighbours came in to help, particularly as he refused to take any food or medicines from his wife's hand. This alone should have rung alarm bells but he did not offer any specific allegations against his wife either to the police or to the Lodge doctors. Nor did he voice any concerns about the manner in which Mabel had died. When Henry Needle died on 4 October 1889, the attending doctor issued a death certificate stating he had died of 'subacute hepatitis, enteric fever, and exhaustion.'

Martha Needle had taken out a £200 insurance policy on her husband's life with The Trustees, Executors and Agency Company. She was dismayed when the administrators only paid her £60, keeping the rest in trust for the two minor children. Martha Needle was furious since she had expected to receive the entire amount. She complained about her deceased husband to anyone who would listen, portraying him as a jealous, irritable and violent man.

With her share of the insurance payout Needle began to keep a boarding house in Richmond. It initially proved profitable, although the work involved in running such a business was relentless and arduous, even with servants.[55] Slaving away in a large house, with meals to prepare, laundry to wash and iron, and general duty of care for the boarders was hardly the future Needle envisaged for herself. So in October 1890 she closed the business and went to live in a smaller residence with her two daughters.

Fourteen months later, Elsie died after three weeks of a painful debilitating illness. Like Mabel, the once-healthy little girl suffered terrible stomach pains, emaciation and fever. Again there was no suspicion that foul play might have been involved. The Lodge doctor provided a death certificate stating that the six-year-old had succumbed to 'gangrenous stomatitis and exhaustion'. Needle then applied for, and was given, Elsie's share of her father's insurance claim. Eight months later, on 27 August 1891, May, aged nearly five, suddenly sickened and died. The doctor declared she had succumbed to 'tubercular meningitis'. Again Needle received her share of the insurance claim. To the doctor and neighbours, she was a devoted and grief-stricken mother made distraught by the loss of yet another daughter – on whom she had taken out a separate insurance policy of £60. From this death Needle received around £120 – the payout on May and also May's share of the money held in trust after her father's death. It was the equivalent of three years' wages of an unskilled workingwoman.

Needle decided to look out for another target. She found one when she went to work as the housekeeper to two brothers, saddle makers Otto and Louis Juncken (sometimes called Yuncken), young men from the German community of Lyndoch in South Australia. Within a few months the housekeeper became engaged to marry Otto, despite vehement protests from his family. Brother Louis Juncken was not only alarmed by Needle's outbursts of anger and screaming, but also because he had once tried to persuade the young widow to have a sexual liaison with him.

In August 1893, Louis Juncken became desperately ill for a fortnight. While he was sick he finally agreed to the marriage, but as soon as he was well enough he took Otto away to try to knock some sense into him. In response, Martha Needle attempted suicide, leaving a pathetic note that said: 'When my body is found, let me be buried with my children.' Her ruse in combination with her 'tragic' past worked, and Otto became completely devoted to her.

In April 1894 Louis fell ill again, but was reprieved when for a short time he was attended by his sister, Emma Jones. This respite was only short-lived, for he was soon ill again, dying in agony on 15 May 1894. (It was later noted that on 10 May Needle had purchased some 'Rough on Rats' from the local chemist, Mr Richards.[56]) Still, no one at the time was suspicious, and the doctors issued a death certificate saying he had died from 'exhaustion, inflammation of the stomach and membranes of the heart'. This was an extraordinary diagnosis considering that the deceased had been a strong, healthy young man just prior to his sudden illness.

Mrs Juncken and another son, Herman, arrived from South Australia two days after this unexpected death, amazed that Otto still wanted to marry his manipulative housekeeper. The new arrivals insisted that he part from her. In Mrs Juncken's contemptuous view, Needle was nothing but a 'hussy'. With prompting from his mother, Herman convinced his lovestruck younger brother that it was unseemly to live in the same house as an attractive widow. Needle was forced to leave. She left a note to Otto signed 'your cast-off housekeeper'.[57]

Needle moved nearby to a modest home in Richmond. One of her first visitors was Herman Juncken, who attempted to reason with her

Martha Needle was the product of a violent household. W. Mason & Co. Photographers, c. 1880s/90s. Photo: National Trust of Australia (Victoria) Old Melbourne Gaol Collection.

about the unsuitability of her plans to marry Otto. Yet he too became beguiled by her beauty and by her demure and charming manner, and he asked if he could call again. Herman now became Needle's new target. Rather stupidly she attempted to poison him over afternoon tea, serving a cup of decidedly bitter-tasting tea. Dr W. R. Boyd, a local medical practitioner, saved Herman's life with an emetic. After three days in bed, Herman returned to visit Needle, only to be poisoned again. He had just enough strength to crawl to a neighbour's house and once again he was saved by Dr Boyd's ministrations. Not as careless or as gullible as the other doctors, Boyd sent some of the vomit for chemical analysis. It contained a large dose – ten grains – of arsenic, enough to literally kill a horse.

Dr Boyd and Herman Juncken went to see the police with this story and also their suspicions about Louis Juncken's sudden demise. With the evidence of the toxicology report, they decided to set a trap for the suburban femme fatale. On 28 May 1894 Juncken called once more on Needle, who again offered refreshments. Just as he put the cup to his lips, the police stormed the parlour and took the cup and teapot into their possession. The tea was found to contain eleven grains of arsenic, enough to kill five men.

Literally caught in the act, Martha Needle knew she would be arrested and tried, so she attempted to commit suicide by swallowing chloroform in front of the police. Charged with the attempted murder of Herman Juncken, Needle was held in custody while the police continued their intercolonial investigations. Louis Juncken's remains were disinterred in South Australia; they contained thirty-four grains of arsenic. The bodies of Henry, May, Elsie and Mabel were also disinterred but the bodies were too decomposed to give results conclusive enough to stand up to interrogation in court. The amounts of arsenic were minute.

Arresting officers Detective Whitney and Detective Fryer were key witnesses at the police magistrate's inquiry in early August 1894. Dr James E. Neild (1824–1906), the Victorian government's forensic pathologist, and government analyst (and former Conservative parliamentarian) Cuthbert Blackett (1831–1902) provided expert testimony on their forensic investigations. Needle was represented by the disreputable lawyer David Gaunson, a supporter of the notorious, wealthy brothel-keeper Caroline Hodgson, also known as 'Madame Brussels' (see pages 18 and 248). Needle was arraigned for the murder of Louis Juncken.

The trial began in the Supreme Court of Victoria before Justice (later Sir) Henry Hodges (1844–1919) on 24 September 1894. Needle was again represented by Gaunson. The Crown case briefly outlined the accused's marriage and the deaths that had befallen her family. The trial mainly dealt with the circumstances of her association with Louis Juncken and his family; what had happened to her three daughters and her husband was far too circumstantial to go to trial. Justice Hodges cross-examined Otto Juncken for about two hours, an unusual development in a criminal proceeding.[58] Of all the witnesses, only Otto provided any positive testimony about the accused's character. He also told the court that Needle was given to fits and could lapse into deathlike trances for up to five hours. The jury was not convinced by his belief in her good character and her innocence. The all-male jury delivered a guilty verdict after the four-day trial and Needle was sentenced to death. She fainted in utter surprise. For once, her superb figure, pretty face and beguiling smile had not had an impact.

In the Old Melbourne Gaol, she was attended by a Church of England priest, the Reverend H. R. Scott, and a Mrs Hutchinson from the Salvation Army. Unlike condemned baby farmer Frances Knorr (see pages 135–143), who sought salvation in her last days before execution, Needle remained impassive and detached, other than to protest her innocence. Martha Needle was executed on Monday, 22 October 1894, refusing any spiritual comfort or prayers. What is surprising is that she had spent most of her insurance money on elaborate graves for her children, which, Otto Juncken testified at the trial, she visited assiduously. She left all her possessions in her will to Otto, to whom she wrote just before her execution: 'Rest assured we will meet again where there is no parting. Your good father, also poor Louis, and my dear little ones will welcome you ...'[59]

Almost a century after her execution, Bruce Thompson wrote a play entitled *The Eye of Martha Needle* for La Mama Theatre, which in 1993 was performed at the Adelaide Fringe Festival.[60] The drama centred on the sexual tensions between the three bachelors and the charming widow. Her murderous elimination of her husband and three little girls was overlooked in the drama.

One of the most bizarre poisoning cases ever occurred in Richmond in Melbourne in late 1904. Rosina Hubbard was arrested for the murder of her mother, Sarah Ann Robins, in September that year. At the inquest, held two months later, James Robins testified that he was the third husband of the deceased, who had produced twenty children by her various unions. Only two of these children were still alive. One daughter, Jane, had married 'a coloured man, thereby incurring her mother's displeasure'. The other, Rosina, therefore expected to inherit her mother's estate, valued at £1400. In August 1903 Rosina gave birth to a daughter upon whom old Mrs Robins doted, and who was promised a significant inheritance.

When Mrs Robins had a serious fall from a horse and cart on 29 September 1904,[61] she was taken to hospital where doctors Boyd and Morton believed she had in fact been poisoned. She died the following day, and her autopsy indicated the presence of large amounts of arsenic and mercury.[62]

Rosina Hubbard was arraigned for the wilful murder of her mother before Justice (Sir) Henry Hood in the Victorian Supreme Court on 20 February 1905. She was defended by the notorious David Gauson, while Mr Finlayson KC appeared for the Crown. Dr Morton was the first witness for the prosecution, then Nurse Ellen Fowler stated that she had suspected mercury poisoning when, as well as other symptoms, she saw how sore Mrs Robins's mouth was. In her testimony, Rosina Hubbard said that she thought her mother might have taken the quicksilver (mercury) herself because she believed that Hubbard was having an affair with her stepfather. When Mr Robins testified, he described himself as 'gentleman', which at the time described a man from the gentry with extended resources of money. He was hardly from this background, particularly as he admitted he had 'only a few pounds' to his name when he married Sarah Wilson in 1895. Since that time he had acquired three houses, presumably those of his wife, who, he noted, owned five homes and had money in the bank.

The defence was keen to establish the widower's motive for murdering his wife – arguing he had been driven by simple greed and the opportunity to secure the life of a gentleman. As the trial proceeded, the relationship between Robins and Hubbard came under intense scrutiny. Every salacious detail was reported in newspapers across the nation. Robins admitted that he had registered his stepdaughter's baby, although he denied knowledge of its paternity. He was still the major beneficiary of his wife's will. Frederick Fox, the pharmacist for the Richmond United Friendly Society dispensary, testified that Robins had asked him for arsenic to poison a dog. He gave him thirty grains. The next witness, Dr Crawford Mollinson, testified that Sarah Robins had died from arsenic poisoning.[63]

The evidence of the expert witnesses threw doubt on the actions of the accused and shifted attention to her stepfather for his purchase of the large quantity of arsenic. He also had motive to kill his wife: first, for her money and property, and second, because he was having an affair with her daughter. In his summing up to the jury Justice Hood began his address by pointing out that the accused 'deserved to be pitied for her condition [she was a little person] ...', although what the exact relationship her appearance had to her actions was left unclear. He asked the jury to consider also that Mrs Robins may have committed suicide when she learned of the illicit affair. The jury retired for an hour and then returned a verdict of 'not guilty'.[64] Rosina Hubbard was discharged.

Despite her close call, a few weeks later Hubbard confessed to murdering her mother with arsenic. She told the police that her mother 'often knocked me around, and was jealous of me, and thought my stepfather and I carried on with one another and called me such terrible names. I was determined to do her in'.[65] She was safe to make such an admission since the principle of double jeopardy in common-law jurisdictions meant she could not be charged with the same offence again.

The story had one final twist when it was reported that Rosina Hubbard had been admitted to Melbourne Hospital on 24 May 1905 and died that day from gastroenteric fever.[66] An inquest was conducted before the coroner, Dr R. H. Cole. There were no suspicious circumstances and a finding of 'death by exhaustion' was given.[67]

CHAPTER 11

The Thallium Killers

In 1944 director Frank Capra released his latest comedy, *Arsenic and Old Lace*. In this madcap film, Mortimer Brewster (played by Cary Grant) discovers that his sweet, genteel, 'maiden lady' aunts, Abby and Martha, have extended their charitable activities to relieving old bachelors of their loneliness by hospitably killing them with a recipe of elderberry wine laced with arsenic, strychnine and 'just a touch of cyanide'. Mayhem ensues – and never a touch of reality.

Arsenic continued to be used occasionally as a killer. Although she was never convicted, mother of three children Irene Crofts told the Supreme Court in Melbourne in November 1948 that she had used arsenic to poison her husband, one of the Rats of Tobruk in World War II. She shocked the court when it was revealed she told the investigator, Detective Dent, that she hoped her husband died.[1] He had been violent and often wrecked the furniture in their house in Richmond.[2] Still, arsenic had fallen from favour as the preferred poison for murder since the distinguished star of British forensic pathology, Sir Bernard Spilsbury (1877–1947), had exposed the solicitor Herbert Armstrong of employing arsenic to poison his wife in 1922.

By the 1930s, a new, more insidious poison was available to the killer in the domestic home. In 1938 newspapers in Australia reported the five murders by Martha Marek, another 'modern Lucrezia Borgia', of various family members. She had used a little known metallic poison – thallium.[3] Her motive was financial benefit from insurance claims. The New Zealand detective writer Ngaio Marsh used thallium in the plot of her novel *Final Curtain*, in 1947.

Thallium first came to public attention in Australia in a report in the *Sydney Morning Herald* on 1 August 1862. It described the discovery of a new substance called thallium by chemist and physicist Dr (later Sir) William Crookes. In the previous year *Scientific America* had praised its therapeutic potential.[4] The product was at first used as a depilatory, although its harsh action made razors a far easier and safer alternative. It was also used in preparations to treat ringworm in children but this had disastrous consequences when thirteen children in Spain died in 1930. Three others were left permanently injured. Even after this tragedy, thallium was still used in Australia to treat this common childhood complaint.[5] But its commercial use soon transferred to vermin control.

Even after the bubonic plague epidemics in Australia in the early twentieth century, public officials had still not managed to eliminate rat infestations decades later. In *Kangaroo*, his 1923 novel set in Sydney, D. H. Lawrence remarked on the prevalence of vermin:

> The battle was against rats, fleas and dirt. The plague affects the rats first, said the notices, then the fleas and then man ... it seemed to his embittered fancy that Sydney harbour, and all the coast of New South Wales, was moving with this pest. It reminded him of the land of Egypt, under the hand of the Lord: plagues of mice and rats and rabbits and snails ... [6]

Despite its reputation since the 1890s as a 'working man's paradise', many people in Australia actually lived in abject poverty. Those in overcrowded inner-city precincts lived in dilapidated housing with few modern amenities. These slums were infested with vermin and diseases. Tuberculosis was prevalent in the post-war period in the inner Sydney suburbs where the thallium dramas were played out. Typhoid and poliomyelitis were also constantly present.

In a survey of 8000 homes in 1945, Melbourne's Slum Abolition Board found that only 1000 of them could be deemed 'tolerably fit'. A

Collingwood family reported that rats 'sit in the kitchen and watch us have dinner'.[7]

In Sydney, in the immediate post-war years, over 250,000 people lived in slums. In 1946 only 13 per cent of homes had refrigerators and only 2 per cent had washing machines.[8] Ashfield Council, which represented inner-city suburbs such as Paddington, Redfern and Rozelle, eradicated 31,000 rats between 1945 and 1947 using 124,000 baits of M109 Rat Paste.[9] This alone was a health hazard since so many unused baits were left in public spaces. Even in middle-class suburbs rats were troublesome in the years just after World War II, often because families had fowls and poultry feed in their back gardens to supplement the meagre government rations.

Rats were certainly attracted to the grain fed to fowls, which in Queensland was often kept in sugarbags, stored under the high, stilted wooden houses. In Brisbane in the early 1950s city council health workers inspected homes for vermin accompanied by packs of excited and vigilant fox terriers.[10] Houses across the nation kept various rat baits readily to hand. The majority of these poisons smelt so disgusting that no one could possibly have used them to lace food or drink undetected. End-o-Rat, M109 Rat Paste, and DDeaTh were far too obvious and noxious to be used on humans – all but 'Thall-Rat', which was sold only in New South Wales, and which had come onto the market in 1939 manufactured by Sayers Allport of North Sydney in convenient 1-, 2-, 4- and 16-ounce sizes.[11]

Between March and October 1952 ten people died and thirty-six were hospitalised in New South Wales from thallium poisoning.[12] In September 1952 the first criminal conviction involving thallium poisoning came before the courts. Four months previously Yvonne Fletcher of Newtown, Sydney, had been arrested for the murder of her two husbands, Desmond George Butler, who died in 1948, and Bertram Fletcher, who died on 23 March 1952. Police prosecutor Sergeant Bush told the central court that investigations had begun when Fletcher was admitted to the Royal Prince Alfred Hospital and his doctors suspected poisoning.[13] Although he never received the sort of publicity that Sir Bernard Spilsbury had received from his expert testimony in criminal cases, the New South Wales government analyst, Thomas McDonald, was instrumental in Yvonne Fletcher's arrest and trial. He suspected thallium had killed Fletcher. Through his investigations of this case, and another in 1953, that of Caroline Grills, McDonald became the world expert on thallium and its effects as a poison on humans. He spent months of research experimenting with thallium in ginger to demonstrate that it was tasteless and odourless. He also established that one-tenth of a grain would be about one-hundredth part of one bottle of Thall-Rat.[14]

Soon after the death of Bertrand Fletcher, police ordered the exhumation of George Butler's remains from Rookwood Cemetery. McDonald undertook the scientific analysis, determining that he had died from thallium poisoning.[15] In the original 1948 inquest conducted by M. J. D. Austin SM, Butler's death was ascribed to natural causes. Peripheral neuritis of unknown origins, affecting the heart was cited.[16] He had died in Broughton Hall, part of Callan Park Mental Hospital, suffering extreme depression. He had lost all his hair, the use of his limbs, and much of his eyesight – all symptoms of thallium poisoning. But no one at the time thought of testing for thallium, and tests for arsenic, lead and strychnine all came back negative.

In June 1952, at the request of the attorney-general, the Supreme Court of New South Wales, consisting of the Chief Justice Kenneth Street (1890–1972), Justice William Owen (1899–1972) and Justice Leslie Herron (1902–73), ordered a new inquest into Butler's death. Joint inquest hearings were ordered into both men's deaths. The new coroner's inquest, conducted by E. J. Forrest SM, opened on Monday, 16 June 1952. Thomas McDonald proved to be a star expert witness as he carefully detailed his research on thallium, its effects and its presence in the remains of Butler and Fletcher. Dr H. B. Taylor, also a government analyst, and Dr C. E. Percy, the government medical officer for Sydney, testified that they had carried out tests on the properties of Thall-Rat after Butler's body was exhumed.[17]

Detective R. G. Fergusson testified that when he went to Yvonne Fletcher's house in Ferndale Street, Newtown, she said, 'I have been expecting to see you. I suppose it is about my husband.' Bertram Fletcher was a well-known identity in Newtown; his sister, Florrie Witchard, lived in nearby Susan Street. Yvonne Fletcher openly stated that her new husband, whom she had married in November 1951 after meeting him at a two-up game, was abusive and violent. Three months into the marriage she had had to leave home because of his brutality. She had gone to the Newtown Police Station for a summons for assault. Her husband refused to give her any housekeeping money, he gambled on Saturdays and was 'very moody'. Fletcher soon asked for money to gamble from his new and increasingly angry bride. He also went around the district saying that his new wife was a 'police moll' and that the two children from her previous marriage had TB (tuberculosis). Fletcher was violent to the little boy, beating him 'black and blue' for no cause.[18]

Even more damaging was a report that she had laughed at his funeral, waving to a man in the street. A neighbour, Mrs Edith Roache, stated that Yvonne Fletcher waved at Herbert Wood, known locally as 'Dago Joe', and that he was a frequent visitor to her house. She also confirmed Fletcher's account of the domestic violence that dominated the new home in Ferndale Street. She had heard the accused screaming 'Don't let him kill my children', as, taking the children with her, she fled the abuse and threats. Fletcher appeared in the street with blood on her face on several occasions. Roache said that Fletcher told her that Bertram Fletcher was telling 'doctors and different people that he was going like Dessie [Butler], and that she had poisoned him'.[19] Roach did not, however, go to the police with this revelation.

In the 1971 play entitled *Mrs Thally F* by John Romeril, the character of Vonny (Yvonne Fletcher) demands of her abusive husband: 'Fancy keeping a girl like me in rags. I don't mean a thing to you, do I? ... You're lowering me, Bluey Fletcher, you're dragging me down to your own stinking level.'[20] This implied that Yvonne Fletcher had 'married beneath her', in the parlance of the day. This was not the case. Yvonne Bogan was an uneducated, rough, working-class woman born in 1922 and bred in the inner-city Sydney slums. Desmond Butler, whom she married in 1943, was employed as cleaner for Grace Bros department store; Bertram Fletcher worked as a rat baiter for Butler and Norman's bottle factory in the industrial suburb of Alexandria. Neither man served in World War II even though both were of military age.[21] Yvonne Fletcher's desperation was driven not so much by the fact that she did not have a bourgeois home with all modern conveniences, but rather that she had married two violent men who were unable or unwilling to support her and her two children.

In her testimony before the inquest on 25 June 1952, Yvonne Fletcher told the proceedings that she believed her second husband had committed suicide with Thall-Rat 'just to get me into trouble'. Somewhat unadvisedly she also said: 'I had plenty of reason to murder my first husband but not my second.' While 'Butler was an impossible man to live with' she had no idea he would end up 'a mental case' confined to a psychiatric hospital. She called for Jesus to aid her in her dark hour.[22] Jesus did not come to her aid; she was ordered to stand trial for the wilful murders of both her husbands.

The trial commenced on 15 September and was presided over by Justice Edward Kinsella (1893–1967), a man of deep sympathies for ordinary people.[23] The eminent barrister C. V. Rooney QC led the case for the Crown. Only two months previously he had secured the conviction of the notorious gangster 'Chow' Hayes for the murder of an associate.[24] Rooney was a formidable opponent in court. Fletcher was represented by Frederick W. Vizzard, a state-appointed counsel, since she lacked the funds to hire an experienced and therefore expensive barrister. Rooney opened the Crown's accusations by showing how easy it was to purchase deadly rat poison. It only required 2/6 to purchase Thall-Rat at almost any local grocery store.

Rooney dealt first with the death of Desmond Butler, explaining persuasively why no one had been initially suspicious of the presence of thallium. Butler's local doctor had been baffled by his symptoms, and had at first attributed them to severe hysteria. Butler was certified insane and committed in May 1948. At first Yvonne Fletcher refused to take him home, arguing that he was violent towards her, but when he was eventually discharged on 21 July 1948, he was weak, confused and totally debilitated. Rooney argued that Fletcher then administered another dose of thallium to her husband.[25] While he lingered, Yvonne Butler went out at night to enjoy herself, leaving Desmond Butler to be fed and cared for by neighbours.[26] He died on 29 July. Much of the remaining testimony followed that given in the second inquest.

Yvonne Fletcher addressed the jury from the dock, telling its members that 'you know as much about the deaths of these two men as I do. I never poisoned my husbands. I do not know who poisoned them or how they were poisoned. I never bought or handled any poisons at any time.' Despite this, however, evidence was supplied in testimony that Bertram Fletcher had indeed brought home Thall-Rat from his workplace in order to dispose of vermin in their home and yard. He had placed it on bread to tempt the rats in the house. Fletcher also told the jury that she received no benefit from insurance on the deaths of either husband, thereby attempting to refute any implied financial motive. With little clear motive, the Crown's case was based upon circumstantial evidence, for like other instances of poisoning the deed was done in secrecy with the effects only emerging over time. How and when Yvonne Fletcher obtained Thall-Rat to murder Desmond Butler was not so clear. However, Crown Prosecutor Rooney painted Yvonne Fletcher as an evil woman, seared by 'black hatred' against her second husband, who was violent and disappointing as a breadwinner.

The jury was not convinced that both men had accidentally ingested thallium and found Yvonne Fletcher guilty of wilful murder on 23 September 1952 after eight days of court deliberations. They took just four hours to reach their verdict that she had poisoned her first husband, Desmond Butler. Justice Kinsella pronounced the death sentence.[27] Yvonne Fletcher collapsed and was admitted to the first offenders section in the hospital at Long Bay jail hospital while her legal counsel decided whether an appeal was appropriate.[28]

For the appeal heard in early December 1952, Fletcher secured the services of J. W. Shand QC for her defence. In the appeal the judges considered the evidence in relation to a recent decision in the House of Lords that quashed a conviction on the grounds that it had been made by wrongfully using one case to substantiate another of similar history.[29] The Court of Criminal Appeal upheld the original judgment against Fletcher, whereupon she requested an appeal to the Privy Council. Her grounds for this were that inadmissible evidence had been used in the trial to wrongfully link two separate incidents. Yvonne Fletcher's appeals were dismissed, but her capital sentence was commuted to a term of life imprisonment. She was assigned to act as cook for the female warders of Long Bay Prison.[30]

Three week after the conclusion of Fletcher's criminal trial another case of thallium poisoning came before the Supreme Court of New South Wales. On the advice of the coroner, an illiterate farmer, Ruby Norton, was charged with the wilful murder on 20 July 1952 of her daughter's fiancé, a truck driver named Allen Williams. She was arrested for the offence on 19 August 1952. Williams was a boarder in Norton's house in Cowra, where her daughter Fay, adopted son Boris, and the Worths – her married daughter and son-in-law – also lived. Norton was implacably opposed to Fay's forthcoming marriage and did everything she possibly could to prevent it. She had placed sugar in Williams's petrol tank so he might have an accident, and she had also purchased rat poison from the local pharmacist, Mr D. G. Kritsch.[31] There was nothing sinister in this purchase, however, since most homes, especially in rural areas, kept vermin poison.

Norton's trial began on 10 October 1952. C. V. Rooney QC again led the prosecution team. Norton's son-in-law, George Worth, testified that Norton took an inordinate interest in the outcome of the Fletcher case, although the timing was wrong for this to have been an inspiration for any attempted murder.

Norton was an incipient radical feminist who evinced a dislike of all men and wished to manage 'a woman-run ranch'. Her husband testified that she had previously tried to poison him. She tolerated George Worth only because he was a good farm worker. Norton's sister, Elizabeth Sinclair, and her aunt, Florence Hill, both testified that Norton was a violent woman who had threatened to kill Williams so that Fay would stay single and remain at home. Despite her motive, the stated intention to get rid of Williams, and the opportunity to lace his food with thallium, Ruby Norton was found not guilty and released.[32]

In 1953 thallium had become the poison of choice. Of the thirty-six admissions to hospital since March that year – some of whom were left with permanent injury – were a young man, disappointed in love, who drank a bottle of thallium in front of his former girlfriend in Hurstville, and a seventy-two-year-old pensioner who attempted suicide using thallium because he was 'in pain'. He was kept under observation on the order of the Lunacy Court.[33] Another trial, this time for attempted murder, involved Beryl Haugh of Leichhardt, who had attempted to kill her husband by putting thallium in his cup of tea. She was sentenced to two years' imprisonment in July 1953; Allen Haugh declared he was 'looking forward to reunion' with his erring wife when she was released from prison and was hopeful 'they could start again'.[34] On 28 June 1953, a dog died in agony outside the Como Hotel in Sutherland, Sydney. It was just one in a spate of thirty-four canines similarly afflicted that day. In the following five days another thirty dogs were poisoned in that same suburb. A reward of £100 was offered to detect and prosecute the cruel perpetrator.[35]

A far more brutal and devastating series of deaths was soon to dominate the pages of national newspapers. Arrested on 12 May, 'Mrs

Caroline Grills, 63, of 12 Gerrish Street, Gladesville' was identified as a possible thallium poisoner.

The serial killings by Caroline Grills belied any stereotype of 1950s, plump, middle-aged matrons who liked to bake and serve afternoon tea to family and friends. Feminine talent was then often judged by how well the homemade sponge cake rose and the lightness of its texture. The photographs that appeared in the press showed a woman tiny in stature, only 130 centimetres tall, with a large, comfortable bosom and wide hips, dressed in a cheap flower-print frock, her grey hair in an old-fashioned roll, and wearing unflattering large-rimmed spectacles. She was smiling and lively, revelling in the attention she had attracted. No matter the appearance she gave, Grills was a killer: ruthless, calculating and amused by her power over life and death in the most mundane domestic settings of inner Sydney. Since 1947 she had murdered her stepmother, two relatives by marriage, and a family friend, as well as attempting to kill two other family members in April 1953. Her actions had left another woman, Eveline Lundberg, her husband's sister, blind and crippled.

At her initial hearing before the central court on 12 May 1953, she denied all the charges, protesting her innocence through her solicitor, E. N. Rowley. Though accused of numerous murders Grills was not remanded in custody but was placed on £300 bail, then a substantial amount that represented an unskilled woman's wage for more than two years. Her husband, Richard Grills, was now a real estate agent with a good income. Moreover, Grills had inherited two houses as a result of her lethal activities.

Caroline Grills had not always lived in comfortable circumstances. Born in 1888 in the working-class industrial suburb of Balmain, her father, George Mickelson, worked as a labourer. At the age of nearly twenty she married Richard Grills, also a labourer, in the local registry office.[36] The Grills went on to have six children, although two sons died. Like many working-class families, the Grills frequently moved from house to house, unable to secure their own home. By the mid-

1940s, however, they lived in Randwick, able to afford this more affluent location with Richard Grills's increased earning power as an estate agent. But Caroline Grills hungered for her own home where she could entertain her extended family and wide circle of friends.

Her opportunity to attain the Australian dream of home ownership presented itself in 1947 when she murdered her stepmother, eight-seven-year-old Christina Mickelson. The old lady was taking an inordinately long time to die so Grill simply decided to hasten the process with thallium-laced food. Her motive was to inherit her father's house in Sydney. Mrs Mickelson was an elderly lady and there was no suspicion that her demise was unusual. Grills later told the court that she was 'old anyway. She used to get pains in her legs. Her legs were all gone. She got that way she could not use her legs at all.' Incapacity in the extremities is a symptom of thallium poisoning.

Not content with this acquisition she then targeted her mother's widowed friend, Angelina Thomas, aged eighty-four, who lived in a comfortable cottage in Leura, in the Blue Mountains. Grills would visit her with fresh fish, then almost impossible to obtain in the Blue Mountains. She made much of the tedious journey and of her expense and effort to obtain only the best and tastiest food for her mother's dear old friend and confidante. The delectable fish dishes were much appreciated by the elderly lonely widow who died suddenly on 17 January 1948.[37] Richard Grills inherited her house in the will. From being a poor girl in Balmain at the end of the nineteenth century Caroline Grills now had two houses upon which there were no mortgages.

Her husband's brother-in-law, John Lundberg (married to Richard's sister Eveline), aged sixty-seven and living in Sydney, was the next to die suddenly and mysteriously, on 17 October 1948. Before his death he had lost all his hair even though he had had no indications of baldness previously. No property was forthcoming on Lundberg's death; from now on Grills's motive for killing was purely for pleasure – to watch those around her suffer and die in painful lingering circumstances while she was the only one who knew the real truth of their sudden afflictions. There was a hiatus for some years when no one died. This was not because Grills had got bored with her hobby; rather, she had simply been unsuccessful, with only severe illness strangely affecting her extended family and friends. Christine Downey, the daughter of John and Eveline Lundberg, took ill on 1 June 1952 after visiting her aunt and uncle.[38]

On 15 February 1953, Caroline Grills's widowed sister-in-law, Mary Nicholson, aged sixty, also died. Grills had been assiduous in her role of caring, self-sacrificing relative, bringing her food and tending to Mary Nicholson's every need.

On 22 April, John Downey, Christine Downey's husband, unexpectedly came home for lunch. He found Caroline Grills as a guest, alone with his mother-in-law, Eveline Lundberg, aged sixty-seven. Downey was suspicious that death followed Grills's presence at meals. When he thought he saw Grills put something into his mother-in-law's teacup, he made an excuse to take the cup back to the kitchen, where he managed to put some of the contents into a clean jar. Mrs Lundberg soon experienced terrible suffering, losing her sight, her hair and the use of her legs. After she was admitted to hospital, Grills brought her home-cooked food to supplement the hospital diet.[39]

In early May, Downey took the tea he had salvaged to the government analyst, Thomas McDonald, who reported that it contained a large dose of thallium. The assistant medical superintendent of Sydney Hospital, Dr F. M. Farrar, later testified that thallium had been discovered in pathology samples provided by Mrs Downey and Mrs Lundberg.[40]

Several days later, on 11 May 1953, Caroline Grills was arrested by Detective Fergusson, who had also worked on the Fletcher case the previous year. The police disinterred the bodies of Christina Mickelson, John Lundberg and Mary Mickelson, all of which contained large quantities of thallium. Angelina Thomas had been cremated so there were no remains.

Appearing in court on Friday, 17 July 1953, on the charges of committing four murders and three attempted murders, Caroline Grills was granted £2000 bail, then the cost of two brand-new Holden sedans. Her counsel, Eric Rowley, argued that his client's health would be adversely affected by incarceration in Long Bay jail and that the case against her was circumstantial. He also argued that Grills '… is known in the district for her philanthropic acts'.[41] Her surface respectability and disarmingly benign appearance belied her cruelty and sadism.

The police searched the Grills's home in Gladesville for evidence, and found one and a half bottles of rat poison on her sideboard. She told Detective Fergusson that 'it is a very good thing to have'. The possession of this product in no way indicated guilt, given that any home would more than likely have rat poison, and Grills had said that she had bought it because one of her neighbours kept fowls, and there were 'always rats and mice where there were fowls'.[42] The police needed to unravel the links between the victims, the motives, the modus operandi and the locations if a conviction was to be assured.

The inquest into the death of Christina Mickelson opened on 11 August 1953. Detective Fergusson detailed the list of victims for whom Grills stood accused of killing or attempting to murder. When asked why she would attempt to kill Eveline Lundberg, Grills pointed out that she had no motive, asking: 'Have I got anything to gain by doing a thing like that?' This rather overlooked that she had benefited financially from the first two deaths. When interrogated about a brown wool frock in which traces of thallium were found, the dress that John Downey said she wore when he saw her deposit something into his mother-in-law's tea, Grills denied the accusation. She told the Coroner's Court: 'Well, that is where you are wrong. I only wear that dress in winter.'[43]

The following day John Downey was the star witness. He described the lunch party and how he had retrieved his mother-in-law's tea. Throughout the proceedings, Caroline Grills laughed and smiled. Her counsel warned her to desist as she was creating a very bad impression.[44]

A blind and feeble Eveline Lundberg then took the stand. She recalled a conversation she had had with Grills around Christmas 1951 during which Grills had reported having a dream in which Mrs Lundberg died and left her all her clothes. Eveline Lundberg found this quite chilling in retrospect.[45]

On 13 August 1953, Coroner E. J. Forrest opposed bail at the conclusion of the inquest. Through her lawyer Grills objected to this refusal to prolong her bail. The matter was heard before Justice Maguire, who likewise ordered that no bail be granted. Grills's counsel, Frank Hidden, continued to argue that since no evidence appeared in the Coroner's Court there was no reason to stop bail. When the inquests resumed on 27 August,[46] now also into the death of Angelina Thomas, Alice Hurry testified that she had seen Grills tear up Mrs Thomas's bed within half an hour of her death. At the time she saw nothing sinister in this, although a previous witness, Mrs Isobel Jones, said that Mrs Thomas kept a lot of money around her bed. Both Richard and Caroline Grills knew about the money.[47] John Lundberg suddenly took ill after holidaying with the Grills family before his death. When he became seriously ill, Caroline Grills volunteered to look after him, often bringing over food she had baked for him.[48]

Other witnesses attested to the sinister way in which Grills could behave on occasions. Jean Lane testified that Grills gave her mother, Mary Mickelson, a lolly even though she knew her to be a diabetic. In fact, she had forced it into her mouth. Whether this was cruelty or a desire to kill her mother was not clear. Grills also advised the younger woman to get her mother to 'attend to her will' because two people mentioned in the old one were already dead. This was a strange remark especially since Grills herself was not a beneficiary.[49] Another witness, Noel Lane, Mary Mickelson's son-in-law, told the court that after Mary Mickelson had been involved in a minor car accident in 1948, Grills declared: 'Your mother has not much longer to live. Get your relations from the country down.'[50] Clearly, money, property and

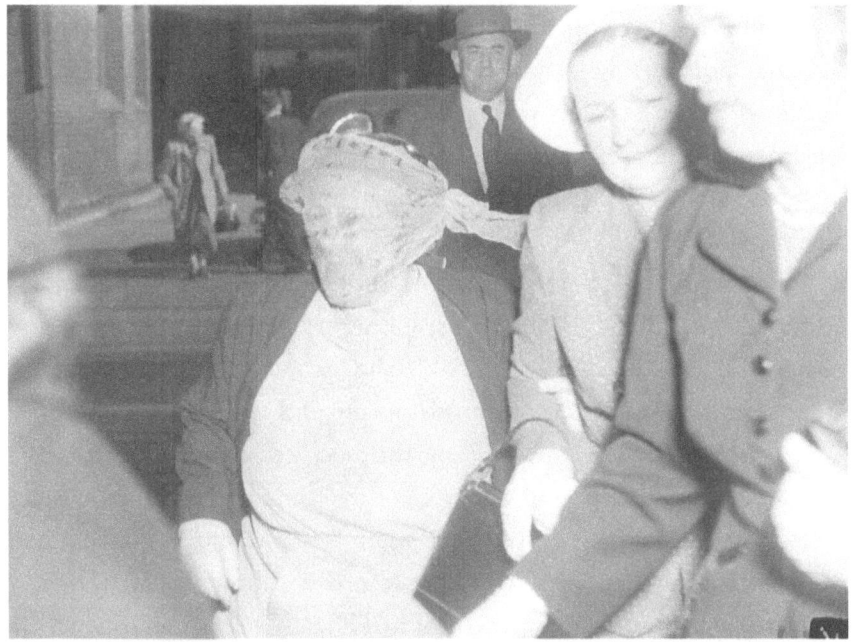

Serial killer Caroline Grills laughed and smiled in court as evidence was heard that the apparent do-gooder had been seen slipping something into an old lady's tea. Photo: Fairfax Media FXT 43229.

real estate were always on her mind, and the relationship between the sick and their estates a preoccupation.

At the conclusion of the inquest on 20 August, Caroline Grills was ordered to stand trial in the Supreme Court of New South Wales on the charge of the murder of her stepmother, Christina Mickelson, and the attempted murder of John Downey and Eveline Lundberg. More investigations were undertaken into the death of Angelina Thomas in the Katoomba Court of Petty Sessions on 27 August 1953. On 29 August Grills was also charged with Thomas's death.

The trial began on Wednesday, 7 October, before Justice Brereton with Charles Rooney QC again leading the case for the prosecution. Grills entered the courtroom with a sheer veil covering her face. Its diaphanous texture could not disguise her cheerful demeanour and laughter despite the seriousness of the proceedings.[51] Rooney opened his case by pointing out that the accused was 'a practised and habitual poisoner who had lost all sense of feeling'.[52] Her counsel refuted the prosecution case, telling the assembled court that this was merely based on evidence of 'similar fact'. It was 'similar fact', however, that had clinched the case against Sarah and John Makin (see pages 126–135).

Rooney proposed that one motive for what seemed to be motiveless crimes lay in Caroline Grills' psychology. She simply loved seeing people suffer; indeed, it was possible she 'experienced a psychological "lift" from administering poison to people and watching its effects'.[53] When he made this observation the accused continued to smile and look around the courtroom cheerily from the prisoner's dock. Detective Fergusson reported that when first questioned, Grills had been defiant, saying: 'Well, you have to prove it, haven't you?'[54]

Much of the evidence at the trial had already been presented at the inquest. One new piece of forensic evidence related to the frocks that Grills had worn in April 1953. The blue dress she wore on 13 April was found not to have any traces of thallium in its pockets; however, the heavy brown dress that John Downey identified as the one she wore the day he removed the teacup for safekeeping did contain thallium in the pockets.[55] In testimony during her trial, Grills denied any knowledge of thallium and its effects, claiming that she had not been aware that Thall-Rat contained thallium until police questioned her. She explained the presence of thallium in the pockets of the brown dress by saying that she had seen a rat in her backyard and taken out some Thall-Rat and bread with which to bait it. When she got some of the poison on her hands she had reached into her pockets to get her handkerchief to wipe them clean. That, she said, was the only way she could explain it.[56]

The jury retired to consider its verdict for a brief twelve minutes. Grills was found guilty of the attempted murder of her sister-in-law, Eveline Lundberg, her friend and confidante for over forty years. When Justice Brereton recorded the death sentence against her, Grills appeared quite unmoved and calm, although the laughter and smiles that had characterised her throughout the trial now ceased. Even Mrs Lundberg was shocked by the verdict despite everything she and her family had endured. In fact, she told the press that no one could be kinder or more helpful than Caroline Grills, particularly to old-age pensioners.[57]

Grills appealed her conviction in April 1954. The appeal was dismissed but her sentence was commuted to life imprisonment.[58] It was expected she would serve fourteen years.[59] In prison Grills became known as 'Aunt Thally' and she took a maternal interest in the younger prisoners, offering them advice and showing concern for their welfare. She died in October 1960 from peritonitis.

The month after Grills' trial and sentence, another salacious case came before the Supreme Court in Sydney. Veronica Monty was charged with attempting to kill her son-in-law, Balmain Rugby League star Bob Ludham, with thallium after the affair they had been conducting while her daughter Judy Ludham attended Mass ended. Prosecutor Charles Rooney played out the dramas connected with all this 'incestuous passion'. Rarely had so much forbidden sex and suffering been publicly aired. The courtroom was packed with eager women awaiting every detail to be exposed and dissected. Monty was acquitted in the Central Criminal Court on 10 December. Her husband promptly sued for divorce, as did Judy Ludham.

As procedures and tests in forensic pathology and toxicology improved, the chances of getting away with murder by using poison or drugs have become increasingly remote – and therefore less frequently attempted. Not until the 1999 conviction of Anu Singh, a young law student in Canberra, for the manslaughter of her partner, Joe Cinque, on 26 October 1997, did another major case grip the public headlines. Singh had injected Cinque with the sleeping drug Rohypnol and then heroin but escaped a murder conviction by reason of diminished responsibility. The case has already entered the annals of international celebrity with Helen Garner's 2004 book, *Joe Cinque's Consolation*; a play by Tom Wright and Lally Katz entitled *Criminology*, performed in 2007; as well as a 2011 episode of former FBI profiler Candice DeLong's popular US cable series *Deadly Women*. Singh completed her master's degree in criminology while on day release from Emu Plains Correctional Centre.[60]

CHAPTER 12

Deadly Manoeuvres in the Nineteenth Century

One of the first cases of husband murder (mariticide) in New South Wales occurred in 1816. Elizabeth Anderson stood accused of the murder of her husband, John Anderson, along with co-defendants James Stock and John Rawlings before Frederick Garling (1775–1848), the newly appointed deputy chief advocate in the Court of Criminal Jurisdiction. This was the superior court in the colony until the Supreme Court was proclaimed in May 1824. And, as was usual at the time, cases were heard with military officers serving as jurors.

At the time of his murder John Anderson was around fifty-five years of age, old for the era. He had arrived as a convict on the *Charlotte*, one of the vessels in the First Fleet. William Bryant and Mary Broad Bryant, the famous absconders who rowed to Timor, were fellow transportees on this vessel. Anderson was a seaman sentenced to seven years' exile and penal servitude for the crime of stealing linen worth £12/2/-. He was convicted in the Exeter Assizes. It's likely that as well as being a sailor his real occupation was as a smuggler, the primary industry in the south-west counties of England in the late eighteenth century. Elizabeth Anderson (née Bruce) was tried and convicted of stealing linen worth 20/- on 10 January 1787. She was transported on the *Lady Penrhyn*, an accompanying First Fleet vessel.

To encourage marriage, social order and sobriety, Governor Arthur Phillip instituted a policy whereby a male convict who married legally would be given a land grant of 30 acres and no assigned labour. For the economically ambitious this was a way to financial and social elevation, perhaps the start of real independence and autonomy. The Andersons' farm at Pitt Town on the Hawkesbury was long established since Anderson was granted his land on 22 February 1792.

The marriage of Anderson and Bruce had been an expedient one, without the slightest pretence of affection or mutual regard. Assigned convicts were forced to work for these newly emancipated, married former inmates, causing all sorts of tensions, resentments and rivalries.

On the evening of 26 February 1816, John and Elizabeth Anderson quarrelled, as they were wont to do on a daily basis, and John Anderson went to bed early. Early in the evening one of the convict servants, Ralph Melkins, testified he heard his mistress (his employer, Elizabeth Anderson) crying out that she had been robbed. He went into the small farmhouse where he found another convict assignee, James Stock. He also heard the other assigned servant, John Rawlings, call out that his master had been murdered. John Anderson was found outside with an apron around his head and a rope around his throat, barely clinging to life. Stock declared that Mrs Anderson had murdered her husband. Another witness, John Trowell, who worked on another farm, reported that some months previously he had been forced to intervene when Anderson had attempted to stab her husband with a knife.[1]

The accused had no legal representation nor were they allowed to give evidence on their own behalf. The military jury considered the evidence and returned a guilty verdict against Elizabeth Anderson and James Stock, who were sentenced to death, with their bodies to be dissected and anatomised afterwards.[2]

Margaret Galvin, convict number 27924 in Van Diemen's Land, left Dublin on the *Arabian* on 12 October 1846, arriving in Hobart Town on 25 February 1847. Illiterate and without any training or skills, like many transported convicts of the mid-1840s she had survived the terrible Irish Famine. After her sentence expired, Galvin married John Coghlan, a milkman and boarding-house keeper in Hobart. He had arrived as a free man on the brig *Portenia* in 1843, later used in the early 'blackbirding' trade to the islands of Melanesia. How Galvin and Coughlan met is not recorded, although they married on 2 April 1849.[3] For most of their marriage they were teetotal but domestic arguments led them to alcohol. By late 1861 John Coghlan was spending every night with prostitutes at 'Blind Tom's' brothel. Margaret Coghlan was infuriated by this betrayal and public humiliation.

On 6 January 1862 a rumour spread through the area around the Church of St John the Baptist in Goulburn Street that the milkman had been brutally murdered and was lying in his bed with his throat cut. As the Hobart *Mercury* reported, the rumour was all too true. Coghlan had been discovered lying naked on his bed in a pool of blood, his throat cut and his head smashed in. The floor of the small bedroom was covered in blood. Margaret Coghlan and another woman who lived in the house, Catherine Lowe, were taken into custody. They were charged with murder in the presence of Hobart's mayor. After some inquiries Lowe was released. Unlike many other women at the time she was native-born to the colony. Coghlan protested her innocence despite her clothes being soaked with blood.

An inquest was convened the following day at James Cousins' Bull Head Hotel in Goulburn Street before Coroner Algernon Jones and seven jurors. All the witnesses, the jury and the coroner went to view the body and the scene of the crime. This was a common procedure in the days before photography. John Coghlan was positively identified and described as a man of around sixty years of age, holding a razor without bloodstains gently in his left hand. A bloodstained water jug was found in an adjoining room. On returning to the hastily convened jury room, the first witness, Lawrence Benson, who was employed by the Hobart Corporation to light the streetlamps, testified that he had known the deceased for fourteen years. On Sunday night, 5 January, he had seen Coghlan alive in the street having just emerged from the Bull's Head Hotel. He then went into Eliza Hooley's house and that was the last time Benson saw him alive. Benson also reported that

Hooley followed Coghlan into her house, shouting: 'If you will give me some money, I will get you some grog.'

Having obtained some money, Hooley went to St Patrick's public house, returning with rum. By the time he entered Hooley's house, Benson testified, Coghlan was not sober, although neither was he 'dead drunk'. Around three o'clock in the morning, as he went about his rounds of putting out the lamps, he saw Margaret Coghlan coming out of her garden, shouting out to her neighbour 'Ellen' across the street. She was drunk and throwing stones. She waited until 6am outside Eliza Hooley's house, becoming increasingly distressed and telling Benson: 'I will murder him. I will have satisfaction.' John Coghlan had publicly humiliated his wife by spending the night with a prostitute in a house directly across the road from his marital home. All their neighbours were able to watch the public spectacle without the slightest bit of difficulty.

Thomas 'Blind Tom' Arnold testified that on the night in question, Mrs Coghlan had bitterly complained to him that 'her husband was away at some of the brothels'. She was visibly upset, and disordered in her appearance and her speech. Constable William Waller stated that the Coghlans had eaten dinner together that night, although there has been trouble between them just before, and Margaret Coghlan had been locked out of her house and caused a public disturbance. He testified that he heard her say: 'Now John, if you give me another chance, I will not drink again for twelve months.' She then 'went onto her knees and called God to witness what she had said'. Waller then confirmed Benson's evidence about Coghlan going to Hooley's house. Constable Waller reported that he had also seen Margaret Coghlan with Constable Cleary around midnight. She had lamented that her husband now chose to spend his nights away from home in brothels. When he saw her again around 3am he inquired why she was not in bed. She demanded he '… get her grog …' followed by 'Oh my God, what will become of me?' She kept repeating the words over and over, he told the coroner's inquest.

He continued that Mary Coghlan had then gone back into her house around 3am, only to come out again crying out 'Oh! My God! Coghlan has cut his throat. Oh constable, he has just come home and cut his throat.' When Constable Cleary viewed the body, however, he said in response: 'That could not be, as it has been done some time.' Mrs Coghlan sat on a chair clapping her hands together in distress. Other police and Dr Cairns were sent for to examine the body, which was already quite cold. At the inquest, Dr Cairns deposed his testimony on the state of the body: Coghlan's throat had been cut while he was still alive. The blows on the head had been done with considerable force as the walls and ceiling of the bedroom were splattered with bloodstains.

When Margaret Coghlan addressed the inquest she denied that she had killed her husband and said that she believed he had committed suicide. When Detective Vickers took the stand straight after Mrs Coghlan, he stated that Constable Cleary had reported on Monday morning that John Coghlan had committed suicide, a patently ridiculous proposition given the severity of the head wounds and the clean razor in his hand. Vickers had arrested Margaret Coghlan for the wilful murder of her husband. On being taken to the Female Factory to be housed with the other convict women, Coghlan admitted that she had killed her husband and revealed where the iron bar she had used to beat him was to be found.

In her statement to police, Coghlan outlined the misery of her marriage, which had started with high hopes and amicability. The peace was ruined by their increasing addiction to rum in large quantities. She said that on the evening of the murder her husband had arrived home drunk and behaved aggressively, knocking her over. He then went to bed, only to wake up and threaten her. She said that she 'turned in passion and got the iron bar and struck him on the head'. When she saw he was dying 'she felt so sorry, that she got the razor and cut his throat. That was between twelve and one o'clock.' The timing in her statement does not appear quite correct and she left out the scenes in the street outside Hooley's house, to which other witnesses attested. The coroner and jury recommended she stand trial for wilful murder.

The trial was heard on 28 January 1862 before the Chief Justice Sir Valentine Fleming, a man of sympathy and consideration. Coghlan was represented by a newly admitted barrister, Mr Cansdell, pleading his first case. As was the legal convention at the time, the attorney-general appeared for the Crown. Much of the evidence repeated that heard in the coroner's inquest. Dr Cairns was closely interrogated to remove any possible belief that the victim had committed suicide. The coroner testified how the accused had broken down and stated in writing that she had 'done a terrible wrong and had offended against Almighty God, and must take the consequences'.

In concluding the Crown's case, the attorney-general argued that insufficient provocation in the legal sense had been offered to account for her crime. Outlining the difference between manslaughter and murder he contended that this was a clear case of murder since it had been a deliberate act. The question of premeditation was not considered. In terms of the legal conventions of the time Coghlan received a fair trial. The jury took only ten minutes to find her guilty of the wilful murder of her husband, for which the penalty was death.[4] The chief justice assumed the black cap and read out the sentence, which included dissection and anatomisation even though this practice had ceased in the United Kingdom a full thirty years before.

The citizens of Hobart were sympathetic to Margaret Coghlan; she was a religious woman despite her grievous crime and intemperate habits. A large petition was assembled to plead for mercy for this now elderly woman. The petition stressed the fact that the Coghlans had been teetotallers and for 'years lived happily together, but had broken the pledge and taken up drinking to excess'. Rum was to blame. These entreaties had no effect and the governor and Executive Council were determined to see the sentence carried out.[5] Attended by the Roman Catholic Bishop of Hobart, Robert Willson, as well as the Reverend

G. Hunter, the Sisters of Charity,* and several benevolent ladies of the diocese, the deeply penitent Coghlan awaited execution.

Margaret Coghlan was executed on Friday, 7 March 1862 in Hobart Town Gaol. She had been lodged in the Female Factory at the Cascades but was moved to the jail several days before she went to the gallows. Reverend Hunter and the nuns attended her until the under-sheriff arrived at the jail to oversee the Supreme Court's decision, followed by the arrival of the jail governor. Coghlan was clothed in deep mourning, with her eyes bandaged. She was so afraid that she trembled and had to be assisted on the walk from her cell to the gallows. In a loud voice she cried out: 'Lord Jesus have mercy upon me', and then, as newspapers reported, she slipped into the eternal. She had, however, prepared a statement with the assistance of Reverend Hunter to be read after her death. In it Coghlan stated: 'I acknowledge fully the justice of my sentence. I deserve this, and a thousand deaths, if that were possible for the horrible crime I have committed. Drink, the curse upon me, strong drink has caused all my misery ... May God have mercy on my soul, for Jesus' sake, take pity on me. O! May all women be particular, take warning of my awful fate ... O! that I had kept my pledge!'[6]

Though temperance and the avoidance of alcohol was a particularly Protestant preoccupation that gathered strength as the colonies moved from their convict pasts, where alcohol had been used a basic trading currency, to a more modern progressive free society in the 1850s, Roman Catholics were not immune to its admonitions. Margaret Coghlan was an elderly woman by the standards of the day when she was executed. Her crime had been brutal, a vengeful fury against a husband who had nightly consorted with prostitutes. But her violence had been fuelled by alcohol. And death by hanging was her penalty.

The story of Margaret O'Donohue, who brutally murdered

---

* The Irish Sisters of Charity, often highly educated women, had arrived in Hobart in 1842, their first mission to attend to those in prison.

her companion in a brothel in Melbourne in 1872, had an entirely different trajectory from that of her fellow Irishwoman Margaret Coghlan, who was legally married and religious. O'Donohue was born in Brandon, County Cork, around 1850 just after the Irish Famine had officially ended. Cork, in the south, had been severely affected by several seasons of blighted crops that had left millions to starve to death, to migrate, or to be permanently affected, physically and emotionally, by the national trauma.

O'Donohue was slight in build and tiny in height, probably due to the effects of poverty and near starvation in her infancy and childhood. At the age of nineteen, she immigrated to Melbourne on the *Lightening*. She found work as a domestic servant in Williamstown before relocating to a better-paid job as a barmaid at Flanagan's Hotel in North Melbourne. She supplemented her income as a 'privateer', a contemporary term for a woman who undertook prostitution on a part-time basis. Usually it was only a short-term measure as most women soon took up the game permanently.

O'Donohue went to live in the Temperance Hotel in Londsdale Street, a location that did not match her occupation or aspirations. In 1872 she moved to 'a low brothel frequented by thieves' in Punch Lane. The whole north-eastern section of the CBD in Melbourne was infested with brothels, not just bordellos and luxurious houses of ill fame such as Madame Brussels's, but also cheap hotels renting out rooms. A local policeman, Constable Dalton, whose beat encompassed these areas, reported that '[w]hen walking the streets as a prostitute, she [O'Donohue] was bold, and would not be told to go away by the police'.[7] O'Donohue based herself in a brothel run by Mary O'Rourke (alias Hewitt and Hewson). The two were close, although at times terrible fights occurred between the women and their pimps. O'Donohue's life was full of violence. She was assaulted by a Mr Jones, by a German client who claimed she had attempted to rob him, and she was admitted to Melbourne Hospital after a brawl with two Irish prostitutes on St Patrick's Day in 1872. This level of altercation and violence was not uncommon at the bottom end of prostitution.

On the evening of 18 August 1872, O'Donohoe, O'Rourke and another prostitute, Anne Crozier, sat down for an amicable glass of rum before a warming fire. Crozier drank so much she fell unconscious and had to be put to bed. When O'Donohue returned to the front room, O'Rourke became abusive, calling her mother a whore. Incensed, O'Donohue seized an axe used to cut firewood and repeatedly smashed O'Rourke over the head, even after she had fallen to the filthy floor. Not content with this almost demented violence, O'Donohue jumped on her victim's back, breaking her ribs, which punctured her right lung. Coming to her senses after the frenzy, O'Donohue tried to stem the bleeding with bandages.

O'Donohue ran out onto the street and found Constable Flanagan in Bourke Street, telling him what she had done. He was so astounded that he said: 'Nonsense'. 'By God, I have,' she replied. 'I smashed her bloody head in with an axe. Come with me and I will show you.' He accompanied her back to the brothel where he found the dead woman lying near a gin case used as a chair. Constable Flanagan called in Dr James Neild, who conducted the autopsy. He found she had been near death from cancer of the uterus and from advanced syphilis, an occupational hazard of streetwalkers and prostitutes in low-class brothels. It is likely that the constant abuse O'Rourke hurled at her attacker had been fuelled by the syphilis, which often ends in bursts of raving and insanity.

When she was taken into the city watch house for questioning, O'Donohue did not deny her actions. She told police: 'I told her a month ago that I would [kill her] for calling my mother a whore. She was constantly abusing me, and calling me a whore, and my mother a whore; and I told her that if she didn't stop, I would murder her, and I have murdered her.'

On 21 August 1872, Margaret O'Donohue went to trial in the Victorian Supreme Court before Justice Sir Robert Molesworth (1806–

90), an aristocratic Irishman. The Crown case was led by Bryan (later Sir Bryan) O'Loughlen (1828–1905), the attorney-general, who came from a distinguished family of lawyers in County Clare in Ireland. O'Donohue was fortunate to have the pro bono services of the distinguished barrister Henry (later Sir Henry) Wrixon (1839–1913), another Irishman from a legal family. He had served as Victoria's solicitor-general for the previous two years. He was ambitious and talented but this case offered little to test his adversarial skills since his client had already confessed to the commission of the brutal crime. A photograph of O'Donohue shows a pinch-faced young woman with low-set eyes and thick eyebrows, described in newspapers as having 'the cast of vice'. Rather, she looks like a poor, hard-pressed working-woman.

No new evidence was presented at the trial. In this case there had been no coronial inquest, but medical evidence did, however, demonstrate that, because of the 'disease from which she suffered', O'Rourke's bones were brittle. An audience in the 1870s understood the unnamed disease to be syphilis. Wrixon was shaken and emotional as he addressed the jury, begging them to recommend clemency on the basis that O'Donohue had heard her mother called 'an objectionable name'. The jury deliberated for just a short time before retuning a verdict of guilty with a strong recommendation for mercy. The gentlemen found it objectionable that a perfectly decent mother, even one whose daughter was a prostitute, should be called a whore. Justice Molesworth pronounced the sentence of death upon the unmoved and silent prisoner.[8]

The premier of the day, James Goodall Francis, was a progressive Liberal. Despite the urgings of Justice Molesworth to hang her, he commuted O'Donohue's sentence to twenty-one years' imprisonment. Given how brutal and savage the crime had been, this was an extraordinary gesture. And lucky for O'Donohue as hers was not the sort of case that aroused public sentiment to petition for mercy. In the end O'Donohue served fourteen years. When she was about to be released, the wardens found that the moths had eaten all her clothes and all that remained was a powdery pile of disintegrating fabric. She was given £5/ 5/- and a modest set of new clothes, and then the prison gate shut behind her. Her fate outside the walls was left unrecorded.

Born in 1860, Danish immigrant Cecilie Andersen was a naive and trusting woman. Widowed young, she fell for a handsome well-born young man called John Fraser, who lived in her Sydney boarding house. Believing her affection returned, she began to lend him large sums of money and to provide free accommodation and board, as well as the comforts of her bed. Yet he had no intention of marrying her – she was simply a useful convenience. The result? He ended up dead and she ended up on trial for his murder in Melbourne in 1894.

Cecilie Andersen immigrated to Sydney with her husband, a bricklayer, in the boom years of the 1880s. With considerable investment going into urban infrastructure and domestic housing, a skilled tradesman could find ample work at high wages. After her young husband's sudden and untimely death, Andersen set up a boarding house in Surry Hills, taking up to a dozen paying guests at a time. Even with servants the work was strenuous, involving long hours to provide food and lodgings for respectable single men. Many of her paying guests were aspiring professionals, such as accountant John Fraser, who in the 1880s had come to Sydney from his family's large pastoral holding, 'Tallygaroopna', near Shepparton in Victoria. This large sheep property had been opened up in 1841, and ran to 160,000 acres (65,000 hectares). Fraser's father, William Fraser, took over the leasehold on 28 February 1866. The elder Fraser had arrived from Scotland in 1841, locating himself first in Van Diemen's Land. As the best land there was already taken, he moved to Wannon in Victoria's Western Districts. Highly respected for his integrity in business and as the largest landholder in the entire district, William Fraser was active in the community, and was particularly proud of his memberships of the Old Colonists Association – which celebrated those who had come as free settlers and not as felons – and the Caledonian Club.[9]

John Fraser frequently boasted to his colleagues and his fellow guests at the boarding house that he stood to become a very wealthy man on the death of his father. He expected to inherit around £18,000, more than a small fortune. Little did Fraser know that the National Bank had taken over the property in 1870 and that his father had only managed to wrest back ownership and control in January 1885. Fraser's belief in his expectations blunted his ambitions. Why did he need to work hard in a dreary office when he would become a man of means and leisure? So although he worked, it was only nominal; he valued far more his reputation as a man about town, attending all the best balls and soirées. Money was merely there to spend maintaining his appearance and his lifestyle.

Fraser soon realised that his quiet Danish landlady was gathering a small capital investment as a result of her hard work and dedication. He started doing her books in lieu of paying rent, but soon moved from the study to the bedroom as he eyed her financial resources. Foolishly, Andersen began lending him money on the expectation that they would legitimise their sexual relationship. Over the years she lent him £445, equivalent to ten years' wages for a domestic servant. But Fraser kept putting off the union, even though he must have known that he could take control of Andersen's capital if he married her since the *Married Women's Property Act* had not yet been passed, and so all a woman's property, inheritances and earnings still went automatically to her husband. It is not clear whether Andersen knew that Fraser was a widower. He had married Mary Howe of Hawthorne in 1872 at the age of twenty-eight. They had had two children – Edgar, born in 1873, and Ruby born two years later.[10]

When William Fraser died in October 1892, the *Argus* provided a splendid if small obituary of the old colonist. What they did not mention was that the drought and the severe Depression of the early 1890s had wiped out all the investments he had worked so hard to win back. In fact, 'Tallygaroopna' was almost worthless and needed to be sold to pay existing liabilities. John Fraser and his numerous siblings were left nothing but debts and resentment as their expectations disappeared. The downturn in the economy affected Fraser even further when he lost his job. Still he did not marry Cecilie Andersen. With his high-society lifestyle about to vanish, he set his sights far higher. To Ellen Lee, a wealthy widow living in Melbourne, he repeated the story of his expectations even though he now knew they were groundless. They married on 28 March 1894. By then, the *Married Women's Property Act* had been passed in Victoria, so the new Mrs Fraser could keep control of everything she had inherited from her first marriage. The couple lived in 'Ellengowan', her spacious and elegant home in Malvern.

Andersen soon heard of this betrayal of her purse and her honour. She went to Melbourne to address the situation. With her she took a revolver should mere words not prove sufficiently persuasive to retrieve her money. Money, however, was not the primary objective – Andersen felt righteously insulted, angry and vengeful. When she had heard in late 1893 that Fraser was engaged, she had gone to plead her case and seek the intervention of his brother-in-law, Thomas Steward, a financial agent. Stuart was not sympathetic, particularly when Andersen swung her revolver around. When she pleaded that 'he is a scoundrel, he has lied and is trying to do me out of my money', Stewart attempted to reason with her. When she said 'But I'll have it [the money]', he replied: 'It is a pity you should fly off like this and get into such tempers; you will entirely lose your head. I hear you go as far as to threaten Fraser's life and that you carry fire arms ... You are acting like a fool ... going on like a lunatic ...' As they parted, Andersen shouted after him: 'I am not done with him.'[11]

On 1 April 1894 Andersen next visited Fraser's brother Thomas, who lived in comfort in Beaconsfield Parade in St Kilda. Unlike prodigal son John, Thomas had worked hard for his own security rather than rely on expectations. Andersen confronted her lover's brother, telling him: 'This is a fine place for revolver practice.' When Thomas Fraser tried to reason with her, she replied: 'I want John to come back to me. If he comes back I will not ask for the money ... I can mesmerise him and get him to do what I wish ... It is cruel that he should leave me to marry another woman.'[12]

The following day Andersen tracked down the newly wedded couple and insisted that Fraser introduce her to his bride. She was angry and shaking, shouting almost uncontrollably. She asked the new Mrs Fraser whether she knew 'what sort of man she had married'. When Ellen Fraser replied that she did (although this is unlikely in the circumstances), Andersen retorted: 'Then more shame on you!' and walked away feeling more aggrieved than ever. In attempt to calm her, Fraser went with her to Princes Bridge and did not return home until late that evening.[13]

Determined at least to restore her capital, Andersen consulted a solicitor in order to begin legal action to recover her money. This was likely to be difficult, given Fraser had no money of his own and he had had 'no occupation' when he married Ellen in March. Fraser threatened a countersuit, and Andersen realised she might lose all her capital to the lawyers and still not retrieve her 'loan'.

The matter went to court where Andersen received a better hearing. She was awarded an order of payment of £445 against Fraser on 14 May 1894 even though he had no way of paying it back unless his wife gave him the money or he was declared bankrupt. Rather than pursue this option, Andersen backed off and entered into a solicitor's agreement in which Fraser would pay her off at the rate of 15/- per week, the outstanding balance to accrue interest at 8 per cent. Such a scheme meant that he would be paying off his debt to her forever. Perhaps she thought it would keep them in touch; that she believed he would make the payment himself every Monday shows how addled her thinking was at the time.

In Melbourne, Andersen stayed with her friend Margaret Healy at the Federal Coffee Place in Collins Street. At the trial Healy testified that her companion talked wildly and obsessively about how she had been betrayed and how she would get her revenge. She related a conversation with the accused:

> I kept him in money, food and tobacco for five or six years ... he said he was coming into a fortune of about £18,000 ... he has injured my pocket and hurt my heart ... I will have satisfaction yet or I will take his life ... I knocked him over when he said he was married, hit him in the mouth and made it bleed ... it is a pity I had not a revolver. I would have done the trick then ...

Andersen was so distressed and anxious she could neither sleep nor eat. She complained constantly that her 'brain burned'.

John Fraser was living on an allowance of £3 per week provided by his brothers. Evidently, the new Mrs Fraser was unimpressed by the story of her husband's caddish behaviour, and she was not a woman who liked a man to sponge off her, whatever his relationship to her. Andersen made an appointment to meet Fraser on 19 June 1894 at the Southern Cross Hotel in Bourke Street in order to finalise their financial arrangements. Since Fraser had consistently refused to sign the agreement in the solicitor's office, Andersen took a room with Margaret Healy and insisted that he meet her there. Fraser agreed, no doubt wanting to avoid another public scene. Hyam Winedrawer, an employee at the hotel, later told the court that 'Mrs Andersen was not sober'. He had also noticed that she had a revolver with her — although why he did not then call in the police was a mystery.[14] After all, women did not normally carry revolvers in their purses at respectable hotels in Melbourne.

Hotel guest William Orr, a mining investor, stated that, even though he was a total stranger, Mrs Andersen had spoken to him of her sorrow that Fraser had not married her. He was entirely perplexed by her confidences. Fraser and Andersen came to the hotel several times on the day of the shooting, first at around 2pm and then again at 4pm. Other employees of the hotel — Mary Egan, Patrick Moran and Henry Morphett — reported that Fraser and Andersen arrived together at the hotel at around 8 pm and had drinks sent to them. They heard shots about an hour later. On entering the room, Fraser was found dead on the bed with head wounds, while Andersen was alive with self-inflicted head wounds. She was taken to Melbourne Hospital where she was treated by the distinguished surgeon, Mr (later Sir) Charles Ryan, the father of the future Lady Maie Casey, chatelaine of Yarralumla.

The trial for the wilful murder of John Fraser opened in the Victorian Supreme Court on 16 August 1894 before Justice Sir John Madden, a man of deep sympathy and compassion. Andersen arrived in court with her head heavily bandaged, and appeared to be confused and disoriented during the brief one-day hearing. Andersen's barrister, Mr Leon, could only plead mitigating circumstances to account for her actions. Medical experts attested that she was not insane when she shot Fraser and then herself. Andersen did not testify.

In his summing up to the jury, the chief justice pointed out that Fraser did not seem a 'man tired of life', so suicide should be ruled out. He spoke with some insight into the distress that led the prisoner to her actions. The jury deliberated for forty-five minutes before reaching a guilty verdict. Andersen received a death sentence, the full penalty of the law.[15] Justice Madden wrote to the governor, Lord Hopetoun, several days after sentencing, reiterating the various ways the condemned woman 'had suffered at the hands of the deceased'. He asked Hopetoun to exercise his prerogative for mercy.[16]

The public realised that Andersen was not a cruel or vicious killer but a woman who had been wronged and discarded. The Danish residents of Victoria and an additional 20,000 citizens petitioned for clemency through the agency of solicitor Marshall Lyle.[17] The Danish consul-general, F. W. Were, was also active on Andersen's behalf. The owner of a highly respected and influential business in Melbourne, Were was the son of importer Jonathon Were, who had been knighted by the kings of Denmark and Sweden for his commercial and cultural expertise and activities.[18] The petitioners pointed out how badly Andersen had been treated, ending with the emotional plea that 'in the present weak, helpless and disabled condition of the unfortunate woman, such an act [hanging] appears to be particularly revolting'.

The solicitor-general reviewed the circumstances of the case on 16 December after Andersen alleged that she had attempted suicide first and that, in a struggle for the gun, Fraser had then been shot.[19] The Executive Council commuted the sentence to twenty years' imprisonment. Once a strong, robust woman, Andersen was now a wreck: unable to walk, partially paralysed and mentally incompetent.

Even as she served her sentence Andersen had not been forgotten. There was constant pressure to secure her release. A group of ladies were active on her behalf, securing the services of solicitor Waldermar Bannow to act for them. A deputation met with the solicitor-general, Agar Wynne MLC, on 3 July 1901. He told them that he had studied the case and believed Andersen should serve a minimum of ten years in prison.[20] Eighteen months later, the new Danish consul-general, Povl Holdensen, made further representations on Andersen's behalf to Premier William Irvine,[21] a prominent lawyer who would become chief justice when Madden retired in 1918. Irvine promised that this 'unfortunate woman, now sixty years of age' and in ill health, would be released on 30 June 1903.

Cecilie Andersen was indeed released on that date and nothing more is known of a fate that had been so blighted by the passion, vengeance and fury of her life.

CHAPTER 13

Killing of Partners in the Twentieth Century

In 1901 the aspiring novelist Miles Franklin published *My Brilliant Career*, an audacious novel about the emotional struggles of its tomboyish hero, Sybylla Melvyn. When her father's drinking threatens to destroy her family's security and social position, Sybylla travels to her grandmother's homestead in New South Wales. There she meets a handsome and wealthy grazier, Harry Beecham. He proposes marriage, as honourable men did. But Melvyn equivocates. It's not that she doubts his intentions. Rather, her reluctance derives from her ambition to become a writer at a time when marriage and motherhood were likely to compromise her freedom and talent. She prefers to choose the uncertainty of life as a writer rather than the conventional security and social obligations of marriage to a well-connected man.

In real life, as the new century began, this was an unlikely plot. Ethel Herringe and Audrey Jacob clearly had not read *My Brilliant Career*, with its precepts of independence and romantic freedom. Instead, when they believed they had been dishonoured and humiliated, both acted decisively – and permanently – to take revenge for broken promises and sexual betrayal.

On Saturday, 22 November 1902, the Melbourne *Argus* reported a strange legal case in New Zealand. The report revealed that a woman, Myra Taylor, had shot her former lover when he refused to marry her, and had instead engaged to marry someone else. On the eve of his wedding, Taylor disguised herself in men's clothing, went to the hotel where he was drinking, and shot him three times. Despite shooting him in front of witnesses, Taylor was acquitted of attempted murder. The paper also reported a case from New South Wales in which a housemaid at the Club House Hotel in Cowra, Ethel Herringe, had shot her employer, a man by the name of Maurice Lee. The tone of the article (subtitled 'A Determined Young Woman') was representative of how this case would be reported in the press. The 'tall and rather prepossessing' Herringe, it revealed, had 'an understanding' with Lee, who had recently returned from serving in the Boer War in South Africa. He had reneged on the marriage, so on the evening of what she thought was to be her wedding night she shot him in front of witnesses. Lee continued to linger in hospital with little hope held for his recovery.[1]

The story might have been presented in a light less favourable to Herringe – she was after all a mere servant who had shot her employer. And there were already hints that she was pregnant, meaning it was a shotgun wedding gone horribly wrong. Furthermore, the victim was a recently returned volunteer for the military engagement in South Africa where the colonies and the recently formed Commonwealth had sent troops as part of an Imperial contingent to fight the rebel Dutch Boers. Lee had served as a sergeant with the West Australian Bushmen's Regiment.

While some saw him as 'a fine stamp of a muscular man', the Reverend Seymour Smith described Lee as 'rather rough and brusque, his language was rough'.[2] Herringe shot her lover in front of this Anglican clergyman, perhaps not the wisest decision on her part. In other circumstances a young single woman in her situation might have borne an ex-nuptial child whose life could have been harsh and even tragic (see early chapters). Yet, by many, Herringe was perceived to be a plucky young woman who had been treated caddishly by a privileged man.

Ethel Herring was born in 1880 to David Herring and Bridget Mary Gray Herring. Several years after her birth her parents decided that plain 'Herring' was too banal, so they added an 'e' to their last name. Before she went to work at the Club House Hotel, Herringe had been employed at 'Melyra', a property near Grenfell in New South Wales, which she left with an excellent character reference.[3]

Many working-class young women of the time did not subscribe to the conventional bourgeois belief in being a virgin when they married, although for this they ran the risk of pregnancy, as Herringe was to discover. Domestic servants also found themselves vulnerable to sexual exploitation by employers and by the sons of the house or establishment where they worked. But from her statements, Herringe did not appear to be a victim but an active agent of her own destiny. Before she became Lee's lover, she had been involved with a friend of her family, another Boer War veteran named Doherty. When he died in South Africa, he left his meagre estate to Herringe. It was later claimed by her supporters that he had been more like a brother than a romantic interest.[4]

When Herringe became pregnant to Lee, she insisted that he marry her – an assertive act for a servant no matter what relationship she had with her employer. Lee gave her an engagement ring, although this might have been to stave off her persistence. Apparently he had been 'engaged' to quite a few other women in the past, perhaps as an enticement into a sexual relationship rather than as a prelude to marriage. A witness at her trial reported that Herringe had stated:

> 'This ring [the engagement ring] has been on a great many girls' fingers but I will show him [Lee] a point about it,' she said. 'If anyone annoyed me I would have their blood, but I am not annoyed with you girls.' On Tuesday I was chaffing her; I said, 'There is a pretty girl coming from Victoria, you will be losing your boy.' She replied that she 'might take him for a while but she will not have him forever.'[5]

Clearly she was determined to secure her rights. On the Thursday, 20 November 1902, Herringe arranged for the Reverend Smith to marry her and Lee after the hotel closed. The setting and secrecy in which the drama played out suggests that Lee had not been party to the arrangement.

At the appointed hour, accompanied by her younger sister Kathleen and another witness named Henry Palmer, Herringe waited for her prospective bridegroom. The Herringes were Roman Catholics and therefore not part of the Reverend Smith's parish. He was surprised to learn that the bridegroom was not her Catholic boyfriend Doherty, but an entirely different man – her employer.[6] She knocked on Lee's door and, to his amazement and dismay, was accompanied in by the wedding party. They all then went down to the kitchen – a strange location for a marriage ceremony. When asked point-blank if he intended to marry Herringe as he had promised, Lee replied that he 'declined'. In response, Herringe said that she would 'give him one more chance'.

By now, the Reverend Smith was alarmed and had a quiet word with Lee about the arrangements, saying he would have nothing to do with the legal papers offered to him. Herringe was infuriated and pulled out a concealed revolver. Two shots were fired.[7] Lee sprang at his assailant and, during the struggle, another shot was heard. Henry Palmer also tried to restrain Herringe. By this time Lee had been shot again. He then went calmly to the bar, poured himself a drink, and departed to bed. His nonchalance, at least, has to be admired. But it wasn't a farce. The bullets were real.

When the local police arrived with the doctor it was clear that Lee was seriously injured, despite his bravado. He refused to name his assailant although he did admit '… regarding the girl, that he had wronged her, and had promised to marry, and that he forgave her'.[8] This statement given on his deathbed five days later was important during Herringe's trial since it offered mitigating circumstances and created a degree of sympathy for the wronged woman among the jury. Just before he died from loss of blood and infection, Lee had taken final leave of Herringe: from prison she returned the engagement ring. An inquest was conducted on 26 November 1902 after which Herringe was ordered to stand trial in the circuit sittings of the New South Wales Supreme Court at Young on 15 April the following year.

Herringe was able to secure the services of a top barrister, (Sir) George Reid KC (1845–1918), who went on to become prime minister in 1905, with a local Cowra solicitor giving instruction. The trial was heard before Sir William Owen (1834–1912), a member of the Scottish gentry who had been educated at Lincoln's Inn. He was regarded as 'a shrewd observer of men and things', an expert on equity and bankruptcy.[9] Reid presented his client as a decent young woman who had been seduced and abandoned by a cad. He pointed out that she had not intended to kill or injure Lee that Thursday night but rather to marry him. Kathleen Herringe, who had given evidence at the inquest, was not called to the stand. Mrs Herringe affirmed that her daughter had been looking forward to marriage and a new life the night before the shootings. At the inquest and the trial Herringe was remorseful, often weeping and sighing. She was so overcome by grief that she was unable to take the stand in her own defence.

Reid was a master tactician in the courtroom. He demonstrated the underlying ruthlessness of Lee's actions, and how the manner in which Herringe had been treated provoked her. Lee's words – 'I won't marry you. You can bloody well shoot!' – were used in evidence for the defence. The purchase of the gun was portrayed as an act of desperation meant to frighten, not injure the deceased. He skipped over the concept of premeditation and calculation – which the jury allowed to slip past as well. Reid concluded his address to the jury by pointing out that the young woman had been 'spurned at the altar' (even though they'd been in the hotel kitchen at the time). There was also some confusion about which shot had killed Lee. It was suggested that it might have been the one that was fired when Palmer intervened, although earlier testimony suggested that this bullet only struck Lee's wrist. The jury retired for a short time and delivered a verdict of manslaughter. Justice Owen sentenced Herringe to only thirty months in prison; in 1894 Cecelie Andersen had been read the death sentence for murdering her absconding lover in Melbourne.

The story did not end with this minimal sentence. The residents of the Cowra and Grenfell districts thought that justice had been heavy-handed and lobbied hard to secure Herringe's early release. This suggests that Lee had not been a popular publican. As the editor of the *Grenfell Vedette*, H. E. Holland, wrote:

> Men of Lee's description are only too common, and every honest man and every honest woman – every brother and sister, every father and mother – should demonstrate their sympathy with this victim – for victim she is. She is not only to face the world; and bear the sorrow that must be hers for the shedding of blood but she has to bear the taunts that will be thrown at her by many less noble than herself.[10]

Harry Holland (1868–1933) was an unusual man to run a small regional newspaper. He was a printer by trade and a militant socialist by inclination. He was a co-founder of the Australian Socialist League in Sydney in 1882. But he wasn't an ideologue, as he demonstrated in the coverage of the Herringe case.[11]

At first the chorus of sympathy and support was locally based. Herringe and her family were popular and respected members of the community. A public meeting was held at Grenfell council chambers on 5 May 1903, attended by more people than the venue had ever seen. A large number were women, many deeply moved by Herringe's situation. Despite Herringe's conviction for manslaughter, she was a heroine for the cause of women's rights. Speakers pointed out the double standard that meant only the girl or woman involved bore the public condemnation for premarital sex and pregnancy.[12]

With the support of the Salvation Army, Hazelton and Holland established the Ethel Herringe Release Committee, with other members helping to circulate petitions in nearby townships. The committee met weekly, keeping up the pressure and publicity. The *Cowra Free Press* opposed this action, concentrating on Herringe's conviction for manslaughter: 'she ... was not entirely blameless' by any means. Cowra Council also refused to allow its buildings to be hired by supporters. But for the most part public opinion swung behind Herringe and the movement to have her released. The local Catholic priest and Protestant ministers endorsed the actions at public meetings.[13]

One important ally was journalist Ada Holman (1869–1949), the new wife of the local member, W. A. Holman (1871–1934), who went on to become the Labor premier during World War I.[14] She had strong links to the influential *Sydney Morning Herald*. Despite her pregnancy and confinement in 1903, Holman worked tirelessly on Herringe's behalf, aided by the feminist and socialist sisters Annie Mackenzie Golding (1855–1934) and Isabella Golding (1864–1940), who were foundation members of the Women's Suffrage League.[15] They were capable and persuasive advocates who organised large petitions, including the signatures of some ten federal MHRs, twenty MLAs and many teachers and other professionals. This was sent to the New South Wales Attorney-General Bernard Wise, close friend and associate of the Holmans, despite the privileged upbringing that saw him educated in England at Rugby School and Oxford University.

The press campaign was not without its obstacles. Wise demanded that Holland retract an editorial of 13 May 1903. He was not convinced that random shootings – which were increasing – should be applauded, however subtly.

Hazelton contacted leading Sydney feminist Rose Scott (1847–1925), who got involved in the Herringe cause, with Hazelton keeping her up to date on local developments. Scott was Australia's best-known and most well-connected feminist at the time, and she could bring to bear impressive weight to any issue. On 27 August 1903, Scott, accompanied by other members of the Women's Political Educational League, made representations to Wise, which were ineffective on this occasion. In September a large public meeting was held in Sydney to support Herringe's cause. Still nothing happened.

In June 1904 Wise resigned his portfolio. Herringe's supporters were not confident that she would be released by the new attorney-general, but the order for release was dated 27 July 1904. Herringe had been in custody since her arrest in November 1902. In prison she gave birth to twins whom she named Mary and Patrick Herringe. They were adopted. Herringe then relocated to New Zealand to start her life again without the ignominy of unmarried motherhood and a conviction for manslaughter attached to her name.[16]

Ethel Herringe may have been sentenced to only thirty months' imprisonment for the manslaughter of her lover before reliable witnesses, but Audrey Campbell Jacob, who killed her fiancé in a classic breach of promise tragedy at a charity ball at Government House in Perth, before dozens of witnesses, was found not guilty. Why? She admitted killing him – although she argued the gun went off accidentally – and some of Perth's most prominent citizens in fact saw her ambush her former fiancé. Did she go free because she was young and pretty, an apparently respectable young Catholic woman before a jury of middle-aged Catholic men? The strategy used by her defence counsel was a brilliant case of obfuscation, appeals to gender and religious stereotypes, and sheer bluff.

In 1925 the committee of the St John of God Hospital organised its major fundraising event with a ball held at Government House, a most exclusive setting. The event began at 8.30pm on Wednesday, 26 August. It is remembered as one of Western Australia's most famous vice-regal functions because that was the evening Audrey Jacob shot her former fiancé Cyril Gidley through the heart in front of the assembled throng. The ball was suddenly the talk of the town, indeed of the nation, with its story of illicit sex, broken promises, a gorgeous young woman and her handsome intended bridegroom, and the overwhelmingly proper setting. Headlines such as SEDUCED,

SCORNED AND SNEERED AT promised the full catalogue of innuendo, titillation and sex among the young who were throwing off the spirit of Victorianism with their fast and, in this case, deadly ways.

Audrey Campbell Jacob was a twenty-year-old art student, and a privileged member of society. Her father was assistant clerk of the court at Fremantle and therefore had the financial resources to allow her to study rather than go out to work at thirteen as less fortunate young women were forced to in the 1920s. One of eight children, she was educated in a Sisters of St Joseph of the Sacred Heart convent at Norseman, in the goldfields, 190 kilometres south of Kalgoorlie. The Dundas field at Norseman had been discovered in 1894, becoming the second largest goldfield in the colony, and a thriving centre. The Sisters of St Joseph of the Sacred Heart was established as an Australian order by St Mary of the Cross (Mother Mary MacKillop). They were an active order of religious sisters committed to good works, education and progressive causes, and by the standards of the day they offered an excellent education for girls. They also encouraged independence, careful thought and charity among their pupils. A talented art student at the convent, Jacob went on to to further her career as a painter who apparently was able to sell over two hundred works while she was still at art school.[17]

Jacob was a modern young woman devoted to the latest dance crazes and popular music. The charleston was first performed in 1923 on Broadway, and soon spread across the Western world, fuelled by the new Hollywood musicals screened in cinemas in Australia. The shimmy that allowed young women to shake in order to make the tassels on their evening dresses move in time with the music also took hold. Flappers, as such girls were called, were outrageous, full of high spirits and ready to turn their backs on the gloomy years of their youth and childhood which had been dominated by casualty lists of the dead and injured in World War I. The scandalous tango of the previous decade was also still popular, along with the foxtrot.

Tea dances and dance parties held in the ballrooms of leading hotels were where young people could meet and enjoy themselves freed from the stricter supervision and chaperonage that had existed before the war. Bands that were beginning to get the feel of jazz performed the latest hits, despite the disapproval of the older, pre-war generation. In 1920 the Princeton-educated short story writer and novelist F. Scott Fitzgerald set the tone for the post-war era, with its 'flaming youth' dedicated to fast cars, fast music, indulgence and sex. His short story 'Bernice Bobs Her Hair', published in 1920, the year his first full-length novel, *This Side of Paradise*, was released, captures the spirit of the modern young woman throwing off her corsets, along with the restrictions and sensible advice of her elders.

When Audrey Jacob became engaged to Cyril Gidley, she was just eighteen. Despite her youth Jacob had already been engaged, to ship's engineer Claude Arundel. She broke it off when the handsome, twenty-five-year-old Gidley from Grimsby, in the north of England, and also an engineer, but on the MV *Kangaroo*, pressed her to take him on as her recognised suitor. She ended her engagement to Arundel.

Jacob had known Gidley for about two years before they became engaged, having met him when his ship was in port. They became officially engaged without immediately telling her parents, and it was announced in three newspapers, including the *West Australian* on 8 October 1924.

Gidley was highly sexually experienced, with a girl in every port of the Far East (as it was then called), diversions when his vessel docked. He also romanced other women quite openly in Perth, still a small community, where news travelled fast. Jacob was far too naïve to realise what she was contending with. She admitted in her testimony that Gidley 'seduced' her and then 'used violence towards her' within six weeks of their engagement. This was clearly a troubled relationship built on threats and recriminations. Later there were hints that Gidley had raped Jacob. But still she continued her engagement. She left home and moved into a flat with another girl in 'Surrey Chambers' on

Audrey Jacob had been seduced and thrown off; in a sensational crime of passion, she shot dead her lover at a ball. Photo: *Sunday Times* 30 August 1925.

St George's Terrace, near Government House, allowing her to escape her parents' watchfulness and disapproval.

At some point the engagement was broken off. On 25 August 1925, Jacob had threatened to shoot Gidley, and then kill herself. Only days earlier, Cyril Gidley had written a letter in which he declared that Jacob had 'threatened me with my life'.[18]

On the evening of 26 August 1925, the band at the St John of God Hospital fundraising ball played all the fashionable melodies and a little jazz, despite the presence of Catholic Archbishop Clune. The dance floor filled with couples dancing the foxtrot. Audrey Jacob, dressed in a Pierrot costume, danced only with her friend Annie Humphreys, who was dressed as Pierrette. Fancy dress parties had become popular after the war, antidotes to the years of mourning black worn by widows and mothers, and the khaki worn by those who had served. In fancy dress, people could assume new identities and behave in ways markedly different from the rigidity required by the black and khaki.

At first Jacob did not see Gidley among the crowd of revellers, but at around 9pm Humphreys spied him and his companion and pointed them out to Jacob. Her reaction was one of amazement since she had been led to believe he had departed for Singapore when the *Kangaroo* left port a few days earlier. He had, however, been unwell and unable to travel or work. Gidley had visited an old school friend of his father, Wilford Mitchell, and his family. Mrs Maude Mitchell was the organiser of the ball and president of the St John of God Hospital Free Ward Committee, and she asked Gidley to attend.[19] He took their daughter Maude Mitchell as his partner to the event.[20]

Audrey Jacob told the court in testimony at her trial that Gidley 'refused to recognise me. He passed me three or four times – more, in fact – but he was very cold. Sometimes he would look at me and put his chin up. Several times as he passed me he gave me a bit of a sneer and then turned away and laughed.' Around midnight Humphreys decided that she would accept the invitation of a young man to dance, leaving Jacob alone to brood. For some time she simply disappeared.[21] As Jacob told the court:

> I was feeling very upset and ill, and my head was aching. I went to my room and I lay down on my bed. I cried about half an hour, I think. I then started to undress. When I opened the drawer I saw a revolver [given to her previously for protection by Claude Arundel] and then I decided to end my life. So I started to dress again. I meant to go to the foreshore to end my life. I didn't put on the Pierrot costume because I didn't want to do it in fancy dress. I picked up the first dress handy, which happened to be a blue costume hanging over the end of the bed. I wrapped the revolver in a handkerchief and went out intending to go down to the foreshore. But on the Terrace I changed my mind and decided to go to the Catholic cathedral first and say my rosary ... I passed the ballroom on the way. They were still dancing. The thought came to me to go and ask Cyril what was the matter ...

A woman about to commit suicide does not normally change into a ball gown and worry that she might appear ridiculous in a fancy dress.

When Jacob returned to Government House she had changed into a 'peacock blue frock' and settled herself on the balcony where she could watch the movements of the people downstairs. Humphreys wanted to leave the ball because she had to catch the 2am transport back to Fremantle where she lived, but Jacob refused to go. She asked her friend to tell Gidley she wanted to see him. Humphreys did as she was asked.

A reporter attending the event for the Perth *Mirror* outlined what happened next:

> I don't think anyone particularly noticed the tallish, slim young girl ... who threaded her way through the dancers as the music was dying away and the crowd was demanding an encore. She made no display of her intentions, gave no sign of rage or hysteria. Near the centre of the hall slightly to the left, a well-dressed young man, dark, nicely featured and attired in full evening dress, was standing chatting to his partner. Until then all the actions of the developing drama had been commonplace. She was noticed by only a few as she approached the man ...
> The report of the revolver woke the dancers to the horror of what had happened. The man was slipping to the floor. They hurried over; believing there had been a joke somewhere; that a cracker had exploded or some humorist was seeking to cause a stir ... Someone bent to feel his pulse. The two young men lifted him up and then I saw a dreadful smear of blood on his lips, increasing as I looked, to a trickle ... then his face had that grey-green pallor that speaks only one thing. His eyes were open, and there was a look of wondering terror in them ... [22]

The band stopped playing the foxtrot, 'Follow Yvette'. A police officer, Constable Wood, was summoned quickly, no doubt from duty in the vice-regal residence. He testified at the inquest that he had heard a shot at around 1.30am. On proceeding to the ballroom, he saw a man lying on the dance floor with blood on his face. He went over to Audrey Jacob and took her by the arm. As he told the inquest: 'As I did so, she said, "I did it", and I then took the revolver from her.'[23]

Witness Claude Kingston covered the dead man with his dinner jacket out of a sense of decency to preserve the dignity of the dead. Many of the young men attending the ball had seen far too much death in all its indignities when they served in the army during the war.

Another witness to the tragedy, Frederick Crowder, stated that he had seen Jacob standing alone and then making her way across the throng on the dance floor: '… with that a shot rang out … as I knelt by his side I heard her say, "Well, I've got you now." She had a revolver in her right hand, at the side of her dress. A policeman arrived and I heard her say, "Get me out quietly and quickly."'[24] Gidley was carried into the cloakroom, where he died very soon after. The proceedings stopped just as he died. The band still concluded the evening by playing 'God Save the King'. Revellers left the scene after giving statements to the police, many unsure of what they had seen happen in such an unlikely venue.

Audrey Jacob was taken into protective custody. While Sergeant Brodie was waiting for the matron of the lock-up, he testified, the prisoner asked: 'Is he dead?' Brodie confirmed that Gidley had died within 'four or five minutes'. Jacob replied that 'he only got what he deserved! … Everybody who knows him will say the same.' Brodie's colleague, Constable Timms, corroborated Jacob's admissions. He stated that when asked why she had 'done such a thing', she replied: 'He had plenty of warning but he took no notice.'[25]

Jacob appeared before Police Magistrate A. B. Kidson the following morning amid a frenzy of press reporters and eager spectators. Remanded in custody, given this was a capital offence, she was charged with wilful murder. Beginning on 3 September, Kidson also conducted the three-day inquest into the circumstances surrounding

Cyril Gidley's death. The lives of both the victim and his alleged killer were laid bare during the proceedings. The stories were sordid and recriminatory, touching on rape, parental abuse, smuggling, blackmail and sexual promiscuity – all paraded before an eager public.[26] Coroner Kidson returned the verdict that Jacob had wilfully murdered Cyril Gidley, and she was ordered to stand trial in the Supreme Court of Western Australia.

The Supreme Court trial opened on 8 October with Hubert Parker (1883–1966), the son of Justice Sir Stephen Parker, presenting the case for the Crown before Justice John Northmore (1865–1968). Both were devoutly religious with his Honour known for leading prayers and Bible readings in his chambers.[27] Jacob was defended by Arthur Haynes, who proved to be a brilliant choice as he skilfully played on the prejudices and sympathies of the jury. He carefully rehearsed his client on how to dress, act and behave in this courtroom drama where reputations would be sullied and defended. Jacob dressed in the 'height of fashion' as a modern middle-class woman – but not as a flapper. Her calm demeanour and self-possession were commented on in the numerous newspaper accounts. She never wavered from her claim that this had all been a terrible accident, unplanned and unforeseen. This was the core legal issue: what had been her intent? Were there sufficient grounds for a plea of provocation, or was it wilful and meditated murder? There was no doubt that she had killed her former lover; the jury had to decide the circumstances behind it. Was it an accidental killing or deliberate?

Jacob told her story in the witness box calmly. She spoke in a clear, low tone, never raising her voice or displaying histrionics. The key part of her testimony involved going to say the rosary in the cathedral after she decided not to commit suicide. When her barrister asked her whether she had any intention to kill Gidley, she simply replied: 'No, none whatsoever'. When further asked whether she intended to harm Gidley, again she was resolute and direct in her response 'No. If I could I would undo what has been done.' The crown prosecutor was not so beguiled. He inquired how well she had practised using her revolver, to which Jacob replied that the event had been her first shot.

Not letting go of the crucial question of the revolver and whether it was accidentally discharged, Parker attempted to force Jacob to re-enact the death scene. This was a tactical mistake in terms of proving her guilt; Jacob appeared before the jury as a fumbling young woman unaccustomed to firearms and their use. When her counsel returned to cross-examine her, the jury began to sympathise with this solid young woman in the witness stand on trial for her life. In the scenario presented by Haynes, Gidley was a promiscuous, cruel and deceitful young man who had seduced and injured the reputation of an innocent convent-educated girl. Haynes's closing address to the jury was brilliant in its conception and execution:

> He would ask them to remember the tumult, which ran through the girl's brain. What did the future hold for her; to be thrown over by the object of her love and for whom she had the closest attachment and between whom there were ties. Life and her outlook presented an emptiness to her; and one could well understand her going home and lying on the bed and sobbing for half an hour; then seeing the revolver and walking out into the night to end her days.

The jury retired to consider its verdict and was back in less than three hours, returning at 8.45pm on 9 October 1925 after they had enjoyed their dinner break. They found the defendant not guilty and she was discharged.

Accompanied by her mother, Jessie Jacob, and a medical practitioner, she returned to her parents' home. The news of the verdict was flashed across the screens at various cinemas. Jacob left Perth and Australia for good, soon after marrying a wealthy New Yorker.[28]

CHAPTER 14

Eugenia Falleni, the 'Man–Woman' Killer

Eugenia Falleni, or, as she was mostly known, Harry Crawford, murdered her 'wife' Annie Burkett Crawford in 1917, dumping her body in Chatswood, Sydney, bushland on or about 1 October, the New South Wales Eight-Hour Day public holiday. When the story of the 'man–woman' murderer eventually came to light in 1920, the press had a field day with the titillating revelations unfolded.* Not only had the accused 'married' and murdered one woman, but since had 'married' another unsuspecting woman two and a half years later. Rather than focusing on the murder and the callous way the victim had been discarded and buried, much of the coverage took the form of ribald speculation about the 'sex pervert' who had married two women, one of whom was a widow with a son.[1]

On 2 October 1917, Ernest Howard, a young employee of Cumberland Paper Mills at Lane Cove, saw what he thought were human remains on his way to work. The body was that of a woman. With the remains were a hatpin, part of a hat, a table knife, an empty whisky flagon, an enamel mug, a glass, a suitcase, a piece of greenstone, and some cheap costume jewellery. The body appeared to have been burned alive. Police at first postulated that it was an alcoholic who had had an accident, hit her head and then fallen into a campsite fire.

---

* The terminology used in this chapter varies. When Falleni is in female apparel I call her 'she' otherwise as Harry Crawford I use 'he'.

The body remained unidentified despite investigations to discover the victim's name. But it was wartime, and enlistments in the army meant that police resources were scarce. The death of an itinerant or homeless person was simply not regarded as important. Newspapers did, however, run stories about the case, and pictures of some of the items found at the scene were included in an attempt to help identify the victim. No relatives came forward to make inquiries or claim the charred remains. Despite the autopsy finding that the woman had ended up in the fire while she was still alive – although unconscious – the inquest delivered an open verdict.

That month, in a cheap boarding house in rough maritime Woolloomooloo, on Sydney Harbour, the landlady, Mrs Henrietta Schieblich, was attempting to eject a troublesome boarder, Harry Crawford, an illiterate, unkempt man who was often drunk and abusive. Crawford told Schieblich that his wife had deserted him and that it was her teenage son, Harry Birkett, who was now residing with him. The boy, who was about fifteen, was harshly treated by his stepfather, constantly abused and humiliated. What the landlady didn't know was that Crawford had attempted to get rid of the boy, quite literally, not long before, going out one night to dig a grave in a remote spot along Bellevue Road. They had taken a ferry out to Watson's Bay with Crawford carrying a shovel for the occasion. When they came to a likely spot, Crawford made the boy dig a substantial hole. This was to be Harry Birkett's grave, dug himself under threat from his stepfather. But Crawford had second thoughts, and so the pair returned to the boarding house, arriving the following morning soaking wet and exhausted. Crawford told his landlady: 'I am going to kill the bastard.'

Crawford's behaviour was often weird and unsettling: he claimed that his rooms were haunted; drunken rages and shouting was common. One day, unwittingly, Mrs Schieblich said to him: 'Perhaps it is your wife that is haunting you. I think perhaps that you killed her.' She decided that the quickest way to make him leave was to tell him that the police had called around making inquiries about him. Crawford disappeared during the night.

She had in fact at one time considered contacting the police; Crawford, who was entirely illiterate, had become agitated when she read him the story of the mysterious charred body. The *Evening News* on 3 October 1917 ran a feature about the mysterious burned woman under the heading 'Was it Murder?'. The article mentioned her black lace stockings and her home-patched shoes. The sight of the shoes made Crawford especially agitated. He had muttered: 'That's her. That's her.' Neighbours also told the police that Crawford had often asked them to read out any articles about murders but not about any other news.[2] Young Harry Birkett was also, Schieblich stated later, upset when he saw the newspaper accounts, crying out: 'Oh, Mother! Mother! Mother! I don't know. I don't know.' This newspaper kept the story running, asking thirteen days later 'Who Patched the Shoes?' No one came forward and the case went cold. Yet no one found Crawford. Why Birkett did not go to the police and report his fears about his mother's safety is puzzling. But he was young and frightened of Crawford, which might have made him keep his fears to himself.

On 13 June 1920, Harry Birkett, now an apprentice tailor in the southern Sydney suburb of San Souci, and his aunt Lily Nugent reported to the police that his mother had been missing since October 1917. Birkett explained that he had believed she was living with Lily in Kogarah. It was the greenstone found in the fire that finally identified her. Nugent recognised it as belonging to her sister, and dental surgeons John McManus and H. G. Vernon at last confirmed that the set of dentures worn by the woman matched those supplied to a Mrs Birkett. Three weeks later, Detective Sergeant Stewart Robson and constables Walsh and Watkins took Harry Crawford in for questioning about the disappearance of his wife. He had been hard to track down since he frequently changed jobs and name, but they had located him working at the Empire Hotel in Annandale.

By this time the police knew that Crawford had been born in Italy. Detective Robson said to Crawford: 'You say your name is Harry Crawford and you were born in Scotland ... Have you any marks on your body that will assist in identifying you as a Scotsman and where you say you were born? ... I believe you are Italian.' When Crawford replied: 'No, I am a Scotsman from Edinburgh', Robson continued his line of interrogation: 'Strip off a little and let me see.' Crawford objected.[3] The ploy was transparent; Robson was not looking for tattoos or ethnic markings. He was looking for something else. Members of the small Italian community in Sydney would undoubtedly have been aware of Crawford's longstanding masquerade and of the existence of a daughter named Josephine Falleni. Despite this, when Crawford suddenly admitted to being a woman during the police interrogation, the police were astounded as they surveyed the stocky, short unkempt man before them. He told them his name was Eugenia Falleni.

Not only did Crawford come from a national group that many Australians of the time looked down on, but he was now marked as a 'sex pervert', and one who was crafty, secretive, and perhaps even murderous.

By the end of the nineteenth century, the new field of sexology had emerged, investigating the basic categorisations of sex, sexual preferences and identity. Richard von Krafft-Ebing's innovative 1886 text, *Pyschopathia Sexualis*, had done much to formulate the concept of homosexuality, thereby forging the connection between practice and preference into a whole identity that defined a person. A cross-dressing woman such as Falleni, who did her utmost to act, dress and live as a man, was believed to belong to the most intractable level of degenerative homosexuality. Havelock Ellis, who had spent time in Australia, also studied sexuality and believed that homosexuality was a congenital abnormality bordering on deformity. Australian jurists, journalists and medical practitioners were aware of these new concepts which began to influence their discourse on sexuality and identity by the 1920s.[4]

The press had previously enjoyed reporting on the criminal cases of the likable larrikin and flamboyant cross-dresser Marion (Bill) Edwards, a mannish woman who enjoyed teasing out all the possibilities of gender alignment and display.[5] Other women who took on male roles were applauded. Flora Sandes, who served in the Serbian Army during World War I, was congratulated by the *Argus* newspaper as 'A Modern Amazon'. A woman called Maud Butler had enlisted in the AIF as a man and she too was praised for serving God, King and Empire.[6] But Harry Crawford/ Eugenia Falleni was not such a loveable character; indeed, she was to prove vicious and devious, determined to preserve her male gender identification at all costs, even murder.

Detective Robson searched Crawford's home at 47 Durham Street, Stanmore, where Crawford now lived with his new wife, Elizabeth Allison, an older woman in her first marriage. On searching the premises the police found a dildo in a locked leather trunk. Marked as Exhibit G1 – and called 'The Article' in the press – it was to be the central feature in the trial.[7] Presumably Crawford had already remarked on its existence to the police to explain how she could pass as a sexually active man. Robson reported that:

> I opened the bag. I got the article from it and asked the accused ... 'Did your first wife know that you were using anything like this?' The accused said, 'No, not until the latter stages of our married life' ... I said to the accused, 'Is this what you referred to as having used on your first wife?' I then took the accused to the Central Police Station where she [sic] was charged [with murder].

'The Article' also caught the medical profession's attention. At a lecture to the British Medical Association Branch in Sydney in 1921, a Dr Palmer brought along the dildo as a 'show and tell', explaining:

'This article was an artificial penis which Falleni had used in her various sexual adventures.'[8]

Its existence suggests that Falleni regarded herself as a man rather than a lesbian, exhibiting gender realignment rather than the desire to become a transvestite. Unlike Marion Edwards, who could play with gender identity for good effect, Crawford/Falleni possessed a transgender identity.

After he was arrested and charged with the murder of Annie Birkett, Crawford attended the Central Police Court on 6 July 1920, where he was refused bail. The press and public were also in attendance, interested to see how the accused would appear in what might be the solution to a longstanding unsolved murder. That next evening the *Evening News* revealed that Crawford was a woman masquerading as a man, sensationalising the case with the headline, 'The Man–Woman'. The public was hooked, eager for further salacious developments and sordid details. The issue of the murder rather paled into insignificance as the sexual elements of the case came to dominate both the court proceedings and the public's appetite for exposure and titillation.

The following day the newspaper carried the bare outlines of the drama, beginning with Harry Birkett's recent report to police that he was concerned about his mother's whereabouts. That she had disappeared nearly three years before did not seem to strike anyone as particularly strange. Nor did the fact that the boy had said he thought she was with her sister, although other evidence suggests that he had told his Aunt Lily that his mother had gone missing years ago. In the midst of the drama, the *Truth* pointed out a universal one on 11 July when it said that Falleni was 'better off as a man', able to earn far more for fewer hours work than as a female in low-paid unskilled labour.[9]

On 14 July 1920 the *Evening Sun* illustrated an article with a full-length photograph of 'Harry Crawford' dressed in a man's suit with shirt, tie and a man's hat. He was short and slightly built, with a rough weather-beaten and wrinkled face that was set into hard lines. The *Truth* on 11 July described the accused as having hollow cheeks, with a 'jaw square and masculine. The features generally are those of a man rather than a woman ... the face is lined and wrinkled and has the appearance of having been shaved.' The crowds gathered for Falleni/Crawford's second appearance at the Central City Court were eager to view this strange person accused of a grotesque crime. Daughter Josephine Falleni, who now worked in a jam factory in Pyrmont, had made statements to the police that day about her mother whom she rarely saw. She had gone to live with her 'father' and Annie Birkett when she was about fourteen but meetings were infrequent after Mrs Birkett disappeared.

Truth, a tabloid newspaper, provided more details about Eugenia Falleni's strange life on 18 July 1920, reporting that she had been married in Italy to a ship's captain named Martello. They had had a daughter Josephine, who had been sent away by her harsh and uncaring mother. The truth actually was that Falleni had never been legally married to anyone, male or female.

When Falleni/Crawford appeared again in court on 28 July, the room was filled with spectators, most of them women. The *Sun* reported on 29 July 1920 that: 'She was still in male attire, and did not appear to heed what was going on in court. She fixed her eyes on the ceiling.'

Eugenia Falleni was born in Livorno, Italy, around 1875, her family moving to the unlikely destination of New Zealand when she was a toddler. Her gender inversion apparently started early. It was possible she was dyslexic since she was unable to concentrate or learn to read and write. In childhood she dressed as a boy and as a teenager sought work in male occupations such as bricklaying. Following the pattern of many disaffected adolescents, at least in their fantasies, Falleni ran away to sea on a cargo vessel plying the South Pacific routes. While on board she became pregnant, to whom and in what circumstances she never revealed. She left her life at sea around 1898, moving first with her little daughter Josephine, born on 19 September 1898, to Newcastle. Josephine later testified that her mother 'was very cruel to me when I was a child. And used to frighten me ... my mother tried

The public pored over every salacious detail in the case of Eugenia Falleni, born a woman but living as a man. Eugenia killed her first wife to prevent the exposure of her secret. Photo: *Daily Telegraph* 7 July 1920.

to smother me when I was a baby.' She was eventually fostered to a Mr and Mrs De Anglis, who lived in Double Bay. They were attached to the child and brought her up with care and affection. In the days before legal adoption these informal arrangements were commonplace.

Falleni resumed her male identity, now with the name 'Harry Crawford', and took on casual work, often in pubs, living in boarding houses for single men. At the age of twelve Josephine was sent out to work as a domestic servant and encouraged to become independent. At first she went out with Mrs De Anglis to clean the large houses in the area.[10] The girl had no idea that her 'father' was her mother until she was much older. She believed that her mother had died and this was the reason her father had had to have her fostered. Mrs De Anglis had apparently tried to protect her charge from too much knowledge.

Crawford started working as a coachman for a Dr Clarke whose practice was located in Lane Cove Road, Wahroonga, on Sydney's North Shore, in 1912. He lived above the stables and generally kept to himself, his leisure time spent in drinking bouts when he was known to become loquacious and a nuisance. Here he met a widow, thirty-two-year-old Annie Bell Birkett who worked as a cook–housekeeper for the doctor's family. Her son Harry, aged around ten, lived with her. Her husband, an English tailor named Harry Birkett, had died in 1906 leaving her few financial resources. Wahroonga was a sparsely settled, quiet area at this time, and the two servants were thrown into each other's company. Initially, Birkett was not impressed by the badly spoken, uncouth and frequently drunk coachman. She had ambitions – to set up a small business for herself – and regarded her work as a domestic as a means to social and economic improvement.

In 1913 Birkett purchased a confectionery shop in Balmain in inner Sydney. Crawford followed her, obtaining work at the local meatworks. He started a campaign to woo the young widow with constant gifts and offers to do odd jobs around the shop. Before long Crawford had moved in. They were married by a Methodist minister in Balmain that year. Crawford then refused to go out to work for a living. Along with his intemperate habits, inability to earn a wage, and hostility to his stepson, tensions soon emerged in the household.

There were more surprises when Josephine Falleni, by then sixteen, turned up to see her 'father'. There had been no mention of a previous marriage or a child. She simply came to live with them. By this stage, Josephine was aware her 'father' was her mother and she reminded him that Mrs Birkett could not be deceived forever. She told 'her': 'She'll find out one of these days. My mother said, "Oh, I will watch it. I would rather do away with myself than let the police find out anything about me."'[11] At the trial there was considerable speculation about how the widow had not realised that her lover was a woman rather than a man.

Josephine started running around with men and became pregnant. This became too much for Birkett, who already disliked her cheeky, disrespectful stepdaughter. Tensions grew so much that Birkett sold her shop and went to live with her sister, Lily Nugent, in Kogarah. For a year or so she went to work for a Dr Binns as his housekeeper in Belgrave Street, Kogarah. Crawford started another romantic campaign to win her back and they were reunited. They went to live in Drummoyne, and a suburb not far from Balmain, where the respectable, sober and conservatively dressed 'Mrs Daisy Crawford' contrasted to her short, bad-tempered, uncouth, and often drunken husband, who spoke only broken English.

Lily Nugent wrote to her sister: 'I have found out something queer about Harry. I don't know what to do, but I'll tell you about it when I see you and get your advice …'[12]

'There's something queer about Harry' is a phrase that has stuck to Crawford/Falleni to the present day. Without doubt, this was when Mrs Birkett discovered her husband was really a woman. She told her sister she intended seeking an annulment, without realising that she didn't need one since she was not actually married. But such an action meant public revelation, something Crawford deeply feared. Neighbours reported at the trial that Crawford and Birkett were a deeply unhappy couple, often arguing. The exact nature of their heated arguments and altercations was not revealed. 'Daisy' Crawford (as Annie Birkett was known) was certainly not a meek, subservient woman, however respectable her aspirations. Even though it was humiliating for her, 'Mrs Crawford' took in washing to make ends meet, with her young son running messages.

The day before the Eight-Hour Day holiday, a neighbour, Mrs Jane Wig, saw Crawford carrying a suitcase and dressed in a gabardine raincoat, although it was not raining. On the day of the public holiday, Crawford went to see another neighbour, Mrs Lydia Parnell, saying that his wife had not come home all night and apparently distressed that she might have run off with another man. Quite out of the blue he asked her son, George Parnell, if there had been anything about a murder or a dead woman in the papers.

On the Monday after the holiday, Harry Birkett returned home from work to find that his mother had gone without leaving a note, which was unlike her since the pair were close. Crawford, who sat drinking whisky at the kitchen table, told him: 'She's gone away with some friends – Mrs Murray and her daughter – to North Sydney.' Harry Birkett had never heard of these friends. Crawford soon arranged for everything in the house to be sold. Had he been more astute, young Harry Birkett would have realised then that something was drastically wrong. Why would his mother not tell him where she was and why would her husband simply sell all her furniture and belongings? They then relocated to Mrs Schieblich's boarding house at Woolloomooloo.

The trial in the Criminal Court before Chief Justice Sir William Cullen (1855–1935) began on 5 October 1920, three years after the disappearance of Annie Birkett. The accused was represented by an inexperienced barrister, A. McDonnell, who was instructed by Maddocks Cohen, while the Crown case was led by the highly experienced W. T. Coyle. Such unequal situations frequently occurred when the accused could not afford good representation or when no barrister was prepared to act pro bono. Crawford appeared in women's clothes, no doubt on the advice of her counsel. The crown prosecutor opened his address by saying:

> I find it difficult to refrain from referring to the accused as he, but when I do you will understand that I mean the accused, who posed as a man, and definitely stated she was a man, and married two women as a man ... all her actions since have been characterised by cunning and deceit.

This was a damning statement; yet a life of utmost deceit does not mean an individual has a proclivity to murder. Much of the trial was concerned with 'The Article' and its use, the source of much amusement on the part of many women in the public gallery. The

English operetta star Dame Marie Tempest and her husband Graham Brown attended the proceedings. Coyle apologised that he had to refer to such indelicate matters. But of course the public could not get enough. Falleni disliked the public and judicial gaze, and insisted on being shielded by a blue screen.

The Crown called twenty-seven witnesses, whereas the defence had only Josephine Falleni, whose mother had now been exposed by newspapers across the country not only as a freak of nature but as a potential murderer. Josephine often cried and was inarticulate throughout most of her testimony. Crawford/Falleni made no admissions or confessions, and even though by the 1920s the accused did at last have the right to testify in his or her own defence, Falleni did not take the stand. She would have made a poor advocate for herself in any case: her English was broken despite living all but two years of her life within the British Empire; she was rough, inarticulate and stubborn. The secrecy and deception that had been her way of life since adolescence could not now be broken even to save her own life. Researchers therefore have no direct evidence of how Falleni perceived herself or viewed the world.

The Crown had a body of circumstantial evidence. An orchardist, James Hicks from North Ryde, testified that he had seen a man coming down Lane Cove Road to the Cumberland Mills where he worked at about 5.30am on Eight Hour Day in 1917. He had identified Crawford in a police line-up. Sergeant Gorman reported under oath that kerosene had been found at the scene of the crime. Government Medical Officer Dr A. A. Palmer, who conducted the autopsy, gave his findings about the cruel and violent way the deceased had died. No one else had a motive to kill Annie Birkett, by all accounts a quiet and modest woman, and given the element of disfiguration nor was it the modus operandi of a killing done by a stranger.

Crawford had a strong motive to kill his 'wife' – Birkett had intended to expose him. This is a strange element of the case. Generally the threat of exposure most affects individuals with a public reputation; but Crawford/Falleni was an illiterate person with a low-paid, casual labouring job with no public reputation to speak of. With little else to go on, it can only be assumed that her identity as a man was so strongly embedded that she would do anything – including murder – to preserve it. Police also discovered that Crawford was in the habit of having affairs with other married women whose husbands were away, often on active service during the war. This occurred while he was married to Birkett as well as afterwards. Dr Palmer, who was fascinated by sexual inversion and its practices, later told the British Medical Association that:

> Each of these women had become aware that Falleni visited the other. One of them, actuated by ill-feeling and jealousy, had made a hole in the weatherboard wall of the other woman's bedroom and, looking through this hole, had witnessed cohabitation between Falleni and the second woman.[13]

The trial reeked of this kind of voyeurism. Yet some people were sympathetic to Falleni. Surgeon Herbert Moran, who wrote about the case in 1939, believed that '[s]ociety had been hunting her all these furtive years and she had become like a creature which when cornered turns with savage claws on the pursuer'.[14] But this overlooks the basic fact that Crawford was largely 'hunted' for murder, and a highly brutal callous one.

The jury was out for some two hours before delivering a verdict of guilty. Eugenia Falleni was sentenced to death, which was commuted to life imprisonment. An appeal was dismissed since there was no new evidence to assess and no one else came forward to confess. Falleni served just ten years before her release. She assumed the identity of 'Mrs Jean Ford' and kept a boarding house in Paddington. She was run over by a car in Oxford Street on 9 June 1938 and buried with Anglican rites at Rookwood Cemetery.[15]

CHAPTER 15

Fighting Back

How the legal system in Australia dealt with women brutalised and tyrannised by violent partners shows surprising sympathy and insight into the motivation of women who fight back. In November 1834, Ann Walsh (alias Smith) stood before the Supreme Court of New South Wales charged with inflicting a mortal wound on her de facto husband, John Taylor. A convicted felon, she had arrived from Cork in 1824 on the *Almorah*. Since the trial was conducted during the still-early days of the colony, the case was heard before a military jury and the chief justice, Sir Francis Forbes (1784–1841). Smith was undefended even though this was a serious offence, but she *was* able to produce witnesses on her behalf. A shoemaker, Charles Daniels, who owned a boarding house in George Street, Sydney, told the court that Smith and Taylor had lived together in his house. Their relationship was volatile, characterised by 'angry words' and violence.[1] On the morning of the fatal assault, 23 October, the couple had argued. In the course of the dispute, Smith got a knife and stabbed Taylor. He was taken to Sydney Hospital where he died a week later. Smith alleged that Taylor threatened her, was constantly violent and had recently struck her with a heavy door bolt. When asked by a juror whether she was drunk on the morning of the attack, she replied that she was not.

Taylor's employer, Gabriel Thompson, a bricklayer of Ultimo, testified that he had visited Taylor in hospital. He was a sober man, unlike most of his other employees, he reported. He told Thompson that on the day of the assault Smith had asked him to go to the public house and get her half a pint of rum, which he did. She consumed this before 8am and then ordered him to get another. When he refused, she knifed him. Thompson believed they had argued about her constant drunkenness, a common problem in Sydney in this period among both men and working-women.

For a woman who allegedly drank heavily and possessed no education, Smith showed herself to be adept at calling and examining witnesses. The chief justice recognised the mitigating circumstances that 'the deceased had previously used violence'. He believed 'a sudden impulse of passion had prevailed over discretion and one which did not call for the extreme severity of the law'. Even in the early nineteenth century, and in what was essentially still a penal colony, rather than give the full weight of punishment, Forbes understood the dynamics that had led to the woman's retaliatory violence.[2] Smith was convicted of the lesser charge of manslaughter – which did not have the mandatory death penalty – and sentenced to transportation for seven years. She died in the harsh secondary detention centre, Moreton Bay Penal Settlement, in January 1839, just prior to its closure.[3]

In the Saturday edition of *Bell's Life in Sydney and Sporting Reviewer*, on 9 April 1859, an unusual article was featured. Murders and domestic assaults were common fare much documented in newspapers. This particular article, though, featured a series of drawings, then uncommon. They depicted a thin depressed-looking middle-aged woman sitting in the dock of a courtroom dressed modestly in a bonnet and a cloak. Her hands were crossed demurely upon her lap. Mary Ann Perry was accused of the brutal murder of her husband, John Perry. The more astounding images were the drawings of the dead man in his bed, and one of the deceased's employer, painting contractor Henry Crane. Mary Ann Perry appeared the epitome of quiet respectability, a far cry from the drunken, riotous, emancipist female defendants more common in court in previous decades.

The couple lived in a small rented house in Burwood, where the Longbottom Government Farm had been established in 1821, and small farms allocated initially to former soldiers in the New South Wales Corps. In 1855 Burwood was one of four inaugural railway stations in the colony. At the murder trial Sergeant William Grimmel testified that Perry was often drunk and abusive towards his wife: they '… lived very unhappily together'. Grimmel had frequently observed Perry drunk in public places, particularly in his current employment of painting the local public house. The local baker, John Blassett, stated that when he went to collect an outstanding payment around Christmas 1858, Mary Ann Perry came to the door, appearing 'very low spirited and melancholy … but not as if she were drunk … She had had words with her husband that morning …'. When Blasset insisted on payment, Mrs Perry said to her morose husband: 'Here's the baker, and he wants his money.' Perry called out from inside the cottage that he would pay on Thursday to which his wife shouted in response: 'Come and tell him yourself!' After that incident the house was always closed.

The butcher, Alexander McCallum, told the court that on Christmas Eve Mary Ann Perry suddenly arrived at his house and asked to be allowed indoors. He offered her a glass of wine. She told him that her husband had 'turned her out' and she wanted to stay the night there. He responded that he could not allow a married woman to stay the night under his roof even in these circumstances. Obviously, Mary Ann Perry was desperate. To go to a tradesman whom she hardly knew and ask for shelter shows that. Some time later she said her husband had gone to Sydney, leaving her destitute. She asked McCallum to buy her pig and some of her furniture. When he went to the house he found it 'topsy-turvy' as if there had been a struggle. He purchased the pig for 30 shillings.

Other witnesses outlined the tensions within the marriage that had been keenly observed by the small community. A Mrs Elizabeth Menzies said she had spoken to Perry on 28 December and asked about her husband. Perry had replied that he had 'gone away that morning'. When asked for further details, she'd replied: 'Good bye,

God bless you!' She spoke of him as 'her poor dear husband ... When I asked her where he had supposed to have gone, she gave me a long sigh, and said he had gone to heaven ...' At this point the police should have been called in to investigate John Perry's sudden disappearance.

Mrs Chitley said that Mary Ann Perry arrived on her doorstep unexpectedly on 29 December saying that her husband had stolen the wages he was to pay the painters and had absconded to Sydney. She asked to be allowed to stay the night even though the two women were not close friends. She came back on New Year's Day, 'dejected and crying', asking again to stay. She did not say at this time what was bothering her or what specifically had occurred. Two days earlier, on 30 December, Perry had tried to sell a black bag, for which she was given 4/-. Later, there was found to be blood inside the leather bag. On 15 January 1859, Perry also tried to sell her furniture to a local builder, William Lucas, and to the pawnbroker, Mrs Barnes. Still the police had not been called.

Finally, on 10 February 1859, Sergeant Grimmel, accompanied by Mr Linden, the owner of the cottage, went to the closed-up house because of a number of complaints of a foul odour. On entering the premises the detective found a man's body on a bed covered by a sheet. It was the decomposing corpse of John Perry. The fully dressed body was by now almost black, with a large gash across his temple. Grimmel later said that he never noticed any smells coming from the cottage, which he generally passed three or four times a day.

An inquest was convened to establish the cause of death. The jury, as was common at this time, visited the scene of the crime and viewed the body themselves. Mary Ann Perry was arrested and committed to stand trial in the Central Criminal Court in April before Justice Samuel Milford (1797–1865), who had served a disastrous term as the inaugural resident judge in the Moreton Bay District in 1857. An aloof, cold man more interested in equity, this sort of case hardly suited his temperament. Perry was too poor to afford counsel. The court

Demure and respectable Mary Ann Perry was found guilty of killing her husband – 'a drunken character'. She received the death sentence but it was commuted to fifteen years in jail. Image: *Bell's Life in Sydney and Sporting Reviewer*, 9 April 1859.

appointed Charles Blakeney (1802–78), who had served as a barrister on the Moreton Bay Circuit of the New South Wales Supreme Court and went on that year to become its first resident barrister.

The case was prosecuted by the attorney-general, Sir William Montagu Manning QC (1811–95), as was the convention in the mid-nineteenth century. He had trained at Lincoln's Inn and was considered highly competent and with excellent judgment. He opened the Crown's case by stating that he believed the murder was committed on 27 December between 10am and 10pm but allowed that this could be disputed. With such a putrefying body the forensic science of the time would have found it difficult to ascertain the time of death. Discussing the issue of motive, Manning believed that the deceased was 'a drunken character', an indication that the Crown intended to be merciful in this case of domestic homicide. Even though this had been a brutal crime, with the victim killed with an axe as he lay asleep on the bed, it was implied that John Perry's drunken and abusive behaviour had contributed to his demise. Abused and battered women, then as now, often killed their assailants when they were asleep or drunk and incapable of retaliating.

The jury retired for an hour, returning with a guilty verdict. Perry was given the death sentence. Justice Milford informed her that 'he held out no hope to you of the commendation of your sentence. You must prepare yourself for death ...' Mary Ann Perry had sat with a degree of depression and resignation throughout the trial and continued to keep her composure. She showed no emotion at all. Criminal cases at this time could not be appealed. Her only hope lay with the Executive Council. The premier, Sir Stuart Donaldson (1812–67), was a man of conservative principles, but even so his Executive Council did commute Mary Ann Perry's sentence to fifteen years' imprisonment.[4]

In March 1928, Norah Schieb was arrested for the murder of her husband, farmer Thomas Schieb from Bingera, near Bundaberg. The case hardly seemed to warrant a long investigation or lengthy trial, for Norah Schieb told the police: 'When I hit my husband with an axe I meant to kill him ... I am glad I killed my husband. I am not one bit sorry.' Queensland had abolished capital punishment in 1922 but Schieb could still have spent the rest of her life in prison if found guilty. What happened in the course of her trial and the judge's sentence, though, indicates that the legal system was able to discern the impact of domestic violence, and to understand that the murder proceeded from prolonged and frequent spousal abuse.

Norah Schieb revealed that on 9 November 1927, Thomas Schieb arrived back at the farm around midday. He had been drinking that morning but was still sober. Later, she saw him drinking from a bottle of gin. When questioned about it, she said they 'began rowing all the time, [with him] wanting me to sign the farm over to him'. They jointly owned the farm and Thomas Schieb wanted full possession, then no doubt to eject his wife. Incessant arguments about his consumption of alcohol characterised this stormy marriage. Later on that day, after constant altercations, he struck her on the face and around the body.

Around 7pm he and one of the workers on the farm, John Barrett, drove off without saying where they were going. Returning an hour later both were 'paralytic drunk'.

Going down into the cane fields to be alone, Norah Schieb thought she would avoid the violence that usually attended these drunken episodes, but her husband followed her and 'started bashing me straight away ... and knocked me down and kicked me on the hip, and screwed my left arm'. A farm worker, Tom Burns, came to her assistance after he heard her screaming. He asked if she would like to be taken into town, presumably for her own safety. Around 10pm, Thomas Schieb had fallen fully clothed onto the bed to sleep off his drunkenness. Norah Schieb told the police:

> Seeing my husband Thomas Schieb was asleep I sneaked
> away down the veranda and down the steps and walked to the
> woodheap at the back of the house, picked up the axe from the
> woodheap and walked up the stairs and sneaked around the
> veranda to my husband's room and stood alongside the bed
> and I hit him three blows on the head with the back of the axe.
> I hit him so he would not wake up. When I hit my husband
> Thomas Schieb with the axe he never moved or spoke ...
> after I planted the axe I came back to my bedroom and laid
> on the bed and went to sleep and woke up about four o'clock
> this morning and about five o'clock I had a wash and went to
> inform Constable Dwyer of South Kolan Police that I had
> killed my husband ...

Like Mary Ann Perry, Norah Schieb waited until her husband was asleep and unlikely to wake before she killed him. This was her defence against constant brutality witnessed by staff and neighbours.

Schieb was arrested for the wilful murder of her husband, standing trial in the circuit sittings of the Supreme Court of Queensland at Bundaberg on 5 March 1928 before Justice Frank

Brennan (1884–1949). The elevation in March 1925 of this former Labor parliamentarian, solicitor and Minister for Health and Public Instruction had been controversial. His was an inherently political appointment; moreover Brennan was initially not a barrister. Brennan had applied to become a barrister in 1924 using the amendment to legislation allowing solicitors of five years' standing to practise at the bar.[5] What he lacked in courtroom experience was more than compensated for by his deep understanding and sympathy for ordinary people, largely arising from his abiding Catholic faith.

The accused could have pleaded guilty since she had confessed to the police that she had killed her husband. But at the trial she pleaded not guilty. Schieb was represented by Edwin J. D. Stanley, the nephew of the chief justice, Sir James Blair. He had begun his career in the Crown Law Office before entering private practice in 1923. Like his uncle, he was a man possessed of an enormous social conscience, as well as a competency that saw him elevated to the bench in 1944.[6] Given the personal characteristics of the presiding judge and her counsel, Schieb could not have been more fortunate in her trial. Justice Brennan soon ascertained through his cross-examination that the defendant had suffered what appeared to be brain damage from the brutality she suffered during her marriage. The police also reported her rambling speech, although this could be accounted for by the stress and trauma brought on by her actions.

During his cross-examination of Dr Egmont Schmidt, who had conducted the postmortem, Stanley questioned closely about the physical and mental state of the accused and the deceased. Dr Schmidt reported that Thomas Schieb was a powerful man physically, unsurprising since he owned a cane farm, which required considerable manual labour. He also believed that while the accused was 'just an ordinary woman ... she was subnormal' in intelligence. The question of whether she was insane or suffering 'mental depression' was canvassed. Dr Schmidt believed – although he was not a psychiatrist and nor did he examine the accused immediately after the offence – that she might have been temporarily insane, and that was what had given her the extraordinary physical power to kill a strong man with an axe; parts of Thomas Schieb's skull had been found two metres from his body.[7]

The all-male jury found Norah Schieb guilty of the lesser offence of manslaughter, and made a strong recommendation for mercy. In his sentencing statement Justice Brennan stated that this had been a violent marriage where the prisoner could quite easily have been killed by her husband. There was no evidence presented in the Magistrate's or Supreme Court that she had been violent, except during the lethal attack. The testimony of witnesses was that the deceased could indeed have killed his wife that day, had it not been for their intervention. Schieb was released since Justice Brennan 'saw no good reason for sending the woman to gaol'.[8]

Although in the late 1920s there was no formal idea of 'battered woman syndrome' or legal apprehension of the cycle of domestic violence, some jurists, members of juries and legal counsel understood the dynamics that led women, so often described as 'perfectly ordinary', to murder their brutal husbands by stealth and with immense savagery.

A violent perpetrator of domestic violence was not always killed by the victim. Sometimes a child acted to end perpetual terror and abuse, often in defence of her mother. In April 1909, teenager Esther Salon, who lived with her family in the regional district of Marengo, near Young in New South Wales, shot her father with a revolver as he tried to choke her mother. Henry Salon had previously attempted to kill his wife in 1903, and had been bound over to keep the peace for six months. He often threatened to kill his wife, causing her to live in constant fear. The coroner reported that Esther's actions had been in protection of another's life and the children's court discharged her.[9] Patricide and matricide are rare crimes, usually only committed in such extreme circumstances.

In May 1937 Kathleen Burnes was charged in Charleville for the wilful murder of her stepfather, Anthony Trioly. Sergeant H. J. Kirk told the Magistrate's Court in the committal hearing that he had gone to the local bowling green where he found the deceased, Mary, his wife, and Kathleen Burnes, his married stepdaughter. Burnes told Kirk: 'I shot him. He came home drunk and was trying to choke Mum. My little sister Nettie came running to my house and told me that dad was drunk and was trying to kill them all. I got my husband's rifle and I saw him trying to choke my mother. I called out for him to let her go. He then rushed at me and I lifted the rifle and fired ... '[10] Burnes was committed to stand trial for wilful murder.

The case was heard before Justice Edward Archibald Douglas (1877–1947) in the circuit sittings of the Supreme Court of Queensland held in Charleville, a small regional community northwest of Brisbane. Douglas was the son of a Scottish aristocrat, John Douglas, a former premier of Queensland. He brought years of living and working on Thursday Island (where at various times his father had been a magistrate), mixing with a rough multi-ethnic community, to the bench. This had equipped with him an experience of life unusual in the judiciary.

Burnes pleaded not guilty to the charge despite her confession to the police. Evidence at the trial revealed that Trioly was frequently violent towards his family, especially when he was drunk. Mary Trioly's sister, Bonnie Campbell, testified that Mary and the youngest daughter, Anthonette (Nettie), lived in constant fear for their wellbeing, safety and lives. Neighbours verified the accounts of the extreme and frequent domestic violence in the Trioly household. On one occasion the deceased had chased Kathleen Burnes and another young woman with a knife, intending to harm them. The defendant was so terrified of her stepfather that she would wake up screaming in the night, terrified that he would enter her marital home and kill her.

Mary Trioly testified that her husband had tried to kill her younger daughter and that when she intervened he had 'kicked her in the stomach'. When she fell over, he 'lifted her to her feet by her hair. He then seized her throat and threatened to choke her.' On the day of his death, Trioly tried to kill his wife and only stopped when he was confronted by his stepdaughter, Kathleen Burnes. Justice Douglas recorded in his notebook that the deceased 'was a dangerous man when under the influence'.

The all-male jury selected from Charleville considered their verdict for just three minutes before entering a not-guilty verdict. To a man, they fully accepted that on the day of his death, the deceased was intent upon violence and perhaps murder against his wife and ten-year old-daughter, and that the defendant had acted to protect them and herself. Kathleen Burnes was discharged.[11]

Unlike Mary Ann Perry's case, a new century had brought a different and more enlightened perspective to cases argued as self-defence. The judges and juries in the cases of Norah Schieb and Kathleen Burnes understood that in both instances the man who had been killed was a violent abuser who terrorised his family, often in the full sight of others. A broader conceptualisation of self-defence was accepted in the case of Schieb, who had killed her abuser when he was drunk and sound asleep.

Both cases were still unusual because, in general, neighbours and employees rarely intervened in marital disputes, even those that appeared rancorous or even dangerous, driven by the customary wisdom that no one should 'come between a man and his wife'. Marriage was a private domain where a man could rule wife and family, literally without inference. The long-standing tradition of a man's 'ownership' of his wife and children was still enshrined in common-law doctrines. Even in the late 1890s everything a woman brought into a marriage passed into the ownership of her husband, as did everything she might receive afterwards; a wife also had no rights over her children at all. These archaic and intolerant laws concerning a woman's right to divorce, legally separate, own property and keep bequests, and to keep her wages were challenged in the later nineteenth century.

In 1857, the United Kingdom passed legislation allowing divorce by petition. South Australia followed with its legislation the following year.

By 1863, all the Australian colonies now allowed husbands to petition for divorce on the grounds of a wife's adultery. Late amendments allowed women to petition on the grounds of adultery with cruelty, drunkenness and criminality.[12] Justice William Windeyer in New South Wales led the reform movement to increase women's rights with regard to matrimony.[13] Women's Property Acts allowing married women to retain their own property and earnings were passed in the 1890s along with rights of custody of their children.[14] Yet, in spite of the immense gains in women's political rights as enfranchised citizens, the informal rule of a husband within the internal dynamics of the family persisted. Indeed, it has persisted into the twenty-first century.

Norah Shieb's case was unusual: women who killed abusive partners when they were asleep, drunk or unconscious were, in general, considered to have committed wilful murder rather than to have been acting in self-defence. This was because the offences were not committed in a moment of imminent threat – for example, the conventional scenario of a 'pub brawl' – instead, they waited until the abuser was unable to retaliate. So of course their actions appear premeditated and the women appear vengeful, sneaky and vicious.

Then in 1979, American researcher Dr Lenore E. Walker published a landmark study entitled *The Battered Woman*. This study sought to understand the complex cycles of violence that characterised a considerable number of domestic environments. Walker specifically focused on why women who experience severe domestic violence persist in a relationship that humiliates, brutalises, and sometimes even kills them. The defence was first tested in Australia in the Ericka Kontinnen trial in 1991 in South Australia, and, accepted in the appeal, the 'battered woman syndrome' has now become a more widely used explanatory argument for defence counsel in common-law jurisdictions.[15]

Erika Kontinnen never denied that she killed Edward Hill. At 7.30am on 28 March 1991, she went to the Angas Street Police Station accompanied by Hill's de facto wife, Olga Runjanjic, to say as much. The levels of sadism, terror, violence and deprivation of liberty the deceased man perpetrated on the two women are almost unbelievable.

Kontinnen was a poorly educated woman with few life or employment skills. She had been involved with Hill's cousin Ronald for nearly a decade before he left her for another woman. However sympathetic he at first appeared, Edward Hill hated women, allegedly because he had contracted syphilis at the age of eighteen. By the time he was just twenty-five, he had thirteen convictions for violence, including assault upon a homosexual with whom he lived in a predatory relationship.[16] His upbringing had been troubled, with an aggressive and violent father. He spent much of his youth in reformatories and boys' homes, and was an avid follower of the mass murderer Charles Manson. At one time, Hill had admitted himself to hospital fearing his violent urges were out of control.[17]

Erika Kontinnen alleged she was forced into a sexual relationship with Hill in 1988. He was then living with his common-law wife, Olga Runjanjic, with whom he later had a son, Archie. Like Kontinnen, Runjanjic had little formal education and was forced to work as a prostitute to supplement the couple's unemployment benefits. With this income they purchased a property at Swan Reach in north-west Victoria. Soon after Kontinnen moved in with the couple, Hill pressured her to purchase the adjoining property in order to start a firewood business. Since she had a job at the local Bridgestone factory and could go guarantor on the loan, Kontinnen was in a position to further the threesome's interests. She agreed.

Almost as soon as the ink had dried, Hill began to be abusive and violent towards her, contending that she now threatened his financial security by taking out a loan which he had no means of servicing. His solution was to force both women to become prostitutes as well as running a telephone sex business. Initially, Kontinnen refused, but the beatings endured by Runjanjic escalated so quickly and became so horrific that she consented.

Hill treated his two 'wives' as slaves – at his beck and call, administering to every whim and fantasy, no matter how abhorrent. He ran a regime of terror, not allowing them to sleep for any extended period or to have any personal autonomy. His physical violence was so severe that both women frequently ended up in hospital. Even then Hill forced them to leave before adequate treatment was completed. On one occasion, Runjanjic had a wound on her head that became infested with maggots, which Hill found highly amusing. He was cruel to Archie in front of the women, throwing him against the wall and even holding his head underwater. Another time he held a shotgun to the little boy's head to terrorise his mother.

Kontinnen and Runjanjic formed a close bond, united by their fear of Hill and their concern for each other, and for Archie. Hill was inordinately proud of his sexual prowess and often brought other women to the house, as well as forcing Runjanjic to have sex with other men so he could watch. This would in turn lead to accusations of infidelity, for which Runjanjic would be then beaten so severely that she would have to be hospitalised. Hill brought gay lovers to the house sometimes. He threatened the women that if either left him, or if he was sent to prison, he would ensure they were both 'executed'. Hill also frequently beat the two women in public, yet no one attempted to intervene or reported the incidents to the police. As in most cases of domestic violence, at certain parts of the cycle Hill could be charming, contrite and easygoing. But these periods became increasingly rare.

Kontinnen and Runjanjic appeared in the Supreme Court of South Australia in May 1991 on the charges of falsely imprisoning Patricia Hunter and causing her grievous bodily harm. Hill, who had also been charged with this crime, was by this time dead. The victim was a longstanding friend of Kontinnen who had been critical of her relationship with Hill. It was alleged that some articles had been stolen from a house in Adelaide where Kontinnen, Hill and Runjanjic lived when they came into Adelaide. Hill alleged that the thief was Hunter. On a pretext devised by Hill, Kontinnen lured her to the Swan Reach property, where Hill beat her with a shotgun. He then handcuffed her to a bed and cut the rings from her fingers even though she had a broken arm that required medical attention. Hunter was then moved to another property and held there against her will for almost a week, from 29 May 1989 to 3 June 1989.

In the original trial, the defendants Kontinnen and Runjanjic denied they knew that violence would be used against Hunter. Yet, at the same time, they contended that they were so terrorised by Hill they had to go along with his plan. The pair were found guilty. In their appeal in 1992, their counsel, K. V. Borick, argued that the case was a notable instance of the 'battered woman syndrome'. He outlined Kontinnen's and Runjanjic's lives with Hill and described how he had terrorised them, keeping them in mortal fear. The work of Lenore Walker, as well as cases in the United States and Canada that had tested the assumptions were cited by defence counsel in the appeal. Chief Justice Leonard King, Justice Christopher Legoe and Justice Derek Bollen accepted the veracity of the syndrome that led women to act abhorrently when they are completely under the control of another person.[18] Kontinnen and Runjanjic were retried in early 1993 and sentenced to three and a half years' jail, which was suspended on payment of a three-year good behaviour bond.

Before being retried for the Hunter case, Kontinnen was tried for the murder of Edward Hill on Sunday, 27 March 1991. The story emerged that early that morning Hill had been particularly aggressive, threatening and attacking Runjanjic with a broom. Her face and legs were injured. The two women took Archie and fled the house, hiding in a park. Since they had no money, they were forced by necessity to return home, where they knew they would be punished. Kontinnen later left the house to service one of her clients. When she returned that night, she decided to read a magazine but when Hill saw her reading without his permission he made her stand at the back of the room. When Archie started to cry, Hill became even more infuriated.

Hill then proceeded to beat Kontinnen. When he finished, he said quietly and matter-of-factly: 'I'm tired. I'm going to get some sleep and all yous [sic] will be dead when I wake up.' Kontinnen got a gun and shot him, although she could not recall these events. The two women fled with the baby and went to a local service station, where Kontinnen called a friend, who urged them to go to the police. Hill was known to the police. The women were reportedly so concerned about their own safety that, on returning to the scene, Kontinnen climbed in through a window to see if Hill was still alive.[19]

Kontinnen's trial outlined the level of violence, terror and threats to which Hill had subjected Kontinnen, Runjanjic and Archie Hill on an almost daily basis. The jury accepted that Kontinnen had acted in defence of herself and the others, and she was acquitted.

When asked by the police: 'How could you still love him?' Runjanjic replied: 'Love is strange, love is blind.' Kontinnen also added: 'Sometimes I felt I loved him.'

Three years later, in 1994, Margaret Raby was charged with the wilful murder of her husband, Keith, who, she testified, had defecated, urinated and vomited on her. She was subject to constant sexual torture and humiliation. He left firearms around their marital home that he threatened to use on a constant basis. In her trial before Justice Bernard Teague in the Victorian Supreme Court she testified that 'I loved Keith very much, with all my heart, and I thought what I could give him, sir, with my love and psychiatric help, we could overcome what he did to me.'[20] Like Kontinnen and Runjanjic, Raby exhibited a common response of women in violent domestic relationships. They love their partner and feel responsible for his behaviour and the subsequent abuse. This sense of responsibility, as well as the attrition of autonomy and escalation of fear, goes some way to explaining why women in such relationships are unable to leave their abuser.

Raby's trial was the first time the battered woman syndrome had been successfully used as part of a defence in Victoria.

CHAPTER 16

Deadly Lovers' Pacts in the Nineteenth Century

Marriage was the bedrock upon which society was founded, and men were in sole charge of the union. Until 1923 in the United Kingdom, the only grounds for divorce was adultery – and the only person who could sue for divorce was a husband. Before that time, a man could be as unfaithful, cruel and violent as he liked. If his wife left him, he kept everything – all her property, all her money ... and the children. It was possible after 1878 for a woman to legally separate from her husband, but she could not divorce and therefore could not marry again. After 1923, adultery became grounds for both husbands and wives to divorce, and in 1937 the additional reasons of cruelty and desertion were added. It was not the 1970s that no-fault divorce became a reality, with a more equal approach to sharing property and care of any children. The very fact that women could be trapped in loveless, cruel or squalid marriages with no recourse or support meant that sometimes the desire for escape could take on a deadly form.

Lucretia Dunkley and her lover, Martin Beech, were executed in 1843 for the wilful murder of her husband Henry Dunkley, a successful farmer from Goulburn. He had been killed with such force that his face had been almost obliterated. Situated 200 kilometres from Sydney, Goulburn was the first regional inland town in the colony of New South Wales. British settlement had been permitted from 1825, although few then ventured so far into this remote and dangerous place. In 1827 William Pitt Faithfull (1806–96) was granted land on the Goulburn plains. The first legal land sales were conducted in 1839. Soon the authorities in Sydney despatched convicts to the area to work in road gangs, many of whom were housed in the Towrang Stockade. Others, like Tom Shepherd transported from Southampton in 1830, worked as 'ticket of leave' (paroled) convicts for private settlers such as Henry Dunkley.

The courts had become accustomed to dealing with disgruntled convicts who took up arms against their assigned masters and injured or killed them. But the circumstance of the wife of a respectable free farmer who appeared to have conspired with her convict lover was particularly unsettling. Her origins were far from respectable as she had been transported from Wales.[1] Suspicions were aroused when Dunkley tried to sell some wheat without her husband's presence. When questioned later at her farm, Dunkley told police that her husband had been murdered by Martin Beech, a ticket-of-leave convict in their employ. On 19 September 1842, almost a week after the crime was later revealed to have taken place, Sergeant John Cook went to the farm and found the body of Henry Dunkley. Beech was arrested and taken to the lock-up in Goulburn.

Dunkley was brought to see Beech where she said that she had no idea why he would kill his master. His clothes were stained with blood, but this, Beech said, came from a bullock he had killed. The police took Beech to the farm to view the body, which he initially denied could be that of Henry Dunkley and obdurately refused to touch when he was asked too. Meanwhile his widow threw herself onto the corpse, which she kissed with a great show of affection and grief.

The story she told was unbelievable. Dunkley alleged that she was asleep with her husband on the night of 13 September 1842, when Beech entered their bedroom and murdered the sleeping man with an axe. She hid under the bed but then helped him conceal the crime. She did not call out for the other convicts and servants to come to her aid or to call the police. This and the fact that the day before her husband's murder she had told people that he was going to Goulburn the next morning point to her as a willing accomplice. At the inquest on 28 September both Dunkley and Beech were held over for the wilful murder of Henry Dunkley.[2]

The trial in the Supreme Court of New South Wales was held before the chief justice, Sir James Dowling (1784–1844), and a civilian jury in Berrima on 5 September 1843. Servants on the farm testified that Mrs Dunkley had conducted a sexual liaison with Beech.[3] Dunkley alleged that her co-accused was solely responsible for the murder, although a report of the inquest says that they had planned to sell Henry Dunkley's property, marry, and move hundreds of kilometres away 'where no one knew what they had done'.[4] It may also have been that she had set Beech up, using their sexual liaison and promises for the future. In any case, Dunkley denounced Beech to police right from the start of the investigation. During the trial she shouted abuse at him, at the crown prosecutor, and at the jury and judge. She frequently laughed and called every witness a liar and a perjurer. By contrast, Beech was composed and calm.

The jury took just five minutes to find the pair guilty of wilful murder. They were both sentenced to be hanged 'without the least hope of human mercy'. Chief Justice Dowling's sentencing remarks are worth examination. Even though he was accustomed to dealing with loud, aggressive and violent behaviour from convict women, Dowling still felt compelled to tell Dunkley that she was 'the Devil in female form … a drunken polluter of the rites of Hymen, the violator of every tie by which the sacred institution of marriage can unite in holy wedlock, yielding to brutal lust and with her paramour, consummating her guilty passion in the blood of her husband'. He also invoked the medieval concept of *petit treason*, now no longer in use in common-law jurisdictions. But in those days, wives and servants were beholden to their 'masters'. If either one took up arms against their lawful master, then the penalty was severe. Dowling also accused Beech of violating his duty to his master by 'murderous treason'.

Dowling was disappointed that 'the humane spirit of the modern age forbids the dreadful severity ... by which the treasons of a murderous wife was expiated by burning alive'; Lucretia Dunkley was lucky that burning at the stake had been outlawed in England in 1790. What had not been known at the trial was that Dunkley was pregnant. She and Beech were executed in Berrima jail on Monday, 9 October 1843[5] and later 'anatomised' and dissected by the local surgeon James Ramsey. Their skulls and the skeleton of the foetus were donated by Dr Ramsay in November 1854 to the Australian Museum, where they were placed on public display.[6]

Sometimes lust and greed produce a volatile mixture that prompts murder. In 1855 Bridget Hurford became the first woman executed in Western Australia. Her supposed lover, Enoch Dodd, was also hanged. Philip Dixon, who had forged the last will of John Hurford, was found guilty of forgery and sentenced to transportation to Van Diemen's Land for the term of his natural life.[7] He was only pardoned because he had turned queen's evidence. At first the accomplices had got away with murder, for the medical practitioner conducting the autopsy, Hannibal Bryan, was later found to be neither qualified nor registered. He was so incompetent he did not know the most basic procedure and could not even use a stethoscope, which, invented in France in 1816, was by then, forty years later, a widespread medical instrument. Bryan found nothing suspicious about the elderly man's sudden death.

John Hurford had arrived as a free man soon after the Swan River Colony was established in 1829. He first went to Augusta and then moved to Wonnerup Inlet near Busselton, where he took up farming. Most of his workers were former convicts, frequently those who found it difficult to find employment, even with significant labour shortages in the new settlement. Hurford was described as an eccentric who worked hard and kept company with vagabonds and tough former felons. In 1851, at the age of sixty-five – then considered ancient – he married. By this stage he was a wealthy man who had accrued a small fortune of £2000. His new wife, Bridget Larkin, was a young widow with three children: Thomas, Bridget and Neddy Larkin.[8] Her husband, a soldier in the 21st Regiment, had recently drowned in Bunbury, and she was desperate to secure her family's security.

From the start Hurford was allegedly abusive and aggressive towards her husband. Not only verbally abusive but on one occasion she had knocked him down, dislodging some of his teeth. After just four years he tired of the constant quarrelling and violence. He went to live with his neighbours, the Greens, after his wife had pushed him out of his bed and onto the floor, the final straw. At the Greens, Hurford lived in one room, being forced to share it with a servant, George Jones.[9] Despite how substantial his own house was – with a separate kitchen, several bedrooms and dairy – sharing with Jones was, for Hurford, far preferable to living with his wife. At the end of six weeks, however, his neighbour explained they needed the room to store barley, and so Hurford was obliged to return home. He was so afraid of his wife that he asked Jones to come and share his bedroom.

On 8 April 1855, Hurford complained of feeling unwell with a severe sore throat. Bridget Hurford gave him some mulled wine. She also asked Jones to sleep in another room to give her husband a chance to rest. Later that night John Hurford was found dead in his bed; his eyes were open and protruding and there were red marks on his neck. The inquest found, on the evidence of 'Dr' Hannibal Bryan, that he had died of natural causes. Witnesses confirmed that the old man had indeed complained of a sore throat, which was swollen. Hurford's will was probated and Bridget Hurford became a wealthy woman.

Later in April, Enoch Dodd confessed to Philip Dixon that he had killed John Hurford and that the whole plot had been Bridget Hurford's idea. On the night of the murder she had urged Dodd to act, with the inducements of a horse and £10 – and the influence of large quantities of alcohol. When he baulked, she stood over him until he had strangled her husband to death. Dodd and Dixon were both ticket-of-leave convicts and hardened men. Yet both found this callous murder of the elderly man who employed them under good conditions repugnant. But that didn't stop Dodd and Hurford ransacking the dead man's belongings.[10]

In September 1855, a lengthy magisterial inquiry was held in Vasse to reconsider the death of John Hurford. On 24 August, Hurford and Dodd had been charged with murder and Dixon with forgery. It was revealed at the inquiry that Bridget Hurford maintained her own home on the property, which had several subdivisions, some with tenant farmers. Several witnesses testified that Hurford had said he would never leave his wife a farthing, and also that the signature on the will was not that of the deceased. A highly literate employee, Andrew Norman, told the magistrates' hearing that he customarily did all correspondence for Hurford and had not been asked to arrange a new will.[11] Neighbour John Green revealed that Hurford had been prepared to sell his property to get away from his wife and that 'several people' had come to view it.[12]

On 4 October 1855, Bridget Hurford and Enoch Dodd appeared before Justice William Mackie (1799–1860), a highly competent jurist trained at Trinity College, Cambridge, and the Inner Temple. He was one of the first free settlers to arrive in the Swan River Colony in October 1829.[13] In this trial he was assisted by a bench of magistrates, but not a jury. His health was poor and there was speculation that he might not be able to take on such a complicated case. Richard Birnie (1808–88) was the advocate-general. He came from a distinguished legal family; his father, (Sir) Richard Birnie, had identified the Cato Street conspirators in the 1820 plot to assassinate the British prime minister and cabinet, the last time in British history that prisoners convicted of high treason were hanged, drawn and quartered.[14] Hurford was defended by Nathaniel Howell, who had arrived in Western Australia in 1853 at the age of twenty-one. Despite his youth and inexperience, Howell was an able counsel, skilled in cross-examination. It was to no avail – Hurford and Dodd were found guilty of wilful murder and sentenced to death.

DEADLY LOVERS' PACTS IN THE NINETEENTH CENTURY

On Monday, 15 October 1855, Bridget Hurford and Enoch Dodd were publicly executed in the new Fremantle jail along with a convict, George Williams, who had attempted to murder a warder. The public eagerly awaited the well-publicised event. Just before 7am a military and police escort took the male prisoners on open carts to the place of execution, where they had to wait some ten minutes before Hurford arrived in a closed cart. Dodd appeared to be very distressed but Hurford was quiet and weak. She had confessed to the crime before her death. A Roman Catholic priest accompanied her to the gallows saying prayers as they walked along. He took charge of her body when it was cut down after hanging for thirty minutes. After Hurford's body was removed from the gallows the two men were hanged. The newspapers commented that many women had attended the executions.[15]

Elizabeth Scott was hanged in 1863 for killing her husband with the help of her lover and another accomplice. She was the first woman to be executed in the colony of Victoria. Her life had been marred by tragedy and brutality that belied a genteel upbringing in England. Scott was born in 1840 in Twickenham, a settlement identified in the Doomsday Book of 1086, on the southern side of the Thames River near the beautiful royal parks of Richmond. When she was twelve, her parents moved to Canterbury in New Zealand before deciding to try their luck on the Victorian goldfields.

For a young girl with a sensitive disposition the goldfields were a rude shock. They were rough, dirty and violent. Most people lived in tents that could be easily transported as the goldfields expanded and moved. Dysentery and cholera were constant reminders of the lack of public health facilities; there were few resources or public infrastructure of any kind. People who came to make their fortunes often became desperate when their rewards did not match their hopes. Robert Scott was one who had initially been fortunate; he had accumulated a considerable financial asset from his prospecting. But as a severe alcoholic he had drunk much of it away. In 1854, believing he was far wealthier than he was, and when she was just fourteen, Elizabeth's parents forced her to marry this uncouth, drunken man of thirty-six. Their daughter did not end up in the life of gentility and luxury they had anticipated.

By the time she was twenty she had borne four children, two of who had died in the unsanitary conditions. Robert Scott set up a grog shanty between Mansfield and Devil's River in the north-east of the colony, an area later famous as the stomping ground of the Kelly Gang. The Scott shanty was on the stock route and isolated from other dwellings. With Elizabeth Scott's fine looks and good manners it soon became a popular meeting place offering food, accommodation and alcohol for the many lonely single men working in the district.[16] Scott was also a shrewd businesswoman who knew how to grow the small business. Before long she fell in love with a nineteen-year-old farm labourer, David Gedge, who was kind, shy and adoring. Like her he was English, having been born at Deptford in Kent, and was accustomed to finer things than the Devil's River grog shanty.

Despite Robert Scott's obsessive watchfulness over his pretty young wife's movements, Gedge and Elizabeth Scott became lovers. They often met when Robert Scott lay drunk and unconscious at night. At other times they met in the nearby stringybark forest. Elizabeth began to plan a life away from the squalor and crudeness, although a quiet young man with no ambition was unlikely to be able to give her a comfortable new life. Elizabeth Scott also had another ardent admirer in the form of their Macao-born general servant, Julian Cross, who despised his employer and the manner in which he treated his wife. Cross was not aware of Elizabeth Scott's liaison with Gedge, and evidence suggests that his attentions towards his mistress remained platonic.

On 13 April 1863, a merchant named Ellias Ellis and his wife, Ellen, stayed at the Scotts' establishment for the night on their way to Melbourne. They had already stayed there three days earlier, on their way to Jamieson, then a small goldfield supply settlement. On that occasion they both saw Elizabeth Scott and Gedge leave the bar at around 5pm, go to the stables and lock the door, and then return again an hour later, coming inside hand in hand. The middle-aged couple said nothing, since it was hardly their business to monitor other people's morals.

During their second stay, on 13 April, the Ellises pitched their tent about 20 metres from the Scotts' house. Elizabeth Scott was starved of feminine company and confided to Ellen Ellis how troubled and unhappy her marriage was. She explained how her parents had forced her to marry when she was still practically a child, and how worried she was that her husband drank so frequently and so much that he was ruining his health and their livelihood. He was suicidal, constantly telling anyone who would listen that he intended to end his misery with a shotgun.

That night Elizabeth Scott asked Mrs Ellis to help her with her husband, who was suffering from delirium tremens. He lay shivering, his teeth chattering, complaining that he was freezing. Mrs Ellis rubbed his feet and suggested that it was time to call in a doctor. Even though there was none nearby, she insisted, in case Elizabeth was later called to account for her husband's death, which seemed imminent. Mrs Ellis stayed to have a nobbler of whisky with him. When she went into the kitchen, she saw Elizabeth Scott and David Gedge huddled at the table deep in conversation. Then Gedge left the two women to talk. After she returned to her tent, Mrs Ellis later heard Robert Scott violently retching.

Around midnight, Ellias and Ellen Ellis were woken by the sound of a single gunshot. Gedge came to their tent and told them that Scott had killed himself. Mr Ellis rushed to the house, where he found Elizabeth Scott in the kitchen. On entering the bedroom he saw the deceased; smoke was still lingering from the gunfire. Scott was lying on his right side, with a pistol near his right knee. Ellis stayed there for about ten minutes, taking note of all the arrangements and conditions in the room, which he later sketched for the trial.[17] He noticed a wound near Scott's left ear. When Ellis returned to the kitchen, Gedge and Julian Cross were there, together with Mrs Ellis. He told them: 'This is a bad job. There'll be a coroner's inquest over this ... it is impossible for a man to have shot himself from the position in which he is lying.' He then said he had attended several inquests and was familiar with the procedures. He believed that this had been a particularly inept attempt to make murder look like suicide. That a right-handed man could shoot himself near his left ear and then lie on his right side was always going to lead to questions. Had he been shot in his right ear, the killers might have got away with murder, given the standards of rural policing and forensic science in 1863.

Ellis berated Elizabeth Scott for leaving a pistol near her husband's reach when she knew he was morose and suicidal.

Cross was sent off on horseback to find help from the police. What Gedge and Scott didn't know was that Cross immediately confessed to them.

The Ellises returned to their tent to try to sleep. Around 4am Gedge came to see Ellias Ellis, claiming that it was the 'blackfellow [meaning Cross] that shot Bob'. What is not clear is whether Cross was part of the plot from the start or brought in only when Gedge bungled the first attempt. Ellis said he would take charge until the police came. When they arrived at around 10am, Ellis conducted them to the room where Robert Scott lay dead.

Elizabeth Scott, David Gedge and Julian Cross were arrested for the wilful murder of Robert Scott and stood before the Chief Justice of Victoria, Sir William Stawell (1815–89), in Supreme Court sittings at Beechworth on 28 October 1863. An aristocratic Irishman, Stawell had been trained at Trinity College, Dublin, and Lincoln's Inn before arriving in the colony in 1843. Scott was represented by barrister George Stephen, the brother of Sir Alfred Stephen, Chief Justice of New South Wales. Dogged by a scandal very early in his career, he eventually set up a practice in Beechworth before embarking on a career as a faith healer.[18]

Julian Cross provided crucial evidence for the prosecution case when he testified that Gedge had told him that he had shot at Scott but the pistol failed to fire. At first Cross did not know what to do but Elizabeth Scott had pleaded with him to kill her husband. So he swallowed some brandy and went into the bedroom and shot the almost comatose man. The men had to later fit the bullet to the pistol while Elizabeth Scott calmly watched. In the trial she denied any involvement in the murder, pleading that it was undertaken entirely without her knowledge or consent by her two admirers. The jury was not convinced, and all three were found guilty and sentenced to death.

No woman had been executed in the colony before then, and this was an uncomfortable start. Elizabeth Scott was a young mother, attractive and personable, a woman who had been married to a drunken brute who had humiliated and belittled her. She could have waited until he drank himself to death, given he was already suffering delirium tremens. Instead, she conspired with her lover, David Gedge, and admirer, Julian Cross, to murder him. As an accessory, she was equally guilty of the capital crime. The three prisoners were kept in Melbourne jail to await their public execution. The sherriff, the official of the Supreme Court who oversaw the punishments handed down, was concerned there would be a considerable crowd to witness this unprecedented act, so he ordered that only forty-five spectators be admitted, much to the disappointment of many Melbourne residents.

On 11 November 1863, the three prisoners were brought from the cells to the scaffold by the jailer, led by Julian Cross. The Anglican Dean of Melbourne, the Very Reverend Hussey Macartney, had attended Scott in her final days and accompanied her to the gallows, saying prayers. Cross was a Roman Catholic from Portuguese Macao and attended by two priests. The Reverend G. Stoddard attended Gedge. Scott was executed first. Her dying words were: 'David, will you not clear me?' He remained silent. She had dressed smartly for her execution in widows' black and carefully arranged and braided-hair.[19]

Judges and juries were tough on married women who were found guilty of killing an unwanted husband. Ellen Thomson was the only woman ever executed in Queensland. The case remains contentious since the circumstances of her husband's death by gunshot in 1886 at Port Douglas in far northern Queensland are open to multiple interpretations. The remarks to the jury by presiding judge, Justice (later Sir) Pope Cooper, were inflammatory and worded in such a way that a guilty verdict for Thomson and her lover John Harrison was inevitable. On her deathbed Thomson dictated an extraordinary confession that revealed that her youngest child was illegitimate, fathered by a man who was not her husband, and that this was her 'guilty secret'. She denied ever plotting to kill William Thomson, although she admitted she hated him.[20]

Ellen Lynch was born in poverty in Cork in southern Ireland in 1846 at the height of the Famine. She and her family endured the full brunt of the disaster since they did not leave Ireland until 1857. Her father died, leaving Ellen, her mother, and Mary, a sister two years her junior, to fend for themselves. The deprivations of her childhood were marked on Ellen's body: she was only 145 cm (4' 9") in height, tiny even for the mid-nineteenth century. Her mother, Mary Murphy Lynch, had a sister, Honora Heffernan, who lived in Goulburn in New South Wales. She had been transported to New South Wales from Cork in 1839 and issued with her 'certificate of freedom' in 1846 after serving her entire seven-year sentence. In Goulburn, Mary Murphy Lynch married another former convict from Ireland. James Heffernan had arrived in the colony in 1840 from County Meath.[21] Although the Lynch family now had a support network and some form of income, the girls did not attend school; Ellen Thomson was almost illiterate when she died.

In 1862, when she was just sixteen, Ellen Lynch married William Wood, then aged thirty-five years old. They stayed in Goulburn where they had five children, one of whom, Victoria, died in 1867. William Wood died in 1871, leaving his family with few resources. Ellen

Wood therefore in 1873 decided to try her luck in Cooktown, a small northern port in Queensland that was the entry point for miners and goods destined for the newly opened Palmer River goldfields.

This was a wild and violent environment where several frontiers operated at the same time. Settlers waged war upon the Indigenous peoples for the control of the land, and intense animosity was directed towards the 18,000 to 20,000 Chinese miners who had come from Canton, Pekin and Macao intent upon acquiring wealth from this single mining field. There were few facilities and little infrastructure in such mining centres and their ports. For the few British women that ventured into these remote and largely lawless places there was always plenty of work as servants, cooks, barmaids – and prostitutes. Cooktown supported some sixty-five registered hotels and over thirty general stores at the height of the gold rush.

How Ellen Wood earned a living for herself and her four children isn't known since she did not refer to it in her confession. After five years at Cooktown the family moved to Port Douglas, the small port near the Daintree River and the Hodgkinson River goldfields. These had opened up in 1876 when British miners left the Palmer River site searching for richer pickings.[22] Wood obtained the post of housekeeper to the elderly William Thomson, who had been the first farmer in the district, taking up a selector's block in October 1877. He also employed Chinese tenant farmers and labourers to produce maize, coffee and coconuts for the expanding population. Under discriminatory legalisation, Chinese people were not permitted to own or take out selections.

In late 1880, Wood gave birth to a daughter whom she named Ellen, and who took the surname Wood. Soon after, she married her employer. This child was later the subject of litigation over her guardianship after her mother's execution. The putative father was William Owen Jones, a resident of Port Douglas and the executor of William Thomson's will.[23] In her deathbed statement she reported that Jones convinced her to make Thomson believe he was the child's father.

The marriage was a disaster from the start. A widower with an adult family, Thomson was then aged fifty-six and he loathed the noise the five children made. Just before her execution in June 1887, Ellen Thomson dictated a letter to the governor, Sir Anthony Musgrave, begging for mercy. In this sad epistle she explained that she had previously asked him and the then premier, Sir Samuel Griffith, during their tour of Port Douglas to provide a school 'to bring my children up the right way, as my husband was so cranky. I banished all the children so that they would not annoy the poor old man …'[24]

Before her execution she detailed what had happened to some of her children: Eve married young and Thomson refused to attend his stepdaughter's wedding; Jemmy had been taken in by the clerk of the court in Port Douglas as 'an act of charity'; and Bob had been despatched to his grandmother in Goulburn. William Thomson resented Nellie (Ellen) because of the speculation about her paternity. She favoured his friend William Jones in looks. So the little girl was often left in the township, although Ellen Thompson did not say with whom.

The couple worked the farm together, labouring hard in the tropical climate, battling constant rain and ever-encroaching vegetation. William owned cattle, and Ellen brought some pigs into the marriage. The farm was not going well financially; Thomson told his wife that the Bank of New South Wales was pressing him for a debt of £100. Arguments were so frequent and menacing that Ellen Thomson stayed in the marital house while William Thomson slept in a smaller building next door. It is not clear when she met John Harrison, a worker on the neighbouring farm 'Bonnie Doon', or when they became lovers. He was an Englishman, fourteen years her junior, and a blacksmith by trade who had deserted the British Army. His photograph in the prison records showed him to be a handsome man with a fresh complexion and fair hair, rather like Heath Ledger. Ellen Thomson was careworn, with grey hair and rough blunt hands that had seen hard work all her life. Her complexion was pitted and deeply ravaged, as if she had suffered smallpox.

William Thomson's second marriage – to Ellen Lynch, a widow with four children – was disastrous. Convicted for her role in his violent death, Ellen was the only woman executed in Queensland. Photo: Queensland State Archives.

There were varying accounts about how William Thomson died on the evening of 22 October 1886. Ellen Thomson stated in her confession that she believed her husband had committed suicide with a bullet to the head. He had said to her that morning he was 'disappointed and miserable for want of money … and did not want to live … the bank would soon foreclose'. She suggested they sell their respective livestock. He was also distressed about the unruly behaviour of his Chinese tenants, whom he could no longer manage. Perhaps his son Bill could come as manager, he wondered. 'The yellow dogs have ruined me and [I] will be putting a bullet through some of them or burning down their humpies about them …' he told his wife.

Ellen Thomson dictated in her jail confession that she went to bed that night around 8pm and was awakened by the sound of a gunshot. She got out of bed and said: 'God Almighty, what's up? I sang out, "Daddy, what is up?" But I got no answer … I went to Marshall's [the

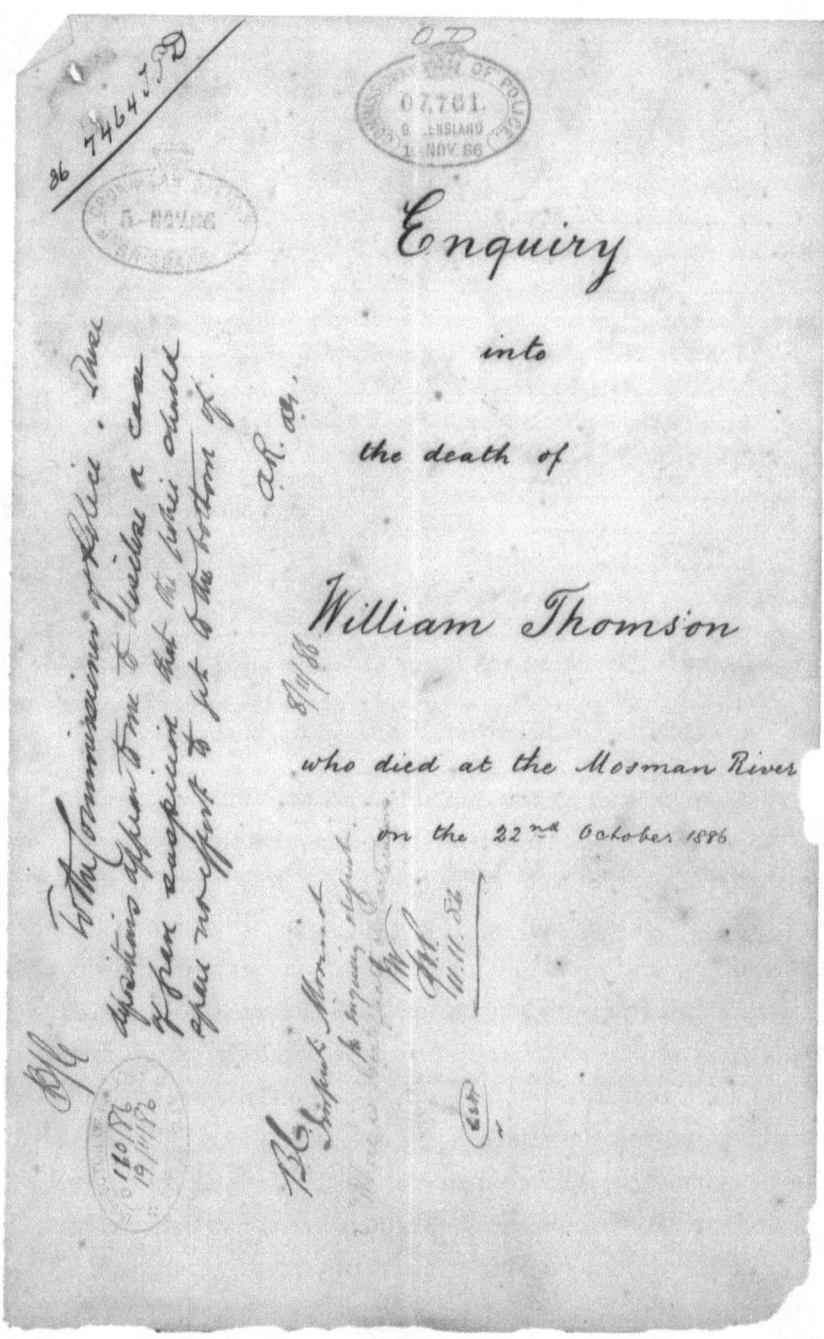

Notes from the statements used as evidence in the trial of Ellen Thomson. Image: Queensland State Archives.

farm where Harrison worked] as there was something wrong with Billy and [asked them] to come on down at once …' She saw Harrison there and spoke to him: 'Is it not a dreadful thing if anything has happened to Billy?' He replied: 'I hope, Mrs Thompson [sic] it is not as bad as you think.' At this time she did not say she had seen her husband lying injured or dead. Marshall and Harrison came to her selection, where they found Thomson dying, too late for medical treatment.

In the trial held in Townsville on 10 and 11 May 1887, a different version of events was presented. Patrick Moran, who worked on the Thomsons' farm, testified that the evening of the shooting he was playing his harmonica when Harrison arrived and started a verbal altercation with Thomson, who said to him: 'I thought you had gone away.' He then accused the young man of 'hawking' (having sex) with his wife, whom he called 'the old woman'. He laughed about her having a 'fancy man'. (It was true enough – for the period she *was* old, since many women died in their mid-forties from the long-term effects of multiple childbirths and rough conditions.) Ellen Thomson had been sitting on the verandah during this argument. When her husband put his hand in his shirt, she called out: 'Look out, Jack, he has got a revolver; you don't know what the old bastard might do.' Harrison then shot him. He said later at the trial that it had been in self-defence.[25] A careful reading of all the testimony favours this version of events.

When other witnesses were called, they stated that there had been two shots. Ah Wing, Ah Loy and Jane Le Ong, a British woman married to Chinese tenant farmer Le Ong, all testified there were two shots, which ruled out suicide. Dr Marley, who at first thought there had only been one shot – through the head – later told both the police inquiry and the Supreme Court trial there were two shots. The crown prosecutor, Virgil Power, brought in another witness, Henry Oubridge, who had shared a cell with Harrison in the lock-up in Townsville. He alleged that the prisoner confided in him that he hoped to get 'the sugar' – meaning the Thomson farm – by killing the owner and marrying his widow. Given that the farm was almost bankrupt, something Ellen Thomson knew well, and that the property had been left to the deceased man's brother, Thomas Thomson, this seems unlikely.

Both accused were represented at their joint trial by a Townville solicitor, not a barrister. Except for Indigenous defendants, there was no public defence for criminal matters until 1903, nor was the accused allowed to speak in his or her own defence. Witnesses could, however, be called. Recently admitted solicitor Jacob Lue was competent and also fully conversant with advances in medical jurisprudence and the particularities of shattered gunshot wounds. In fact, he was more competent on this matter than Dr Marley who, he reminded the court, had changed his mind about the deceased's injuries. But his arguments were to no avail, with so many witnesses testifying that they had heard two shots.

Justice Pope Cooper, a vain and opinionated man who had trained at the University of Sydney with the future inaugural prime minster, Edmund Barton, was resentful that his career remained stuck in northern Queensland.[26] In his address to the jury, Justice Cooper said that 'in every case of murder the law assumes that murder has been committed until the contrary is proven'. This was completely incorrect; in common law, the accused is considered innocent until proven guilty beyond reasonable doubt. His words gave the jury an indication of Cooper's own opinion. They took some time to consider their verdict, some ten hours before declaring that they found both the accused guilty as charged. Thomson and Harrison were both sentenced to death. Unfortunately, no appeals were allowed for criminal cases in Queensland until 1903, even though, given the judge's partiality and misdirection to the jury, in this case there should have been one.

Thomson and Harrison were taken to Brisbane and housed in Boggo Road jail. Despite her lack of education and her inexperience with legal matters, Ellen Thomson had been perceptive enough to realise she had not been given a fair trial. What she had really been found guilty of was adultery. She wrote to the governor saying that witnesses had given false testimony and asking that 'Pope Cooper may never be allowed to sentence another woman in Queensland without first having heard both sides of the story'. She also demanded considerable compensation for her children and that Father Denis Fouhy be given guardianship of her daughter Ellen.[27]

On 2 June 1887 the Executive Council did consider the convictions and sentences but did not recommend mercy – the executions were to proceed. In the press there had been considerable agitation about these imminent executions, strengthened because one was the mother of a large family. Many citizens were outraged when the Executive Council decided to release Lewis Shaw, who had been convicted of kidnapping and killing New Guineans bound for the colony's sugar plantations in 1885. With a conservative government sympathetic to the sugar planters in power, Shaw's fate had altered. Also a black American, Jacob Stevenson, who had been convicted of rape, then a capital offence, was pardoned.[28] Yet in the Harrison–Thomson case, despite the conflicting evidence and testimony, the executions proceeded.

At 8am on the morning of Monday, 13 June 1887, the prisoners were taken from their cells and escorted to the gallows. This was not a public execution, which Queensland had banned as early as 1851. Right to the last minute Thomson was confident that she would be reprieved. Accompanied by the Sisters of Mercy and Father Fouhy, she continued to protest her innocence. On the gallows she said: 'I never shot my husband and I am dying like an angel.' Her sole concern was for her little daughter Ellen.

Various accounts of the execution were printed in newspapers. The most graphic was on 17 June by William Lane, who wrote under the pseudonym 'The Sketcher' for the radical newspaper *The Boomerang*. He later went on to edit *The Worker* and found a utopian colony in Paraguay. Lane believed that Thomson was guilty but was impressed that she had died 'game'. Dressed in black, looking pale and gaunt, Ellen Thomson carried her crucifix. Lane then went on to detail the horrors of the procedure. The rope had cut into Thomson's neck, severing her jugular vein. Those around her were spattered with her blood. All the officials, doctors, jail staff and clergy were 'sickened' by the grotesque spectacle. After this, John Harrison was executed, and to the distress of all present, the same thing happened.

Queensland had never permitted the dissection or anatomising of the bodies of those executed. Yet in this unique case in the colony's history, 'Professor' Gustav de Blumenthal, a German-born phrenologist, was permitted to examine the skulls of Thomson and Harrison; this, despite the fact that phrenology (a method of ascertaining a person's character by examining the structure of the skull) had by now been largely discredited. Without any medical or scientific qualifications, de Blumenthal pronounced that Ellen Thomson had been combative and destructive, with 'the moral propensities small and the sexual love–amativeness, exceedingly large'. Her lover was apparently also possessed of these qualities, as well as selfishness, and had wanted 'old Thomson dead far more than he did old Thomson's wife'.[29]

The following week, the largest newspaper in the colony, the *Brisbane Courier*, reported in full the decision of the Supreme Court in the matter of the guardianship of Ellen Wood, described as illegitimate. Father Fouhy sought guardianship in line with her mother's dying wish, yet William Thomson's will stated that she should be given into his brother's care. He was entitled by law to do this because, until new legislation was passed four years later, women had no custody rights even to their legitimate children. Thomson's actions were simply driven by spite. However, since the child was illegitimate – the biological daughter of William Jones – and bore her mother's first married name, the court decided that Ellen Wood should be given into the care of Father Fouhy, who then sent the little girl back to Port Douglas to be cared for by Father Brady. She was to be raised in the Roman Catholic faith as her mother had wished.[30]

Acknowledgments

I should like to acknowledge my debt of gratitude to all those at HarperCollins who laboured on my manuscript to turn it into a book.

The archivists at the State Archives of Tasmania were helpful in sending electric records of several cases. Jane Wassell at the Queensland State Archives helped me track down several significant Queensland cases.

Librarians at the University of Queensland Library, most notably those in the Law Library, helped me locate relevant sources and legal commentaries.

Trudy Cowley, part of the splendid team at the Female Factory Research Group in Hobart, interrupted her honeymoon to send me records she had collected. This generosity to a fellow historian goes beyond the call of duty.

Endnotes

Introduction
1. Nancy Gray, 'Dumaresq, William John (1793–1866)', www.adb.anu.au/biography/dumaresq-william-john-2239; refer also to Alan Atkinson, *The Europeans in Australia: A History, Volume 2: Democracy*, Oxford University Press, Melbourne, 2004, pp. 140–141.
2. Charlotte Anley, *Prisoners of Australia: A Narrative*, J. Hatchard, London, 1841, pp. 25–26. [Viewed online. Italics are in the original document.]
3. Brenda R. Weber, 'Situating Exceptional Women', *Nineteenth-Century Gender Studies*, Vol. 5, no 1, 2009. [Viewed online.]
4. Clothilde Rougé-Maillart et. al., 'Women who kill their children', *American Journal of Forensic Medicine and Pathology*, Vol. 26, No. 4, 2005, p. 320 [viewed online]; Geoffrey R. McKee, *Why Mothers Kill: A Forensic Psychologist's Casebook*, Oxford University Press, New York, 2006. McKee suggests that many suffered from mental illness or substance abuse.
5. Martin Daly and Margo Wilson, *Homicide*, Aldine de Gruyter, New York, 1988. This deals with the issue at length.
6. P. R. Wilson, *Murder of the Innocents: Child-Killers and their Victims*, Rigby, Adelaide, 1985, p. 52.
7. M. P. Wilkins, 'A Comfortable Evil: Female Serial Murderers in American Culture', PhD thesis, Penn State University, 2004, p. 5. [Viewed online.]
8. Kathy Laster, 'Arbitrary Chivalry: Women and Capital Punishment in Victoria, 1842–1967' in David Phillips and Susanne Davies, *A Nation of Rogues: Crime, Law and Punishment in Colonial Australia*, Melbourne University Press, Carlton, 1994, p. 169.
9. Peter Vronsky, *Serial Female Killers: How and Why Women Become Monsters*, Berkley Books, New York, 2007; Michael Kelleher and C. L. Kelleher, *Murder Most Rare: The Female Serial Killer*, Praeger, Westport,

Connecticut, 1998; Martin Daly and Margo Wilson, *Homicide*, Aldine de Gruyter, New York, 1988.
10. Lindy Cameron and Ruth Wykes, *Women Who Kill: Chilling Portraits of Australia's Worst Female Murderers*, The Five Mile Press, Scoresby, 2010, p. 3.
11. Judith Knelman, 'Women Murderers in Victorian Britain', *History Today*, Vol. 48, No. 8, 1998, p. 14.

Chapter 1 Lethal Abortion in the Nineteenth Century
1. John Keown, *Abortion, Doctors and the Law: Some Aspects of the Legal regulation of Abortion in England, 1803–1982*, Cambridge University Press.
2. Viewed in online version of *The Sydney Gazette and New South Wales Advertiser* 8 August 1828.
3. *British Medical Journal* Vol. 1, 1868, pp. 127, 175 and 197.
4. Gideon Haigh, *The Racket: How Abortion Became Legal in Australia*, (Melbourne University Press, 2008), *op. cit.*, pp. 14–15.
5. Shurlee Swain and Renate Howe, *Single Mothers and Their Children: Disposal, Punishment and Survival in Australia*, Cambridge University Press, Melbourne, 1995, p. 45.
6. *South Australian Register* 12 December 1882.
7. *Argus* 30 July 1886.
8. *Ibid.*
9. David Dunstan, 'Gillott, Sir Samuel' http://www.adbonline.anu.edu.au/biography/youl-richard-4900/text8201.
10. *Queanbeyan Age* 29 September 1886; refer also to Lynn Finch and Jon Stratton, 'The Australian Working Class and the Practice of Abortion, 1880–1940', *Journal of Australian Studies*, No. 23, 1988, pp. 45–64.
11. A. M. Mitchell, 'Youl, Dr Richard (1821–1897)', http://www.adbonline.anu.edu.au/biography/youl-richard-4900/text 8201
12. *Argus* 30 July 1886.
13. R. G. De B. Griffith 'Holroyd, Sir Edward Dundas (1828–1916), http://www.adbonline.anu.edu.au/biography/holroyd-sir-edward-dundas-3784/text5983
14. Robert Miller, 'Williams, Sir Hartley (1843–1929)', http://www.adbonline.anu.edu.au/biography/williams-sir-hartley-4856/text8111

15. Marian Aveling, 'Purves, James Liddell (1843–1910)', http://www.adbonline.anu.edu.au/biography/purves-james-liddell-4419/text7215
16. *Argus* 5 November 1886; Ruth Campbell, 'Madden, Sir John (1844–1918), http://www.adbonline.anu.edu.au/biography/madden-sir-john-7453/text12981. Sir John Madden, later the Chief Justice of Victoria, was the second most expensive QC.
17. *Argus* 26 November 1886.
18. Cited in Ruth Teale, *Colonial Eve: Sources on women in Australia 1788–1914*, OUP, Melbourne 1978, p. 134.
19. *Gippsland Times*, 1 July 1891.
20. *Portland Guardian*, 1 July 1891.
21. *Adelaide Advertiser*, 25 May 1898; 27 October 1898.
22. *Argus*, 26 November 1895.
23. Patricia Sumerling, 'The Darker Side of Motherhood: Abortion and Infanticide in South Australia, 1870–1910', *Journal of the History Society of South Australia*, Vol. 13, 1985. Viewed online.
24. South Australian Archives, Police Department GRG5/2/160, 25 February 1897, cited in Sumerling *op. cit.*
25. *Ibid.*
26. Peter Bartlett, 'Downer, Sir John William (1843–1915), http://www.adbonline.anu.edu.au/biography/downer-sir-john-william-6007/text10261
27. *Barrier Miner,* 6 March 1897.
28. Ronald Elmslie and Susan Nance, 'Smith, William Ramsay (1859–1937) http://www.adbonline.anu.edu.au/biography/smith-william-ramsay-8493/text4941
29. *South Australian Register*, 9 March 1897.
30. W. D. Refshauge, 'Shepherd, Arthur Edmund (1867–1942), http://www.adbonline.anu.edu.au/biography/shepherd-arthur-edmund-8412/text14775
31. *Adelaide Register*, 11 April 1908.
32. *Adelaide Register*, 15 April 1908.
33. *Barrier Miner,* 16 August 1908.
34. *Brisbane Courier*, 19 December 1898.
35. *Argus*, 19 January 1899.
36. *Argus*, 3 February 1923.

37. *Argus*, 13 January 1899.
38. *Argus*, 13 January 1899.
39. Bryan Gandevia, 'Neild, James Edward (1824–1906), http://www.adbonline.anu.edu.au/biography/neild-james-edward-4288/text6939
40. *Argus*, 14 January 1899.
41. Haigh, *op. cit.*, p.19.
42. *Bathurst Free Press and Mining Journal*, 17 January 1899, p. 2.
43. *Western Mail*, 3 January 1899.
44. *Ibid*, p. 20.
45. *Argus*, 23 January 1899.
46. Argus, 26 January 1899.
47. *Argus*, 26 January 1899.
48. *Argus*, 26 January 1899.
49. *Argus*, 26 January 1899.
50. *The West Australian*, 3 February 1899.
51. *Western Mail*, 3 February 1899.
52. *The West Australian*, 3 February 1899.
53. *The West Australian*, 3 February 1899.
54. *The West Australian*, 23 February 1899.
55. *South Australian Register*, 23 February 1899.
56. *South Australian Register*, 24 February 1899.
57. *The North Western Advocate and Emu Bay Times*, 27 February 1899.
58. *The West Australian*, 28 February 1899.
59. *Argus*, 13 March 1899.
60. *Morwell Advertiser* 27 April 1900.
61. Haigh, *op. cit.*, p. 21.

Chapter 2 Lethal Abortion in the Twentieth Century
1. C. A. von Oppeln, 'Crowther, Sir William Edward Lodewyk Hamilton (1887–1981), http://www.adb.anu.edu.au/biography/crowther-william-edward-lodwyk-hamilton-12374/text22237
2. *Examiner* (Launceston), 30 August 1905; *Hobart Mercury* 24 August 1905 and 28 August 1905.
3. *Sydney Morning Herald*, 21 September 1905.
4. *Sydney Morning Herald*, 20 September 1905.

5. *Sydney Morning Herald*, 15 November 1905.
6. Katie Spearritt and Kay Saunders, 'Is There Life after Birth? Childbirth, death and danger for settler women in colonial Queensland', *Journal of Australia Studies*, No. 29, 1991, pp. 64–75.
7. Attorney-General (NSW) v Jackson [1906] HCA 90; (1906) 3 CLR 730 (12 April 1906).
8. J. M. Bennett, 'Blacket, Wilfred (1859–1937)', http://www.adb.anu.edu.au/biography/blacket-wilfred-5260/text8865
9. *Sydney Morning Herald*, 11 May 1906.
10. Neville Hicks and E. J. Lea-Scarlett, 'Beale, Octavius Charles (1850–1930)', http://www.adb.anu.edu.au/biography/beale-octavius-charles-5165/text8675
11. *Western Mail* (Perth), 19 December 1908.
12. *Argus*, 11 December 1909.
13. Geoffrey Serle, 'Schutt, William John (1868–1933)', http://www.adb.anu.edu.au/biography/schutt-william-charles-8362/text14673
14. Hope v R [1909]; HCA 6 (1909); CLR 257 (15 March 1909).
15. *Argus*, 20 March 1909.
16. *Adelaide Advertiser*, 23 May 1910.
17. J. McI Young, 'Hood, Sir Joseph Henry (1846–1922)', http://www.adb.anu.edu.au/biography/hood-sir-joseph-henry-6725/text11615
18. Norma Marshall, 'Maxwell, George Arnot (1859–1935)', http://www.adb.anu.edu.au/biography/maxwell-george-arnot-7533/text13139
19. *Argus*, 21 June 1910; *Hobart Mercury*, 23 June 1910.
20. *Adelaide Register Adelaide*, 22 July 1910; *Argus*, 24 April 1912.
21. *Barrier Miner*, 13 January 1923.
22. Zoe Carthew, '"She had not a Baby Face": The death of Bertha Coughlan', *Provenance: The Journal of the Public Record Office of Victoria*, No. 5, 2006, p. 44.
23. *Barrier Miner*, 3 February 1923.
24. Cited in Gideon Haigh, *The Racket: How Abortion Became Legal in Australia*, Melbourne University Press, Melbourne, 2008, p. 35.
25. Janet McCalman, *Struggletown: Public and Private Life in Richmond, 1900–1965*, Melbourne University Press, Melbourne, 1984, p. 131.
26. *Argus*, 5 February 1923; Carthew, *op. cit.*, pp. 31–46.

27. Haigh, *op. cit.,* p. 33–34.
28. Carthew, *op. cit.,* p. 33.
29. *Ibid.*
30. *Ibid.,* p. 39.
31. *Ibid.,* pp. 38–39.
32. *Sydney Morning Herald,* 2 March 1923.
33. Carthew, *op. cit.,* pp. 33, 41–42.
34. *Sydney Morning Herald,* 2 March 1923.
35. *Cairns Post,* 8 March 1923.
36. *Barrier Miner,* 9 March 1923.
37. *Sunday Times* (Perth), 11 March 1923.
38. Elise B. Histed, 'Mann, Sir Frederick Wollaston (1869–1958)', http://www.adb.anu.edu.au/biography/mann-sir-frederci-wollaston-7473/text13023
39. *Argus,* 21 April 1923.
40. *Adelaide Advertiser,* 17 September 1924.
41. *Argus,* 24 January 1924.
42. *Adelaide Advertiser,* 20 February 1924.
43. *Brisbane Courier,* 10 March 1925.
44. *Cairns Post,* 26 March 1925.
45. *Burnie Advocate,* 12 January 1928.
46. *Barrier Miner,* 20 February 1928.
47. *Argus,* 12 January 1928.
48. *Launceston Examiner, 18* January 1928.
49. *Hobart Mercury,* 18 February 1928.
50. *Advocate,* 12 January 1928.
51. *Argus,* 17 November 1928.
52. *Adelaide Mail,* 23 November 1929.
53. *Cairns Post,* 25 May 1923.
54. *Brisbane Courier,* 4 August 1928.
55. Cited in *Western Argus* (Kalgoorlie), 29 December 1931.
56. Ann Farmer, *By Their Fruits: Eugenics, Population Control, and the Abortion Debate,* Catholic University of America Press, Washington DC, 2008, pp. 90–91.
57. Meredith Foley, 'Goodisson, Lillie Elizabeth (1860–1947)', http://www.adb.anu.edu.au/biography/goodisson - lillie-elizabeth-6422/text 10983.

58. Stephen Garton, 'Jones, Reginald Stuart (1902–1961)', http://adbonline.anu.edu.au/biogs/A140665.htm
59. *Argus*, 5 January 1915; 24 March 1915.
60. W. M. Hughes, 'Can Motherhood Deaths be Prevented?', *Australian Woman's Weekly*, 27 August 1935.
61. *Canberra Times*, 5 March 1935; Heather Radi, 'D'Arcy, Dame Constance Elizabeth (1869–1950)', http://www.adb.anu.edu.au/biography/d'arcy-dame-constance-elizabeth-5880/text10005. She was a devout Roman Catholic, which may have also informed her strong opinions.
62. *Age*, 7 August 2004. Refer also to 'Billy Hughes's Family Secret', *Rewind*, ABC Television, 8 August 2004.
63. Cited in Haigh, *op. cit.*, p. 48.
64. *Argus*, 3 August 1938.
65. *Morning Bulletin* (Rockhampton), 18 April 1938.
66. Haigh, *op. cit.*, pp. 40–43.
67. *Courier Mail*, 7 March 1945.
68. Deposition submitted in Case 40, Supreme Court of Queensland, Criminal Depositions, Queensland State Archives (QSA), CC 399: case of Vera Humphries, 22 February 1943.
69. *Courier Mail* (Brisbane), 7 April 1943.
70. *Ibid.; Cairns Post*, 2 June 1943.
71. Cited in Haigh, *op. cit.*, pp. 43–44.
72. *Hobart Mercury*, 23 August 1944.
73. Ross Johnston, *History of the Queensland Bar*, Bar Association of Queensland, Toowong, 1984, p. 91.
74. QSA SCT/CC 417 depositions 46–70, 1946, case 52 of 1946; *Courier Mail*, 27 March 1946.
75. *Courier Mail*, 27 April 1946.
76. *Western Australian*, 2 March 1949.
77. *Courier Mail*, 4 May 1949.
78. *Hobart Mercury*, 5 March 1949.
79. *Burnie Advocate*, 4 May 1949.
80. *Canberra Times*, 27 January 1950.
81. *Sydney Morning Herald*, 11 March 1950.

Chapter 3 Baby Killers in the Nineteenth Century

1. http://www.capitalpunishmentuk/fempublic.html
2. Annette Ballinger, *Dead Women Walking: Executing Women in England and Wales, 1900–1955*, Ashgate, Aldershot, 2000, p. 1.
3. Judith A. Allen, *Sex and Secrets: Crimes Involving Australian Women Since 1880*, Oxford University Press, Melbourne, 1990, pp. 29–30.
4. 'Luttrell, Edward (1756–1824)', http://adb.anu.edu.au/biography/luttrell-edward-2381/text3135
5. Paula Byrne, *Criminal Law and Colonial Subject, New South Wales 1810–1830*, Cambridge University Press, Melbourne, 1993, p. 255.
6. William Hunter, 'On the Uncertainty of the Signs of Murder, in the Case of Bastard Children', *Medical Observations and Inquiries by a Society of Physicians in London*, Vol. 6, 1784, reproduced as an eBook.
7. K. J. Kramar and W. D. Watson, 'The Insanities of Reproduction "Medico–Legal Knowledge and the Development of Infanticide Law"', *Social and Legal Studies*, Vol. 15, No. 2, 2006, p. 241.
8. Byrne, *op. cit.*, pp. 255–56.
9. Helen MacDonald, *Human Remains: Episodes in Human Dissection*, Melbourne University Press, Melbourne, 2005, p. 54. I have consistently used the spelling McLauchlan as reported in the press. In the official archival record of executions in Hobart in 1830 she is called Mary McLaughlin alias Sutherland, though other records call her McLaughlan. TSAL EC4/1. The Tasmanian State Archives and Library kindly sent me all the records concerned with her case electronically.
10. Helen MacDonald, A Dissection in Reverse: Mary McLaughlan, Hobart Town, 1830, *Lilith*, Vol. 13, 2004, p. 16.
11. MacDonald, *Human Remains*, pp. 54–55.
12. MacDonald, 'A Dissection in Reverse', p. 17.
13. G. H. Stancombe, 'Scott, James (1790–1837)', http://www.adb.anu.edu.au/biography/scott-james-2641/text3671
14. MacDonald, *Human Remains*, pp. 59–62.
15. *Hobart Town Gazette and Van Diemen's Land Advertiser*, 2 March 1822.
16. Female Factory Research Group, *Convict Lies: Women at Cascades Female Factory*, Research Tasmania, Hobart, 2009; Kay Daniels, *Convict Lives*, Allen and Unwin, Sydney, 1999; Joy Damousi, *Depraved and Disorderedly:*

Female Convicts, Sexuality and Gender in Colonial Australia, Cambridge University Press, Melbourne, 1997.
17. MacDonald, *Human Remains*, pp. 65–68.
18. Peter Crisp, 'Hone, Joseph (1784–1861)', http://www.adb.anu.edu.au/biography/hone-joseph-2195/text2833
19. E. R. Pretyman, 'Baylee, Pery (1784–?)' http://www.adb.anu.edu.au/biography/baylee-pery-1757/text1957.
20. R. P. Davis, *The Tasmanian Gallows: A Study in Capital Punishment*, Cat and Fiddle Press, Hobart, 1974, pp. xii–xiii; James Boyce, *Van Diemen's Land*, Black Press, Melbourne, 2008, pp. 168–69.
21. *Hobart Town Courier*, 4 April 1829. This announced his appointment as assistant surgeon to the colony.
22. M. Clark and C. Crawford (eds), *Legal Medicine in History*, Cambridge University Press, Cambridge, 1994, p. 174.
23. MacDonald, *Human Remains*, pp. 73–76.
24. A. Alison, *Principles of the Criminal Law of Scotland*, Blackwell, Edinburgh, 1832, p. 159.
25. Roger Smith, *Trial by Medicine: Responsibility in Victorian Trials*, Edinburgh University Press, Edinburgh, 1981, pp. 148–150.
26. H. R. Thomas, 'Thomas, Jocelyn Henry Connor (1780–1862)', http://www.adb.anu.edu.au/biography/thomas-joclyn-henry-connor-2726/text3843; P. R. Eldershaw, 'Burnett, John (1781–1860)', http://www.adb.anu.edu.au/biography/burnett-john-1855/text1826
27. MacDonald, *Human Remains*, p. 77.
28. MacDonald, 'A Dissection in Reverse', p. 19.
29. 'Bedford, William (1781–1852)', http://www.adb.anu.edu.au/biography/bedford-william-1760/text1963
30. Ida McAuley, 'Bisdee, John (1796–1862)', http://www.adb.anu.edu.au/biography/bisdee-john-1786/text2013
31. *Tasmanian and Austral–Asiatic Review*, 23 April 1830.
32. MacDonald, 'A Dissection in Reverse', p. 20.
33. *The Sydney Gazette and New South Wales Advertiser*, 6 April 1833.
34. *Hobart Colonial Times*, 31 July 1857.
35. *Ballarat Star*, 4 August 1864; *The Australian Advertiser* (Adelaide), 9 August 1864, has a long article on the incident.

36. MacDonald, *Human Remains*, pp. 49–51.
37. MacDonald, 'A Dissection in Reverse', pp. 13–15.
38. *Hobart Town Courier*, 15 May 1835.
39. Details of the case are contained in Decisions of the Nineteenth Century Tasmanian Superior Court, *R v Masters; Hobart Town Courier*, 12 May 1838.
40. Peter Bolger, 'Bedford, Edward Samuel Pickard (1809–1876)', http://www.adb.anu.edu.au/biography/bedford-edward-sameul-pickard-2962/text4311
41. For more details refer to Kramar and Watson, *op. cit.*; Hilary Marland, *Dangerous Motherhood: Insanity and Childbirth in Victorian Britain*, Palgrave Macmillan, London, 2000.
42. Smith, *op. cit.*, pp. 146–147; Tony Ward, 'The Sad Subject of Infanticide: Law, Medicine and Child Murder', *Social and Legal Studies*, Vol. 8, No. 2, 1999, pp. 163–180.
43. J. M. Bennett, 'Hargrave, John Fletcher (1815–1885)', http://www.adb.anu.edu.au/biography/hargrave-john-fletcher-3718/text5835.
44. *Sydney Morning Herald*, 26 November 1867.
45. M. Carter and A. A. Morrison, 'Harding, George Rogers (1838–1895)', http://www.adb.anu.edu.au/biography/harding-george-rogers-3712/text5825
46. A. Rahmentula, 'Real, Sir Patrick (1846–1928)', http://www.adb.anu.edu.au/biography/real-sir-patrick-8169/text14281
47. *R v Judge*, Queensland State Archives (QSA) Supreme Court Records, CCT 7/N42.
48. *Brisbane Courier*, 2 May 1885.
49. *Brisbane Courier*, 30 April 1885.
50. Ross Johnston, *History of the Queensland Bar*, The Bar Association of Queensland, Toowong, 1984, p. 99.
51. *Queensland Law Journal*, Vol. 1, 1885, pp. 61–62.
52. Cited in Ruth Teale (ed.), *Colonial Eve: Sources on Women in Australia 1788–1914*, Oxford University Press, Melbourne, 1978, pp. 142–43.
53. *Ibid.*, p. 137.
54. *Argus*, 21 December 1870.
55. S. M. Ingram, 'O'Loghlen, Sir Bryan (1828–1905)', http://www.adb.anu.edu.au/biography/o'loghlen-sir-bryan-4331/text7028

56. Petition on behalf of Maggie Heffernan, *Women's Sphere*, December 1900, cited in Teale, pp. 139–140.
57. J. McI. Young, 'Hodges, Sir Henry Edward Agincourt (1844–1919)', http://www.adb.anu.edu.au/biography/hodges-sir-henry-edward-aginscourt-1092/text 11549
58. The case is detailed in *Women's Sphere*, December 1900, and reprinted in Teale, *op. cit.*, pp. 139–40.
59. Letter to the editor by Marshall Lyle (dated 22 February), *Argus*, 23 February 1900.
60. *Bendigo Advertiser*, 21 December 1901, p. 3.

Chapter 4 Baby Killers in the Twentieth Century
1. Senate debates, 18 March 2010.
2. *Sydney Morning Herald*, 11 February 2009.
3. *Brisbane Courier*, 4 March 1901.
4. C. T. Beck and J. W. Driscoll, *Post-partum Mood and and Anxiety Disorders,* Jones and Bartlett, 2006.
5. Judith Wheelwright, 'Nothing in Between: Modern Cases of Infanticide', in Mark Jackson (ed.), *Infanticide: Historical perspectives on child murder and concealment, 1550–2000*, Ashgate, Aldershot, 2002, pp. 270–72.
6. *Adelaide Advertiser*, 11 May 1910.
7. Norma Marshall, 'Maxwell, George Arnot (1859–1935)', http://anu.edu.au/biography/maxwell/george/arnot-7533/text13139.
8. R. G. DeB. Griffith, 'à'Beckett, Sir Thomas (1836–1919)', http://anu.edu.au/biography/à'beckett-sir-thomas-2860/text4073
9. *Brisbane Courier*, 23 April 1913.
10. *Argus*, 18 April 1915.
11. *Argus*, 16 June 1915.
12. Queensland State Archives (QSA) Supreme Court Criminal Sittings SCT/CC 297, item ID 95745, trial of Nellie Spiers for concealing a birth, 7 July 1924.
13. Robert Likeman, *'Tis but the Time: The life of Lieut-Col. Espie Dods, DSO MC AAMC*, Slouch Hat Publications, McCrea, Victoria, 2007, for more details.
14. *Cairns Post*, 14 January 1952.

15. *Age*, 28 April 2005.
16. *The Mail* (Adelaide), 13 October 1951.
17. *Adelaide Advertiser*, 22 December 1951. The files in this type of case are not opened for scrutiny by researchers for 65 years.
18. Readers are advised to consult Matthew Benns, *When the Bough Breaks: The True Story of Child Killer Kathleen Folbigg*, Bantam Books, Sydney, 2003. This is the most well-documented account of this case, apart from the record of the trials and appeals.
19. *R v Folbigg* [2008] NSWSC, 24 October 2003.
20. *Ibid.*, refer also to Malcolm Brown (ed.), *Cold-blooded Murder: True Crimes that Rocked Australia*, Hachette, Sydney, 2008, p. 166; Paul B. Kidd, *The Australian Crime File*, Five Mile Press, Rowville, Victoria, 2005, pp. 39–44.
21. *R v Folbigg* [2008] NSWSC, 24 October 2003.
22. *Ibid.*
23. *Ibid.*
24. *Ibid.*
25. *Ibid.*
26. Belinda Morrisey, 'Monstrous Semantics: The Case of Criminal Diaries', *Australian Feminist Studies*, No. 65, 2010, p. 301.
27. *Ibid.*, pp. 137–47.
28. 'Of Woman Born', *Australian Story*, ABC Television, 15 March 2004.
29. *Ibid.*.
30. *R v Folbigg* [2008] NSWSC, 24 October 2003.
31. *Ibid.*
32. *Ibid.*
33. *Ibid.*
34. *Folbigg v the Queen*, HCA Transcripts S59/2003.
35. Sharmila Betts and Jane Goodman-Delahunty, 'The Case of Kathleen Folbigg: How Did Justice and Medicine Fare?', *Australian Journal of Forensic Sciences*, Vol. 39, No. 1, 2007, pp. 10–24. [Accessed online 1 December 2011.] The authors are both psychologists.
36. *Ibid.*, pp. 246–68 for summary of the trial; Brown, *op. cit.*, pp. 177–80. Key points of the original trial can be read in the 2007 appeal: *Folbigg v R* [2007] NSWCCA 371.
37. *R v Folbigg* [2003] NSWSC, 24 October 2003.

38. *R v Folbigg* [2005]NSWCCA 23 judgement, delivered 17 February 2005 before Sully JA, Dunford J and Hidden J.
39. *Folbigg v the Queen* [2005] HCAT trans 657, 2 September 2005.
40. *Folbigg v R* [2007] NSWCCA 371.
41. *Daily Telegraph*, 9 July 2003; Benns, *op. cit.*, p. 287.
42. Peter Lalor, *Blood Stain: The True Story of Katherine Knight, the Mother and Abattoir Worker who Became Australia's Worst Female Killer*, Allen and Unwin, Sydney, 2002, p. 305.

Chapter 5 A Baffling Case: Keli Lane
1. *R v Keli Lane* [2011] NSWSC 289, 15 April 2011. Much of the material on this case can be located in the court records online.
2. *Ibid.*
3. Article by Jane Cadzow, *Newcastle Herald*, 15 April 2011.
4. *Ibid.*
5. Rachael Jane Chin, *Good Girl: The Story of Keli Lane and her Missing Baby, Tegan*, Simon and Schuster, Sydney, 2011, p. 25. Readers are advised to consult this excellent book for more details, along with Justice Whealy's sentencing, which is available online.
6. Chin, *op. cit.*, p. 45 and pp. 53–54.
7. *Australian*, 31 August 2010.
8. *Newcastle Herald*, 15 April 2011.
9. *R v Keli Lane* [2011].
10. *Ibid.*
11. Chin, *op. cit.*, p. 48.
12. *Sunday Telegraph*, 17 April 2011.
13. Emma Martin, 'We knew she was hiding something', *Who* magazine, 25 April 2011.
14. *Manly Daily*, 10 August 2010.
15. *R v Keli Lane* [2011].
16. *Ibid.*
17. To protect his identity and that of his daughter with Lane, I have not used his surname.
18. Refer to Chin, *op. cit.*, Chapter 9.
19. *R v Keli Lane* [2011].

20. *Ibid.*
21. Chin, *op. cit.*, Chapter 17.
22. *Ibid.*, p. 259.
23. *Ibid.*, p. 255.
24. *Sunday Telegraph*, 17 April 2011.

Chapter 6 The Deadly Baby Farmers
1. H. L. Adam, *Women and Crime*, T. W. Laurie, London, 1911, p. 176.
2. Kathy Laster, 'Frances Knorr: She killed babies, didn't she?' in M. Lake and F Kelly (eds), *Double Time*, Penguin, Melbourne, 1985, p. 18.
3. *Pall Mall Gazette*, 19 December 1899.
4. Carol Herben, *From Burren Street to the Gallows: The John and Sarah Makin Story*, J. and C. Herben, Fairy Meadow, 1997, p. 3.
5. Heather Radi, 'Makin, Sarah Jane (1845–1918)', http://adbonline.anu.edu.au/biogs/AS1051.htm
6. *Ibid.*, p. 11.
7. *Australian Town and Country Journal*, 19 November 1892.
8. *Ibid.*
9. *Bathurst Free Press and Mining Journal*, 17 November 1892. This provides a word for word account of Clarice Makin's testimony.
10. Herben, *op. cit.*, p. 87.
11. *Sydney Morning Herald*, 7 March 1893.
12. Woods, *op. cit.*, p. 396.
13. Judith Rowbotham and Kim Stevenson (eds), *Criminal Conversations: Victorian Crimes, Social Panic and Moral Outrage*, University of Ohio Press, 2005, Athens, p. 214, available as an eBook.
14. *Sydney Morning Herald*, 24 March 1893.
15. Suzanne Edgar and Bede Nairn, 'Salomons, Sir Julian Emanuel (1835–1909)', http://adb.anu.edu.au/biography/salomons-sir-julian-emanuel-4532/text7423
16. *R v Makin and Wife* [1893] NSWLR 1 at 22; *Sydney Morning Herald*, 31 March 1893.
17. Quoted in Woods, *op. cit.*, p. 399.
18. *Sydney Morning Herald*, 13 August 1892.
19. *Sydney Morning Herald*, 12 August 1893.

20. Herben, *op. cit.*, p. 173.
21. Sharpe, *op. cit.*, p. 116.
22. Sharpe, *op. cit.*, p. 116.
23. *Age*, 6 September 1893.
24. *Age*, 9 September 1893.
25. Simon Cooke, 'Candler, Samuel Curtis (1827–1911)', http://adb.anu.edu.au/biography/candler-sameul-curtis-12839/text23177
26. Lucy Sussex, '"God Help My Poor Baby!" The Case of Frances Knorr' in K. Greenwood (ed.), *The Thing She Loves: Why Women Kill*, Allen and Unwin, Sydney, 1996, p. 100.
27. *Herald*, 6 December 1893. 'The home was a religious organisation in Chelsea', Alan Sharpe, *Crime and Punishment: 50 Crimes that Shocked Australia*, Kingsclear Books, Crows Nest, 1997, p. 115.
28. *Ibid.*
29. *South Australian Register*, 2 December 1893.
30. Sussex, *op. cit.*, p. 102.
31. Kathy Laster, 'Knorr, Frances Lydia Alice (Minnie) (1867–1894)', http://adbonline.anu.edu.au/biography/AS10272b
32. Barbara Yazbeck, '"Deviant Motherhood" in the Late Nineteenth Century: A case study of the trial and execution of Frances Knorr and Emma Williams for child murder, MA thesis, University of Melbourne, 2002, Chapter 2, p. 36.
33. Sussex, *op. cit.*, p. 104.
34. *Ibid.*
35. *Argus*, 4 January 1894.
36. *Argus*, 16 January 1894, gives a full account of the execution.
37. Sussex, *op. cit.*, p. 105.
38. P. R. Kidd, *The Australian Crime File: The 'Best of' Bollection of Notorious True Crime Stories*, The Five Mile Press, Rowville, Victoria, 2005, p. 165.
39. The author visited the Old Melbourne Gaol Museum in September 2011. Women killers are disproportionately represented among the exhibits.
40. Penelope Hetherington, Baby Farming In Western Australia: The case against Alice Mitchell, 1907', *Studies in Western Australian History*, Vol. 25, 2007, pp. 88–89. Readers are advised to consult this article for more details concerning this case and its aftermath; refer also to Jennifer Worrall, 'Baby

Farming' in Jenny Gregory and Jan Gothard (eds), *Historical Encyclopedia of Western Australia*, Perth, UWAP, 2009, p. 118.
41. *Western Australian*, 6 March 1907.
42. *Western Australian*, 9 March 1907.
43. P. B. Kidd, *Australia's Serial Killers: The Definite History of Serial Multicide in Australia*, Macmillan, Sydney, 2000, p. 42.
44. *Western Australian*, 9 April 1907.
45. Hetherington, *op. cit.*, p. 78.
46. Hetherington, *op. cit.*, pp. 76–79.
47. *Western Australian*, 18 February 1907.
48. Hetherington, *op. cit.*, p. 80; S. Thompson, 'Infant Mortality' in Gregory and Gothard, *op. cit.*, pp. 478–79.
49. Margaret Brown, 'Cowan, Edith Dircksey (1861–1932)', http://adb.anu.edu.au/biography/cowan-edith-dircksey-5791/text9823. She was the first woman elected to a house of parliament in Australia in 1921.
50. *Western Australian*, 6 March 1907.
51. E. J. Edwards, 'McMillan, Sir Robert Furse (1858–1931)', http://adb.anu.edu.au/biography/mcmillan-sir-robert-furse-7424/text12919; G. C. Bolton and G. Byrne, *May It Please Your Honour: A History of the Supreme Court of Western Australia from 1861–2005*, Supreme Court of Western Australia, Perth, 2011), pp. 104–105, 137, 167–68.
52. *Western Australian*, 11 and 13 April 1907.

Chapter 7 Child Killers in the Nineteenth Century
1. *Sydney Herald*, 24 March 1842.
2. *Colonial Times*, 16 July 1852.
3. *Hobart Town Courier*, 10 July 1852.
4. Archives Office Tasmania (AOT) CSO 50/21 and 50/22. [These sources were kindly sent to me by historian Trudy Cowley.]
5. *Hobart Town Courier*, 16 July 1852.
6. Peter Bogner, 'Salier, George (1813–1892)', http://adb.edu.au/biography/salier-george-4531/text7421.
7. *Hobart Town Courier*, 4 August 1852; Trudy Cowley, 'Mary Sullivan, murderer' in Female Factory Research Group, *Convict Lives: Women at Cascades Female Factory*, Research Tasmania, Hobart, 2009, pp. 157–60.

8. *Colonial Times*, 3 August 1852.
9. *Argus*, 14 August 1852.
10. *South Australian Register*, 5 November 1895.
11. Michael Cannon, 'Emma Williams: The prostitute compelled to drown her own child" in *The Woman as Murderer: Five who paid with their lives*, Today's Australian Publishing Company, Mornington, Victoria, 1994, p. 127.
12. *South Australian Register*, 5 November 1895.
13. Cannon, *op. cit.*, p. 112; Barbara Yazbeck, '"Deviant Motherhood" in the Late Nineteenth Century: A case study of the trial and execution of Frances Knorr and Emma Williams for child murder, MA thesis, University of Melbourne, Melbourne, 2002, Chapter 3.
14. Ruth Hoban, 'Sutherland, Sulina Murray McDonald (1839–1909)', in http://adb.edu.au/biography/sutherland/sulina/murray/mcdonald/4674/text7727
15. *Argus*, 19 October 1895.
16. G. Serle, 'Champion, Henry Hyde (1859–1928)', http://adb.edu.au/biography/champion-henry-hyde-5548/text9457
17. C. R. Badger, 'Strong, Charles (1844–1942)', http://adb.edu.au/biography/strong-charles-4658/text7697
18. *Barrier Miner*, 30 October 1895.
19. *Barrier Miner*, 5 November 1895; *Argus*, 5 November 1895.
20. Cannon, *op. cit.*, p. 145.
21. Details of the case are taken from the trial contained in *The Queen v Marie Christensen*, November 1896, Supreme Court of Queensland, Queensland State Archives (QSA) SCT/CC 127; Sean Gouglas and J. C. Weaver, 'A Postcolonial Understanding of Law and Society: Exploring criminal trials in colonial Queensland', *Australian Journal of Legal History*, Vol. 14, 2003 [Viewed e-journal online.]
22. Evidence of Budlo Lefu in *R v Christensen*.
23. *Brisbane Courier*, 26 September 1896.
24. Details of the inquest may be found at QSA JUS/N245, File 370/96. My thanks to archivist Jane Wassel for locating these files.
25. Gouglas and Weaver suggest this line of argument.

Chapter 8 The Wicked Stepmother: Martha Rendall

1. *Sunday Times* (Perth), 17 December 1950.
2. Paul D. Kidd, *Australia's Serial Killers: The definitive history of serial multicide in Australia*, Pan Macmillan, Sydney, 2000, p. 58.
3. Anna Haebich, *Murdering Stepmothers: The execution of Martha Rendell*, UWAP, Nedlands, 2010. In the contemporary documents the executed woman is called often Martha Rendall and I have followed this name through my text.
4. *Ibid*, p. 141.
5. *Ibid*, pp. 183–88.
6. *Ibid*, p. 49; Sarah Morris described her married life at the inquest into the deaths of her three children, cited in the *Western Australian*, 11 August 1909.
7. S. T. Shulman, 'The History of Pediatric Infectious Diseases', *Pediatric Research*, Vol. 55, No. 1, 2004, pp. 163–76 for more details.
8. *The Australian Home Companion*, 7 April 1860; *Adelaide Advertiser*, 9 February 1895.
9. Lionel Rose, *The Massacre of the Innocents: Infanticide in Britain 1800–1939*, Routledge & Kegan Paul, London, 1986, pp. 10–12.
10. *West Australian*, 21 May 1932.
11. *West Australian*, 21 May 1909.
12. R. V. Southcott, 'Cleland, Sir John Burton (1878–1971)', http://adb.edu.au/biography/cleland-sir-john-burton-5679/text9595.
13. M. Roe, 'Cumpston, John Howard Lidgett (1880–1954)', http://adb.edu.au/biography/5846/text9935. He became the inaugural Director-General of Federal Health.
14. *Sydney Morning Herald*, 17 August 1909.
15. *West Australian*, 11 August 1909.
16. *Sydney Morning Herald*, 17 August 1909.
17. *Sunday Times*, 12 September 1909.
18. *West Australian*, 11 August 1909.
19. Haebich also concurs with this interpretation in her book.
20. G. C. Bolton and G. Byrne, *May It Please Your Honour? A History of the Supreme Court of Western Australia from 1861–2005*, Supreme Court of Western Australia, Perth, 2011, p. 135; Gregory and Gothard, *op. cit.*, p. 525.
21. Haebich, *op. cit.*, p. 1. [e-Journal edition.]

22. *West Australian*, 2 October 1909.
23. Haebich, *op. cit.*, p. 11.
24. *West Australian*, 7 October 1909.
25. Kidd, *op. cit.*, p. 55.

Chapter 9 Child Killers in the Twentieth Century
1. *Adelaide Advertiser*, 26 March 1935.
2. *West Australian*, 27 March 1935.
3. *Age*, 12 April 1935.
4. *Western Argus*, 17 July 1934.
5. *Adelaide Advertiser*, 18 December 1937.
6. *Sydney Morning Herald*, 13 August 1950.
7. *Canberra Times*, 24 October 1950.
8. *Argus*, 24 October 1950.
9. *Argus*, 20 December 1950.
10. Paul R. Kidd, *Australia's Serial Killers: The Definitive History of Multicide in Australia,* Pan Macmillan, Sydney, 2000, pp. 200–201; P. R. Wilson, *Murder of the Innocents: Child Killers and Their Victims,* Rigby, Adelaide, 1985, pp. 48–52.
11. *Ibid*, p. 200.
12. *Sydney Morning Herald*, 10 April 1980.
13. Kidd, *op. cit.*, p. 230.
14. *Ibid.*, p. 231.
15. 'Babysitter "was killer"', *Age*, 2 April 1980.
16. Wilson, *op. cit.*, p. 50.
17. *Ibid.*, p. 51.
18. Michael Grant and John Hazel, *Who's Who in Classical Mythology*, Routledge, London, 2002, pp. 212–14.
19. *R v Fitchett* [2008] VSC 258 (18 July 2006). All statements and evidence are taken from the court records.
20. *R v Fitchett* [2008] VSCA (18 July 2008], from Justice Nettle's sentencing statement.
21. *Ibid.*, from section entitled 'Moral Culpability'.
22. *R v Fitchett* [2008] VSC 258 (18 July 2006), *op. cit.*.
23. Justice Nettle's sentencing statement, *op. cit.*

24. *The Queen v Fitchett* [2010] VSC 393.
25. *R v Fitchett* [2008] VSC 258 (18 July 2006).
26. *Ibid.*
27. *R v Fitchett* [2009] VSCA 150 (25 June 2009).

Chapter 10 Poisoners of the Nineteenth Century
1. Katherine Watson, *Poisoned Lives: English Poisoners and Their Victims 1750 to 1914,* Hambledon, London, 2004, p.7.
2. *Ibid.*, p. 190.
3. Sir Sydney Smith, 'The History and Development of Forensic Medicine', *British Medical Journal,* 24 March 1951, p. 604.
4. *Ibid.*, p. 34.
5. See Katherine Watson, 'Medical and Chemical Expertise in English Trials for Criminal Poisoning, 1750–1914', *Medical History,* Vol. 50, No. 3, 2006, pp. 373–90 for further details.
6. *Sydney Gazette and New South Wales Advertiser,* 25 September 1823.
7. *Adelaide Register,* 23 June 1920.
8. Allan Peters, *Dead Woman Walking: Was an Innocent Woman Hanged?* Bas Publishing, Seaford, Victoria, 2008, p. 23. Readers are advised to consult this fascinating and well-researched account.
9. *Ibid.*, pp. 28–30.
10. *Worker,* 19 October 1895.
11. Peters, *op. cit.*, pp. 61–64.
12. 'The Last Statement and Confession of Elizabeth Woolcock to Mr Bickford', 16 December 1873 in J. Towler and T. J. Porter, *The Hempen Collar: Executions in South Australia 1838–1964,* Wednesday Press, Parafield Gardens, 1999, pp. 72–73. It was originally published in the *Adelaide Observer,* 3 January 1874.
13. *Ibid.*
14. *South Australian Advertiser,* 3 December 1873.
15. *South Australian Register,* 5 December 1873.
16. *Ibid.*
17. *Ibid.*
18. Robin Milhouse, 'Andrews, Richard Bullock (1823–1884)', http://www.adb.anu.edu.au/biography/andrews-richard-bullock-2889/text4139.

19. *South Australian Register*, 5 December 1873.
20. Renate Howe, 'Bicknell, James (1816–1895)' http://adb.anu.edu/biography/bickford-james-2993/text4375.
21. *South Australian Advertiser*, 31 December 1873.
22. *Yorke's Peninsular Advertiser and Miners' News*, 25 May 1874.
23. Peters, *op. cit.*, pp. 291–94.
24. 'Elizabeth Woolcock', http://en.wikipedia.org.wki.Elizabeth_Woolcock; Peters, *op. cit.*
25. Peters, *op. cit.*, p. 301.
26. *Australian*, 18 May 1841.
27. Ann Jones, *Women Who Kill*, The Feminist Press, New York, NY, 2009, pp. 145–57.
28. Martha Rutledge, 'White, James (1828–1890)', http://adb.anu.edu/biography/white-james-4837/text8073.
29. Cited in Alan Sharpe, *Crime and Punishment: Fifty crimes that shocked Australia*, Kingsclear Books, Crows Nest, 1997, p. 100.
30. The coronial inquiry was concerned with Louisa Collins' character. Refer to Wendy Kukulies-Smith and Susan Priest, '"No Hope for Mercy" for the Borgia of Botany Bay: Louisa May Collins, the last woman executed in NSW, 1889', *Canberra Law Review*, Vol. 10, No. 2, 2010.
31. Sharpe, *op. cit.*, p. 102.
32. *Ibid.*, p. 100.
33. William Guy and David Ferrier, *Principles of Forensic Medicine*, fourth edition (first published in 1844), p. 177 [read as an e-book]. Guy was the inaugural professor of forensic medicine at King's College, London.
34. Smith, *op. cit.*, p. 605.
35. Sharpe, *op. cit.*, p. 101.
36. This was reported in Central Criminal Court papers, July 1888, inquest no. 786, cited in Kukulies-Smith and Priest, *op. cit.*, p. 148.
37. *Argus*, 24 July 1888.
38. Kukulies-Smith and Priest, *op. cit.*, p. 148.
39. *Sydney Morning Herald*, 18 July 1888.
40. Cited in Kukulies-Smith and Priest, *op. cit.*, p. 144.
41. *Sydney Morning Herald*, 6 November 1888; 9 November 1888.
42. *Sydney Morning Herald*, 9 November 1888.

43. Kukulies-Smith and Priest, *op. cit.*, provide an excellent coverage of the legal issues on this matter.
44. *R v Collins* [1888] NSWSupC2. The full judgment can be read in the *Brisbane Courier*, 10 December 1888.
45. *NSW Parliamentary Debates* (LA), 19 December 1888. His biography can be read at http://adb.anu.edu/biography/melville-ninian-4184/text6725
46. Kukulies-Smith and Priest, *op. cit.*, pp. 154–55.
47. *Ibid.*, p. 155.
48. *Ibid.*, p. 157.
49. *The Bulletin*, 12 January 1889.
50. Mrs Foran gave this long interview to the *South Australian Register*, 20 June 1894.
51. *South Australian Register*, 4 April 1876.
52. *South Australian Register*, 13 July 1876.
53. *South Australian Register*, 15 March 1877.
54. www.victoria.mypeoplepuzzle.net/familygroup.php?/familyID=F47
55. Kidd, *op. cit.*, p. 23.
56. Much of this evidence comes from the court proceedings. Refer to the *Argus*, 3 August 1894, for an account of the police court hearing.
57. *Argus*, 16 June 1894. This issue contains a series of letters written by Martha Needle and Otto Juncken.
58. *Argus*, 25 September 1894.
59. Cited in http://www.familytreecircles.com/martha-needle-34559.html
60. Kidd, *op. cit.*, p. 30.
61. *Northern Miner*, 15 November 1894.
62. *Sydney Morning Herald*, 18 November 1904.
63. *Argus*, 21 February 1905.
64. *Ibid.*
65. *Western Australian*, 10 March 1905.
66. *Barrier Miner*, 24 May 1905.
67. *Kalgoorlie Western Argus*, 18 July 1905.

Chapter 11 The Thallium Killers
1. *Canberra Times*, 5 November 1948.
2. *Western Australian*, 7 December 1948.

3. *Courier Mail*, 10 May 1938.
4. *Courier Mail*, 27 March 1929; *Townsville Daily Bulletin*, 2 April 1919.
5. Noel Sanders, *The Thallium Enthusiasms and Other Australian Outrages*, Local Consumption Publications, Sydney, 1995, p. 45. Readers should consult this wide-ranging account.
6. D. H. Lawrence, *Kangaroo* (1923) [read as an e-book].
7. Kate Darian-Smith, *On the Homefront: Melbourne in wartime, 1939–1945*, Oxford University Press, Melbourne, 1990, p. 102.
8. Kay Saunders and Raymond Evans (eds), *Gender Relations in Australia: Domination and negotiation*, Harcourt Brace Jovanovich, Sydney, 1992, p. 185.
9. Sanders, *op. cit.*, Chapter 1.
10. I lived in the middle-class northern Brisbane suburb of The Grange in the early 1950s and remember the excitement for local children when the pack of yapping fox terriers made its way around the area looking for rats. Our parents were not quite so enthusiastic about this implied slur on bourgeois standards of respectability. The fox terrier was then not a suitable pet, given its reputation as a working animal doing dirty jobs.
11. Sanders, *op. cit.*, pp. 18–19.
12. *Sydney Morning Herald*, 19 June 1953.
13. *Courier Mail*, 20 May 1952.
14. Richard Hall, 'Clues Under the Microscope: Great Sydney crimes', *Sydney City Monthly*, 28–31 August 1982, pp. 29–30.
15. *Courier Mail*, 20 May 1952.
16. *Sydney Morning Herald*, 11 June 1952.
17. *Sydney Morning Herald*, 21 June 1952.
18. *Sydney Morning Herald*, 17 June 1952.
19. *Adelaide Advertiser*, 18 June 1952.
20. John Romeril, *Mrs Thally F* in R. Fisher (ed.), *Seven One-Act Plays*, Currency Press, Sydney, 1983.
21. Their names do not appear on the Australian War Memorial Service records for World War II.
22. *Adelaide Advertiser*, 26 June 1952.
23. Martha Rutledge, 'Kinsella, Edward Parnell (Ted) (1893- 1967)', http://adb.anu.edu.au/biography/kinsella-edward-parnell-ted-1074/text19051

24. *Sydney Morning Herald*, 29 May 1952.
25. *Argus*, 17 September 1952.
26. James Holledge, *Australia's Wicked Women*, Horwitz, London, 1968, p. 36.
27. *Argus*, 24 September 1952.
28. *Canberra Times*, 29 September 1952.
29. *Courier Mail*, 10 December 1952.
30. *Courier Mail*, 30 August 1954.
31. *Sydney Morning Herald*, 20 August 1952.
32. Archive Office, NSW: CP, Supreme Court and Courts, *R v Ruby May Norton*, 10/10484, cited in Clair Scrine, '"More Deadly Than the Male" – The Sexual Politics of Female Poisoning: Trials of the thallium women', *Limina*, Vol. 8, 2002, p. 130. Testimony of witnesses is taken from the court case.
33. *Sydney Morning Herald*, 19 June 1953.
34. *Courier Mail*, 31 July 1953.
35. Cited in Sanders, *op. cit.*, pp. 9–10.
36. Stephen Garton, 'Grills, Caroline (1888?–1960)', http://adbonline.anu.edu.au/biogs/A140381.htm
37. *Sydney Morning Herald*, 15 August 1953.
38. *Argus*, 9 July 1953.
39. *Sydney Morning Herald*, 15 August 1953; *Burnie Advocate*, 8 October 1953.
40. *Burnie Advocate*, 13 August 1953.
41. *Canberra Times*, 8 July 1953.
42. *Sydney Morning Herald*, 12 August 1953.
43. *Argus*, 12 August 1953.
44. *Argus*, 11 August 1953.
45. *Courier Mail*, 14 August 1953.
46. *Argus*, 21 August 1953, reported the inquest would resume the following week on that date.
47. *Argus*, 15 August 1953.
48. *Launceston Examiner*, 20 August 1953.
49. *Argus*, 19 August 1953.
50. *Launceston Examiner*, 18 August 1953.
51. *Truth*, 16 August 1953, cited in Scrine, *op. cit.*, p. 132.
52. *Sydney Morning Herald*, 8 October 1953.

53. *Sydney Morning Herald*, 9 October 1953.
54. *Courier-Mail*, 13 October 1953.
55. *Sydney Morning Herald*, 8 October 1953.
56. *Sydney Morning Herald*, 14 October 1953.
57. *Adelaide Advertiser*, 16 October 1953.
58. *Adelaide Advertiser*, 10 April 1954.
59. *Argus*, 24 September 1954.
60. Miranda Devine, 'Her new career's to die for', *Sydney Morning Herald*, 4 June 2005.

Chapter 12 Deadly Manoeuvres in the Nineteenth Century

1. *Sydney Gazette and NSW Advertiser*, 22 June 1816.
2. *R v Anderson* [1816] NSWKR 5; *Sydney Gazette*, 22 June 1816.
3. Tasmanian State Archives. Marriage of Margaret Galvin and John Coghlin (sic) CON 52/1/3, researched from online records.
4. *Hobart Mercury*, 29 January 1862.
5. *Brisbane Courier*, 15 March 1862.
6. *Bell's Life in Sydney and Sporting Chronicle*, 8 March 1862.
7. Michael Cannon, *The Woman as Murderer*, Today's Publishing Company, Mornington, Victoria, 1994, p. 42.
8. *Sydney Morning Herald*, 27 August 1872. Cannon writes that the jury did not recommend mercy. Newspaper accounts of time attest that it did.
9. *Argus*, 17 October 1892. Obituary of William Fraser.
10. *Traralgon Record*, 22 June 1894. This article provided a good deal of background information.
11. *Argus*, 1 August 1894.
12. Cannon, *op. cit.*, p. 87.
13. *Argus*, 1 August 1894.
14. *Ibid.*
15. *Argus*, 17 August 1894.
16. Cannon, *op. cit.*, pp. 91–92.
17. *South Australian Register*, 12 December 1894.
18. Weston Bate, 'Were, Jonathon Binns (1809–1885)', http://www.adb.anu.edu.au/biography/ were-jonathon-binns-2783/text3963
19. *Barrier Miner*, 17 December 1894.

20. *Argus*, 4 July 1901.
21. *Barrier Miner*, 23 June 1903.

Chapter 13 Killing of Partners in the Twentieth Century
1. *Adelaide Advertiser*, 21 November 1902.
2. *Evening News*, 21 November 1902.
3. Cited in Juliet Peers, 'The Case of Ethel Herringe' in Kerry Greenwood (ed.), *The Thing She Loves: Why Women Kill*, Allen and Unwin, St Leonard's, 1996, p. 56.
4. *Ibid.*, p. 57.
5. Cited in *Ibid.*, pp. 57–58.
6. *Grenfell Vedette*, 6 May 1903, cited in *Ibid.*, p. 59.
7. *Adelaide Advertiser*, 21 November 1902.
8. *Kalgoorlie Western Argus*, 25 November 1902.
9. Martha Rutledge, 'Owen, Sir Langer Meade Loftus (1862–1935)', http://adb.anu.edu.au/biorgraphy/owen-sir-langer-meade-loftus-8499/text13813. Sir Langer was the son of Sir William Owen.
10. *Grenfell Vedette*, 29 April 1903, cited in Peers, *op. cit.*, p. 62.
11. AWSS, 'Holland, Henry Edmund (Harry) (1868–1933)', http://adb.anu.edu.au/biorgraphy/holland-henry-edmund-harry-6708/11579
12. Peers, *op. cit.*, pp. 62–63.
13. *Ibid.*, pp. 63–64.
14. Heather Radi, 'Holman, Ada Augusta (1869–1949)', http://adb.anu.edu.au/biorgraphy/holamn-ada-augusta-666710/text11583
15. Beverley Kingston, 'Golding, Annie Mackenzie (1855–1934)', http://adb.anu.edu.au/biorgraphy/golding-annie-mackenzie-6416/text10971; J. A. Allen, *Rose Scott: Vision and Revision in Feminism*, Oxford University Press, Melbourne, 1994 [read as an e-book].
16. Peers, *op. cit.*, p. 68. This chapter provides more details on the aftermath of this intriguing case.
17. Jacob made this statement in her testimony in the courtroom at her trial.
18. Testimony of William Murphy, customs officer, Perth; letter written by Cyril Gidley on 16 August 1925, cited in the *Mirror*, 12 September 1925.

19. Jill Matthews, 'Ballroom Tragedy, Courtroom Drama', in Greenwood, *op. cit.*, p. 32; Claude Kingston, *It Don't Seem a Day Too Much*, Rigby, Adelaide, 1971.
20. *Mirror*, 12 September 1925, reporting on the evidence of Maud Mitchell at the inquest.
21. Matthews, *op. cit.*, pp. 32–32.
22. *Mirror* (Perth), 27 August 1925.
23. *Mirror*, 12 September 1925.
24. Reported in *Western Australian*, 4 September 1925. This newspaper reported the trial. References from these proceedings come from this newspaper.
25. *Mirror*, 12 September 1925.
26. Matthews, *op. cit.*, p. 34.
27. Bolton and Byrne, *op. cit.*, p. 99.
28. *Ibid.*, p. 154.

Chapter 14 Eugenia Falleni, The 'Man–Woman' Killer
1. Ruth Ford, 'The Man–Woman Murderer: Sex fraud, sexual inversion and the unmentionable "Article" in 1920s Australia', *Gender and History*, Vol. 12, No. 1, 2000, pp. 158–95.
2. Alan Sharpe, *Crime and Punishment: Fifty Crimes That Shocked Australia*, Milson's Point, Currawong Press, 1982, pp. 174–76.
3. *Barrier Miner*, 20 August 1920. Evidence before C. H. Gale SM at Central Police Court, Sydney.
4. Ford, *op. cit.*, pp. 163–64.
5. Kay Saunders, *Notorious Australian Women*, ABC Books, Sydney, 2011, Chapter 5.
6. Ford, *op. cit.*, p. 175.
7. Herbert Moran, 'Portrait of an Invert' in *Viewless Winds: Being the Recollections and Digressions of an Australian Surgeon*, Peter Davies, London, 1939, pp. 230–36.
8. Cited in Ford, *op. cit.*. p. 180.
9. Suzanne Falkiner, *Eugenia: A Man*, Pan Books, Sydney, 1988, pp. 6–17. Readers are recommended to consult this well-researched account; Carolyn Strange, 'Falleni, Eugenia (c. 1875–1938)', http://adbonline.

anu.edu.au/biogs/AS10153.htm. Cited in Falkiner, *op. cit.*, p. 40. The details of the court case can be found in newspapers such as the *Sydney Morning Herald*.
10. *Ibid.*
11. *Kalgoorlie Western Argus*, 24 August 1920, reporting evidence at the last day of the hearing at Central Police Court.
12. Cited in *Ibid.*, p.23.
13. Cited in Ford, *op. cit.*, p. 181.
14. Moran, *op. cit.*, p. 230–36.
15. Strange, *op. cit.*

Chapter 15 Fighting Back
1. Testimony of Charles Daniels at the trial of Ann Smith, *Sydney Gazette* and *New South Wales Advertiser*, 5 November 1834.
2. *R v Smith* (no. 2) [1834] NSWSupC 124; *Sydney Herald*, 17 November 1834 and 20 November 1834.
3. Convict Records NSW, 4/4549, Reel 690, p. 024.
4. This case can be followed in the *Sydney Morning Herald* account of the trial of 5–7 April 1859. The coverage is particularly detailed. Notice of commutation of sentence is contained in a list of sentences 3 May 1860.
5. Malcolm Cope, 'Brennan, Frank Tennison (1884–1949)', http://www.adbonline.anu.edu.au/biogs/A070408b.htm.
6. Ross Johnston, *History of the Queensland Bar*, Queensland Bar Association, Toowong, 1984, pp. 91–92.
7. All testimony is taken from the transcript of the trial. Queensland State Archives (QSA) Supreme Court Trail Records, ID 787407.
8. *Rockhampton Bulletin*, 7 March 1928.
9. *Kalgoorlie Western Argus*, 13 April 1909.
10. *Argus*, 27 November 1936.
11. QSA Justice E. A. Douglas Notebook 11/3/1937 -20/5/1937 ID 18554; *Courier Mail*, 18 May 1937.
12. Ruth Teale, *Colonial Eve: Sources on Australian Women in Australia 1788–1914*, OUP, Melbourne, 1978, pp. 166–68.
13. Hilary Golder, *Divorce in 19th-Century New South Wales*, University of New South Wales Press, Sydney, 1985, page 215.

14. Katie Spearritt, 'New Dawns: First wave feminism 1880–1914' in Kay Saunders and Raymond Evans (eds), *Gender Relations in Australia: Domination and Negotiation*, Harcourt Brace Jovanovich, Sydney, 1992, pp. 325–47.
15. B. F. Bartal, 'Battered Wife Syndrome Evidence: The Australian experience', British Society of Criminology Conference, July 1995, published September 1998 and available online; E. A. Sheehy et al, 'Defending Battered Woman on Trial: The Battered Wife Syndrome and its limitations', *Criminal Law Journal*, Vol. 16, 1992.
16. Details of this complicated case can be located in court records available online; refer to *The Queen v Runjanjic The Queen v Kontinnen*, Nos 226 and 227 of 1991 Judgment, No 2951 [1991] SASC 2952; [1991]56 SASC 114; Joanna Brodie, '"All Yous Will be Dead in the Morning": The Kontinnen case' in Kerry Greenwood (ed.), *The Thing She Loves: Why Women Kill*, Allen and Unwin, Sydney, 1996, pp. 44–53; Nan Seuffert, 'Domestic Violence, Discourses of Romantic Love and Complex Personhood in the Law', *Melbourne University Law Review*, Vol. 8, 1999.
17. Nigel Hunt, *Sunday Herald Sun*, 12 April 1992.
18. *The Queen v Runjanjic The Queen v Kontinnen*, Nos 226 and 227, *op. cit.*
19. Belinda Morrisey, *When Women Kill: Questions of Agency and Subjectivity*, Routledge, 2003, p. 85.
20. *R v Raby* Supreme Court of Victoria (unreported), 17 October 1994, cited in Seuffert, *op. cit.*, p. 1.

Chapter 16 Deadly Lovers' Pacts in the Nineteenth Century
1. *Sydney Morning Herald*, 5 October 1842.
2. *Australasian Chronicle*, 4 October 1842.
3. Details of the widely reported case can be read in the *Sydney Morning Herald* 9 September and 15 September 1843.
4. *Sydney Morning Herald*, 5 October 1842.
5. *Morning Chronicle*, 21 October 1843.
6. *Empire*, 6 November 1854.
7. G. C. Bolton and G. Byrne, *May It Please Your Honour: A History of the Supreme Court of Western Australia from 1861–2005*, Supreme Court of Western Australia, Perth, 2012, p. 29.

8. *Ibid.*
9. *Perth Gazette and Independent Journal of Politics and News*, 14 September 1855.
10. *Sunday Times* (Perth), 19 September 1909; Alan Sharpe and Vivien Encel, *Murder! Twenty-five True Crimes*, Kingsclear Books, Crows Nest, 1997.
11. *Perth Gazette and Independent Journal of Politics and News*, 14 September 1855.
12. *Ibid.*
13. J. H. M. Honniball, 'Mackie, William Henry (1799–1860)', http://adb.anu.edu.au/biorgraphy/mackie-william-henry-2410/text3191
14. Ann-Mari Jordens, 'Birnie, Richard (1808–1888)', http://adb.anu.edu.au/biorgraphy/birnie-richard/2997/text4385
15. *Perth Gazette and Independent Journal of Politics and News*, 19 October 1855.
16. Paul B. Kidd, *The Australian Crime File: The 'Best' of Collection of Notorious True Crime Stories*, The Five Mile Press, Rowville, Victoria, 2005, pp. 189–95.
17. *Maitland Mercury and Hunter River General Advertiser*, 7 November 1863. This is a lengthy account of the trial.
18. 'Stephen, George Milner (1812–1894)', http://adb.anu.edu.au/biorgraphy/stephen-george-milner-1294/text 3771
19. *South Australian Advertiser*, 26 November 1863.
20. Ellen Thomson, Brisbane Gaol, 23 May 1887, Queensland State Archives (QSA) PRI/6 01/01/87–31/12/1907, Prisoners under sentence of death, Sheriff's Office, Prison Department.
21. NSW Convict Index, 4/4404 reel 1022, 950.
22. Raymond Evans, Kay Saunders and Kathryn Cronin, *Race Relations in Colonial Queensland*, University of Queensland Press, St Lucia, 1988 (first published 1975), pp. 282–84.
23. The case in Criminal Jurisdiction of the Supreme Court of Queensland in October 1887 was fully reported in the *Brisbane Courier*, 22 October 1887.
24. QSA Justice Department File A/18487 01/01/87- 31/12/87, Supreme Court of Northern District, Townsville.
25. *Brisbane Courier*, 11 May 1887.

26. Ross W. Johnston, *History of the Queensland Bar*, Bar Association of Queensland, Toowong, 1984, pp. 65–68.
27. Cited in Marion Purnell, 'Ellen Lynch (1841 (sic)–1887, the only woman to have been legally hanged in Queensland)', http://www.easystreet.com.au/lynch_ellen.html
28. *Sydney Morning Herald, 3* June 1887.
29. *The Boomerang*, 17 June 1887.
30. *Brisbane Courier* 22 June 1887.

Index

Ambrose, Mabel 8, 28–38
Andersen, Cecilie 251–257
Anderson, Elizabeth 241–242
Anderson, John 241–242
Andrews, Charles 206–209, 210, 211, 212
Anley, Charlotte 1–2, 10
Atkinson, Alwyn 93–94

Beaney, Dr James 'Champagne Jimmy' 16
Beck, Valmae 11
Beech, Martin 303–306
Bevan, Freda 61, 62
Blain, Frances 22, 23
Bonfiglio, Frank 46–57
Booth, Elizabeth 145, 146
Booth, Ethel 145–149
Borden, Lizzie 9
Borgia, Lucrezia 195, 205, 223
Boswell, Charles 'Carlo Adolph de la Lebedur' 31
Brady, Joan 62
Bradley, Mary Ann 196
Brian, Kathleen 62
Brown, Gladys 62
Brown, John 155–62
Bryant, James 71
Brussels, Madame 18, 219, 248
Burkett, Annie 274–86
Burnes, Kathleen 295–297
Butler, Desmond George 225–230

Calloway, Rose *see* Hamilton, Mrs
Cameron, Rodney 133
Carter, Eliza 20

Cassey 162–65
Christensen, Marie 162–66
Cogdon, Ivy 182–84
Cogdon, Patricia 182–84
Coghlan, John 242–248
Cohen, Lilian 63
Collins, Louisa née Hall 7, 205–212
Collins, Michael 'Mick' 207–211
Coppock, Elizabeth 80
Costello, Mary 155–62
Coughlan, Bertha Evelyn 46–54, 56
Courtenay, Emma *see* Williams, Emma
Crawford, Annie *see* Burkett, Annie
Crawford, Harry *see* Falleni, Eugenia
Crofts, Irene 223
Crowther, Dr Bingham 39–40
Curnow, Lauren 93
Cuthbert, Dr James 172, 173, 174

Dissratia, Mrs *see also* Ambrose, Mabel 30, 32
Dodd, Enoch 306–309
Dow, Amelia 61–62
Downey, Elizabeth 44–46
Dubberke, Thekla 28–38
Dunkley, Henry 303–305
Dunkley, Lucretia 303–306

Elburn, Elizabeth *see* Radalyski, Olga 'Madame Olga'
Ellis, Ellen 310–313
Ellis, Ellias 310–313

Fairbairn, May *see* Harpur, Melissa 'Madame Harpur'

Fairbairn, Melissa *see* Harpur, Melissa 'Madame Harpur'
Fairburn, Elsie 22, 26, 27, 28
Fairburn, Melissia *see* Harper, Melissa
Fairburn, Dr Brierley 22
Falleni, Eugenia née Harry Crawford 274–86
Falleni, Josephine 277, 280–83, 285
Ferry, Agnes 90–91
Fitchett, David 188–94
Fitchett, Donna 5, 188–94
Fletcher, Bertram 225–230
Fletcher, Yvonne 225–230, 231, 234

Folbigg, Craig 94–107
Folbigg, Kathleen 94–108, 122,

Coghlan, Margaret (née Galvin) 242–47
Gaze, Dr William 29, 31, 34, 35, 36, 37
Gedge, David 310–313
Gidley, Cyril 7, 265–273
Gillies, Duncan 110, 111, 112, 113, 114, 115, 116, 118, 119, 120, 121–22, 123
Gillies, Julie, mother of Duncan 111, 118
Giovinazzo, Alma 182
Grills, Caroline 7, 226, 231–39
Guizzardi, Dominica 182
Guizzardi, William 182

Hamilton, Mrs 18, 19
Hanlon, Sidney 40
Hanlon, William 40
Harper, Melissa 'Madame Harpur' 21–28
Harpur, 'Madame' *see* Harper, Melissa
Harrison, John 314, 316, 319–22
Haugh, Beryl 231
Heffernan, Maggie 86–88
Herringe, Ethel 259–65
Hill, Edward 298–302
Hindley, Myra 9
Hodgson, Caroline *see* Brussels, Madame
Holmes, Annie 23–25
Hope, Florence 42–43
Hubbard, Rosina 220–221

Hughes, Helen 59
Hughes, W. M. 58, 59
Humphries, Vera 60
Hurford, Bridget 306–309

Jackson, Margaret 40–42
Jacob, Audrey Campbell 7, 258, 265–273
Judge, Annie Magann 83–85

Knight, Kathy 108
Knorr, Frances 135–43, 144, 158, 162, 219
Kontinnen, Erica 6, 298–302

Lane, Keli 4, 10, 109–124
Lane, Robert 109, 110, 123
Lane, Sandra 109, 110, 120, 123
Lane, Tegan 4, 109, 113–124
Lee, Jean 9
Lee, Maurice 259 260–263
Lefo, Budlo 163–64
Lonsdale, Emma 91
Lundberg, Eveline 232–239
Lynch, Ellen *see* Thomson, Ellen)

Mackellar, Lily 65–66
Makin, John 126–135, 140, 144, 238
Makin, Sarah 126–135, 140, 141, 143, 144, 238
Maloney, Mary 1–2
Marek, Martha 223
Markham, Harriet 26
Masters, Sarah 75–79
Mathews, Mrs 21
Mayo, Dr Helen 25
McCallum, Isabel 44–45
McDonald, Edna 63
McDonald, Emily 89–90
McDonald, Thomas 226
McGregor, Sarah 1
McLauchlan, Mary 8, 10, 66–76
McLeod, Topsy 163, 165
Medea 5, 187–88
Melville, Julie *see also* Gillies, Julie 113, 117, 118

INDEX

Miller, Alexander 24
Mills, Jean 26
Milward, Margaret 48, 49, 50 51, 52, 53, 54
Mitchell, Alice 4–5, 143–150
Mitchell, Hannah Elizabeth 'Nurse Mitchell' 46–57
Mitchell, Margaret 'Queenie' 48, 52, 54
Moore, Helen 184–87
Moore, Patricia 5
Morris, George 170,
Mowat, Laura 60

Nairne, Charles Ross 68, 69, 70, 73, 74
Needle, Martha (née Charles) 143, 159, 162, 213–220
Neild, Dr James E. 29, 30, 32, 137, 218, 249
Norton, Ruby 230–31
Nugent, Lily 276, 279

O'Donnell, Mary 69
O'Donoghue, Margaret 247–251
Olga, 'Madame' *see* Radalyski, Olga

Patterson, Varna 63
Peacock, Dr Samuel 16–17, 18, 19
Pennington, Clara 44–46
Perry, John 288–292
Perry, Mary Ann 288–292, 297
Pinti, Livia 182

Raby, Keith 302
Raby, Margaret 302
Radalyski, Olga 'Madame Olga' 28–38
Rendall, Martha 7, 9, 167–78
Richter, Allen 181–82
Richter, Alma 181–82
Robertson, Margaret 16–17
Robins, Sarah Ann 220–221

Robinson, Sarah Jane 205
Rollings, Eugene 180–81
Runjanjic, Olga 6, 298–302

Salon, Esther 295
Schieb, Norah 297, 298
Schieb, Thomas 298
Scott, Elizabeth 6, 309–13
Scott, Robert 309–13
Sherman, Lydia 205
Short, Harriet 80–82
Smith, Madeline 9
Smith, Susan 179
Spiers, Nellie 91–93
Stevens, Mary 179–81
Sullivan, Mary 5, 10, 152–55
Sutherland, Sulina 159

Taylor, Elizabeth 16–21, 26
Taylor, John 287–88
Taylor, Myra 258–59
Thomson, Ellen 314–22
Thomson, William 314–22
Tod, Travice 28–38
Trioly, Anthony 295–297
Tucker, Laura 25–28

Walsh, Ann 287–88
Warburton, Julia 17–20
West, Isabel Scott 182
Whitford, Bertha 42–43
Williams, Allen 230–31
Williams, Frederick 'Fred' 144–62
Williams, Emma (née Courtenay) 155–62
Williams, Mary 80–82
Wilson, Mary 156–57
Woolcock, Elizabeth 7, 196–204
Wournos, Aileen 9
Yee Lee, Minnie 44–46
Youl, Dr Richard 18, 30

ABOUT THE AUTHOR

Professor Kay Saunders, AO, is the author of *Notorious Australian Women*.

She is currently writing the history of Bond University.

www.ingramcontent.com/pod-product-compliance
Lightning Source LLC
Chambersburg PA
CBHW022027290426
44109CB00014B/783